ITALIAN CULTURAL LINEAGES

In *Italian Cultural Lineages,* Jonathan White seeks answers to the elusive questions, What is Italian culture and what is Italian identity? By tracing Italian life and art through selected themes – viewing, fantasy, passion, capital cities, justice, reputation, and lifestyle – White offers new ways of perceiving Italian cultural history and tradition. In doing so, he challenges readers to discern the rich, often subtle connections that bind together these themes.

Italian Cultural Lineages is primarily concerned with the elements that unify Italians, however geographically dispersed they may be. Drawing on extensive archival and historical research, White shows how Italian cultural traditions that often appear to be extinct are, in fact, enduring – pushed out of the mainstream or submerged at some given point in history, only to resurface and take on new meaning at a later date. Other more marginal currents might disrupt and fragment Italian identity, politically and socially. However, White proposes that these new challenges to Italy and Italian culture offer lessons in tolerance that have the potential to produce a much stronger, more inclusive culture, primed to welcome the marginal into an expanded spirit of all that counts as Italian.

(Toronto Italian Studies)

JONATHAN WHITE is Professor in Literature at the University of Essex.

JONATHAN WHITE

Italian Cultural Lineages

To Hal and Jeff
In warm friendship
Jonathan

UNIVERSITY OF TORONTO PRESS
Toronto Buffalo London

© University of Toronto Press Incorporated 2007
Toronto Buffalo London
Printed in Canada

ISBN 978-0-8020-9230-4 (cloth)
ISBN 978-0-8020-9458-2 (paper)

Printed on acid-free paper

Toronto Italian Studies

Library and Archives Canada Cataloguing in Publication

White, Jonathan Charles, 1945–
   Italian cultural lineages / Jonathan White.

(Toronto Italian studies)
Includes bibliographical references.
ISBN 978-0-8020-9230-4 (bound)
ISBN 978-0-8020-9458-2 (pbk.)

1. Italy – Civilization.   2. Italians – Social life and customs.
I. Title.   II. Series.

DG442.W55 2007   945   C2006-906345-1

Publication of this book was facilitated by a grant from the
Research Promotion Fund of the University of Essex.

University of Toronto Press acknowledges the financial assistance to
its publishing program of the Canada Council for the Arts and the
Ontario Arts Council.

University of Toronto Press acknowledges the financial support for
its publishing activities of the Government of Canada through the
Book Publishing Industry Development Program (BPIDP).

Contents

List of Illustrations vii

Acknowledgments ix

Introduction: Kangaroos, Papyrus Scrolls, and the Poetics of Cultural History 3

1 Modes of Viewing: From Vasari to Film and Television Culture 28

2 Fantasy, Science, and Hyperreality: From Ariosto and Galileo to Las Vegas 59

3 Passion in the Operatic Repertoire 87

4 Capital Contrasts: Naples and Turin a Century before Unification 103

5 Justice and the Individual, Torture and the State 144

6 Italy's Romantic Reputation 176

7 Lifestyles High and Low in Changing Post-Unification Urbanism 218

Notes 277

Bibliography 303

Index 317

List of Illustrations

1.1 A *mondo nuovo* with children viewing images in it 29
1.2 The *imbonitore* of a *mondo nuovo* shows mother and child the 'distances and prospects' of a range of views 33
1.3 A *mondo nuovo* from Venice, last half of the eighteenth century 34
1.4 Image of a *mondo nuovo*, first quarter of the nineteenth century 37
1.5 Placido Domingo as Cavaradossi from Puccini's *Tosca* 56
1.6 Catherine Malfitano as Tosca in her suicide leap from the ramparts of the Castel Sant'Angelo 57
1.7 The same picture with the cars of Rome's modern traffic removed 57
7.1 Telemaco Signorini, *The Ward of the Mad Women of St Boniface in Florence* 256
7.2 Angelo Morbelli, *Those Left at Christmas* 258
7.3 Angelo Morbelli, *Holiday at the Pio Albergo Trivulzio* 259
7.4 Angelo Inganni, *Urban Chimneysweep* 261
7.5 Angelo Inganni, *View of the Piazza del Duomo with the Figini Portico* 263
7.6 Angelo Inganni, *View of the Piazza della Loggia under Snow* 264
7.7 Laura Antonelli as Giuliana Hermil in Visconti's *L'Innocente* 270
7.8 Giancarlo Giannini as Tullio Hermil and Jennifer O'Neill as the Countess Teresa Raffo in *L'Innocente* 271
7.9 Dirk Bogarde as Professor Aschenbach in *Death in Venice* 273

Acknowledgments

That this book has come to fruition is largely owing to the support of institutions, colleagues and friends around the world. After publication in 2001 of my earlier book, *Italy: The Enduring Culture*, I was fortunate to be awarded two fellowships at opposite ends of the earth, which provided wonderful opportunities to research, discuss, and write up chapters of the present volume. First, at Columbia University in New York, Professor David Freedberg and his staff at the Italian Academy for Advanced Studies in America welcomed me and my year group of 2002–3 fellows, and provided us with ideal academic companionship and conditions of scholarship. Professor Freedberg leads this Academy by example. He published in the very year that we were there his outstanding and award-winning study of Galileo and his intellectual circle of the Academy of the *Lincei* (Lynxes), The advantages of Columbia's Butler Library, furthermore, have to be experienced to be believed. I was often able to find books published earlier in the same year, already catalogued and on the open shelves for borrowing. The library's sizable historic holdings on Italian subject matter had begun with books purchased or bequeathed by its own first professor of Italian, Lorenzo Da Ponte, during a time when the institution was still called Columbia College and located in lower Manhattan. (Da Ponte, Mozart's most famous librettist, had emigrated from London to the United States in the early 1800s, and lived variously in Pennsylvania and New York City for the remaining three decades of his life. Introducing young Americans to Italian language and culture was only one of several pursuits during his years in America.)

I had not long left New York than I took up a fellowship at the Humanities Research Centre (HRC) of the Australian National University. There the deputy director, Dr Caroline Turner, as well as permanent fellows Paul Pickering, Glen Barclay and Alastair Maclachlan, were constantly both supportive and intellectually challenging. As at Columbia, I had the benefit of co-fellows from around the world with whom to discuss, in particular, the advantages and pitfalls of different approaches to cultural history that are in contention in our age. I hope some of the critical thinking that I was exposed to while in places as different as New York and Canberra proves of value to others who read this volume.

Return to my home institution, the University of Essex, has been rewarding, even after periods of privileged scholarship overseas. I am supported by a thriving School of Humanities and Comparative Studies. Individual studies are fuelled by different disciplinary inputs, in creative ferment with one another. I am keenly aware of the wider stimulus I gain from working among people who study a range of cul-tures and histories. Particular thanks go to my long-term departmental colleague, Hazel Horsnell, for help with the material production of the book. I am also greatly indebted to the staff of the Albert Sloman Library at Essex, in particular to members of its inter-library loans section, who were so helpful in fulfilling my various requests.

At a later stage, my editors at the University of Toronto Press, Anne Laughlin and Ron Schoeffel, in conjunction with their painstaking copy-editors Robert Giannetto and John St James, offered everything that a writer could wish for by way of encouragement and watchful insights about the book under production.

Above and beyond institutions I have mentioned, my greatest good fortune in the writing of this book has been the support of colleagues and friends. I warmly appreciate the long-term relationship between us at the University of Essex and our colleagues at the Università degli Studi di Palermo, with whom we have held two specialized *convegni*, one in Palermo and another in Colchester. Remarkable dedication to common endeavours has been shown by Palermitan friends of long standing: Elio di Piazza, Daniela Corona, Michele Cometa, Patrizia Lendinara, Alessandra Rizzo, Marcella Romeo, and Federica Mazzara.

In North America, Italianists of many kinds gather at conferences of two fine groupings, the American Association of Teachers of Italian and the American Association of Italian Studies. Mainly through these associations, but also at the annual convention of the Modern Language Association, I have made lifelong friendships. Among those who have been of greatest inspiration over the years are Regina Psaki, Massimo Lollini, Graziella Parati, Gabriella Romani, Luca Somigli, Carol Lazzaro Weiss, Daniela Bini, Andrea Ciccarelli, Millicent Marcus, Giuseppe Tosi,

Nicoletta Pireddu, Christopher Kleinhenz, Fabian Alfie, and Joseph Luzzi. The list grows longer and longer, and even those named here are by no means all who have come to mean so much to me.

Similarly, in the United Kingdom and Republic of Ireland, Italianists meet up mainly through the Society for Italian Studies (SIS), quite apart from networks between departments. Joe Farrell, Michael and Ann Caesar, Sylvia Ross and Mark Chu are only five among many whom I perhaps would never have met were it not for the SIS. On British and Irish soil, as elsewhere, the intellectual vibrancies of our common culture of study, Italian culture make for inspiring gatherings.

In Australia and New Zealand the professional association of Italianists is the Australasian Centre for Italian Studies (ACIS), a body generously supported by the Cassamarca Foundation, based in Treviso, Italy, under its president, the Honourable Dr Dino De Poli. I was kindly invited by Gino Moliterno and David Moss to deliver the opening address to the 2001 ACIS conference titled 'The Importance of Italy,' where I met Australian and international scholars, including for the first time Peter Bondanella of the University of Indiana at Bloomington. In Canberra at a later stage, during my 2003 fellowship at the HRC, I also met Federica Zullo, who deepened my understanding of modern Italian television.

Art historians Jules Lubbock and Maggie Iversen, close friends and near neighbours in London, have provided constant intellectual stimulus and good cheer. Across the Atlantic, Sante Matteo has, more than anyone else, closely read, responded to, and challenged my interpretations of Italy. It is to him that quite a number of attunements and corrections to the present book are attributable, though I would hasten to add that all of what may be its remaining faults are my own in origin and perpetration. In a different part of my life, Marina Warner has recently joined our department at Essex. Marina is Italian on her mother's side and has recently been made a Commendatore by the Italian Republic, where her work is widely read and much admired. The opportunity to discuss with her various aspects of Italian culture has been a great boon to me, so original are her perceptions and her formulation of them. Like others, I have been inspired by her presence among us, and look forward to what I hope will be many productive years in the same institution.

My brother and sister, Nicholas and Charlotte, my daughters Jessica and Kate and their mother Janet, and my stepson William are unending sources of joy, as is now the additional generation of Brendan and Rose Coll. As delightful as these newcomers are, I think too with gratitude of those who have meant so much to me but are now gone forever: in particular Peter and Sylvia Andrew, Vincent Buckley, Francis Barker, and my parents.

Three close companions, none of them Italianists, albeit matchless critical thinkers in wide fields of endeavour, are the persons in whose company it is my privilege to spend much of these richly rewarding years of my life: Peter Hulme, Aijaz Ahmad, and Susan Oliver.

ITALIAN CULTURAL LINEAGES

Introduction: Kangaroos, Papyrus Scrolls, and the Poetics of Cultural History

'What sort of perceptibility should the presentation of history possess?' asked Walter Benjamin,[1] driven to the question by his belief, which he worked into almost everything he wrote, that 'being past, being no more, is passionately at work in things.'[2] We could do worse than use Benjamin as one important benchmark in our own attempts (as he put it) at 'distilling the present, as inmost essence of what has been.'[3] I have written the present book on Italy out of a complementary conviction; namely, that to capture this passionate historicity in the things we treat requires so remarkable but also so subtle an intelligence and sensitivity that the ways we write the past aspire to certain conditions of poetry. We have a greater chance of achieving such a goal, or at least of getting close, if we set out with the conscious ideal of doing so.

In the following study I explore Italian culture in terms of seven themes – viewing, fantasy, passion, former royal capitals, justice, reputation, and lifestyles – and posit the existence of complex and fascinating lineages of each. I shall not attempt to offer a definitive explanation of my term 'lineages' at this point, partly because I have more to say about it in a first chapter, on modes of viewing from Vasari through to film and television. Indeed, I search for new ways of focusing cultural lineages in the case of each of the themes treated in the book. Nonetheless, in these introductory pages I do offer some first accounts of what we might understand by the concept, which I hope prove useful. For instance, it needs to be affirmed from the beginning that lineages of a culture are not essentially of one sole typology, susceptible to theoretical definition, but are instead protean by nature. They are multiform and intersecting. Many cohabit in the same historical spaces. Their existence is for the most part best confirmed through empirical exploration, which is what I attempt in the book. Some of these lineages have outcomes in the present that can be studied directly, and others, by contrast, involve discontinuities of tradition that render certain past Italies, at first unintelligible to our imaginations, all the more challenging to us as scholars as we attempt to reconstruct what has disappeared from view.

I am aware of the extreme difficulty in achieving the subtlety that I dream of in this task of re-imagining past configurations of a culture such as Italy's, because of the near impossibility of balancing philosophical speculation with empirical research, and expressive metaphors with factual exactitude. Nonetheless, I also believe that if scholars in the humanities do not preoccupy themselves with such considerations, we are all likely to be intellectually poorer. So the project I venture here is an invitation to collaboration, in freshly charting not just Italian cultural history but also other traditions as well.

In one of the best articles ever written on how difficult, but also how necessary, it is to get inside history, E.P. Thompson wrote, 'History ... is made up of episodes, and if we cannot get inside these, we cannot get inside history at all.'[4] While keenly assenting, I should like to hold on firmly to the idea of intricate cultural lineages, alongside that of episodes. Throughout this book I shall need to treat both, sometimes together, since several of the lineages I seek to trace run through different historical episodes, obviously changing as they do so.

We cannot talk of any of these things without conceptual hypotheses. Thompson stressed the need for them, as well as for 'empirical evidence to enforce or to break down these hypotheses,' such that there arises (quite properly) a 'friction between "molecular" research and "macroscopic" generalization.' He went on to affirm that 'in any vital intellectual tradition this dialectic, this abrasion between models and particulars, is always evident' – thereby producing a hypothesis of his own about the nature of cultural lineages of the intellectual variety.[5]

Since I am deeply persuaded of the need for Thompson's 'dialectic ... between models and particulars,' I have naturally attempted wherever possible to achieve that level of cogent internal debate at the heart of my explorations. The one thing that Thompson had perhaps not adequately included in his own 'model' of vital intellectual traditions is their tendency to ask questions, quite as much as they hypothesize and bring to bear evidence. So – models, particulars, and *questions*. In all that follows, it is this triangulation for which I am striving.

Let me begin my meditations on Italian cultural history, therefore, by making several generalizations of a macroscopic kind before proceeding to 'abrade' them somewhat, first by general probing, then by a more 'molecular' form of investigation. In point of fact, the alternation between and even the interpenetration of molecular research and macroscopic generalization is ceaseless. One is forever engaging with them separately or in unison – but hopefully not just as some set-piece strategy, or they become a dull routine.

Italy led the West in urbanization and in trade and banking, which fostered the first possibilities of a post-feudal culture. Perry Anderson has brilliantly shown how 'the simultaneous eclipse of the Empire and the Papacy made Italy the weak link of Western feudalism.' The Italian peninsula did not follow the predominant Western European trend towards feudal absolutism. 'The premature development of *mercantile capital* in the North Italian cities ... prevented the emergence of a powerful reorganized *feudal* state at the national level.' As Anderson also goes on to point out, these urban concentrations were still surrounded by feudal agrarian structures: 'urban enclaves within the feudal mode of production ... essentially existed in dynamic *tension* with the countryside.' But over time they came to dominate and exploit the feudal modes of production of the *contado* (rural area), for the enhancement of their own post-feudal dynamic. 'The communes customarily combated certain basic institutions of agrarian feudalism: vassalage was often expressly banned within the towns, and serfdom was abolished in the countryside controlled by them. At the same time, the Italian cities systematically exploited their *contado* for urban profit and production, levying grain and recruits from it, fixing prices and imposing meticulous crop regulations and directives on the subjugated agricultural population.'[6] In avoiding the prevailing paradigm of absolutist feudal monarchy, and pioneering instead mercantilist modes of production, Italy was anticipating, sometimes by several centuries, the rise elsewhere in Europe of post-feudal capitalist structures, centred upon and largely driven by multiple competing urban economies, themselves hegemonic over their agrarian hinterlands of supply.

In what respects does the world still see its cultural agenda set by Italy, even perhaps the inauguration of an endgame to capitalist modes and structures that have predominated as our historical episteme since the demise of feudalism?[7] Could we be witnessing a so-called end of history in no way conforming to Fukuyama's model of the final triumph of a Western capitalist mode; instead, its transformation into something unprecedentedly *post*-capitalist in configuration that no one has begun successfully to theorize? Our focus is Italian culture, seen from as many interdisciplinary angles as possible. So it is crucial to recognize, amid the general clamour about Italy in crisis, those few voices that are saying that once again, in these very conditions in which Italy finds itself, other Western cultures might be wise to see presages of their own future. The political commentator Martin Jacques, for instance, writing of the 'conditions for Italy to become the political laboratory of Europe' – Western Europe, that is, since he made an exception of formerly communist Eastern Europe – saw as early as 1994 that 'however acute the crisis of the political class elsewhere, Italy remains the only country in which the political system has experienced meltdown.' But he suggested nonetheless that 'somehow the Italian experience chimes with what is happening in other Western democracies. Everywhere there is a crisis of the political class ... From being Europe's odd man out, Italy is rapidly acquiring the status of paradigm.'[8] *Re*acquiring the status of paradigm would be my own immediate gloss on Jacques's remark.

We who spend our lives studying Italy are often forced to contemplate rapid or even violent changes in it, by no means all for the good. How will it maintain itself or recuperate its losses as the third millennium presents inevitable choices of renewing distinctive aspects of Italian culture or losing them forever? Will Italy go on inventively reusing aspects of its past in solving current crises, or will it resort to modes of social, economic, and political self-renewal divorced from its past, which no degree of familiarity with its long and involved history could allow us to predict? Might it slide towards some terrible abyss, obliterating the greatness of earlier times? These urgent questions, because they are directed towards an unknown future, are impossible to answer fully at the present time. But that does not lessen their importance as speculative enquiries.

In framing issues concerning Italy's past and present, and particularly the intricate lineages of connection and disconnection between them, I have had to adapt and hone a host of tools from disciplines other than that of my initial training, literary criticism, using one and then another as the occasion demanded. Although this need for a fluid and broad-based approach might at first make the tasks of analysis seem more daunting, I take inspiration from three thinkers who have been preoccupied with similar notions of historical and cultural lineage.

First, it was a key thesis of Benedetto Croce that all history is contemporary history, since any plotting of the past is inevitably undertaken from within a cultural present: 'It is only some concern of present life that can spur us to enquire into a past fact.'[9] ('Solo un interesse della vita presente ci può muovere a indagare un fatto del passato.')[10] Knowingly or not – and it is clearly best to do so knowingly – we are *interrelating* ourselves to the past or to the cultural 'other' through our studies of it: 'for however (even exceedingly) remote the facts contained ... the history is really always responsive to the present need, the present situation, into which those events convey their reverberations.'[11] ('Per remoti e remotissimi che sembrino cronologicamente i fatti che vi entrino, essa è, in realtà, storia sempre riferita al bisogno e alla situazione presente, nella quale quei fatti propagano le loro vibrazioni.')[12] Or rather, we discover by our chartings of continuity and discontinuity the complex routes by which our arrival came about, so cross-hatched and intricately grained is this historical present in its own right.

Our struggles to create the future emerge from this same meditation. 'If we are enveloped in the past, if the past is, in fact, ourselves, then how can we rise superior to it? There is only one route, that of thought, which does not break the link with the past but grows upward out of it in an ideal growth, and converts it into knowledge ... Goethe once said that the composition of histories is a way of unburdening ourselves of the past. Historical thought grasps the past to turn it to use, and transfigures it into its object, and thus the composition of history is our liberation from history.'[13] ('Come metterci disopra del passato, se vi siamo dentro, ed esso è noi? Non v'ha che una sola via d'uscita, quella del pensiero, che non rompe il rapporto col passato ma sovr'esso s'innalza idealmente e lo converte in conoscenza ... Scrivere storie – notò una volta il Goethe – è un modo di togliersi di sulle spalle il passato. Il pensiero storico lo abbassa a sua materia, lo trasfigura in suo oggetto, e la storiografia ci libera dalla storia.')[14]

That final, Goethe-flavoured note of 'liberation from history' on Croce's part is more of a nineteenth- or early-twentieth-century ideal than a twenty-first-century one. It is part of the idealism in Croce that appealed to so many during his own times, and, in its own right, an early kind of 'end of history' argument, in so far as it suggested a reaching beyond crises of the past and present. The terrible century since Croce wrote those words has caused mistrust on our part of any such idealism, which is perhaps why many of us seek deeper entry into history, rather than rely on some promise of liberation from it. For liberation implies escape; even if this was not intended by Croce in his original formulation. Moreover, we would prefer to *face* the crises and legacies of history, not seek some transcendence from them. Somewhat reluctantly, therefore, we put Croce to one side in our studies, for all his compelling accounts of what drove us to historicizing pursuits in the first place.

I doubt very much, for instance, that anything like Croce's idealized 'liberation from history' is the goal of my second chief example, Aijaz Ahmad, a Marxist cultural critic who has written impressively on Italy, especially on Gramsci and Italian Fascism, but whose main area of study is South Asia, specifically India and Pakistan. Ahmad uses the Italian context for some illuminating cross-cultural comparisons with contemporary Indian realities. But I am concerned here only with his most general notion. He begins his recent book, so appositely entitled *Lineages of the Present* (itself not without New Leftist intellectual traditions linking it back to Anderson's great *Lineages of the Absolutist State*), with a sense of how ineluctably the past is always with us. 'No present,' Ahmad writes, 'is ever *sui generis*, no lives are ever lived simply in the present tense, and each generation is called upon to address, in its own present, those unresolved conflicts of the past which remain in modulated forms a substantial part – at times a *fatal* part – of the present.'[15] This for Ahmad is the most urgent meaning of his title term 'lineages,' clearly highly political for him, especially in the tumultuous historical present of South Asian realities. As specialists, by contrast, in different aspects of Italian culture, we too are surely forced into recognizing the urgency arising from such 'unresolved conflicts of the past.'

Much that is unresolved in the case of Italy relates to founder ideologies of the nation, which, although focused on unification, were disparate from the start, fractured and further fragmented with the passing of the decades, and only partially realized. My third thinker about historical lineages, Antonio Gramsci, understood profoundly that looking at movements such as the Risorgimento has always been intrinsically difficult because of 'the inconsistency and gelatinousness of the organism being studied,' namely the nation under construction ('la scarsità degli elementi oggettivi "nazionali" ai quali fare riferimento, per la inconsistenza e gelatinosità dell'organismo studiato').[16] So while there may indeed be many lineages, to call them *Italian* is often simplistic and misleading. For, as Gramsci was to ask rhetorically in another meditation on the Risorgimento from the *Prison Notebooks*, 'How can one talk of "traditions, mentalities, solutions" in the case of Italy as such?' His reply was that 'the traditions, mentalities, problems and solutions were multiple, contradictory, often highly individual and arbitrary by nature, and were not at the time seen in unitary ways.' ('Come si può parlare di "tradizioni, mentalità, problemi, soluzioni" propri dell'Italia? ... Le tradizioni, le mentalità, i problemi, le soluzioni erano molteplici, contradditorî, di natura spesso solo individuale e arbitraria e non erano allora mai visti unitariamente.')[17] Thus, even though the Risorgimento may well be one of those 'episodes' of which Thompson writes, it is more difficult to 'get inside' than most because of the sheer contradiction, inconsistency, and gelatinousness in what ought to have been, but clearly wasn't, a finely articulated quiddity – namely Italy itself.

My task throughout this book is to suggest that traditions, mentalities, problems, and solutions can nevertheless be traced, even if they rarely apply to the entirety of what has always been called Italy (long before it existed as a nation state). In our positing the existence of such cultural lineages, Gramsci's scepticism about whom we may name as either their subjects or their agents is a healthy one, and it is just as relevant to many other periods before and after the Risorgimento. Likewise, a sense of utter complexity in the subject matter under discussion – nothing less than its *multiple, contradictory, individual,* and *arbitrary* nature – is what has made the writing of this book such an exciting challenge.

The remainder of this introduction constitutes what Kenneth Burke called a 'representative anecdote' (a concept I will return to a little later). It tells of a courtly exchange of some useless – because they were largely unopenable – papyrus scrolls from Herculaneum, for a gift of kangaroos originating from the fledgling colony of New South Wales, or just possibly from Britain's other early penal colony in what we now call Tasmania. The parties to the reciprocal gift-giving, which took place between 1816 and 1819, were the Bourbon ruler of Naples, previously known as Ferdinand IV, but later known, in his second restoration after 1815, as King Ferdinand I of the Two Sicilies; and the other the British prince regent, acting largely through his foreign secretary Lord Castlereagh, at home and his new plenipotentiary,[18] Sir William A'Court, at Ferdinand's court in Naples. King Ferdinand's gift came first, largely, it seems, as a form of thanks for Britain's help in restoring him to his former throne. Britain responded with its strange gift a couple of years later.

The kangaroos were placed in a menagerie on the Vomero hill overlooking Naples. As for the papyrus scrolls, after other eminent persons had failed in the task of unfurling them, Britain's leading chemist and inventor, Sir Humphry Davy, was brought in by the prince regent to try unlocking their secrets using such techniques as would not lead to their further crumbling away. Davy's diffidence about collaborating with the

Neapolitan authorities in their important Museum of Archaeological Antiquities, once he had transferred there in order to experiment on more supplies of the precious papyrus scrolls, can be seen as an unproductive way of seeking to prise open the cultural archives of another nation and people. This raises for us once again Benjamin's question as to how a certain 'perceptibility' in the presentation of history might best be achieved, particularly when dealing with a culture other than one's own.

This episode from the Romantic era connecting Naples with Britain,[19] and via the latter with an unspecified, faraway colony in Australia, leads us to appreciate how extraordinary the links between near and far cultural realities may be. Such links confirm the bizarre claim that something as apparently insignificant as the movement of a butterfly's wing in one part of the globe can have repercussions elsewhere on the planet. In our apprehension of such extraordinariness, a tantalizing poetics of cultural history emerges. Experiencing this poetics from the outset encourages us to be on the lookout for similar intensities 'passionately at work' within the several lineages of Italian culture traced in the following chapters of this book.

During this early period of Ferdinand's second restoration he seems to have been so grateful to various European powers for having seen off the French that he lavished numerous gifts on other courts and states. Among his posssessions were papyrus scrolls, which came from the ongoing unearthings of Herculaneum, the smaller of two main cities buried after the eruption of Vesuvius in AD 79, ruins of which had been accidentally discovered in 1713 during the sinking of a well. As the future protagonist of this narrative, the scientist Sir Humphry Davy, put it, 'The persons who have the care of the MSS. found at Herculaneum, state that their original number was 1696, and that 431 have been operated upon or presented to foreign governments.'[20] Elsewhere he had stated more exactly that '24 have been presented to foreign potentates.'[21]

The terms of the original gift of papyrus scrolls to the British prince regent were worked out and then communicated to William A'Court in April and May of 1816, in other words, fairly early in this post-war period of Ferdinand's own restoration. Twelve scrolls were to be sent to Britain, was stated in correspondence from Ferdinand's Interior Ministry, and they were to be 'amongst the best conserved of those still unopened.' The scrolls were mostly in Greek, but one was in Latin, from what can be ascertained of them in their unopened state. Along with those to be sent were two already opened papyrus scrolls in fine condition and mounted under glass, containing the second and the eleventh of Epicurus's books on nature. The gift was also to include four further *modern* volumes on the Herculaneum finds, including Philodemus's *Treatise on Music*, and a reprint of Epicurus's same two books on nature from the papyrus originals.[22] This sending of both an ancient text on nature and a modern edition of it is piquant, certainly to us, and maybe to the original recipient of the scrolls, judging from his choice of that reciprocal gift of kangaroos. Already we begin to see an instance of courtly European diplomacy during the Romantic age, touching things recently discovered both from the Classical world and from the New. From a site rich in Roman remains, one European power has amassed an exceedingly large collection of ancient artefacts. Another has not so very long ago been mapping and subsequently colonizing faraway lands, sending a series of convict ships on long voyages to settle one such, and, among other things, has seen brought back on returning vessels exotic species of New World fauna. What could be more logical than to seek favour with the other European power, each by means of a gift of bestowing something found in abundance, in connection with Old and New World discovery?

Once received in Britain, the twelve papyrus scrolls that were not already opened proved a devil. Sir Humphry Davy's attempts to open them, of which he wrote in the newly founded *Quarterly Journal of Literature, Science and the Arts* in 1819, and later briefed the Royal Society in 1821, were only partially successful. Before either of these public revelations took place, English authorities had requested of the Neapolitan court that Sir Humphry be allowed to come to Naples to continue his experiments on further papyrus scrolls, which they begged he be supplied. The Neapolitans obliged by allowing him to work in the great museum that already by then housed so many of the treasures from Pompeii and Herculaneum, including hundreds more of the papyrus scrolls, mostly in far poorer state than those already opened. However, as Sir Humphry revealed to the Royal Society, continuing with the experiments in Naples meant having to collaborate with a whole class of jealous 'unrollers' (*svolgitori* as he called them, adopting their own term)[23] of these manuscripts on home soil.

But what about the kangaroos? Exactly how such animals had reached London from Australia in the first place is a mystery. We first note that kangaroos were going to be sent to Naples in 1818. Presumably Sir William A'Court had communicated to his superiors in England the personal situation of King Ferdinand, which included a reason why such a gift might be welcome. Lady Blessington in her Neapolitan Journals fills us in here by means of a pen portrait of a new woman in Ferdinand's life, the Principessa Partanno (later titled the Duchess of Floridia), 'a Sicilian lady of high birth, who being left a widow with a large family, and no longer in her *première jeunesse*, captivated Ferdinand, soon after the death of his Queen, Caroline, the sister of Marie-Antoinette.'[24] According to Lady Blessington, Ferdinand had bestowed upon this mature Sicilian widow 'his left hand, the title of Princess, and a large revenue.' He proceeded to buy for her as a birthday gift a villa on the Vomero overlooking Naples, which was built from designs by the architect Antonio Niccolini. This villa had large and beautiful gardens where, in Lady Blessington's words of the succeeding years, 'trees, plants, and flowers of every country are skilfully raised. Grottos, of considerable extent, are perforated in the huge rocks that intersect the grounds; a bridge of fine proportion and of cut stone, is thrown across a vast chasm to unite them. Terraces of marble well executed, representing fauns, satyrs, and nymphs, with vases, and groups of sculpture ornament the garden.' As though this romantic scene with its neoclassical leftovers were not enough, Ferdinand also included in the grounds of the Villa Floridiana, named after the Duchess of Floridia (by then his morganatic wife) a *parco zoologico*, or menagerie. Lady Blessington went on to say, 'A menagerie is, in my opinion, the only drawback to this charming place, as the roaring of the lions, and screams of the other wild beasts, are little in harmony with so Arcadian a spot.'

Lady Blessington does not mention the kangaroos themselves. The first and only contemporary *published* record of their existence comes in General Pietro Colletta's *History of the Kingdom of Sicily*, which first appeared posthumously in 1834. His account is a fascinating reaction of the period under study:

> A villa on the Vomero which twenty years previously a certain Lulò, favourite of Queen Caroline of Austria, had built, purportedly for lascivious assignations with her, was bought and enlarged by the minister Saliceti, and then by his heirs sold on to the king, who gave it to his wife, calling it Floridia, after her. He added other grounds and buildings, and with prodigal hand embellished them all. Pastured there were animals from America of luxuriant size called Kangaroos, which by singular deformities often walk on their forepaws, and have a long and curled up tail. Eighteen such obscene beasts were obtained for a stipulated price of a similar number of not yet opened papyrus scrolls from Herculaneum, Sir William A'Court handling the exchange.

Una villa sul Vomero che venti anni prima un tal Lulò, favorito della regina Carolina d'Austria, avea fabbricata, e dicevasi per le secrete lascivie, fu comprata ed ingrandita dal ministro Saliceti, e poi dagli ededi venduta al re, che la donò alla moglie, chaimandola, dal titolo di lei, Floridia. Vi aggiunse altre terre, altri edifizi; e con prodiga mano tutti que' luoghi abbellì: vi si alimentavano per lussuriante grandezza i Kangarou animali dell'America, per deformità singolari, camminando spesso sulle zampe anteriori, e la coda lunga e ravvolta; e, per pattovitto prezzo di diciotto così oscene bestie, furono dati all'Inghilterra altretanti papiri non ancora svolti dell'Ercolano, trattando quel cambio sir William Accourt.[25]

It is an account rich in revelations as well as obvious mistakes. As documentation of the times, whatever its unintended misinformation, it positively exudes fascinating cultural attitudinizing. We already know from the Neapolitan diplomatic records that the original gift from Ferdinand to the prince regent consisted of only twelve unopened papyrus scrolls, a further two already opened, and four modern tomes of editions of Herculaneum texts. Curiously, this does add up to Colletta's total of eighteen. So he is half correct about what was given originally by Ferdinand to the prince regent. That being the case, can we anywhere but in Colletta's text find eighteen of these 'obscene beasts' from *America*?

I have looked hard for these kangaroos in both English and Neapolitan archives. Although in the former I can trace a certain number of them, I cannot find as many as eighteen. Moreover, in neither the Neapolitan nor English archives, and certainly not in all of Sir Humphry Davy's writings on the papyrus scrolls, do I find corroboration of Colletta's point that this was a brokered exchange of Old World courtly diplomacy. All the evidence would seem to hint, on the contrary, that Ferdinand made his original gift in 1816 without obvious calculation of anything in return. He did indeed act through Sir William A'Court. He even offered A'Court the use of a Neapolitan frigate to take the mahogany caskets in which the eighteen items were stowed as far as Toulon or Marseille on a part-sea, part-land route back to Britain, which would have been typical during these post-war years.[26] The symmetry involved in Colletta's account of several years later (for each papyrus scroll, one kangaroo) bears witness to an incessant urge in the writing up of cultural history: the urge to project a deeper patterning than is actually furnished by the messy realities of the past.

General Colletta's disgust with the kangaroos as 'obscene' and 'deformed' is quintessential cultural history in its own right. To illustrate what I mean, here is an example that demonstrates a reaction similar to Colletta's, and suggests how cultivated opinion in Europe towards New World fauna might be a curious mixture of fascination and disgust. Sir Walter Scott was offered a pair of emus for the grounds of the large country house he had constructed for himself at Abbotsford on the Tweed River. His residence and grounds constituted a monumental example – if ever there were one – of bricolage. For instance, in his building materials, Scott incorporated stones from ruined abbeys, from imitations of the same, and even an old door to Edinburgh Jail that he was offered when it was being junked. But his bricolage, incorporating historical memorabilia and exotica, did not stretch to the inclusion of 'emusses' – as he delightfully pluralizes the term. In his journal for Tuesday 17 July 1827, Scott writes:

> Here is a whimsical subject of affliction. Mr. Harper, a settler who went from this country to Botany Bay, thinking himself obliged to me for a recommendation to General McAllister and Sir Thomas Brisbane, has thought proper to bring me home a couple of Emusses. I wish his gratitude had either taken a different turn or remaind [sic] as quiescent as that of others whom I have obliged more materially. I at first accepted the creatures, conceiving them in my ignorance to be some sort of blue and green parrot which though I do not admire their noise migh[t] scream and yell at their pleasure if hung up in the hall among the armour. But your Emus it seems stand six feet high on his stocking soles and is little better than a kind of Kassowari or Ostrich. Hang them, they might [eat] up my collection of old arms fro [sic] what I know.[27]

In his edition of Scott's journal W.E.K. Anderson notes that it took Scott at least a fortnight to rid himself of the impending gift of the emus. In a letter to his publisher Robert Cadell after his insolvency, Scott continued in this vein: 'In this dilemma & not willing to affront a good & kind man I have written to Mr Somerville Writer Edinr. (Mr. Harper's friend) to get his permission to transfer the birds to the King and [if] Mr Harper will give his consent I would wish them sent with every due precaution by the next steamboat to the Royal Menagerie at the tower. Do for gods sake seek out Mr Somerville without loss of time and try to get me free of the Emusses; the matter is pressing for I expect every moment to see the Emusses arrive here followed by the whole mob of Melrose and Darnick.'[28] Anderson had this to add: 'It seems that the King was already provided with Emus, and that Harper himself called on Cadell to assure him "that his Emus are as inoffensive as Turkies – feed on natural grapes, and follow him in the quietest manner."' Scott then solicited the Duke of Buccleuch, thinking he might like them. Poor Scott had been made insolvent only the year before, in January 1826, and his assets put in the hands of trustees. His wife died shortly afterwards. At the time of the emus, he was already hoping to buy back the copyright to his novels, which had been acquired by his trustees. Perhaps the prospect of feeding two exotic six-foot-high birds was the last straw.

Why do I dwell on this amusing tale of reaction to Australian fauna? My larger point is that too often in cultural history we narrow our focus to only one context. I would urge that, in particular when dealing with opinions, attitudes, and reactions, wherever possible there should be a wider trawl for illuminating inter-cultural comparison. For there exists something like a 'spirit of the age,' as William Hazlitt was to call it in the title of his famous book of 1825. I contend that, although representative of different parts of Europe, General Pietro Colletta's and Sir Walter Scott's sensibilities are closer in kind to one another than either of them are to our own historical temper. I also contend that one of the highest and most constant goals of cultural history should be to move from analysis of incident to the plane of what is revealed *through* incident about the *zeitgeist* or historical *episteme* – the terms for spirit of the age are themselves multiple, if often foreign![29] At many points in this book I seek to go through that analytical gear change from specific instance to general condition, which may be difficult when already travelling at speed through so much historical material that is local and initially requiring close focus.

The aim of seeing homologies between the part and the whole in culture has been brilliantly defined by Clifford Geertz: 'Hopping back and forth between the whole conceived through the parts that actualise it and the parts conceived through the whole that motivates them, we seek to turn them, by a sort of intellectual perpetual motion, into explications of one another.'[30] My only caveat – developed further in chapter 3, on passion – is that Geertz's formulation does not sharpen our wits sufficiently to uncover cases where the specific is not necessarily and inevitably an expression of the general. Geertz's formulation suggests that it is *our activity of interpretation* that is in the final analysis all-important in the realization of cultural history. By his reckoning it is *our* seeking to turn part and whole into 'explications of one another' that is crucial and dynamic: crucial *because* dynamic (an 'intellectual perpetual motion' on our parts) in the history-producing process. But to my perception, alongside this tracing of homologies between the local and the general – synecdoches of culture, so to speak – we must elaborate a counter-hypothesis to Geertz's. The specific example studied (and this applies especially to works of art) may not unerringly be either representative of, or for that matter, in Geertz's terms, 'motivated' by 'the whole.'

For instance, Mozart and Da Ponte's opera *Don Giovanni* (which I will treat in greater detail in my third chapter) has everything to do with surrounding culture. But its greatness is such that it reveals more about the culture than vice versa. The homology does not work reciprocally, in other words, according to Geertz's beautifully symmetrical model of interpretation. Nothing in the *ancien régime* to that point could have helped us to anticipate the nature of this opera. Rather, the specific case follows the one-way logic of what Adorno meant when he made a pronouncement fundamentally at odds with Geertz's later principle of interpreting culture. Geertz's point, again, is that interpretation works best as an intellectual perpetual motion, from the part to the whole and from the whole back to the part. Adorno's point, while scarcely less brilliant as a formulation, is somewhat less gratifying for interpreters, since it claims that in the case of major works of art there cannot be an adequate 'deducing' of their meaning from the circumambient 'totality' of culture. 'The specific work can never be reconstructed or deduced from the historical totality; on the contrary, the totality is contained within its most minute cell.'[31] In other words, the culture does not 'include' or in any real sense 'explain' the great instance. To the contrary, Adorno's is a larger and also more counter-intuitive claim: a work such as *Don Giovanni* 'contains' the totality! And it does so not only in its entirety as a work of art, but 'within its most minute cell.' This recourse to scientific language on Adorno's part is interesting in terms of the narrative of 1816–20 that I have related here.

So what actually happened to the kangaroos, and how many of them could there have been? I found the first note of intention to make a gift of kangaroos in 1818 in the Public Records Office in London among the collection of diplomatic interchanges between Naples and England of that year. Evidence of the kangaroos is of a different kind than almost all the other documents in the file. It consists of a few hastily written pencil notes. These notes were encountered only intermittently in a box otherwise dedicated to items of more formal diplomacy, mostly touching on the petty crimes of British naval seamen in Naples, on trade agreements or, occasionally, on larger affairs of state in Britain's relatively amicable and untroubled dealings with Naples during these years. Some of the latter documents, which I encountered while looking for references to kangaroos, were originally sent from Naples in letter code, and only turned back into readable English once in Britain. These largely refer to Prince Metternich's policies, either in Europe generally, or with specific regard to Naples, whose Bourbon sovereign was to a considerable degree under Austria's political influence during these years. This is another aspect of all that I would claim cannot and should not be excluded from consideration when reading through an archive with a predetermined quest in mind. Almost inevitably, as in my case in seeking to capture some elusive kangaroos in diplomatic files of almost two centuries ago, other things in an archive will draw one's attention. In letting ourselves be distracted by such apparent miscellanea as Metternich's activities, and Neapolitan attitudes toward them, the overall work acquires the potential to achieve the cultural specificity that Geertz famously called 'thick description.'

Oddly, the marsupials due to be taken to Naples are overlooked by Castlereagh in England over the subsequent winter. Their keeper in the Kings Mews is forced to write a reminder about 'these unfortunate kangaroos,' as he calls them. (Might this be the same menagerie at the tower of London where, a few years later, as we have seen, the sovereign already possessed a sufficiency of emus and would not want Scott's pair?) Plans are then laid to take the kangaroos out on 'the first Ship of War or Store Ship destined for the Mediterranean.' But when a boat is found, it is not one sailing a direct passage. The kangaroos are to be transported first to Malta in one vessel and then forwarded at the next available opportunity, while those in charge were enjoined to make sure 'to feed them during the Passage to Malta at a Rate of five guineas for each.' Sir William Hamilton writes that 'directions have been given to the Clerk of the King's Stables at the Royal Mews, to cause the five Kangaroos to be put into the proper Cages and sent aboard the Ann.'[32] This particular mention of the kangaroos, and of the number five, is the last time I can trace them at all until they mysteriously reappear as eighteen in number in Colletta's posthumous text almost fifteen years later. (Colletta had died in 1831, and the first edition of his *History* did not appear until 1834.)

Clearly some kangaroos had eventually and successfully reached Naples, and been placed in the menagerie of the Villa Floridiana. Possibly by the time that General Colletta saw them there they had multiplied in the Neapolitan climate, so like parts of Australia. That may be the cause of the numerical discrepancy in the various documents. What we can say with certainty is that nobody with direct Australian interests was involved in the diplomacy between King Ferdinand and Sir William A'Court. The circulation of gifts is confined to Old World protagonists, which is perhaps one reason why a person of General Colletta's distinction in Neapolitan society could be ignorant about the exact New World origin of the kangaroos he saw. Any reading elsewhere in his *History of the Realm of Naples* will reveal Colletta a highly educated man for his day, with a clear sense of Naples' position on the political, social, and economic map of Europe over hundreds of years. It is only such matters concerning New World exotica that show him to be out of his depth. The age had not yet dawned in which even the most modestly educated children the world over would associate kangaroos with Australia (although it is possible that Colletta was using the term 'America' loosely to reference the New World in general).

I was dealing earlier with learning of a rather different kind. For the gift of papyrus scrolls and the task of furthering cultural knowledge about the ancient world by means of them had fallen to the English scientist and inventor Sir Humphry Davy. The English authorities vaunted his fame when they asked permission for him to work in Naples on further exemples. Castlereagh wrote to A'Court in August 1818: 'I am commanded by the Prince Regent to acquaint you that Sir Humphry Davy, the most eminent of our Professors in various branches of natural Science purposes during the course of his Travels on the Continent of Europe, to reside some time in the course of the Autumn in Naples, and that a Series of Experiments which he has conducted in this City before he left England has given him reason to hope that he will be able to lend a very effectual assistance in unrolling the Herculaneum Manuscripts.'[33] Davy's discipline was not history itself, though in this particular matter of the scrolls his goal certainly was to broaden historical and literary knowledge. Rather, his activities related to what he understood best, namely chemical science, in which he was possibly Europe's most advanced researcher of this age. His early book of 1799, *Researches, Chemical and Philosophical, Chiefly Concerning Nitrous Oxide ... and its Respiration*, went so far as to recommend that the said laughing gas be used as an anaesthetic in surgical procedures. Though the medical suggestion was not taken up, the gas was inhaled in fashionable social gatherings, obviously to much hilarity.[34]

A fellow of the Royal Society since 1803, Davy was to become its president in 1820, immediately following the aforementioned episode in Naples. He had published many important papers already, given countless lectures to learned societies, and shortly beforehand had reported on his most famous invention, the safety lamp for miners. The challenge of opening these papyrus scrolls now rests with him, at the Regent's own request. They become indeed the physical *matter* on which he must for a while conduct his ongoing experiments. He tends to discuss them in subsequent lectures and articles in terms of their chemical properties.

As with our own enquiry into cultural history, Sir Humphry frequently in his experiments changed direction, and tried opening scrolls by some new chemical means when an earlier attempt had not been entirely or even modestly successful. He experimented with soaking the scrolls in stronger or weaker solutions, and with heating them once immersed to greater or lesser degrees. Most were not so much charred as dampened, and of an earthy consistency, since volcanic ash did not settle over Herculaneum to the extent it did over Pompeii, the latter having been nearer to the eruption and more entirely enveloped in the pyroclastic surge that we now understand shot forth from Vesuvius. The consistency of the *papyri* was therefore that of peat. 'My experiments soon convinced me that the nature of these MSS. had been generally misunderstood; they had not, as is usually supposed, been carbonized by the operation of fire, and they were in a state analogous to peat ... Moisture, by its action upon vegetable matter, produces decomposition, which may be seen in peat bogs in all its different stages.'[35]

Katie Trumpener has worked this same literal term – peat bog – into an effective trope in her figuring of Irish history as the bog beneath much of the land. One of the interesting things about Trumpener's deployment of this trope is the way the bog is recognized as a morass that envelopes or engulfs history at the same time that it preserves it. Culture has over time sunk down into and been penetrated by the bog, metaphorically at any rate. That culture of which she writes so well survives to an extent *within* the bog, and its later manifestations are essentially emanations from the vastnesses *of* the bog. By contrast the draining of the bog leads to a desiccation and destruction of material history.[36]

My own quest for subtler ways of accessing and talking about Italy's past bears comparison with Trumpener's exploration of Irish cultural history. However, I am concerned that we focus not only on the matrix of history, or repository of its remainders (bog or papyrus scroll, as it may be), but also on the figure of the researcher into it, Sir Humphry Davy in the specific instance. Renowned scientist from a country that is a close ally of the Kingdom of Naples and the Two Sicilies, he is attempting experiments to recuperate stores of ancient learning from their different states of decomposition. Castlereagh himself has been requested by the prince regent, as he puts it in that letter to Sir William A'Court, to leave 'nothing untried to open to the Public these valuable Stores of ancient Literature.' The English minister has sought 'to engage his Sicilian Majesty to give to Sir Humphry Davy in his researches the opportunities which he may require for applying to the Manuscripts now under examination at Naples, or to any other more favourable to his purposes, the results of his Experiments.'[37]

The relevant opportunities have indeed been made available to Davy, though they have led to tensions between him and his Neapolitan hosts. What most impresses me at this stage is the fervour with which the main experimenter, with so much backing both from England and, by means of diplomacy, from Naples itself, is seeking to piece together bits and pieces of tantalizing cultural relics. The best of the scrolls have long since been opened by the Neapolitans themselves. But Davy is convinced that any new and collateral pieces of ancient literature that his experiments may bring to light could alter the way the entirety of what has already been discovered is understood. A fragment could further illuminate the grasp of the ancient world that has been pieced together so far.

It is this last point that most nearly approximates our own quests for understanding, and the enterprises by which we seek to bring them to fruition. At the local level we are looking at Davy looking at the ancient world. But more fundamentally ours is an attempt to comprehend as fully as possible a number of different lineages in Italian cultural history and only incidentally this particular moment in British and Neapolitan relations within the flow of them. Davy's use of chemical hypotheses, subtly altering his various experiments for recuperating papyrus relics in different stages of decomposition, is highly analogous to our own tacking and weaving by means of hypothesis and analysis. His discoveries extend all the way from *papyri* where the characters have been erased by damp penetration or by processes of detaching sheet from sheet, to others that are entirely legible when opened. Similarly, there are things we can know with ease about a particular cultural reality from Italy's past, but there are also contiguous factors, shrouded in mystery, that tantalize our desire for fresh discovery.

Like Davy we must be prepared for archival whiteout – places, in other words, where there has been total fissuring or erasure of what was once in the culture. 'Of a few, particularly the superficial parts, and which probably were most exposed to air and water, little remains except the earthy basis, the charcoal of the characters, and some of that of the vegetable matter, being destroyed, and they are in a condition approaching to that of the MSS. found at Pompeii, where the air, constantly penetrating through the loose ashes, there being no barrier against it as in the consolidated tufa of Herculaneum, has entirely destroyed all the carbonaceous parts of the Papyrus, and left nothing but earthy matter.'[38] Just as Davy discovers that many of the papyrus scrolls that he opens have had the charcoal inks of their written characters disappear over time, we often find just enough evidence that something has occurred, but *not* sufficient enough to piece together what it was. Sometimes, too, our frustration is with explorers who have gone before, who by their clumsy methodologies have managed to damage the archive. 'The persons charged with the business of unrolling the MSS. in the museum, informed me that many chemical experiments had been performed on the MSS. at different times, which assisted the separation of the leaves, but always destroyed the characters. To prove that this was not the case with my method, I made two experiments before them.'[39]

At this point we are in a highly sensitive area. Who should have access to the cultural archive and to what degree? In particular, should an archive of one nation be open to scholars from afar as well as near, and if so, on what terms? We are frequently arrogant about our own methodologies, and such arrogance is particularly unwelcome to others when they figure us as the cultural interloper. From the way he writes on this sensitive issue, Sir Humphry seems hardly aware of the sensibilities he might have been ruffling. 'I did not think it proper to communicate the details of my method to the operators in the museum; for though it possesses great simplicity, yet it must be performed with care, and is a gradual process, and might be injurious in unskilful hands, and ought to be executed by an accurate manipulator, and one acquainted with the science of chemistry.'[40]

Here we have the renowned chemist from abroad, handling the most valuable Neapolitan archive of ancient learning, and arrogantly implying that, simple though his method of opening papyrus manuscripts is, it would be unwise to impart it to a 'native' practitioner. We may laugh at this, but I submit that it is a situation replicated over and over in our own scholarly world. The interloper will not trust the persons already in the field, is convinced he or she is possessed of a superior new methodology of access to truth, and precisely out of this conviction decides to 'patent' the methodology for personal use solely. Always reasons are given for attempting to patent the access route. The claim is invariably based on notions of superiority. The new expert, in this case Davy, is in fact all the while behaving like a colonizing overlord. Obviously if one has a closed mind towards those in the same field of enquiry, one cannot benefit from their experience. One has, precisely, *prejudged* that experience as unworthy of attention.

The prejudgment on Davy's part, this closure of his mind to Neapolitan experts, is in effect what Superintendent Rosini of the Office of the Papyrus Scrolls in Naples complains of in a letter to the Neapolitan Minister of Internal Affairs:

> Your Excellency has communicated to me ... that Cavaliere Davy desires to copy some lines of papyrus scrolls already opened so as to compare them with those upon which he is working, in the hope that by such means he may decide at first glance on the author and on the nature of the work, without being obliged to open fully papyrus scrolls of little value; of all this you require me to give my opinion. To do so it is my duty to tell you that I do not understand at all how from reading a few lines of an opened scroll one can decide at first glance on the authorship and on the nature of a different work, much less how one can do so without reading the work itself.
>
> Mi ha partecipato S.E ... che il Cavaliere Davy desidera di far copiare alcune linee de' papiri già svolti per poterli paragonare con quelli intorno ai quali si sta adoperando, perché con questo mezzo egli spera poter decidere a primo lancio dell'autore, e della natura dell'opera, senza essere obbligato a svolgere sino alla fine papiri di poco valore; laonde Ella m'impone d'informarla col parere sull'oggetto. In esecuzione è mio dovere dirle che io non comprendo affatto, come dalla lettura di poche linee di un papiro svolto possa decidersi a primo lancio dell'autore, e della natura di un'altra opera, e molto meno, come ciò si possa fare, senza leggere l'opera stessa.[41]

Monsignor Rosini goes on to say that there is a schedule involved in the museum's own work, from the opening of manuscripts, to their republication in modern editions, and then to the business of interpretation; this last stage requiring time and reflection if truth is to be discerned. In particular, Rosini does not wish for advance publication abroad of what the Neapolitan monarch has already decided will be best handled in editions under the imprimatur of his Herculaneum Academy. Piecemeal publication of orts and scraps of papyrus scroll by the likes of Davy could lead to false knowledge, which the Neapolitan academicians would be obliged to correct before the public of all Europe, partly compromising even themselves in the process.

Davy, for his part, is convinced that the Neapolitans under Bourbon rule are stretching out publication almost to the crack of doom. 'From the characters of the persons charged with their publication, there is very little probability of their being, for many years, offered to the world, which is much to be regretted; for though not interesting, from their perfection as literary works, they would unquestionably throw much light upon the state of civilization, letters, and science, of the age and country to which they belonged.'[42] It all comes down to the question as to what constitutes 'the literary world' that Davy appeals to at the end of his first relation. Someone who had by now turned antagonistic to Davy, the Neapolitan secretary of state for internal affairs, even more boldly refers to 'the literary republic' in speaking of the dispute. This internal minister, in a letter to the Neapolitan minister of foreign affairs, is appealing that this *repubblica letteraria* not be compromised by irregular acts of publication on the foreign chemist's part.[43]

If the literary 'world' or *repubblica* is one that truly minimizes the importance of all political and national boundaries, well and good. But it normally doesn't. And in such cases there must be protocols. When Davy had submitted his first requests, one of them had been for 'Permission to make these experiments within a room in the Museum from which all persons not employed by the maker of these requests are excluded, or to make them out of the Museum in a proper laboratory.'[44] These are not exactly the words of a person who has thought out the meaning of his own term, the literary world. And possibly the fact that he is a *chemist* trying to access ancient literary documents – practising, so to speak, a certain 'interdisciplinarity' – makes him less than fully sensitive (as someone who was more of a classical scholar might be) to what Monsignor Rosini calls these documents' 'nature.' I tread carefully at this point, from my own deep belief in what sophisticated deployment of one discipline in the service of another can bring by way of developing knowledge. But I have to admit that the charge being made by Rosini is not without merit for our times as well as for his and Davy's: namely, that to make valid comparisons you need sufficient evidence from the works being compared. Rosini is a classical *litterateur* of his day, and he is implicitly criticizing Davy for lack of training, not in chemistry (which is his undisputed forte), but in classical letters. Davy is not, according to Rosini, in a position to discover authorship and subject matter from the scraps of writing he has managed so far to open. He ought to immerse himself at the very least in the already available archive before proclaiming himself to be in a position to extend it.

One of my reasons for sensitivity to this entire fracas is that I am a non-Italian who has dared now to write a second book on lineages in Italian culture. One has to be perpetually on one's guard to the charge, stated or unstated, that one is somehow trespassing on another people's lives and histories. At the same time it is of vital importance that one not lose one's nerve in genuine attempts – attempts one should remain proud of – to fathom something beyond one's ken. Plainly the example of Davy, for all his fervent desire to open ancient documents successfully, is somewhat negative. We sense his unwillingness to dialogue with contemporary Neapolitans, however learned, and his shortcomings in getting to know the prior state of knowledge of a field he was so confident he could expand.

This brings to mind another dictum of the same period from the hand of Giacomo Leopardi. It is a two-part judgment that complicates, but in a most interesting way, the whole issue of studying cultures other than one's own. Leopardi's principal case was a point so general that it is really only a truism: namely that 'it is impossible for a foreigner to know perfectly another nation' ('impossibile a uno straniero il conoscere perfettamente un'altra nazione'). But his associated point is trickier, and was applied specifically to his own culture. 'Italians,' he claimed, are 'sensitive above all other peoples about their reputation; a truly strange fact, considering the little or even non-existent national esteem which exists among us, most certainly less than in other countries' ('delicatissimi sopra tutti gli altri sul conto loro: cosa veramente strana, considerando il poco o niuno amor nazionale che vive tra noi, e certo minore che non è negli altri paesi').[45] This latter part of Leopardi's judgment would seem to remain largely valid in our own times. But merely saying so does not make this enterprise of writing on Italian cultural history any less fraught with risk.

On the one side lies the Scylla of never being able fully to experience the culture as an Italian might, on the other the Charybdis of Italian touchiness about being analysed by anyone but themselves. Possibly both dangers are best just faced head on. As far as Italian touchiness goes, it must be braved. The really great analytical documents in and about this culture – works such as Leopardi's *Zibaldone* or Gramsci's *Prison Notebooks* – are no longer widely read by Italians themselves, except for a small and possibly shrinking class that still tackles the kind of long work that is all the more brilliant for its vast scope. (Another example of the type of work in question, though not one about Italy, would be Benjamin's

Arcades Project, which, applicable to what we are talking about here, is largely about a different culture from that of Benjamin's upbringing.) As for the risk of not ever being able to experience with the sensitivity of an insider, one can retort that there is not in any case one Italian culture but many, such that very few Italians have 'insider' access to a wide gamut of the many variations of Italianness. Furthermore, as anyone with a modicum of sense will attest, there are truths that *only* an outsider can begin to see clearly or analyse dispassionately.

Another point I would make about Italian cultural history is that never before have there been so many people both inside *and* outside Italy, particularly in the United Kingdom and the United States, engaged in its pursuit. Ideally one should be ceaselessly attending to studies both from within Italy and abroad. It is against all reasonable protocols of a 'literary republic,' either in Davy's day or our own, to pretend to hegemony over a domain of learning, the main archives of which are superintended in that other country whose ancient or modern culture one wants best routes into. To claim, as Davy did, that one brings to an entire field of learning a new methodology of access, while refusing to impart its techniques to the very keepers of the archive, is counter-productive. To do so in ways that reveal that one is not very conversant with what has already been successfully accessed and stored within that archive is worse than counter-productive. It demonstrates obtuseness, even from the world's leading chemist of the day.

The visitor from another European culture, Sir Humphry Davy, and those he wished would leave him to his own chemical devices in Naples, alone with their unopened papyrus scrolls, eventually reached a stand-off. After two successive winters in Naples, Davy simply went home, and thereafter made his reports on matters concerning papyrus scrolls among men of learning in his own culture.

I have been using this story of cultural interchange between Naples and England as an instance of what the American philosopher-critic Kenneth Burke in 1945 called a 'Representative Anecdote.' Burke seemed to accept our need to use representative anecdotes, often even as tropes, but no sooner began discussing them than he raised some problems.

> Men seek for vocabularies that will be faithful *reflections* of reality. To this end, they must develop vocabularies that are *selections* of that reality. And any selection of reality must, in certain circumstances, function as a *deflection* of reality. Insofar as the vocabulary meets the needs of reflection, we can

say that it has the necessary scope. In its selectivity, it is a reduction. Its scope and reduction become a deflection when the given terminology, or calculus, is not suited to the subject matter which it is designed to calculate.[46]

Burke does not warn us off representative anecdotes entirely, and even implies, in his way of playing the point about 'deflection,' that if suited to the subject matter they may act as an instructive 'calculus.' But he does also mention pitfalls and cases of unsuitability. I have chosen to use selective representations – some in the form of anecdotes, others as 'exemplary instances' of a general case – throughout this book. My plea is that without them no ambitious attempts to formulate what has actually gone on and been significant in the evolution of a culture such as that of Italy would be possible. If we sought to avoid reductions entirely, we would be trying always to describe a totality that is beyond all scope of being captured. Our 'vocabularies' would not be able to leave anything out because no one thing would be admitted as representative of many other cases.

A danger, and it is not one I have managed to avoid entirely, is that while attending to one representative aspect of a culture, many others – and important ones at that – may be occluded in the process. For instance, despite the highly political nature of several of the chapters that follow, the present introduction does not present large political perspectives, only descriptions of intercultural sensitivities and their significance. On the other hand, I have taken pains to stipulate that even when not looking to fathom the overall historical situation one gains wider insight. Simply sifting through a diplomatic file in search of kangaroos, one might stumble as I did on reports, originally in code, on Metternich and on Neapolitan attitudes to him. Over and over again in cultural history, what at first may seem small matters and what one surmises will be (and remain) momentous change places, back and forth, in the mind. And this, it now seems to me after many years of study, is entirely as it should be. One of the hardest things to estimate of a prior moment in culture is how relatively important various matters were. We usually start our enquiries by exporting into the past our own hierarchies of importance. It is quite a jolly irony that these always need to be radically revised by the time one is capable of anything like thick description of that other culture, and no matter whether, and how much, our own culture may be lineally descended from it. For the priorities of cultures, as of individuals, change imperceptibly over time, and over the longer term the differences become dramatic.

Sir Walter Scott knew Sir Humphry Davy, from a meeting in 1805, also in his later capacity as president of the Royal Society, and furthermore because Davy had married an Antiguan-born daughter of the neighbouring Kerr family from Kelso, to whom Scott believed himself related. Davy stayed at Abbotsford in 1820. Did they speak about scrolls or kangaroos? The former would have been a likely topic, since Davy had not long been back from conducting his chemical experiments on these peaty relics of ancient culture. Kings of Naples and prince regents would probably have been mutual interests, maybe rolled together into one culturally comparative subject in their discussion. Scott was certainly also highly interested in Herculaneum, and was to visit it and Pompeii some years later on his trip to Italy shortly before he died. These last details and accompanying speculations are hardly representative. On the other hand, as cultural history of people's lives, and of their consuming interest from afar in aspects of Italy – great enough to cause them in old age to travel there to experience such realities in person – they are significant.

Scott's own lifelong fascination with the past would lead him towards the end of his life to speak of the 'curious history' that was so elusive to an enquirer, and which he contended might be pieced together from fragments and miscellanea – if only the necessary continuities might be recovered.[47] I have sought to recover the continuity of one such highly curious history in this introduction, out of fragmentary knowledges that we are able to piece together about some papyri and kangaroos that were courtly gifts almost two centuries ago.

1 Modes of Viewing: From Vasari to Film and Television Culture

How do we conceptualize the world, including our own or any other culture within it? In particular, what devices or technologies have provided – or currently provide – ways of bringing what is historically or geographically distant into a frame of reference and mode for viewing?

There is a way by which we may conceptualize modes of popular viewing of things both far and near in time and space. I call this conceptualization a 'cultural cosmorama,' which is admittedly a metaphor, but one grounded in an account of actual optic boxes of the eighteenth and early nineteenth centuries. These viewing boxes used to be rather loosely called cosmoramas. The technical term that modern Italian scholars have taken to calling them is *pantoscopi*.[1] But when they flourished, in the eighteenth century especially, they were mainly called *mondi nuovi* ('new worlds'), or some variant thereof, because of what they promised by way of imaginary access to other times and places, just from peeping into them (see figure 1.1). What seem to have been their contexts of use and the 'prospects' they made possible? And how should we compare the knowledge that they provided and the wider imagining that they stimulated in the public with all that later cinematic and televisual modes of viewing have made possible, both cognitively and imaginatively?

Lines of development in Italian culture were very different to a High Renaissance painter and thinker such as Giorgio Vasari, compared with how people during the age of Enlightenment saw them, or indeed with how we ourselves do several centuries later. Vasari had a mighty sense of continuities in his charting of the lives of artists, through to what he saw as an apex of achievement during the generation and in the individual works of Michelangelo. In Vasari's text, simple though it may be in its

Figure 1.1 A *mondo nuovo* with children viewing images in it, last quarter of the eighteenth century. Attributed to G.M. Graneri. Courtesy Museo Nazionale del Cinema, Turin.

grand lineaments, there occurs a specific moment where he says something compelling about a totalizing 'cosmography.' Vasari sought and achieved this quality in Duke Cosimo I de' Medici's remodellings of the Palazzo Vecchio in Florence as a residence and seat of power – not surprisingly under Vasari's stewardship. The textual moment comes in Vasari's description of the palazzo's *Sala del Guardaroba*, a room embellished with Ptolemaic maps and representations of exotic flora and fauna, as well as events upon which, and persons upon whom, hinged momentous turns of history.

The words I wish to draw attention to are part of Vasari's account of the chief artist involved in the decorations of the room, Ignazio Danti, 'very excellent in matters of cosmography, and of rare talent' ('nelle cose di cosmografia eccellentissimo, e di raro ingegno'). This Renaissance map room, according to Vasari, was a 'capriccio ed invenzione' of Duke Cosimo's own devising, something designed to gather 'all things relating to heaven and earth in one place, without error, so that one could see and measure them together and by themselves' ('per mettere insieme [ad] una volta queste cose del cielo e della terra giustissime e senza errori, e da poterle misurare e vedere ed a parte e tutte insieme').[2] The important point to be remembered, particularly in relation to the popular optic devices of the succeeding Enlightenment age, is one well put by Juergen Schutz, in his analysis of the room's frescoed map cycle and of the rarities from Duke Cosimo's collections. Schutz stresses that 'like the decorations found in many other Renaissance *studioli*, the decoration of the *Guardaroba* aspired to mirror the sum of wisdom attained by humankind, in the form of a complete representation of the physical cosmos and a selection of the men who had governed it or labored to understand it ... A theological order was ... implied by the rising tiers of plants, animals, lands, men, and constellations.'[3]

Vasari's notion of having some means or device – here the artistic program of the *Sala del Guardaroba* itself – that enables acts of dynamic configuring of where we stand in relation to larger trajectories of history or wider realms of geography is crucial to my study. For it is at this point that I come to one of the main notions of this chapter – the idea of an analogous 'cultural cosmorama,' into which I claim we inevitably gaze from one phase of our lives to another, making comparisons (consciously or not) between what we see in it from the past or the unknown, and our immediately surrounding culture. Some aspects of my meta-phor do, of course, change over time. For instance, we move from an implicitly theological ordering of such a room as Duke Cosimo's to the 'encyclopaedic' optic box of the Enlightenment (whether it be called *scatola, cassella*, or more popularly in Venetian, the 'mondo niovo'), commonly mounted in piazzas during that period and operated by a travelling *inbonitore*, and then to the binding secular experience of the modern age, the television screen.

As a culture, we return constantly to the screen of that other small 'box' – whether television set or computer monitor makes little difference to my argument – for knowledge and entertainment. Domestic in its placement, or sometimes professional, it purveys fixed or moving images received mainly from external transmissions with which we usually have lamentably little direct input. Sometimes, as in the images of the destruction of the two World Trade Center buildings that have dominated our cultural imagination of late, even 'live' videotaping of events comes from those who find themselves doing so by happenstance, who are, in other words, in the grip of factors of 'recording' and 'representation' largely beyond their own controlling power.

Let us concern ourselves for a moment with these shifts in conceptual paradigms, initially from one model of knowing, Duke Cosimo's Renaissance map room, to that later one, the optic boxes or *mondi nuovi*. Even as I discuss aspects of the latter, I shall throughout be claiming that at this millennial cusp, we too are positioned in a cultural sense (in spite of actual technologies of presentation having gone through a series of further paradigms) as though before an optic device such as the portable cosmoramas.

For my larger philosophical claim is that scenes and events of the past, including different geographies than those where we may be positioned at any particular moment, present themselves for our contemplation in a changing succession within the metaphorical cosmorama of our minds. These images challenge us, as students of culture, to attain to higher understandings of how the various aspects of a vast cultural history interrelate and also how they correspond to what we see when we raise our heads and seek to read the present directly. But when we do look up, we often find that matters of our own times are themselves not free from obscurities, arising in the course of their transmission to us. Reality being always more complex than any single interpretation or 'snapshot' of it, the projections in the 'cultural cosmorama' that we are trying to interpret rarely seem like the full truth of any given moment of our vast inheritance, including even the present. The snapshots are simply too 'static,' too frozen as single moments in an evolutionary continuum.

Admitting, however, this inevitable incompleteness of any attempt to understand the relationship between changing projections in the cosmorama, there is no excuse for not attempting to prise open each angle of interpretation as wide as possible, starting from the earliest. The cosmorama was a device during the age of the Enlightenment, capable of producing, as a consequence of its exotic displays of other states and places, considerations of how the present might be recast in some imagined future. The best single representation for understanding the uses of these popular eighteenth-century optic devices is a line engraving by Gaetano Zompini of one such 'mondo niovo' (Venetian spelling), from his 1753 collection of engravings *Le Arti Che Vanno Per Via Nella Città di Venezia* (see figure 1.2), one of sixty such engravings executed between 1746 and 1754, representing the common street occupations of Venetians.[4]

Precisely because of the cosmorama's nature as a device for gazing into, there are two common terms – *distances* and *prospects* – of importance in our discussion of it, and which assume more than their ordinary meaning. More than being merely spatial markers, the terms gradually take on temporal significance as well.

The two terms are taken directly from the rubric to the line engraving by Zompini. As the rubric makes clear, for the cost of one soldo the contraption's owner – the so-called *imbonitore* – showed the *mondo niovo, con dentro lontananze, e prospettive*, 'in which are distances and prospects' (or perspectives). In discursive terms, the new world, and hence the *lontananze* (distant views) and *prospettive* (perspectives) which it comprises, are literally *dentro*, 'inside,' the device (see figure 1.3).[5] They are images (*vedute*) that we don't see, but which we are encouraged in this image that we *do* see, of the *boy seeing them*, to imagine as exotic topographies. They enter into *our* imagination as viewers, in other words, precisely by being indirectly rather than directly represented.

Already in this first of several images of cosmoramas that we are considering closely, the words *lontananze* and *prospettive* take on slightly more than their technical significances, and suggest, tropologically, that images of a whole 'new world' really are projected *within the device*. The distances and prospects are internal to the device, in technological terms, but in terms of the imaginary they know almost no bounds. In short, the technology of a popular, relatively small street device mounted on trestles, becomes a means of escaping, in geographical terms, far beyond the Venice of the device's present emplacement in Zompini's engraving. (Sometimes the profusion of such devices gets considered in terms of a history of pre-cinema. But we must be careful not to conceptualise those optic devices merely in relation to the later technol-

Modes of Viewing: From Vasari to Film and Television Culture   33

In sta cassela mostro el Mondo niovo
Con dentro lontananze, e prospetive,
Vogio un soldo per testa; e ghe la trovo.

Figure 1.2 The *imbonitore* of a *mondo nuovo* shows mother and child, for the price of one *soldo*, the 'distances and prospects' of a range of views (*vedute*). Gaetano Zompini, engraving from *Le Arti Che Vanno Per Via Nella Città di Venezia* (1753). Courtesy Biblioteca Querini Stampalia, Venice.

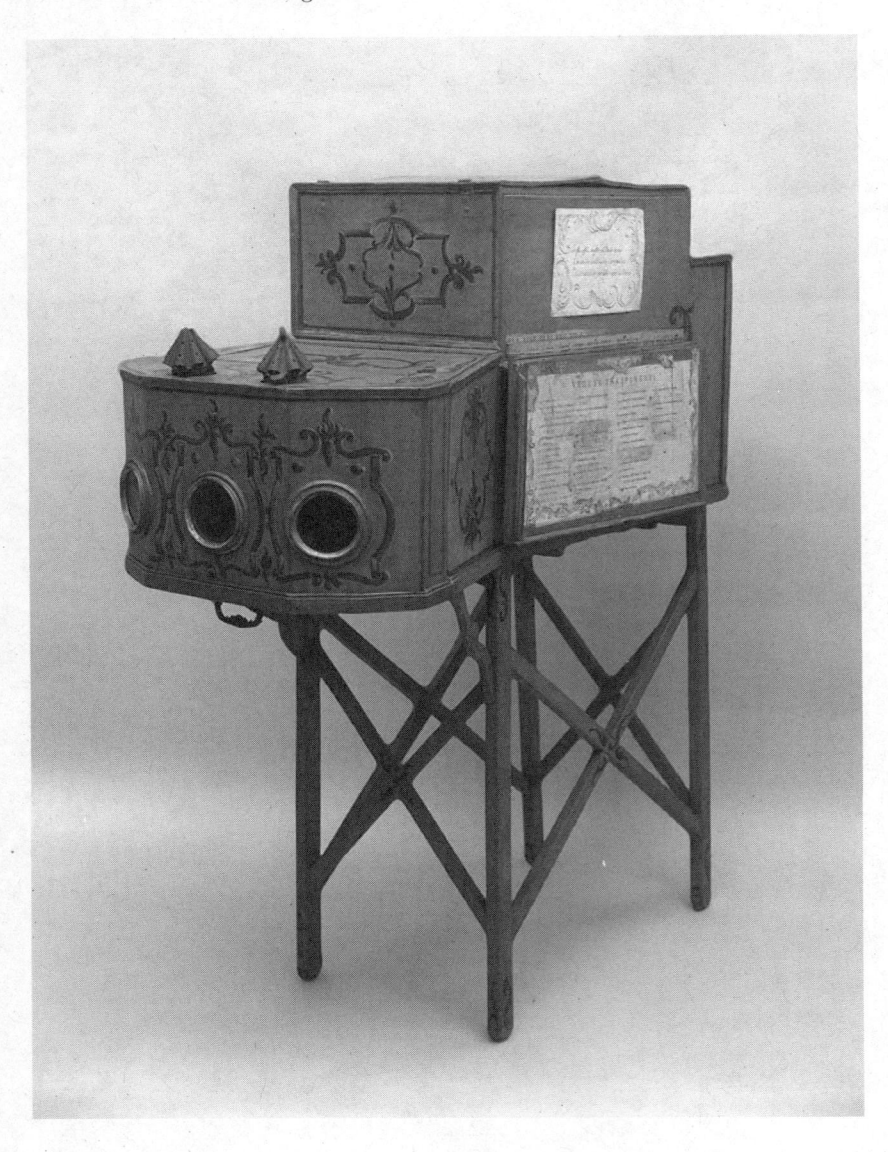

Figure 1.3 A *mondo nuovo* from Venice, last half of the eighteenth century. From the collection by Maria Adriana Prolo (1908–91). Courtesy Museo Nazionale del Cinema, Turin.

ogy and art form of film. Their meaning in their own time was not so that cinema might eventually come into being. And they can have other meanings for us in our own time as well.)

The device was almost always wielded by its owner, the *imbonitore*, and such images as we possess of its usage (most of them, but by no means all, Italian) show viewers who are almost always women or children. So we must imagine the *mondi nuovi* as devices for popularization of knowledges at social levels other than those of already learned classes and persons. The scenes, or *vedute*, shown in them were usually dropped vertically by strings or *spaghetti*. These *vedute* formed part of a vast artisanal production in their own right, from mainly only four European cities: London, Paris, Augsburg in southern Germany, and Bassano nel Grappa, where the famous *bottega* of the Remondini was especially important. What they made possible by way of contemporary imagining of worlds beyond that of any given viewer is well attested by one of the chief students of them, the Paduan scholar Carlo Alberto Zotti Minici: 'Journeying – the possibility of moving in space and time (as in the case of images of mythical cities) – and finding oneself placed simultaneously within realities utterly different from those imposed by one's own physical being, is all realised by means of viewing ... The 'Mondi Nuovi' and the optic views, mainly dedicated to the topographical genre, furnished their spectators with the wings of ubiquity, appeasing the desire for far-flung experience.' ('Il viaggio, la possibilità di muoversi nello spazio e nel tempo (nel caso di raffigurazioni di città mitiche) e di trovarsi contemporaneamente in realtà del tutto dissimili da quelle imposte dal proprio essere fisico, si realizza attraverso la visione ... I Mondi Nuovi e le vedute ottiche, in massima parte dedicate al genere topografico, fornirono ai loro spettatori le ali dell'ubiquità, appagando il desiderio di tentare esperienze lontane.')[6]

The term 'new world' has a special resonance of otherness with respect to Venice, since the commonly denominated New World of the Americas was precisely one of which she had not been able to share in the colonization, as had other nations of Europe. In short, literally unable to exploit this New World because of the greater geopolitical distance she stood from it, its *representation* in Venice had, in consequence, less interrupted routes into the imagination of Venetians than it might have, say, for persons in London, Lisbon, or Amsterdam, so involved as those centres of New World colonization were by then in complex transatlantic extensions of their power. As a toy of the Enlightenment therefore, the cosmorama's compelling images, when deployed in a place like Venice, could be all the more directly utopian in kind. Of the relationship between the decline of Venice's former glory and this turn towards 'new worlds' in which the imagination held great sway, Gian Piero Brunetta has written: 'Placed in Venice, so pulsating with life, but at the same time condemned by symptoms of immanent mortality, the box of the Mondo Nuovo finds its natural citizenry. Venice is the stage upon which can be witnessed an interchangeable profile of hundreds of other possible places experienced and inhabited by the collective imagination.' ('Nello spazio veneziano pulsante di vita, e al tempo stesso condannato dai sintomi della mortalità imminente, la cassetta del Mondo Nuovo trova la sua cittadinanza naturale. Venezia è lo scenario entro cui possiamo scorgere il profilo intercambiabile di centinaia di altri possibili luoghi vissuti e abitati dall'immaginazione collettiva.')[7]

Consider now another example. It is a poem of 1761 by Carlo Goldoni entitled, not surprisingly, 'Il Mondo Nuovo,' which is an indulgent panegyric on the life of a young daughter of the aristocratic Balbi family.[8] The poem refers to one such 'industriosa macchinetta' as Goldoni calls the device, which displays marvels and, 'in virtue of its crystalline optics,' is able to project flies such that they appear horses: 'mostra all'occhio maraviglie tante,/ Ed in virtù degli ottici cristalli/ Anche le mosche fa parer cavalli.'[9] The words are echoed in another engraving of a *mondo nuovo* from the early nineteenth century (see figure 1.4), with the inscription beneath it as follows:

> Sirs, before late evening comes
> You shall see highly strange marvels
> Two giants astride two frogs
> And a fly that fires artillery.

> Signori, avanti che la sera è tarda
> Vedrete maraviglie affatto strane
> Due giganti a cavallo di due rane
> E una mosca che tira di bombarda.

We are told by Goldoni in his poem of 1761 that such devices are commonplace now in the public squares, especially during the time of carnival, and that their 'inventors' (as he calls them) are able to gather together crowds who are mad for their views of battles, and ambassadors, regattas, queens, and emperors.

It is my belief that those distances and perspectives discussed already

Figure 1.4 Image of a *mondo nuovo*, first quarter of nineteenth century. A. Orio. Courtesy Museo Nazionale del Cinema, Turin.

in relation to Zompini's line engraving of a cosmorama have in Goldoni's poem become projections of time more than of space. What is apparent in the reading of the poem is that historical as well as mythical subject matter had always been a prime realm of treatment in these *mondi nuovi*. And what that in turn makes possible is the idea that a retainer can build one such 'new world' specifically to represent the past, present, and a little bit of the future history of distinguished members of the family of his patron. (Not surprisingly, Balbi is Goldoni's main patron, too.)

Fundamental to so crystalline a poetic discourse as Goldoni deploys in this poem is the notion of clear historical perspectives opened up by the world of the invention, the *mondo nuovo*; it is itself a locus for projections back and forth in time, and thus a way of recounting a particular story from past into present, and from present into presentiments of a future. This is why I have used the device as emblematic in this chapter. It seems to me that we need to be highly aware, philosophically speaking, of the time spectrum that these popular cosmoramas opened up, particularly the notion of the 'new world' as an *unfolding future*. For if we could prove that such a sense of unfolding futurity had become self-reflexive – projected onto Venice itself, so to speak – then that would constitute a very important piece of evidence as to how open to questions of its own future this society was by the time of its fall.

But quite apart from Venice, if this optic device, so universally portrayed as a toy for women and children and very much a thing of popular rather than learned culture, could be said to possess such extraordinary temporal and self-reflexive properties, at least *in potentio* – that is, in terms of a *possible* imaginary apprehension of the world in all its variety – that would make it philosophically of towering importance to our sense of the birth of modernity within the Enlightenment age, and to all such considerations of time and self-reflexivity from that moment to the present.

It would be impossible in small compass to detail all the optic devices of the Enlightenment age that were contemporary with the *mondi nuovi*, never mind the unfolding realities of, and treatises upon, magic lanterns, cabinets of curiosity, cosmoramas, dioramas, panoramas and the like, onwards towards the age of the photographic plate, the moving images of cinema, and right down to our own postmodern moment of multi-media, television, and the internet. Nonetheless, surely it *is* of compelling significance that as of several decades ago we domesticated the television for viewing the world beyond ourselves, calling it the 'tube,' and even – in England at any rate – 'the box,' while in America and Australia it is often referred to as 'the idiot box.'

The leading Italian historian of the cinema, Gian Piero Brunetta, defines lines of connection between, on the one hand, the magic lantern and the art form of cinema, and on the other, between the portable cosmoramas of the eighteenth century and the television set. As he stresses, 'Upon the screen begin to converge, in an ever increasing degree, all our great dreams and collective desires, so as to become coordinated with those of viewers far away in other continents ... We continue to gaze into the depths of the "box" in search of new "distances" and "prospects."' ('Verso il piccolo schermo cominciano a confluire, in misura crescente, tutti i grandi sogni e desideri collettivi e a sintonizzarsi con quelli di spettatori sparsi in altri continenti ... Continuiamo a guardare verso il fondo della "cassela" alla ricerca di nuove "lontananze e prospettive."')[10] Epoch-changing events in New York and Washington in 2001 have shown that it is now not merely collective dreams and desires, but horrifyingly real collective nightmares that can reach us from the small screen at the very time of their unfolding. So the metaphorical cultural cosmorama that my chapter has been concerned to define is more complex than ever in the case of television.

There have been histories of television's development in Italy, perhaps none more useful than Aldo Grasso's, for a sense of the programs that were actually on offer year by year, the nation's various preferences, and critical reaction to the medium.[11] Elena Dagrada has written illuminatingly on the interrelations between television and its critics.[12] And David Forgacs gives at once the most focused and sophisticated reading of the place of television within the overall spectrum of cultural consumption in Italy since the Second World War.[13] These studies and others are important sources, but I go on to develop something rather different, an understanding of television as part of a larger *poetics* of viewing.

As a last threshold between all that came before this modern paradigm and the televisual age itself, let us review the longer lineage traced so far. A good way of doing so is to contrast briefly modes of viewing in Italy to this point with approximately the same developments evident over a vastly shorter historical period in another nation. Aijaz Ahmad, whose work on lineages of the present I mentioned in my introduction, and who certainly comes from a culture – that of India – where cinema and television have a huge present market, has reported to me a strange fact of his own lifetime, which seems like a compressing of the couple of centuries it has taken us in Europe to go from one viewing box, the *mondo nuovo*, to another, the television set. Ahmad has attested, 'Cosmoramas were ... a great delight in the days of my rural, pre-electricity childhood in the Northern Indian countryside.' The language development theorist Ruqaiya Hasan, like Ahmad born in Uttar Pradesh before Partition, recently confirmed his remembrances, describing small wooden boxes similar to the Italian *mondi nuovi*[14] that we have been considering.

What Ahmad and Hasan's evidence suggests is that Italian cultural lineages, though highly particular in themselves, are related to global trends, and that some of the same general paradigms of viewing studied here have been observed in cultures far removed from Italy and indeed from Europe. The important difference is one of historical time frames, themselves often governed by interrelations between residual feudal modes of production and emergent capitalistic ones. Nations such as India have seen more stark historical contrasts of the residual and the emergent than Italy. Pre-modern, early modern, and ultra modern modes of viewing that have more or less replaced one another progressively in Italy, in a cultural unfolding across several centuries, have had more overlapping time frames in India.

On the day in 1992 that Judge Giovanni Falcone and his wife and bodyguards were blown up on their way to Palermo from the airport at Punta Raisi, I had arrived on the other side of Sicily, in Catania. I had come to study – in hindsight I still find there to be a terrible irony in this – the great late-medieval fresco of the *Triumph of Death* in the National Gallery of Sicily in Palermo, and to try to obtain a fresh understanding of death as a factor preoccupying the Sicilian mentality. After hearing on a shop radio of the car-bombing at Capaci, I found myself obliged to contemplate a triumph of death far more real than any I had imagined in setting out on my quest. There were a couple of matters that I experienced in the national processing of this tragedy, both of them televisual, and both of which have left an indelible imprint on my imagination, such that a great deal of my thinking about television culture, Italian television culture in particular, comes back to those instances.

First, I went a few days later to the town of Racalmuto, in the south-west of the island, as part of trip to fathom Sicily's preoccupation with death. I wanted to speak with surviving members of the family of Leonardo Sciascia, the writer who, to my reckoning, had had the canniest things to say on the subject. I found his relatives gathered in a modest sitting room, some of the elderly members of the family with tears in their eyes, as they watched on television the national funeral procession through the centre of Palermo of the coffins of Judge Falcone, his wife, and his bodyguards. I had come, let me stress, to discuss their own recently deceased family member with them, and here they were mourning the death of another man, who had learned so much and quoted so often from the older writer, Leonardo Sciascia, even, particularly, regarding the matter of Sicilian fascination with death. They were gathered around the instrument that focused and transmitted for them, as for all other members of the nation, this event so important in the history of the Italian people. I could not easily, or for long, talk to these people about their kinsman, but I could watch and share this momentous occasion with them in a kind of phatic communion of common grieving. As any other decent Italians would have done, they graciously included me.

During the same week, in the evenings, the various television *canali* (channels) became a kind of public piazza space. What I mean is that of the several channels (local and national) on my hotel television in

Palermo, most had groups of people, known and unknown to viewers, discussing Falcone, the nation's ills and how to overcome them, and the need to hasten the election of a new president in view of the premature retirement of the outgoing one. The situation seemed a modern instance of what had been identified long ago by Tommaso Garzoni in his Venetian publication of 1610, *La Piazza Universale*. However, instead of this being a real piazza where political discussion took place, as is still common throughout Italy, the various television channels themselves had become a *virtual* piazza, potentially more spacious and various in what they could attend to and bring into people's homes. Each discussion group on the channels of this virtual *piazza universale*, this totality of Italian television networks, was focusing on the same tragic set of circumstances. As a viewer, one could pass from one group to another simply by changing channel, as though walking about and overhearing the various public groupings in a real piazza. One was in no way excluded as an intruder upon a regular grouping. Of course, it was not possible to make one's own voice heard in any of the conversations, but one could hope that someone in the many discussions would manage to express feelings close to one's own.

The actual cosmoramas I have been dealing with were essentially devices mounted in piazzas. I have traced my paradigm of the cultural cosmorama into the home, in terms of what I have called the binding secular experience of modernity, television itself. But my present instance – this terrible moment in recent Italian history of the killing of Falcone – also takes us, precisely by means of the domesticated box into which we gaze, back into a virtual *piazza universale*, or, at the very least, onto a *piazza nazionale*, where we must go on examining matters of common interest. In Italy, as elsewhere, television is secular modernity's main visual paradigm. To expand on our sense of how it functions as that, we need to deepen our understanding of the specific Italian format I have been discussing, the televisual piazza. This is best approached now through more ordinary examples, rather than through moments of unusual bonding during the bereavement for a national figure cruelly murdered.

Already at the inception of national television broadcasting by RAI in 1954, the cultural commentator Luigi Barzini predicted that the advent of television would render inevitable this parallel with the piazza. At the same time, he saw the country finally 'reduced' to a unity that had always eluded it. Barzini felt that the unity in question might prove psychologically somewhat disturbing, considering the mutual eyeballing that it would enforce upon all – an encounter with truths that had so far been kept from view, so to speak. 'In a short space of time the instrument will be literally everywhere ... in the church hall, in the public bathhouse, in trattorias, and in the most modest of homes. The capacity to instruct and to move with the combination of word and image and soundtrack is enormous. The possibilities for good and for bad are equally vast. Italy will be, in a certain sense, reduced to a single country, an immense piazza, a forum in which we shall all be constrained to look each other in the eye.' ('Tra breve, senza dubbio, l'apparecchio sarà letteralmente dovunque, dove ora sono radio-riceventi, in parrocchia, nello stabilimento di bagni, nelle trattorie, nelle case più modeste. La capacità di istruire e commuovere con l'immagine unita alla parola e al suono è enorme. Le possibilità di fare del bene o del male altrettanto vaste. L'Italia sarà, in un certo senso, ridotta ad un paese solo, una immensa piazza, il foro, dove saremo tutti e ci guarderemo tutti in faccia.')[15] Barzini's prescience possibly went too far, exaggerating in its concluding remark just how much honest stocktaking the new medium might constrain Italians to. But he correctly saw the medium as a contested site for political wrangling over what is 'good' and what is 'bad.' Both parts of his further prediction – television as an extension of the already existent Italian piazza, and television as a solvent of the factors of difference within the nation – have been enormously important aspects of its perceived role in Italy.

Several programs in the history of Italian television have used the piazza in its status as the hub of Italian sociality. For instance, the made-for-television setting of the rather downmarket *I fatti vostri* was itself named Piazza Italia. This popular program was watched at home in the middle of the day, in particular by old people and housemakers, in great numbers according to statistics from Auditel. It concentrated on *cronaca nera* (i.e., sensationalist) news items, drawn from the whole nation. *I fatti vostri* has recently changed into *Piazza Grande: La fortuna in piazza*, the same sort of program, broadcast at lunchtime as well, and its title even more significant for the focus on the televisual piazza setting. People who are housebound can connect via such programs not only with the traditional sociality of the Italian piazza, but also with a host of lurid events, the poring over of which is a long-standing Italian tradition.

In the 1990s, more serious television programs about political and social issues were introduced. *Milano-Italia*, hosted by Gad Lerner, focused mainly upon the rise of the Northern League and on the problems connected with this in Italian social and political life. In *Samarcanda*, hosted by Michele Santoro, there was real discussion about, and commitment to, the anti-mafia movement. Since 2002, *Ballarò* has been a continuation of these earlier programs. Named after a famous and popular marketplace along streets of Palermo's *centro storico*, *Ballarò* is transmitted after dinner on the RAI 2 network. Considerably more serious in its coverage than *I fatti vostri*, invited guests sit out in a typical piazza (actually another television mock-up) to discuss current issues and events. *Festival Bar*, a program that has roots in an earlier public contest shown on television (*Cantagiro*), is a summer competition of musical variety performances. Unlike other programs mentioned so far, it goes to *actual* piazzas and conducts outside broadcast television in different cities and regions, culminating a final show from the Arena in Verona.

A further example, so axiomatic that we might be in danger of forgetting its similarity with the other instances I have mentioned, is the pope's televised open-air mass every Sunday from the Piazza San Pietro in Rome. Many Italians who formerly went in person each Sunday to their parish church now connect with church ritual via this televisual 'mass spectacular.'

Slightly different from the piazza, but also a paradigm of interconnectivity for Italian television viewers, is the studio made to seem a *salotto*. Some of the multiple discussion formats that overtook television channels at the time of Falcone's murder conformed to the more intimate *salotto* in dimension or layout, even though my earlier point was that in their totality, and by switching from one to the other, one obtained the sensation of an entire televisual piazza. In my last chapter, on 'lifestyles,' I suggest how the seventeenth and eighteenth century *salotto* was transformed in certain nineteenth century fashion shops, so as to displace emphasis from their actual commercialism. The traditional *salotto* has now gone through a further metamorphosis and become a televisual format. What seems important in this newest transformation is preservation of its function as both a public *and* an intimate institution, for *conoscenti* and for extroverts certainly, but also as a mode for drawing people together in a group bonding process, which is equivalent almost to the dynamic of an extended family.

The challenge for Italian television, therefore, has always been whether the sense of an extended family could be stretched to include the entire nation. Bruno Vespa, of the Italian Right and quite close to Silvio Berlusconi, hosts a program on RAI 1 called *Porta a Porta*, in which invited persons sit in a circle on comfortable chairs, as in a real *salotto*. Before his latest term as prime minister, Berlusconi participated in *Porta a Porta* during the electoral campaign in 2001, even signing on the program one evening his 'Contract with Italians,' the promises he made and programs he offered if elected to govern. The atmosphere of such programs is smart and civilized, as befits the paradigm of the *salotto*, which comes from the rich past of European culture. Bad grace is as unacceptable as wittiness is mandatory. This dual compulsion functions as an effective means of internal policing that is implicit in the *salotto* format, which in turn means that the program is not, nor ever could be, a venue for radical protest, for that would be to fissure the *salotto* paradigm of good form with its opposite, bad form. Television of this kind does not easily countenance such internal contradictions.

Maurizio Costanzo – of the *Maurizio Costanzo Show* – was a long-running Italian institution. The program, first launched in 1982 and only recently taken off air, was certainly a grandiose version of the *salotto* format. This relatively highbrow program had a big audience in spite of the late hour it aired. Topics ranged from homosexuality to intricacies of Italian politics, with perhaps the most important factor being the presence of the showman personality of Maurizio Costanzo as anchor of this Canale 5 (Berlusconi channel) broadcast. Costanzo had had a long passion for the Italian theatre, and the 'set' of his talk show first travelled in an itinerant way from theatre to theatre in Italy before establishing a fixed location in the Teatro Parioli in Rome.[16] Costanzo has also been an anchorman for the variety program *Buona domenica* (complete with scantily clad showgirls and wearyingly upbeat razzmatazz), which runs for a full five hours on Sunday afternoons.

Maurizio Costanzo in part owes his televisual longevity to the patronage of media boss and twice prime minister, Silvio Berlusconi, on whose networks he appears. Not so fortunate have been other television personalities of national standing, who have seen their programs removed because they were unpopular with Berlusconi, even though they were on RAI (i.e., state-run networks), and therefore technically not part of the prime minister's direct television fiefdom. Enzo Biagi, a major Italian journalist and intellectual, but someone neither very radical nor very leftist, saw his program about Italian culture and politics, *Il fatto*, not reconfirmed in the RAI agenda for 2002 when he and the show found disfavour with his prime minister. Michele Santoro, who hosted another cultural and political discussion program called *Sciuscia* on RAI 2 after dinner, likewise had to go when Berlusconi gave the thumbs-down sign. The dynamics of the removal of individual programs always varies, and responsibility for figures such as Biagi and Santoro being taken off air can never with complete ease be pinned on Berlusconi alone. Nonetheless, the nation was witness to acrimony between each of them and the prime minister, and some time later they were no longer hosting their programs. The end results of quarreling with so powerful a figure speak for themselves. This transpired in spite of the fact that when Berlusconi first came to power in 1994 there was a fierce national debate over whether anti-trust legislation was required in order to curtail his political domination of Italian television.[17]

A law established in 1984–5 first recognized the full right of private television channels to operate under licence in Italy, which a number (including some owned by Berlusconi) had already been doing under more makeshift legislation since the early 1970s. Since 1985 the major Italian television networks have been denominated a duopoly: the state-run RAI networks on the one hand and Silvio Berlusconi's channels on the other.[18] The very factor of a prime minister owning channels and pulling strings in a not entirely transparent way has been much remarked upon and written about. But increasingly with his leadership of Forza Italia and his two terms as prime minister, Berlusconi has been manoeuvring his way into, and seeking hegemony over, the politics of RAI channels as well as his own. There has been, therefore, an incremental risk over the years of a reversion of Italian television to the status of monopoly. Charges have been levelled, from the Left especially, that this reversion has already tacitly occurred, and that the former state television network is now dominated by Berlusconi, or at least run with his (only slightly offstage) surveillance and control.

This intensely political atmosphere in which Italian television has to make its way in our times is, at any rate, a change from some of its earlier simplicities. To take the measure of that initial period, consider what cultural commentator Umberto Eco had to say in his 1963 *Diario minimo* about what he called the 'Phenomenology of Mike Bongiorno.' The following constitutes an important sociocultural critique, applicable to so much television, not just Italian programming. It refers to a relatively early period of the medium, and ostensibly only one show personality, but with its important message that 'culture has a critical and creative function,' the passage exemplifies qualities of expressive intelligence that are so often lacking in television.

> Idolized by millions of people, this man owes his success to the fact that from every act, from every word of the persona that he presents to the telecameras there emanates an absolute mediocrity along with (the only

virtue he possesses to a high degree) an immediate and spontaneous allure, which is explicable by the fact that he betrays no sign of theatrical artifice or pretence. He seems to be selling himself as precisely what he is, and what he is cannot create in a spectator, even the most ignorant, any sense of inferiority. Indeed, the spectator sees his own limitations glorified and supported by national authority ... Mike Bongiorno is not ashamed of being ignorant and feels no need to educate himself. He comes into contact with the most dazzling areas of knowledge and remains virgin, intact, a consolation to others in their natural tendencies to apathy and mental sloth. He takes great care not to awe the spectator, demonstrating not only his lack of knowledge but also his firm determination not to learn ... Mike Bongiorno hasn't the slightest inkling that culture has a critical and creative function.[19]

Idolatrato da milioni di persone, quest'uomo deve il suo successo al fatto che in ogni atto e in ogni parola del personaggio cui dà vita davanti alle telecamere traspare una mediocrità assoluta unita (questa è l'unica virtù che egli possiede in grado eccedente) ad un fascino immediato e spontaneo spiegabile col fatto che in lui non si avverte nessuna costruzione o finzione scenica: sembra quasi che egli si venda per quello che è e che quello che è sia tale da non porre in stato di inferiorità nessuno spettatore, neppure il più sprovveduto. Lo spettatore vede glorificato e insignito ufficialmente di autorità nazionale il ritratto dei propri limiti ... Mike Bongiorno non si vergogna di essere ignorante e non prova il bisogno di istruirsi. Entra a contatto con le più vertiginose zone dello scibile e ne esce vergine e intatto, confortando le altrui naturali tendenze all'apatia e alla pigrizia mentale. Pone gran cura nel non impressionare lo spettatore, non solo mostrandosi all'oscuro dei fatti, ma altresì decisamente intenzionato a non apprendere nulla ... Non lo sfiora minimamente il sospetto di una funzione critica e creativa della cultura.[20]

For many decades, widespread distaste for television has arisen from its tendency, so extraordinarily well defined here in 1963, to sustain and consolidate people's 'natural tendency to apathy and mental sloth.' In speaking up for the 'critical and creative function' of culture, and implicitly against ways of using media such that they reproduce mediocrity on a ever-widening scale, Eco is in fact defending television as a potentially remarkable window onto the world and as a tool for understanding and creative wonderment.

The passage states that 'dazzling areas of knowledge' often elude Bongiorno. The point is simply that he in no way responds adequately or with a will to understand such matters. Bongiorno's very complacency and mediocrity endorse an extension of the same qualities in viewers. What is being patiently established by Eco is culture's reproductive function. Just as mediocrity begets mediocrity, so a critical and creative culture would tend to reproduce itself under incommensurably better uses of the medium. In the passage Eco signals a warning about the reproduction of mediocrity, but he implies, too, a stimulus, pointing towards television's potential for critical thinking and creativity. It also serves to present Umberto Eco himself as antithetical to the type of showman he is describing. In an extraordinary and certainly non-self-referential way, Eco's writing exemplifies the critical and creative intelligence being demanded from television.

Umberto Eco was the most important critic of early Italian television, having worked for television studios of the RAI in Turin between 1954 and 1958. Although he subsequently transferred to the major Italian publishing house of Bompiani and then into his brilliant academic career,[21] he has continued commenting on television through the decades in newspaper articles. He has always done so as a semiotician in the widest sense, for he is someone who watches and reads television's many 'signs.' He is often at his most genial and witty when describing the tacky content that appears so frequently on Italian home networks, and he fashions similar critiques of American productions as well. Sometimes in his writing this makes for hilarious cross-cultural comparisons of televisual kitsch from both sides of the Atlantic. The fact that Eco comments so frequently indicates that he sees constant changes in both Italian and American culture, changes he is able to read merely by watching their television.

Many other Italian writers, in the early decades especially, were far more severe in testifying to the worthlessness of television. Leonardo Sciascia declared as late as 1980 that for him television 'is like writing a book in water: nothingness, void: I totally refuse to watch it.' ('Per me la televisione è come scrivere un libro sull'acqua: il nulla, il vuoto: ho un rifiuto totale a vederla.')[22] Alberto Moravia likewise testified to detestation and almost total avoidance. Having said from the outset in the 1950s that Italian television was 'a sub-Italy, a series-B Italy' ('una sotto-Italia, un'Italia di serie B'), he followed up in later years with a remark scarcely more complimentary: 'The remote control seems to me an instrument of neurasthenia. I never watch television, but once when I was bed-ridden from an operation and used the remote, it made me lose my mind. I saw everything and nothing.' (Il telecomando mi sembra uno strumento di nevrastenia. Non vedo mai la TV ma una volta ero immobilizzato a letto per una operazione e lo usai mi fece perdere la testa. Vedevo tutto e niente.')[23]

Pier Paolo Pasolini was possibly the most savage public critic of Italian television. Even though the medium was still in its infancy, he wrote tirades against it as an instrument of the devil, no less! While fulminating against it as 'mass-' or even 'sub-'culture, he famously suggested that its programmers should put it to use in launching an equivalent *mass* reading of books. Reading, he argued, unlike television, is 'not a phenomenon of subculture, but of culture' ('la lettura ... che al contrario della televisione, non è un fenomeno di sottocultura, ma di cultura'). Bizarrely, Pasolini seemed to suggest that not just serious discussion programs, but also even light entertainment shows should be put 'at the service of this new task, so noble, altruistic, and scandalously contradictory' (a disposizione di questo nuovo compito, così nobile, altruistico e scandalosamente contradditorio).[24] Pasolini knew, however, that this particular consumer culture would not commit to a scheme that, however undeniably noble and altruistic, 'scandalously contradicted' its very premises. The total effect of his argument is therefore not really to suggest that he believes in this patently unrealisable suggestion. Rather, Pasolini leads the reader to the point of seeing, in the unnegotiability of the medium and its programmers, why such a scheme would never be realised, thereby confirming television's enduring sub-cultural status.

Pasolini's particular loathing for television arose because he saw it as a formless, uncreative medium. 'In substance television so far has offered nothing which constitutes stylistic and precise rapport between form and content. The content of television has been so weak and unavailing, so barren and partial, that up till now it has not been able to give it any form. It's useless for me to confront the problem of television if I know that in doing something on television I shall either have to forget myself or sell my soul to the devil.' ('In sostanza la televisione non ha offerto, sinora, niente che fosse un fatto stilistico, preciso, che ponesse i rapporti fra forma e contenuto. Il contenuto della televisione è talmente labile e inefficiente, talmente infecondo e parziale che sinora non ha potuto dare nessuna forma. È inutile che io affronti il problema della televisione se so che per fare qualcosa in televisione debbo dimenticarmi, oppure vendere l'anima al diavolo.')[25]

This was a strong objection, but not uncharacteristic of criticism levelled at television in the early days of the medium. (Pasolini spoke these words in 1962.) We should note that just as in Eco's outright putdown of the phenomenology of Mike Bongiorno, so, too, in this criticism by Pasolini of the same period, there exists a loophole of positive possibility. In fulminating against what the medium of television has produced 'so far,' Pasolini implicitly allows for the idea that, under radically changed conditions, television with precise rapport between form and content – in short, television that was critical and creative in ways that would no doubt delight Eco too – might at some point emerge.

Italo Calvino, by strong contrast, seemed wistful about television, as might be expected of a fabulist. But even he reports late in his life that while constantly expecting some amazing program from it – and this above anything shows how positive was his stance towards its potentiality as a medium – he had gone on looking and waiting in vain:

> I am convinced that there is in it some understanding of the world's events, that a coherent history and one motivated in all its series of cause and effect is beginning somewhere, not beyond reach of our verification, and that it contains the key to judging and understanding all the rest. It is this conviction which holds me glued to and fixated upon the screen, with dazed eyes, while my frenetic clicks of the remote make appear and disappear interviews with ministers, lovers' embraces, deodorant ads, rock concerts, arrested persons hiding their faces, the launch of space rockets, gunfights in the Wild West, leaping ballerinas, boxing matches, quiz competitions, samurai duels. If I do not stop and look at any of these programs it is because the program that I seek is another, and I know it is out there. I am sure that it is none of these, and indeed that they are transmitting these precisely to trick and discourage anyone like me who is convinced that that other program is the one that counts.

> Io sono convinto che un senso negli avvenimenti del mondo ci sia, che una storia coerente e motivata in tutta la sua serie di cause e d'effetti ci stia svolgendo in questo momento da qualche parte, non irraggiungibile dalla nostra possibilità di verifica, e che essa contenga la chiave per giudicare e comprendere tutto il resto. È questo convincimento che mi tiene inchiodato a fissare il video con gli occhi abbacinati mentre gli scatti frenetici del telecomando fanno apparire e scomparire interviste con ministri, abbracci d'amanti, pubblicità di deodoranti, concerti rock, arrestati che si nascondono il viso, lanci di razzi spaziali, sparatorie nel West, volteggi di ballerine, incontri di boxe, concorsi di quiz, duelli di samurai. Se non mi fermo a guardare nessuno di questi programmi è perché il programma che cerco è un altro, e io so che c'è, e sono sicuro che non è nessuno di questi, e questi

li trasmettono solo per trarre in inganno e scoraggiare chi come me è convinto che sia l'altro programma quello che conta.[26]

In the passage Calvino seems like one of the questing personae of his own stories, constantly yearning in the face of quotidian reality for a more glorious achievement, 'the one that counts.' The jumble of the quotidian is amusing in its own right: deodorant ads with samurai duels and leaping ballerinas, etc. All replicate the world's diversities, but none is sufficient in itself to requite his longings of a different order.

Not for nothing did Calvino so love the Renaissance poet Ludovico Ariosto, a figure capable of hauntingly representing the unrequited love of an Orlando in the midst of a thousand other goings-on. If in considering Calvino's remarks we displace emphasis from the ostensible topic of television programs, it becomes evident that he is really referring to a way of thinking about what we expect from works of art. Calvino is displaying an amusingly urbane frustration at not finding some ultimate work, finer than all the others. Part of why this is amusing as well as painful is that Calvino stirs us to imagine the welter of beguiling compensations of the actual world, as well as the 'transmitters' who want us to be taken in by such inferior distractions, even as our further dream remains unfulfilled. Wry pain of this order is hardly surprising from a writer who was about to put long meditations on the necessary conditions of great art into his lecture series for Harvard, *Six Memos for the Next Millennium,* which only his death prevented him from finishing or delivering in person.

I treat Calvino's specification of a lineage of fantasy in Italian culture in my very next chapter. In that chapter also, the *desiderata* he spells out lecture by lecture in the *Six Memos* are discussed in terms of his ideals for art works that will come after his own decease, ideals richly exemplified in Calvino's text by works already in existence. It is therefore hardly surprising that at the very time he was moving towards those late definitions of the deepest conditions of art, Calvino was bemused by never finding a more historic representation of world events, or (beyond all the sensational or humdrum kitsch) just one glorious program on the television channels he surfed, a program that *counted indisputably* as only a work of greatness could for a mind of his subtlety. Perhaps such achievement was simply not to be found on Italian television. It is a measure of Calvino's moving optimism (moving because it was frequently discouraged) that he believed it was there even while eluding his search.

Italian television has been mixed in quality since its beginning. However, there is one claim, made by Eco, which has wide concurrence among critics and cultural commentators. It is that, more than any other factor since Unification in 1860, the establishment of a national television network did much, linguistically and socially, to unify this intrinsically fissiparous nation.[27] Tullio De Mauro is possibly television's strongest advocate. In his studies of the modern Italian language, he has suggested how the range of modalities spoken on different television programs has led to greater lexical variety and a rich gamut between formal and informal uses of the language. Television, he affirms,

> has brought the more educated classes towards an abandonment of dialect and the total adoption of Italian in every circumstance and social rapport. Among less educated and poorer classes of minor cities, where the powerful Italianization produced by progressive urbanization of the country and by post-elementary education has not been so influential, it has introduced a model of spoken Italian ... to a context until recently firmly dialect speaking ... For the poorest of all classes in Italy, for the peasant sub-proletariat, television has constituted a model of culture and of the possibility of verbalisation, an incentive to overcome longstanding inarticulacies and to break old silences.
>
> Ha portato i ceti più colti verso l'abbandono totale della dialettofonia e l'adozione integrale dell'italiano in ogni circostanza e rapporto sociale. Tra i ceti meno colti e più poveri dei centri minori, là dove non può avere operato la potente azione italianizzante della urbanizzazione progressiva del paese e della scuola postelementare, ha portato un modello di italiano parlato ... in un ambiente fino a ieri compattamente dialettofono ... Per i ceti dell'Italia più miserabile, per il sottoproletariato contadino, la televisione ha costituito un modello di cultura e di possibilità di verbalizzazione, un incentivo a vincere antichi torpori, a rompere vecchi silenzi.[28]

What this argument does not do is protest against the disappearance of dialects, gradual in some areas, almost complete in others. Such concern is largely absent from De Mauro's trumpeting of Italian unification around the rich linguistic variety of its television. The point was not a neutral one. Interestingly, Pasolini, in an open letter to Italo Calvino published in *Paese sera,* which even cites De Mauro's opinions on language as ones he is fighting against, was infuriated by what he saw as television's manner of *reducing* to a narrow conformity the varieties of

Italian now spoken.[29] So for him, unity was bought at the high price of conformism. And conformism itself was, by Pasolini's reckoning, largely in the interests of consumerism, the culture which he repeatedly claimed was most served by television. As a consequence of this conformism, brought about in language as in so much else, according to Pasolini, readers could scarcely follow the dialectal speech used in his own earlier novels.

Italians themselves are television's best and most severe critics; perhaps this is because an early wave of commentators on television programs, including Eco and Pasolini, trained them in various strategies for 'reading' the medium and raising their awareness about how individual images promulgated by it are used affectively. There were, for instance, excellent critiques available from a wide variety of commentators about gross manipulation of news broadcasts treating the protests against the 2001 G8 Summit in Genoa. Very little police brutality was directly shown on either RAI or the Berlusconi channels. Indeed, protesters against the summit were largely demonized by television commentaries, but the various television coverages largely backfired in their intended affect because widespread popular criticism throughout Italy challenged their biases. The brutality that had actually been meted out to protesters was largely revealed in other sources – print journalism, foreign television networks, alternative online sites such as Indymedia.org, and radio networks like Radio Gap or Radio Onda Rossa.

At certain historic moments, the very opposite of this type of inadequate and biased Italian television coverage has occurred, revealing events that, for whatever reason or none, have been shown without much concealment or editing. Many Italians can attest to the fact, for instance, that they saw on television searing images of clandestine immigrants from Albania landing on the Pugliese coastline in the summer of 1991, and witnessed their subsequent maltreatment by Italian authorities. These images radicalized numbers of Italians into greater empathy for the plight of *extracommunitari*. (Empathy, however, was by no means universal, for this issue is highly contested ground in Italian politics.)

Mention of Albania in this context leads naturally to consideration of the film *Lamerica*. Gianni Amelio's intriguing work of 1994 presented to Italians an outside perspective on their own Italianness; in particular, it showed the way their culture is interpreted in the nearby and poor nation of Albania, which easily receives Italy's various television network broadcasts. The film concerned Italian conmen who were implicated in the 1980s and early 1990s in some of the worst scams, tricking Albanians out of their money with the promise, never intended to be fulfilled, of setting up a shoe factory in the poorer nation. This promise of investment was itself likened in the film to Italy's fascist conquest of Albania during the early 1930s. Italian entrepreneurs of the 1990s were seen as no better than their earlier fascist equivalents in their attempt to exploit Albania's many weaknesses. A further parallel existed in the title. Italy, for these desperate Albanians, became the same beacon of hope that America – *Lamerica* – was for Italians during earlier generations of migration across the Atlantic. Italian viewers of the film were thereby enabled and encouraged to read in the poor Albanian *clandestini* a replication of the plight of earlier generations of poor Italians.

But above all, the film *Lamerica* gave Italians a new, and largely negative, perspective onto their own television programs. For Italy had only become a nation of hope for the hundreds of Albanians shown seeking to reach it in a creaky overfilled vessel at the close of this film because of how they had understood the country from Italy's own television broadcasts. The film's release in 1994 was only three years after Italians had been so horrified at the conditions of such boatloads of poor Albanians seen landing on their southern coastline, in Puglia. The movie was, in a sense, a 'pre-history' and 'explanation' of the events of 1991, which Italians had already witnessed via their television news. But Italians who saw this film could also now understand with a deeper level of shock just how much of what gets broadcast on Italian television is not a truthful representation of Italian culture, but rather a meretricious purveyance of false dreams and expectations. *Lamerica* thereby became a vehicle for intense cross-cultural comparison of overly glamorized Italy with genuinely impoverished Albania – with the further cross-cultural parallel of Italy serving as a false America, just as America itself had dashed the built-up expectations of so many earlier Italian migrants.

For Italians, much of what gets broadcast may be considered to be in the realm of the 'national unconscious.' If so, much of that unconscious was dredged up to consciousness here. Italians saw Albanians having to understand Italy only in terms of what gets televised, and were thereby enabled to realize themselves how very inadequate and distorted such a knowledge base is. Although Italians are used to seeing the same glamorized images, they have other everyday realities of Italy (many highly negative) with which to balance them. With this film, Italians were made aware of how Italy gets interpreted by another, considerably poorer society through television broadcasts only, without the rest of the country's *non*-televisual reality as a counterbalance. This was an important *self-*

othering moment for some Italians, and at the heart of it lay questions concerning the many deep untruths, and distortions of life in Italy as promulgated on its television networks.

Projections in the popular *mondi nuovi* were frequently images of different times and places. Television vastly extends such possibilities. An extraordinary example is furnished by Michelangelo Antonioni and his cinematic team, who made a long program in three parts on modern China in 1972. It was shown in black and white on the National Program in 1973 and again in a colour version on *Retedue* in 1979. Or consider historical programs. In 1974 a relatively hagiographic treatment of Garibaldi's South American years from 1834 to 1848 was offered, while in the same year another program entitled *Bronte: Chronicle of a massacre that history books do not relate* (*Bronte: Cronaca di un massacro che i libri di storia non hanno raccontato*) told the 'other side' of the Risorgimento, which chronicled the brutal putdown by Garibaldi's 'thousand' of a popular uprising in 1860 in the small town of Bronte in Sicily.[30] Here was evidence, if any were needed, of television being used vigorously to promote an 'alternative' history to that which is normally sanctioned and made sacrosanct.

Projections across time, on the part of television, include the various recyclings of art works in other forms. Over the years there have been several adaptations of classic Italian novels, chief among them Manzoni's *I promessi sposi*, itself a projection back in time to Milan and the surrounding region during the seventeenth century. The first version of 1967 achieved average viewing figures of more than eighteen million people for each of its eight episodes. A 1989 version broadcast on RAI 1 was seen by an average of more than fifteen million viewers per episode. Like the first version, this one was much used in Italian schools to bolster interest in Manzoni's novel, even if its many departures led one important critic to declare: 'What is most missing in this adaptation – it would be better to say this spectacular – is precisely Manzoni himself, the author. Salvatore Nocita's *I promessi sposi* is a western, a cloak and dagger film, an American mini-series ... indeed many things, but not the novel of Alessandro Manzoni.' ('Ciò di cui più si sente la mancanza in questo scenaggiato – sarebbe meglio dire kolossal – è proprio lui: l'Autore. *I promessi sposi* di Salvatore Nocita sono un western, un film di cappa e spada, un miniserial americano ... insomma tante cose ma non il romanzo di Alessandro Manzoni.')[31] As though to cover over the inadequacies of this 'mini-series,' in the very next year, RAI 1 produced a satirical cabaret version in five episodes, complete with popular variety acts and a supposed interview with Manzoni himself.[32] The butt of the satire was not so much Manzoni's novel, as it was RAI 1's own adaptation of the previous year. While this may be an instance of television locking itself into a closed circuit of self-referentiality, there is a more significant factor. For better or worse, what is evident is Italian television's persistent attempt to revamp legacies of a vast cultural heritage for the substantially non-reading public of the modern televisual age. Such 'adaptations' may never win the approval of the Pasolinis and Adornos of this world, but it is a repeatedly proven fact that in the wake of televisual or cinematic versions of classic texts, the original book has vastly augmented sales figures. So in an ironic way, a portion of Pasolini's 'scheme' for the mass medium of television to promote the minority culture of reading is constantly being realized by classic adaptations.

Let me end with a televisual image from a different adaptation, which concerns the soprano Catherine Malfitano as Puccini's Tosca in her suicidal leap from the ramparts of the Castel Sant'Angelo in Rome. Rada Films, which was responsible for the production and transmission (along with RAI) of the adaption, sent me two pre-production stills for my earlier book on Italy, one of them of Placido Domingo as the painter Cavaradossi singing his last aria before his execution, the other of Tosca's leap (see figures 1.5, 1.6). I was overjoyed, until I realized that, in the case of the suicide leap, one could see cars below in the streets of Rome.

We could not use the image, I immediately decided, because to do so would be to confuse periods, which the television production itself managed to avoid through the angles of its actual shoot (*after* these pre-production stills were taken). When I contacted my publishers to communicate my sad decision to exclude the image, they were amused, saying (more or less), 'You want the image but not the cars in it. No problem.' So the picture we finally published was the pre-production still *without cars* (figure 1.7).

We gaze into cultural cosmoramas, and our current paradigm is televisual. But our age has ever new ways of cosmetically removing those complicating bits of 'the real past or present' that we are squeamish to include. And I myself have collaborated in one such clean-up! It seems useless to protest that we shall ever understand the complexities of a culture if we distort and 'improve' the projections of it – the *lontananze e prospettive* – in our collective cosmoramas by means of which we meditate upon and recount our common history. For we have always changed reality in the processes of representing it. After all, the *vedute* painted

Figure 1.5 Placido Domingo as Cavaradossi from Puccini's *Tosca*. Pre-production still of the TV version of the opera broadcast live in 1992 to 107 countries worldwide. Courtesy Rada Films, Rome.

Figure 1.6 Catherine Malfitano as Tosca in her act 3 suicide leap from the ramparts of the Castel Sant'Angelo.

Figure 1.7 The same picture with the cars of Rome's modern traffic removed. Pre-production stills courtesy Rada Films, Rome.

some two hundred or more years ago for viewing in *mondi nuovi* were often beautifications or intensifications. One has to understand cultural history not by removing all such changes as arise in acts of representation, but by considering these along with the rest of reality that they further complicate.

As an act of faith in past, present, and future, I have chosen to adapt further, for the cover of the present book, the original pre-production still of Catherine Malfitano in the role of Tosca, a character from a plot set in 1800. This character commits suicide at the end of Puccini's opera, which was written a century later, by throwing herself off the Castel Sant'Angelo in Rome to escape her royalist pursuers. My overall subject of this chapter is 'viewing,' as the first of several cultural lineages that I am concerned with studying here. Because what we actually see when we view long traditions is an overlay of later upon earlier material factors in a culture, I have allowed for further digital development of the image, including, once again, suppression of the cars that form the street traffic of Rome almost a century after Puccini composed the opera.

After all, most of what we actually see when we view any culture is a historical palimpsest, a layering of age upon age. Our own age is only the thin outer skin, transparent enough in places to allow us to perceive much that remains as an integral fabric from former ages, the past inextricably woven into the present so to speak. And although I have moved from an analogy of layering to one of weaving, I would claim that this is because any given culture manifests both these processes, often simultaneously. Cultural history reveals other things too, and necessarily so, because the phenomenologies of any given moment in the vast developments of a culture are so exceedingly complex. In the succeeding chapters of this book I am concerned with tracing other changes and what remains from them within Italian culture, subject though all such changes and remainders are to the still further complications of 'representation' that I have also been discussing.

2 Fantasy, Science, and Hyperreality: From Ariosto and Galileo to Las Vegas

In a 1968 written elaboration of answers he had given in a television interview on relations between science and literature, Italo Calvino began to outline one of the most important lineages in Italian culture in terms of just a few of its salient figures from the High Renaissance onwards. 'The ideal way in which Galileo regarded the world, even as a scientist, is nourished by literary culture. So much so that we can draw a line from Ariosto to Galileo to Leopardi and call it one of the mainstreams of our literature.' ('L'ideale di sguardo sul mondo che guida anche il Galileo scienzato è nutrito di cultura letteraria. Tanto che possiamo segnare una linea Ariosto-Galileo-Leopardi come una delle più importanti linee di forza della nostra letteratura.')[1] The possibility implicit in Calvino's critical remarks as well as in some of his fictional writing – we could call it a working hypothesis – is that for hundreds of years (and still now, potentially) 'speculative fantasy,' or the engagement of the mind in realms of the fabulous, may have kept two major aspects of our culture – science and literature – in a closer relationship than we commonly imagine.

If Calvino was right about the existence of such a lineage and his identification of key figures in it, could we not – considering the kinds of writing that he himself was engaged in producing for most of his life – include him as an important latter-day exemplar? My concerns, however, are larger than a mere exegesis of literary qualities that Calvino partly derived from earlier writers and sustained with creative bravura of his own. At their widest they have to do with the nature of both literary and scientific speculation. How far may fantasy be seen as a necessary component of both? In an age when we know that the humanities and the sciences have gone so many separate ways, our enquiry concerns what they may still have in common, perhaps characteristics that are largely unrecognized even by practitioners and students.

There is considerable evidence of a direct link from Calvino back to Ariosto, so much did the modern author display love of his literary ancestor in the redeployment of chivalric-romantic themes and actions in his own fictions, in the multiple references to and occasional essays on aspects of Ariosto, as well as in his editing of an abridgement of *Orlando Furioso* for popular appreciation in Italy. However, the important lineage here, by Calvino's own reckoning, also takes in Galileo and Leopardi, in what I believe is essentially an intertwined tradition of literary and scientific speculation. In such a tradition, science and literature have not yet, and indeed do not ever, fundamentally split. They may not ever be one and the same thing, but they can operate in discursive unison. Centuries before Calvino, Galileo too had adored Ariosto and annotated his poetry with gusto, as he did in the cases of Dante, Petrarch, and Tasso.[2] He was, for instance, very rude about Tasso, constantly comparing his *Gerusalemme Liberata* unfavourably with Ariosto's *Orlando*: 'Leave be your little madrigals, Madonna Armida; otherwise Goffredo, if he has any brain, will notice that you're a schemer, and send you off to a bawdy house. We might, having read such a narration, compare one by Ariosto, to see the diversity of their styles, and with how much finer a manner, gracefully and affectingly, the latter's heroines, whether Isabella, Olympia or Lidia, recount their situations.' ('Madonna Armida, lasciate stare i madrigaletti; altrimenti Goffredo, se averà cervello, s'accorgerà che voi siete una mariola, e vi manderà in bordello. Possiamo, letta questa narrazione, legger una di quelle dell'Ariosto, per vedere la diversità dello stile, e con quanto miglior maniera e quanto più affettuosamente e leggiadramente raccontino i lor casi, o vogliate Isabella, o vero Olimpia, o vero Lidia, o qualsiasi altra.')[3] Leopardi, in turn, adored Galileo's dialogues and treatises. There is much reference, direct and indirect, to Galileo in his *Zibaldone* (*Miscellany*) and *Operette morali* (*Moral Opuscules*), his strikingly early *Storia dell'astronomia* (*History of Astronomy*), and the only slightly later *Errori popolari degli antichi* (*Popular Errors of the Ancients*), not to mention a number of key quotes from Galileo in Leopardi's *Crestomazia italiana* (*Anthology of Italian Prose*), some of which I use for exemplification in what follows.

It is valuable also to test our explorations of such a hypothesis about ongoing linkage between science and literature against a very different order of fantasticated materiality within late-modern culture and postmodernity, usually referred to as hyperreality, as defined by Jean

Baudrillard and Umberto Eco. I am aware that by contrasting aspects of the fantastical that have been passed down through *literary* or *scientific* lineages of culture with *visual* and *solid* iconic creations of the hyperreal in plazas, hotels, malls, and casinos, there is an incongruity of scale and of form. But my basic question is whether such realms of the hyperreal are not different in more fundamental respects from the other lineage of fantasy I shall be inspecting. If so, are the differences of consequence to the future? Clearly, the importance of the questions dwarfs the issue of incongruity in what we are comparing.

Is Las Vegas something signally new, a different order of creativity from anything we may have analysed from the past, or just a reshuffling of constituents of old gestalts in a tarted-up format? Can we, in the terms of Robert Venturi and his co-authors' famous 1972 treatise, still 'learn from Las Vegas'?[4] In short, in relation to what has appeared over the horizon even since Baudrillard and Eco wrote their seminal essays on the emergent phenomenon, what exactly *is* hyperreality in the new millennium? How does it reconfigure a culture such as that of Italy – the exemplary one for this enquiry – which, along with just a few others, it raids for images, ideas, and artistic context? Above all, does hyperreality mainly relate by similarity to, or by difference from, earlier traditions of scientific and literary-fantastical speculation?

Let me return to the opening considerations by focusing on Calvino's main claim as to the nature of cultural interconnectivity over several centuries. From what he had been saying, the lineage in question was one with little bifurcation between speculation that is scientific and speculation that is fantastical. In essence, they are one and the same, having about them what in his great *Six Memos for the Next Millennium* (*Lezioni americane: Sei proposte per il prossimo millennio*) he defined more precisely as the qualities of *leggerezza, rapidità, esattezza, visibilità,* and *molteplicità* – lightness, quickness, exactitude, visibility, and complexity, to give their English equivalences.[5] It is of compelling interest to see how he glosses the common qualities between those earlier figures – Ariosto, Galileo, and Leopardi – in what he calls their 'line-of-force' connections. Calvino is ostensibly responding to the question as to why he had recently claimed – with intent, but also hyperbolic 'lightness' – that Galileo was the greatest of Italian writers; however, much more than the initial claim is glossed in his answer.

> In the *Zibaldone* (Miscellany), Leopardi admires Galileo's prose for being elegant and precise at one and the same time. And we have only to look at

the choice of passages from Galileo that Leopardi includes in his *Crestomazia* (Anthology) of Italian prose to realize how much the language of Leopardi – even Leopardi as a poet – owes to Galileo. But, to get back to what I was saying a moment ago, Galileo uses language not as a neutral utensil, but with literary awareness, with a continuous commitment that is expressive, imaginative, and even lyrical. When I read Galileo I like to seek out the passages in which he speaks of the moon. It is the first time that the moon becomes a real object for mankind, and is minutely described as a tangible thing, yet as soon as the moon appears one feels a kind of rarefaction, almost of levitation, in Galileo's language. One rises with it into an enchanted state of suspension. It was no coincidence that Galileo admired and annotated Ariosto, cosmic and lunary poet that he was ... So much so that we can draw a line from Ariosto to Galileo to Leopardi.

Leopardi nello *Zibaldone* ammira la prosa di Galileo per la precisione e l'eleganza congiunte. E basta vedere la scelta di passi di Galileo che Leopardi fa nella sua *Crestomazia della prosa italiana*, per comprendere quanto la lingua leopardiana – anche del Leopardi poeta – deve a Galileo. Ma per riprendere il discorso di poco fa, Galileo usa il linguaggio non come uno strumento neutro, ma con una coscienza letteraria, con una continua partecipazione espressiva, immaginativa, addirittura lirica. Leggendo Galileo mi piace cercare i passi in cui parla della Luna: è la prima volta che la Luna diventa per gli uomini un oggetto reale, che viene descritta minutamente come cosa tangibile, eppure appena la Luna compare, nel linguaggio di Galileo si sente una specie di rarefazione, di levitazione: ci s'innalza in un'incantata sospensione. Non per niente Galileo ammirò e postillò quel poeta cosmico e lunare che fu Ariosto ... Tanto che possiamo segnare una linea Ariosto-Galileo-Leopardi.[6]

The passage suggests that many rich cultural links are at stake in the final hypothesis. Each point Calvino makes is an invitation both to look at the evidence for ourselves and to elaborate on the analytical scaffolding offered. We are challenged to question, furthermore, whether Calvino's own writings, fictional and non-fictional, possibly extend the lineage under examination.

Let us begin, as Calvino does, with Leopardi, who serves as a bridge between our modern period and the much earlier times of Ariosto and Galileo. We can, furthermore, for convenience of understanding and economy of space, organize many of the opening aspects of our discussion around a commonly shared interest on the part of all of these authors in the moon. Leopardi is preeminently the poet of moon and moonlight and the speculations which they inspire – 'gran poeta lunare' (great lunar poet), as Calvino called him in a letter to *Il Corriere della Sera* in 1967.[7] In a multiplicity of places in his *Canti* in particular, Leopardi makes the moon a focus for some of what we have come to know through subsequent historical criticism as the most essential resonances in the whole of Italian Romanticism. In his poems the moon is usually felt as a far off celestial body, paradoxically companionable precisely because it is distant, unknowable, and above all, indifferent to the sufferings that are the ordinary lot of humans, the poet included. For example, 'You rise in the evening, and travel / contemplating deserts, then rest.' ('Sorgi la sera, e vai, / contemplando i deserti; indi ti posi.') Or '... now turns the year upon this hill / where I came full of pain to marvel at you: / and you hung then over that wood / as now you do, and illuminate it all.' ('... or volge l'anno, sovra questo colle / io venia pien d'angoscia a rimirarti: / e tu pendevi allor su quella selva / siccome or fai, che tutta la rischiari.') These and other such quotes from Leopardi in his *Canti* form part of a fine analysis by Calvino, who attests that 'the miraculous thing about his poetry is that he simply takes the weight out of language, to the point that it resembles moonlight' ('il miracolo di Leopardi è stato di togliere al linguaggio ogni peso fino a farlo assomigliare alla luce lunare').[8]

But the curious thing – and Calvino, in a number of other places, bears witness to this – is that Ariosto and Galileo had gotten to the moon before Leopardi, so to speak, and vastly affected his appreciation of it as a celestial body. Consider for a moment not one of the *Canti*, but an essential part of the 'Dialogo della Terra e della Luna' ('Dialogue Between the Earth and the Moon') from Leopardi's *Operette morali* (*Moral Opuscules*), first published in 1824:

> MOON. Excuse me, Madame Earth, if I answer you a little more freely than becomes one of your subjects or servants, as I am. But really, you strike me as rather vain if you think that all things in every part of the world are like your own; as if Nature were only intent on reproducing you in everything she did. I say that I am inhabited, and from this you conclude that my inhabitants must be men. I inform you that they are not; and although you accept the fact that they are different creatures, you assume that they have the same qualities and live under the same conditions as your people; and you bring up the telescope of some scientist or other. But if this telescope doesn't see more clearly in other cases than in this one, I must believe that its eyesight is

as good as your children's, who discover in me eyes, mouth, nose – which I don't know anything about.

LUNA. Perdona, monna Terra, se io ti rispondo un poco più liberamente che forse non converrebbe a una tua suddita o fantesca, come io sono. Ma in vero che tu mi riesci peggio che vanerella a pensare che tutte le cose di qualunque parte del mondo sieno conformi alle tue; come se la natura non avesse avuto altra intenzione che di copiarti puntualmente da per tutto. Io dico di essere abitata, e tu da questo conchiudi che gli abitatori miei debbono essere uomini. Ti avverto che non sono; e tu consentendo che sieno altre creature, non dubiti che non abbiano le stesse qualità e gli stessi casi de' tuoi popoli; e mi alleghi i cannocchiali di non so che fisico. Ma se cotesti cannocchiali non veggono meglio in altre cose, io crederò che abbiano la buona vista de' tuoi fanciulli; che scuoprono in me gli occhi, la bocca, il naso, che io non so dove me gli abbia.[9]

The cumulative effect of the argument here is not unlike a moment of observation early in *The Dean's December*, one of Saul Bellow's most philosophical novels. In that novel, Bellow's main character, a college dean named Corde, hears a lone dog barking and imagines it to be 'a protest against the limits of dog experience (for God's sake, open the universe a little more).'[10] Leopardi also is entering the plea that we not live in mental straitjackets, a principal one being our tendency to imagine all that is *other* in terms of what is *not* other, but rather the same. On Leopardi's part, this is a complex argument against anthropomorphism and in favour of our seeking to 'open the universe a little more' than our earth-bound prejudices will normally allow. In its light, swift, precise way, this argument is closely indebted to a passage from Galileo, which Leopardi himself was to anthologize in the *Crestomazia*, published in 1827. Indeed, Galileo is being subtly – if somewhat indefinitely – conjured into Leopardi's passage as the scientist (*fisico*) with the telescopes.

Leopardi's argument here virtually repeats that famous earlier intervention by Galileo. Galileo was investigating what is learned by contemplating the moon – in particular, what we *cannot know* with certainty. The moon forces us to consider the likely existence of conditions other than our own, which therefore cannot be characterized by us precisely because they are beyond our conceptual framework. The highlight of the earlier author's passage, quoted in Leopardi's *Crestomazia* from what is possibly Galileo's most important work, the *Dialogo sopra i due massimi sistemi del mondo, tolemaico e copernicano* (*Dialogue concerning the two chief world systems, Ptolemaic & Copernican*) of 1632, runs as follows:

> Whether on the moon or some other planet, grasses or plants or animals similar to our own have developed, or whether there are rains, winds, and thunder, as in the case of the earth; I do not know, but think not; and much less that it be inhabited by humans. But I do not suppose that, if there be no creations similar to our own, we necessarily must conclude that there is no life process there. May there not be some other beings which are begotten, develop, and dissolve, not only different from our own, but quite beyond our imagination or capacity to conceive. And since I am sure that to someone born and nourished in an immense wood, amongst beasts and birds, and who had no conception of the element of water ... it would be impossible to conceptualize fish, the ocean, boats, fleets, and naval armadas; likewise – indeed far more – may it happen that on the moon, so remote an interval from us, and by chance so different from the earth in composition, there be substances and operations not only strange but quite beyond our grasp; such indeed as do not resemble anything that we know, and are therefore beyond conception. Whatever we may imagine to be there must pertain either to things we have already seen, or to some combination or part of things already beheld, just such as are sphinxes, sirens, chimeras, centaurs. I have many times wondered over these matters. And at length it appears that I come up with things that are not, nor ever could be on the moon, but with not a single thing that I believe is or could be there; except by way of vague generality; that is to say, things which might embellish it, acting and moving and living, but perhaps in a way utterly different from our own.

> Che nella luna, o in altro pianeta, si generino o erbe o piante o animali simili ai nostri, o vi si facciano pioggie, venti, tuoni, come intorno alla terra; io non lo so, e non lo credo; e molto meno, che ella sia abitata da uomini. Ma non intendo già come, tuttavoltaché non vi si generino cose simili alle nostre, si deva di necessità concludere che niuna alterazione vi si faccia, né vi possano essere altre cose che si mutino, si generino e si dissolano, non solamente diverse dalle nostre, ma lontanissime dalla nostra immaginazione, e in somma del tutto a noi inescogitabili. E siccome io son sicuro che a uno nato e nutrito in una selva immensa, tra fiere e uccelli, e che non avesse cognizione alcuna dell'elemento dell'acqua ... non si potrebbe già mai figurare i pesci, l'oceano, le navi, le flotte, e le armate di mare; cosí, e molto piú, può accadere che nella luna, per tanto intervallo remota da noi, e di materia per avventura molto diversa dalla terra, sieno sustanze, e si

facciano operazioni, non solamente lontane, ma del tutto fuori d'ogni nostra immaginazione, come quelle che non abbiano similitudine alcuna con le nostre, e perciò del tutto inescogitabili. Avvegnaché quello che noi ci immaginiamo, bisogna che sia o una delle cose già vedute, o un composto di cose, o di parti delle cose, altra volta vedute, che tali sono le sfingi, le sirene, le chimere, i centauri. Io sono molte volte andato fantasticando sopra queste cose; e finalmente me pare di ritrovar bene alcune delle cose che non sieno né possan esser nella luna, ma non già veruna di quelle che io creda che vi sieno e possano essere; se non con una larghissima generalità; cioè cose che l'adornino, operando e movendo e vivendo, e forse con modo diversissimo dal nostro.[11]

This is an impressive argument, which strikes at the heart of conditions of unknowability in science. Galileo is trying to understand what might possibly provide a bridge from the known to the unknown, and at every attempt he meets a barrier to thought. For his argumentation continually leads him back, ineluctably, to the realization that we can only conceptualize in terms of knowledge we already possess, and therefore we are imprisoned within these bounds. We cannot, not even by utmost willpower and imagination, leap to an understanding of things that are, by definition, quite different from every building block used to conceptualize them. Those building blocks of understanding are themselves boundaries, which cannot be transcended. No matter how we use them, we will construct permutations or combinations of the already known.

And yet, all the while there is a tension here as Galileo, up against the very grain of things unknowable – because beyond limits of human conception – shows how his mind is nevertheless drawn compulsively into speculation. He has his speaker in the dialogue confess to being caught up in a particular repeated act: *sono molte volte andato fantasticando sopra queste cose* (I have many times wondered over these matters). In the original dialogue the speaker changes from Sagredus to Salviatus at this point, a factor that is ignored in Leopardi's anthology. But this does not really alter our assumption that the cognitive activities being addressed must pertain to Galileo. A dictionary translation into English of Galileo's word *fantasticando* – daydreaming – doesn't capture all that is hinted at in the original.[12] In the context here, *fantasticando* certainly seems to suggest a strong act of fantasizing and of hypothesizing on Galileo's part, for the instance resonates with the role fantasy may play in scientific reasoning and speculation, a thought close to the formulation by Calvino.

But there is more to the dynamic of this passage than meets the eye. For inside it is another implicit, if unacknowledged, thinker/poet, who had beaten much this same pathway of lunar speculation – had been *fantasticando sopra queste cose* – a century before Galileo, and is an unnamed presence, tutoring and enticing him along the way. That figure is Ariosto, beloved author to Galileo of the poem he ceaselessly dwelt upon and praised, *Orlando Furioso*. Indeed he remarked on Ariosto's poem so variously that to list all the reasons for his loving it would make for a lengthy departure from my argument. But one of the reasons reminds us of a quality Calvino much admired centuries later: namely, to use Galileo's own words for it, the 'racy speed expressed by Ariosto in many places' ('velocità di corso espressa dall'Ariosto in molti luoghi').[13] At the literal level Galileo means the speed of knights and ladies on their steeds and of their adventures per se. But speed is also appreciated as a quality in writing itself – preferred specifically to 'weightiness' – in another illuminating passage by Galileo, this time on discursive argumentation, also anthologized by Leopardi and commented upon by Calvino, as practically the most important definition of prose style in the Italian language.

A passage which Galileo focuses on in the thirty-fourth canto of Ariosto's poem is the stanza describing how, among all the things on earth that have wound up on the moon, people's wits are the principal thing lost. In Ariosto's poem the knight Astolfo is guided by St. John the Evangelist, in a chariot not unlike Elijah's, through the space separating the terrestrial paradise from the moon, to fetch back Orlando's wits (*senno*) taken from him by God as a punishment for his loving beyond all measure the pagan princess Angelica. The '*Senno d'Orlando*' (Orlando's sanity, so to speak) proves to be in the largest of many flasks of people's missing wits, because his loss is the greatest of all on earth. These '*varie ampolle*' – to use Ariosto's incipiently scientific Renaissance terminology for the storage vessels of all the human sense gone missing from their original bearers – together make up a mountain on the moon. One particular *ampolla* in the mountain pile is filled with that portion of Astolfo's own sanity, which is not whole; the idea being that none of us has retained perfect wits from birth through to maturity and beyond. Whatever we have lost of our sanity becomes a minor phial, or as it might be, a major demijohn, of this heap of all persons' lost *ampolle* (vessels) of sanity on the moon's surface.

The actual stanza favoured by Galileo is one which rehearses some of the universal causes of our losing our wits, and therefore of their flying to the moon. The utter inescapability of some loss of sanity is emphasized by the wordplay of the final line of the Ariosto quotation:

> Some in love lose it [their sanity], others in honours;
> Others in coursing the sea in quest of riches;
> Others in placing their hopes in their Lords;
> Others believing in magical follies;
> Others in gems, still others in painters' works,
> And others in something other, which more than all other they cherish.

> Altri in amar lo perde [il senno], altri in onori;
> Altri in cercar scorrendo il mar, richezze;
> Altri ne le speranze de' Signori;
> Altri dietro a le magiche sciochezze.
> Altri in gemme, altri in opre di pittori,
> Et altri in altro, che più d'altro apprezze. (XXXIV, 85)

What is interesting is that in his annotation of this material, Galileo was so caught up in the fun of listing that he added two lines of his own, in place of those with Ariosto's clever wordplay in them. (Salman Rushdie, in a review article on Calvino, attests to how fabulists love lists.)[14] In other words, before ever reaching Ariosto's crowning summation in the close of the stanza – 'Of sophists' wits and astrologers' gathered there / And of poets' as well, so much abounded' ('Di sofisti e d'astrologhi raccolto / E di poeti ancor ve n'era molto') – Galileo prefers to insert a kind of jaunty variant. Interestingly, it is a variant that satirizes a new age that has come to pass mainly since the time of Ariosto, and it consists of curio collectors that populate Galileo's early seventeenth-century world. 'Some in onions identify exotic flowers, / and some in ancient medals have their delights.' ('Chi in cipolle raccor di estranei fiori, / E chi in medaglie antiche ha sue vaghezze.')[15]

Ariosto's idea that all that goes missing (not just sanity, but much else as well) lands up on the moon, is perhaps another way of utilizing the unknowable qualities of the moon for poetic purposes. The moon being from the beginning a symbol of the unknowable, we might as well infuse it precisely with what we have lost and cannot find for all our searching. It becomes, therefore, a locus for representation of fruitless quests on Earth. Instead of despairing at this, as a metaphysic of meaninglessness, Ariosto turns the whole matter of our human madness – literally the *sense-less-ness* of all our questing (Orlando's for Angelica being representative) – into an extended joke about *all lost sanity* having migrated to that other place. Calvino, in his synopsis of the poem, well sums up Ariosto's principal poetic premises: 'The moon is a world as big as ours, seas included. There are rivers, lakes, plains, cities, castles, just as with us; yet *other* than our own. Earth and Moon, just as they have interchangeable dimensions and form, so too they invert the functions of one another: seen from up there, it is the Earth which can be called the world of the Moon; for if men's reason is conserved up there, the implication is that on Earth there remains only folly.' ('La Luna è un mondo grande come il nostro, mari compresi. Vi sono fiumi, laghi, pianure, città, castelli, come da noi; eppure *altri* da quelli nostri. Terra e Luna, cosí come si scambiano dimensioni e imagine, cosí invertono le loro funzioni: vista di quassú, è la Terra che può esser detta il mondo della Luna; se la ragione degli uomini è quassú che si conserva, vuol dire che sulla Terra non è rimasta che pazzia.')[16]

Ariosto is nothing if not indulgent in his reckonings. He compares God's having likewise deprived Nebuchadnezzar of his sanity for seven years with Orlando's offence, which is such that his total time without his wits is but a three-month period. Much of what has gone missing on earth, like mercy and piety, lords' trust and women's beauty, is genial satire on Ariosto's part. 'Only of folly is there neither great or little there / for it remains below, and never from hence departs.' ('Sol la pazzia non v'è poca né assai / che sta qua giù né se ne parte mai.')

A point to remember in our consideration of the fantasy deployed by Ariosto is that it seemed to have amused Galileo and inspired him in his development of a more extended and telescope-aided appreciation of the moon and its spots. Many now would agree that Galileo was both a great scientist and a great writer. Far from dispensing with Ariosto's fabulist appreciation of the moon's surface, and postulating the infinitude of things that may be on the moon in an entirely different way, Galileo is inspired by this most fantastical poem of a century earlier. All the evidence suggests that, as a result of appreciating Ariosto's imagination at full stretch in the treatment of lunar and cosmic matters, Galileo was influenced along the literary and speculative pathways of his own writings. Most specifically, Ariosto's fantasy about the moon is fundamental to Galileo's own careful thinking about things knowable and unknowable. In short, fantasy is not a literary mode which Renaissance science was obliged to dispense with and leave behind as something inhibiting thought. Rather, in the hands of one of the most brilliant scientific practitioners of early modernity, it is a tool for extending what is at once science's key realm and its modus operandi, namely speculation.

We come, by a natural turn of the argument, to consider one of Galileo's fundamental ideas on the discursive handling of knowledge. It is an idea that Leopardi anthologized in his *Crestomazia*, and it seems later to have deeply influenced Calvino, for he recycled Galileo's piece of early seventeenth-century counsel on the finest form of discourse in his *Six Memos for the Next Millennium*, which was written in the last year of his life.

In the passage, Galileo is striving to define what difficult discursive thinking is really like and what it is about. To that end he considers the derivation of the word *discorrere*, to discourse, in the word *correre*, to run. (I have had to translate the latter as 'to course' in the following to keep this sense of derivations more intact in English.)

> The number of those who in difficult matters discourse well is much fewer than of those who discourse badly. If discourse about a difficult problem were like carrying weights, where many horses are able to support more sacks of grain than a single one, I would consent that many discourses do more than just one: but 'to discourse' is like 'to course,' and not like 'to carry,' and a single Berber stallion will course faster than a hundred Frisians.

> Il numero di quelli che nelle cose difficili discorron bene, è minore assai che di quei che discorron male. Se il discorrere circa un problema difficile fusse come il portar pesi, dove molti cavalli porteranno piú sacca di grano che un caval solo, io acconsentirei che i molti discorsi facesser piú che un solo: ma il discorrere è come il correre, e non come il portare; ed un caval barbero solo correrà piú che cento frisoni.[17]

What impresses immediately in Galileo's own discourse here is its felicitous brilliance. With comic brio he juggles, on the one hand, a set of interrelated distinctions between persons who discourse well and others who do not, lightness and weightiness, racing and carrying, as well as, on the other hand, that fundamental correlation (embedded even in the etymology and meaning of the verb *discorrere*) between a horse's swiftness and the necessary celerities of expression. Additionally, the argument climaxes, in the starkest but also the most clinching contrast of all, in the implied idea of a race between a single speedy Berber horse and one hundred Frisian drays. On Galileo's part there is a fine subtlety of thought in operation here, which has nonetheless managed to find 'exactitude' (Calvino's term) in exemplificatory imagery from popular life to make his meaning easily grasped.

With writing of this kind in mind, Leopardi claims early in the *Zibaldone* that Italian is a language whose peculiar province is the imagination. But he also quickly asserts in the same passage that this does not detract from its suitability for scientific expression as well. Importantly, Galileo's influence emerges in Leopardi's argument as one of his two examples of 'precise efficacy and sculpting' in writing. Galileo's passage is certainly an instance of a precise 'sculpting' of the syntactic musculature of expression.

When it comes to the French language, the division Leopardi notes between cold scientific or mathematical precision, which he claims that French is well suited to, and imagination, which cannot be so well handled by it, gets bridged in his example of Galileo's Italian. This claim could be exemplified by Galileo's passage about discourse.[18] Elsewhere in Leopardi's *Zibaldone*, Galileo is cited as the very model of precision balanced with elegance.[19] However, opposite opinions and speculations also frequently emerge as a kind of intellectual counterpoint. For instance, in the matter of Galileo's Italian, Leopardi claims elsewhere that it is *not* elegant in areas where it is precise and mathematical, but that it is nonetheless always extremely *pure*.[20] The overall impression, nonetheless, is that Leopardi keenly appreciated Galileo's prose as a supremely subtle, imaginative, and precise instrument of speculative thought. This has been put memorably by Franco Gabici in a fine article on Leopardi's appreciation of Galileo: 'Borrowing an image from astronomy, we could say that Leopardi completed a thorough orbit of the work of Galileo, in search of its hidden face, that is to say Galileo the writer.' ('E mutuando una imagine dall'astronomia, possiamo affermare che Leopardi ha compiuto una vera e propria circumnavigazione dell'opera di Galilei, andando alla riscoperta di un *volto* nascosto, vale a dire il Galilei scrittore.')[21]

With some sense of this vibrant and often fabulist tradition informing literature and science behind us, the next stage in the discussion is provided by Calvino's own use of Galileo's passage as a touchstone for what he has to say in his section on *rapidità*, or quickness, in the 1985 Charles Eliot Norton Lectures that he was to have delivered at Harvard in 1985. Having postulated that 'the horse as an emblem of speed, even of speed of the mind, runs through the whole history of literature, heralding the entire problematics of our own technological viewpoint' ('Il cavallo come emblema della velocità anche mentale marca tutta la storia della letteratura, preannunciando tutta la problematica propria del nostro orizzonte tecnologico'), Calvino has led up to this instance in Galileo's writing by means of a brilliant series of examples from other works in our literary history.

First, Calvino dwelt on how, in a notable point in the *Decameron*, horse travel is used by Giovanni Boccaccio as an implicit metaphor for 'correctness of style' ('la proprietà stilistica') and 'agility of both thought and expression' ('agilità dell'espressione e del pensiero') in the pacing of narration in the art of the novella. Next he turns to Thomas De Quincey's essay of 1849 'The English Mail Coach,' in which 'the technical perfection of the vehicle' ('la perfezione tecnica del veicolo') becomes a means for 'the transformation of the driver into a blind inanimate object' ('la trasformazione del guidatore in un cieco oggetto inanimato'), bringing us to the very brink of modernity. Calvino claims that De Quincey had already seen how travellers may be placed 'at the mercy of the mechanical inexorability of the machine' ('in balia dell'inesorabile esattezza d'una macchina') and 'the vision of sudden death' of two vehicles colliding or, just possibly, by the good grace of God, managing in the nick of time not to.[22]

Calvino's final example before the one from Galileo takes us rapidly through a phase of thinking in the *Zibaldone* in which, a full century before the futurists, Leopardi (possibly the most underestimated of the great Romantics outside Italy) was preoccupied by speed of travel as instantiation of 'vivacity,' 'energy,' 'strength,' and 'sheer life of ... feeling.' Calvino shows us where Leopardi turns these thoughts in a literary direction, such that they become a concern for 'speed and conciseness of style' (the words are Leopardi's own). According to Leopardi, such speed and conciseness 'please us because they present the mind with a rush of ideas that are simultaneous, or that follow each other so quickly that they seem simultaneous, and set the mind afloat on such an abundance of thoughts or images or spiritual feelings that either it cannot embrace them all, each one fully, or has no time to be idle and empty of feelings.' ('La rapidità e la concisione dello stile, piace perchè presenta all'anima una folla d'idee simultanee, o così rapidamente succedentisi, che paiono simultanee, e fanno ondeggiar l'anima in una tale abbondanza di pensieri, o d'immagini e sensazioni spirituali, ch'ella o non è capace di abbracciarle tutte, e pienamente ciascuna, o non ha tempo di restare in ozio, e priva di sensazioni.')[23] Such a thought process was clearly seen positively by Leopardi, as it was subsequently by Calvino.

Calvino does not point out the origin of such realizations by Leopardi, but rather directs us to Galileo's passage concerning rapidity of discourse, which was known to and indeed anthologized by Leopardi. Calvino comments: '"Discoursing," or "discourse" for Galileo means reasoning, and very often deductive reasoning. "Discoursing is like coursing": this statement could be Galileo's declaration of faith – style as a method of thought and as literary taste. For him, good thinking means quickness, agility in reasoning, economy in argument, but also the use of imaginative examples.' ('"Discorrere," "discorso" per Galileo vuol dire raggionamento, e spesso ragionamento deduttivo. "Il discorrere è come il correre": questa affermazione è come il programma stilistico di Galileo, stile come metodo di pensiero e come gusto letterario: la rapidità, l'agilità del ragionamento, l'economia degli argomenti, ma anche la fantasia degli esempi sono per Galileo qualità decisive del pensar bene.')[24] Calvino's ongoing discussion here – as to the deep connection between scientific thinking on Galileo's part, and his skill in and conception of writing – is an implicit demonstration as to why in a new millennial age of remarkable and sometimes frightening scientific achievements, we might do well to look back to some of the methodological and stylistic foundations of contemporary expository thinking as expressed by this early modern scientist.

But what of Calvino himself? He had emerged from his role as a Partisan at the end of the Second World War. He had even committed in the final lines of his first novel, *The Path to the Spiders' Nest* (*Il sentiero dei nidi di ragno*), what Salman Rushdie avers was the 'last example on record of a bad sentence' in his entire career. (For interest, the sentence reads: 'And they walk on, the big man and the child, into the night, amid the fireflies, holding each other by the hand.'[26] 'E continuano a camminare, l'omone e il bambino, nella notte, in mezzo alle lucciole, tenendosi per mano.'[27]) What are some features of his next developments, and how do they relate to the cultural lineage of fantasy that I have been following?

It is particularly noteworthy that, after that first novel, Calvino entitled his trilogy of tales of the 1950s, which is most keenly based on the narrative modes of *romanzi cavallereschi* by Ariosto and others, *Our Ancestors* (*I nostri antenati*). In doing so, it is as though he were announcing not so much that we are directly born of such fantastical persons as his protagonists, as that we too have important origins – our ancestry, so to speak – in the traditions of narrative which give rise to them. (I am referring to his main figures in this trilogy, the non-existent knight, the cloven viscount, and the baron in the trees.) In other words, we have a birth in lineages of storytelling as well as our biological genealogy, and our psychologies too have a genealogy, fabulist in large measure and deriving from characters of narrative no matter how strange.

Even as he begins the trilogy, Calvino seems to allude to the possibility of a vacuum, where identity should exist but may not. He describes a line of mounted paladins being reviewed by Charlemagne before the red walls of Paris. In the armour that keeps them 'stiff in their saddles' ('impettiti in sella') quite as though it were such metal casings – and not the bodies within – that provided stability and musculature, they make a combined noise, 'a surf-like sound ... from warriors snoring inside the metallic throats of their helmets' ('un russare di guerrieri incupito dalle gole metalliche degli elmi').[28] Within so few words we are already at the border between personality, on the one hand, and the impersonality of objects without identity, on the other.

However, the case is even more multiple, more complex (to adopt again that last value term from among his later 'memos' for our new millennium). When the eponymous, inexistent knight of this first part of Calvino's trilogy is introduced, his very inexistence is paradoxically denoted by Calvino not in terms of lack of identity, but rather plenitude – so much, indeed, that it exceeds those of the regular knights who do in fact exist. Even in introducing himself, this figure, whose fantastical name is Agilulfo Emo Bertrandino dei Guildiverni e degli Altri di Corbentraz e Sura, cavaliere di Selimpia Citeriore e Fez, speaks with an impersonal voice, seemingly produced from non-bodily objects, as though he may indeed lack identity: 'a metallic voice from inside the closed helmet, with a slight echo as if it were not a throat but the very armour itself vibrating.' ('La voce giungeva metallica da dentro l'elmo chiuso, come fosse non una gola ma la stessa lamiera dell'armatura a vibrare, e con un lievo rimbombo d'eco.') By the close of the chapter, however, he can be declared to be 'a model soldier; but disliked by all' ('un modello di soldato; ma a tutti loro era antipatico).

By employing a narrative technique of astute fantasy, which is *within* traditional chivalric-romantic modes of narration, Calvino produced a working 'imaginary' of modern alienation specific to the age of late modernity in which he was writing. (Importantly, too, his own career emerged during a period immediately after the devastations – in Italy as elsewhere – of the Second World War.) It is as though the *empty* spaces of existence posited by this trilogy of updates of chivalric-romantic narration (updates each set retrospectively in a past age of European conflict) were, oddly, what denoted the *plenitude* of every aspect of those fantastical traditions of our common culture of 'the marvellous.'

There may be some element of residual satire directed towards fascism in what Calvino provides in his accounts of Agilulfo, a being whose uniform *is* himself – 'possessor of the finest whitest armour, inseparable from him, in the whole camp' ('possessore della piú bella e candida armatura di tutto il campo, inseparabile da lui'). As historians of fascism are well aware, belonging to such a party and movement often offered the outward uniform of conformism, rendering the need to sustain a personal inner conscience unnecessary. But in Calvino's writings things are always more multiple, more complex. Agilulfo, for all that he is a suit of armour filled by a non-existent knight, is also Calvino's pertinent fabulist's way of posing, not of avoiding, problems of existence so soon after the war. Calvino, at bottom, is just as interested in those others in his narrative who, when they take off their armour, are 'content at being distinct and differentiated human beings once again' ('soddisfatti a ritrovarsi persone umane distinte e inconfondibili').

The sharp fantastical contours of the story of a non-existent knight therefore focus for us more clearly what it is or might be to be *existent*. Fantasy at this point of the 1950s serves the ends of helping readers to get a firmer grip on what is real. There are haunting descriptions of the scenes of battle, not unlike a moment in William Shakespeare's *Henry V* in which a character named Williams, a common soldier, articulates the nightmare vision of 'all those Legges, and Armes, and Heads, chopt off in a Battaile,' strewing the battlefield. In Calvino's case, the scene consists of dead soldiers still partly wearing their armour; 'as if the armour was filled not with whole bodies but with stuffed guts which spilled out of every gash' ('come se le armature fossero riempite non da corpi interi ma da visceri ficcati lí a casaccio'). It is partly by having one figure in the narrative who has no body within his suit of armour that this vision of those who were once living and whole, and precisely *not* random vessels of piled together blood and guts (as in death they seem), can be appreciated for its full horror. As I have been stressing, this seems like a reflection on the prior carnage of the Second World War in Europe. Calvino even has his most 'existent' character, a young and inexperienced knight named Rambaldo, react to the knockabout character named Gurdulú in a way that raises a fundamental philosophical doubt. When Gurdulú becomes covered in soup, Rambaldo imagines 'the world being nothing but a vast shapeless mass of soup in which all things dissolved and tinged all else with itself' ('il mondo non fosse altro che un'immensa minestra senza forma in cui tutto si sfaceva e tingeva di sé ogni altra cosa').

The Non-existent Knight, although the first tale in the eventual Italian edition of *Our Ancestors* as a trilogy, was the last to be published singly, in 1959. The enduring issues of existence and of non-existence that it explores are taken about as far as the fantastical postulates of Calvino's narrative will allow. In the next tale of the trilogy, *The Cloven Viscount* (*Il visconte dimezzato*), we touch on an earlier (1951) fabulist meditation into *split* existence; or to call it in terms of the popular psychology of the day, split personality. Calvino takes from popular psychology the idea of split personality and, by means of his fabulism, premises it on the literal notion of a split person: one whose two halves, divided in battle by a cannon ball, thereafter go on living separate existences. The Manichaean vision here is of all the good in a person surviving in only half of his being, while the evil lives on in concentrate in the other half. If this alone does not suggest the divisions in the moral and perceptual universe during the world war in Europe, the tale's geographical and historical setting reinforces the point. The story is set during the late seventeenth-century Bohemian wars between Christians and Infidels in Austria and Turkey, and mixes almost unbearably gory fantasies of war (Goya's *Horrors of War* series would be an apt comparison) with realistic components: 'Over the bare plain were scattered tangled heaps of men's and women's corpses, naked, covered with plague boils and, inexplicably at first, with feathers, as if these skinny legs and ribs had grown black feathers and wings. These were carcasses of vultures mingled with human remains.' ('In groppi di carcasse, sparsi per la brulla pianura, si vedevano corpi d'uomo e donna, nudi, sfigurati dai bubboni e, cosa dapprincipio inspiegabile, pennuti: come se da quelle loro macilente braccia e costole fossero cresciute nere penne e ali. Erano le carogne d'avvoltoio mischiate ai loro resti.') This scene of horror is a prelude to the narrative moment – which, even more importantly, might be considered a *philosophical* moment – when Calvino's character, Viscount Medardo di Terralba, is cloven in two. For as the 'good' Medardo expresses it, 'That's the good thing about being halved; that one understands the sorrow of every person and thing in the world at its own incompleteness.' ('Questo è il bene dell'esser dimezzato: il capire d'ogni persona e cosa al mondo la pena che ognuno e ognuna ha per la propria incompletezza.') In brief, as in other cases of this narrative trilogy, the fantastical tale operates as allegorical symbolism for a general condition.

The third tale in Calvino's trilogy is *The Baron in the Trees* (*Il barone rampante*), which was published in 1957. Twice as long as each of the other two novellas, it is set in Calvino's own Ligurian region of Italy before and after the French Revolution. In the story, a child of the Ligurian aristocratic *ancien régime*, in a fit of peak over family dinner, climbs into the trees of their estate. Though it is presumed his inclination to protest will soon pass, he prolongs his revolt for the rest of his life, never again touching ground, even when he dies in premature old age by being swept off his perch and out to sea by an out-of-control flight of balloonists. Although Baron Cosimo Piovasco di Randò's individual act of revolt is sustained up to the moment of his death, he suffers over the course of his life a series of defeats in each of his personal desires for fulfillment and, more generally, in his utopian ideas for society. Therefore, the tale is about the failure to produce revolution under circumstances where there was good cause for one. As the tale's main narrator, the Baron's brother, puts it: 'In fact, all the causes of the French Revolution were present among us too. Only we were not in France, and there was no revolution. We live in a country where causes are always seen but never effects.' ('Insomma, c'erano anche da noi tutte le cause della Rivoluzione francese. Solo che non eravamo in Francia, e la Rivoluzione non ci fu. Viviamo in un paese dove si verificano sempre le cause e non gli effetti.') One suspects that with that remark in 1957, Calvino was indicting those many conditions of political stagnation that were stifling deep-structural change in Italian society in the postwar period. Of course, this may have been true for many other societies too.

The evidence culled from an inspection of only the first stage of Calvino's career in fantasy-based fictions, and from key moments in his non-fictional essays over the span of his life, including his great last work, *Six Memos for the Next Millennium*, suggests an enormously engaged and philosophically thoughtful writer. Calvino was keenly preoccupied with past, present, and, not least of all, future conditions. Those last 'memos,' in which he gathered a kind of summa of his wide reckonings in the world of literature, were intended for this new millennium, which he knew he would not personally live to see. He had such a positive set of wishes for those who would outlive him that he bequeathed his hopes in the form of striking counsels, which were premised on readings in significant former literary achievements. Those readings of the past are written in ways that exemplify (like so much of Calvino's writing before them) the very qualities of the bequest – lightness and rapidity, to mention only two. Throughout, Calvino manages to convey an impression that the literature of the future might also be quite different in kind from anything that has gone before, yet no less culturally valuable.

What happens when we turn from that long intellectual and creative cultural tradition, so vibrant in Calvino, to another fantastical set of phenomena – replicas of past icons in Las Vegas and other 'way out' environments? A learned approach might be to avoid consciously snubbing hyperreality with any of the standard high-minded prejudices characteristic of, as Eco puts it, 'the European visitor' and 'American intellectual.'[29] Eco talks about the 'crèche-ification of the bourgeois universe,' and about works that are not facsimiles but 'fac-differents.' His amusing analysis of what he calls 'the reconstructive mania' and 'industry of absolute iconism' of a 'bricolage, haunted by *horror vacui*,'[30] all make up in reading pleasure for the tedium and disappointment that might otherwise be experienced without the aid of his jovial and serene wit. For example, consider what he has to say about his discovery in California of three-dimensional 'replicas' in waxwork or glass of Leonardo Da Vinci's Last Supper: 'not the way it looks now in Santa Maria delle Grazie, but the way we suppose it must have looked when Leonardo painted it, or rather – better – the way Leonardo ought to have painted it if he had been less shiftless ... The voice has warned you that the original fresco is by now ruined, almost invisible, unable to give you the emotion you have received from the three-dimensional wax, which is more real, and there is more of it.'[31] Eco's ability to be so sardonically comic undermines what might have been a first impulse to moralize at the sheer 'artistic or philosophical pretensions' (to use his own words) of so much of this stuff, when, that is, it is not going still further downmarket, into a 'savage taste for the amazing, the overstuffed, and the absolutely sumptuous at low price.'[32]

The laughter Eco stirs in his readers and the indulgent mood he tends to foster in these 'Travels in Hyperreality' certainly encourage us to avoid the tendency of crude moralizing in our own analyses. But I believe we are, nonetheless, obliged to ask whether this culture of 'fakes' (especially ones built to new agendas since Eco's great descriptions of the genre in 1975) does not over time have a tendency to degrade other, more valuable traditions of the fantastic, or worse still, completely displace them? Enormous plastic replicas of the Seven Wonders of the World and impossibly large gambling casinos with dinky, 'repro' Venices are not just examples of vulgar capitalistic trash. Nor are they mere grand-guignolesque whimsies. They may well be both, and neither might matter per se. More importantly, they might also spell disaster for the life force that once coursed through other, greater traditions. Those other and earlier traditions were not financed, as hyperreality so often is, by brute capital that has been extorted by means of ever larger structures of exploitation on behalf of leisured classes that do not themselves labour to produce. Very importantly, in the copying of works from the past in a relentless ethos of 'authenticity,' does hyperreality not get caught up in a logic of the finite, rather than fostering what we might expect from enduring art and culture, namely infinitude?

Even so, I have to confess to being uneasy about my own drift here, back towards analysis with a moralizing edge. Indeed, I am obliged to enter a reservation. The nature of the debate requires that we at least pose the question whether hyperreality, such as we currently witness in Las Vegas, rather than being just a vulgarizing of previous gestalts that its builders replicate in fragmented form, does not actually change those gestalts in the process, and in ways that are at first difficult to understand? If the answer to this question is yes, then it is because as perceivers and interpreters we are caught up in arrangements that seem recognizable, but often turn out not to be so. Even in our acts of identifying what bits and pieces from our common culture and history are being referenced by all those material replicas, we experience a dynamic estrangement from what has gone before. Designers of specific instances of hyperreality may distract our attention in this way for a purpose, perhaps as a cover-up for other factors about their creations that they are less keen to have scrutinized critically.

From at least the time that Robert Venturi, Denise Scott Brown, and Steven Izenour published *Learning from Las Vegas* in 1972, we have received plenty of counsel not to prejudge the lifestyles evident in such cities, nor the environments built to accommodate them. Perhaps a key point of reckoning, however – and one that could be taken right back to these authors' analyses of thirty years ago – is a question of whether the environment in Las Vegas was not always less a *response to* lifestyles than a way of pre-determining them?

Much of *Learning from Las Vegas* is based on two main propositions, which I hope not to oversimplify. The first is that if we come to the Las Vegas 'Strip' with eyes trained by appreciation of great classical models of architecture and of urban planning, particularly those based on the Old World cultures of Italy or Britain, we will not appreciate the very terms of difference from which this other culture began. To quote Venturi and his co-authors: 'Essential to the imagery of pleasure zone architecture are lightness, the quality of being an oasis in a perhaps hostile context, heightened symbolism, and the ability to engulf the visitor in a new role: for three days one may imagine oneself a centurion at Caesar's Palace, a ranger at the Frontier, or a jetsetter at the Riviera rather than a salesperson from Des Moines, Iowa, or an architect from Haddonfield, New Jersey.' Or: 'The Strip shows the value of symbolism and allusion in an architecture of vast space and speed and proves that people, even architects, have fun with architecture that reminds them of something else, perhaps of harems or the Wild West.'[33] In these two quotations alone, concepts of 'lightness' and of 'speed' are addressed in ways which predate Calvino's use of such terms in the following decade. So a question arises: Did Venturi and his co-authors in the 1970s already appreciate Las Vegas as a visual and spatial culture for some of the same values Calvino was to select for the enduring literary culture he envisioned on behalf of the new millennium?

The second main justification is, in a strange way, contrary to the first, namely that the Las Vegas Strip organizes meaning not so differently than the Roman Forum did for its time and context: the implication being that one just has to be broadminded enough in cultural relativities to understand such deeper similarities. Already in these quotations we notice that Last Vegas will encourage in ordinary Americans a role playing as persons of other times and places. But the further point is that those other times and places are, after all, not so completely other as all that. As the authors assert elsewhere in the text, 'The agglomeration of Caesar's Palace and of the Strip as a whole approaches the spirit if not the style of the late Roman Empire with its eclectic accumulations.' And elsewhere: 'Like the complex architectural accumulations of the Roman Forum, the Strip by day reads as chaos if you perceive only its forms and exclude its symbolic content. The Forum, like the Strip, was a landscape of symbols with layers of meaning evident in the location of roads and buildings, buildings representing earlier buildings, and the sculpture piled all over.'[34] What is very much at stake is a question we have followed in the case of the lineage traced in literature by Calvino; namely, how much in each newly created work is derived from past gestalts? In terms of Las Vegas, what is old and what is new in the 'buildings representing earlier buildings'?

I want to focus the remaining discussion mainly on one recent building in Las Vegas. Its designers were ambitious to replicate not merely an earlier building, but an entire city. I am referring to the hotel-casino-mall-resort (for it is all these things at once) named *The Venetian*. It was built by the will and force of capital of its owner, Sheldon Adelson (in an earlier life an impoverished Boston taxi driver), in the late 1990s for a cost of two and one half billion dollars. This complex seeks to incorporate into its structures a replica of nothing less than the city of Venice –

Fantasy, Science, and Hyperreality: From Ariosto and Galileo to Las Vegas   81

canals, gondoliers, and a myriad other cultural paraphernalia. As a result my other main question – what happens to the exemplary culture of Italy in these New World transmogrifications of it? – is well served by analysis of this one instance of the far wider, ongoing constructions of the culture of the hyperreal.

During the building of those parts of the complex that were to replicate aspects of the real Venice, Sheldon Adelson came out repeatedly with orders to his teams of advisers, builders, painters, and costumiers to 'interpret it exactly the way its supposed to be. Don't change history.'[35] The ultimate arbiter of the exactitude of the complex's reproduction of history was, of course, Adelson himself. However, as Eco had warned us long ago, what constructors of hyperreal replicas actually want to offer is always 'more and better than the original.' So even this other term also used by Calvino – exactitude – in the realm of hyperreality is a fast and loose one. Adelson's Rialto Bridge would not have his particular Grand Canal running under it, but rather a street of Las Vegas itself as a come-on to gamblers.

This same Rialto Bridge, in order to minimize one kind of American horror at the ordinary act of walking, would have motorized travelators to take people across. Aldelson certainly was speaking the language of hyperbole in his claims that 'Venice came to Las Vegas' (rather than the reverse), and that in terms of the marble (mostly concrete or polystyrene in any case) 'We have to provide the weathering and the aging *immediately.*' All this was developed to satisfy one half of the urge at the heart of hyperreality, desire for the authentic. But then the other half of that urge – an impulse for the inauthentic – resulted in Adelson's gondolas becoming motorized in ways unseen by the romantic couples being steered about by their gondoliers with fake Italian accents. In short, there was a dictatorial arbitrariness about what was to look like the real Venice, and what Adelson felt he could alter or improve on, so as to give that essential feeling of more and better. As the BBC television critique of the program would point out about the completed complex, 'The clock tower in St Marks is perfect in every detail – except for the fifteen-story neon tower that sits atop it.'

As for not changing history, one commentator on the motorized gondolas points out that this was 'redefining how you operate one of these things. Perhaps the Venetians are going to take tips.' In relation to an earlier remark in *Learning from Las Vegas* that a client might imagine himself 'a centurion at Caesar's Palace ... rather than a salesperson from Des Moines, Iowa,' Adelson certainly sought to give his patrons an alternative experience to going to Venice, but one that by his lights somehow incorporated the best of what being in Venice could offer without all the hassle of foreign travel, or of coping with anything *offputtingly* culturally other. 'We can get a better Venice here every day,' he crowed once the complex was completed.

One of my greatest concerns pertains to the urge on Adelson's part – presumably second-guessing his clients' desires to stay in America at all costs – to incorporate into *The Venetian* the exotic of the other in ways that make redundant any actual need to *travel to* that other locale in order to experience it. Certainly in the process of domesticating the culturally other, the desert town that was once much simpler and less strange itself – a 'Strip' of neon and casinos and parking lots established to amuse that tired salesperson from Des Moines – has grown into a garish panoply of reproduction: Versailles, Venice, Paris, Rome, the Seven Wonders of the World, and many other marvels of past culture. These are mainly lodestones for pulling shoppers into upmarket malls, and gamblers into ever 'classier' casinos, using the time-honoured hyperreal technique of masquerading as something other than merely malls or casinos. As a result, there is an 'uncertaintizing' effect intended by the designers to disorient patrons with respect to both place and purpose.

Are you having an uplifting Venetian holiday, as may seem to be the case? Surely rather you are gambling money away, while being *distracted by the notion* that you are having an uplifting Venetian holiday. The drag on on your wallet is, in a sense, countered by something 'more,' something 'better,' which provides a distracting *uplift* in spirits. *The Venetian* is a fantastical blend of a neon present with a fake-marble and 'immediate' past. To represent it there could be no vulgarity finer than the one used by the London wide boy employed by Adelson as foreman of works. He is captured by the BBC program on one particularly difficult day during the construction, saying that his team has got into a 'right cluster fuck.'[36] In compressing everything of the past into a cluster, and then 'screwing up' this nodal point of prior realities, the hyperreal (in the case of *The Venetian*) steamrolls away time and change, and thereby can be said to take away the intrinsic value of cultural complexity. How can we best remind ourselves of what such complexity might have gone on meaning to us, supposing it were not under erasure by the hyperreality in question?

In closing, I would answer this question by turning back to the other tradition examined earlier in the chapter. There is a passage in Galileo

Fantasy, Science, and Hyperreality: From Ariosto and Galileo to Las Vegas 83

that presages one in Calvino, which in turn is taken up, altered, and carried on anew by Salmon Rushdie. Altogether this line of connection between artists alive to a *fundamental fantasticality* at the heart of our everyday historical realities constitutes a marveling response, in this case, to what is possible in the seemingly simple human use of script. Galileo, Calvino, and Rushdie help us to see anew the marvel of writing, which we may have begun taking for granted because of so many other amazing inventions, not the least of which in recent times is the Internet (although writing is still at the heart of that invention too).

Galileo leads up to what he has to say about the creation of the alphabet by expressing wonderment about the intricacies of music, poetry, architecture, and navigation:

> When can I ever stop marveling if I look at what humans have discovered by way of the fixing of musical intervals, and instructions and rules to wield them to the admirable delight of hearing? What shall I say of so many and such diverse instruments? Or with what sense of marvel does not the delivery by excellent poets fill anyone who attentively considers the invention of conceits and their unfolding? What shall we say of architecture? Or the art of navigation? But above all stupendous inventions, what eminence of mind was that of the person who imagined a way of communicating the most intricate of thoughts to whomsoever, however great the interval in space or time. To be able to speak with those who are in the Indies; to speak with those that are not yet even born and, who will not be this side of a thousand or ten thousand years from now? And by what means! With various rearrangements of twenty paltry letters on a piece of paper.

> S'io guardo quel che hanno ritrovato gli uomini nel compartir gl'intervalli musici, nello stabilir precetti e regole per potergli maneggiar con diletto mirabile dell'udito; quando potrò io finir di stupir? Che dirò dei tanti e sí diversi strumenti? La lettura dei poeti eccelenti, di qual meraviglia riempie chi attentamente considera l'invenzion de'concetti, e la spiegatura loro. Che diremo dell'architettura? che dell'arte navigatoria? Ma sopra tutte le invenzioni stupende, qual eminenza di mente fu quella di colui che s'immaginò di trovar modo di comunicare i suoi piú reconditi pensieri a qualsivoglia altra persona, benché distante per lunghissimo intervallo di luogo e di tempo? Parlare con quelli che son nell'Indie; parlare a quelli che non sono ancora nati, né saranno se non di qua a mille e dieci mila anni? E con qual facilità! con i vari accozzamenti di venti caratteruzzi sopra una carta.[37]

Implicit in Galileo's notion of the global intercommunicability of writing is the idea that in the combination of letters on paper the consciousness of one person may be taken up, through the act of reading, by that of another, possibly far away in both space and time.

Calvino quotes this passage in *Six Memos for the Next Millennium* and remarks on a further implication not spelled out by Galileo, 'We should also add the immediate connection that writing establishes between everything existent or possible' ('occorre aggiungere comunicazione immediata che la scrittura stabilisce tra ogni cosa esistente o possibile').[38] More importantly, in the closing words of his trilogy *Our Ancestors*, Calvino had already produced his own tribute to, or rather a variant on, this idea of an 'infinite' in writing: 'Ombrosa no longer exists ... perhaps it was ... embroidered on nothing, like this thread of ink which I have let run on for page after page, swarming with cancellations, corrections, doodles, blots, and gaps, bursting at times into clear big berries, coagulating at others into piles of tiny starry seeds, then twisting away, forking off, surrounding buds of phrases with frameworks of leaves and clouds, then interweaving again, and so running on and on until it splutters and bursts into a last senseless cluster of words, ideas, dreams, and so ends.' ('Ombrosa non c'è piú ... Forse c'era solo ... un ricamo fatto sul nulla che assomiglia a questo filo d'inchiostro, come l'ho lasciato correre per pagine e pagine, zeppo di cancellature, di rimandi, di sgorbi nervosi, di macchie, di lacune, che a momenti di sgrana in grossi acini chiari, a momenti si infittisce in segni minuscoli come semi puntiformi, ora si ritorce su se stesso, ora si biforca, ora collega grumi di frasi con contorni di foglie o di nuvole, e poi s'intoppa, e poi ripiglia a attorcigliarsi, e corre e corre e si sdipana e avvolge un ultimo grappolo insensate di parole idée sogni ed è finito.')

The richness of that collocation – 'words, ideas, dreams' – is enacted here in Calvino's very passage, with its indication of the infinite possible directions a writer's thoughts may move while engaged in mental adventuring, implicitly taking the reader along also. Writing becomes an analogue of nothing less than the mysterious human act of thinking, even as it is a means of achieving that perhaps even more mysterious activity of the human race, namely communication. I have quoted the exact passage in Calvino that Salman Rushdie singles out from the ending to *The Baron in the Trees* in his review of *Our Ancestors*, which appeared in 1981, the year Rushdie received the Booker Prize for *Midnight's Children*. Rushdie says of this passage that it displays an interest in 'narration as a process.'[39]

It does somewhat more than that, as Rushdie, who may have had the very passage in mind when composing another in *Midnight's Children*, surely knew. When his narrator of that novel, Saleem Sinai, focuses on the 'white dot of consciousness' he is speaking both of the art of narration and the mysteries of human thought and intellection as such: 'I preferred the messier type, whose thoughts, spilling constantly into one another so that anticipatory images of food interfered with the serious business of earning a living and sexual fantasies were superimposed upon their political musings, bore a closer relationship to my own pell-mell tumble of a brain, in which everything ran into everything else and the white dot of consciousness jumped like a wild flea from one thing to the next.'[40] I am not claiming that Rushdie had direct knowledge of Galileo's thought about the 'various rearrangements of twenty paltry letters on a piece of paper.' Rushdie's passage is not really about writing as such, though it does describe the fantastical 'leakage' of one idea into another that is characteristic of his own narrative style in this novel. Rather than describing writing, it is about the phenomenal open-endedness (and a possible tendency to pell-mell tumbles) in all human thinking, something the ending of *The Baron in the Trees*, which Rushdie was reading and commenting on precisely in the period of his own novel, conveys no less brilliantly.

A direct comparison with both Rushdie's key notion and Calvino's is the earlier passage by Leopardi dealing with 'a rush of ideas that are simultaneous, or that follow each other so quickly that they seem simultaneous, and set the mind afloat on such an abundance of thoughts or images or spiritual feelings that either it cannot embrace them all, each one fully, or it has no time to be idle and empty of feelings' ('una folla d'idee simultanee, o così rapidamente succedentisi, che paiono simultanee, e fanno ondeggiar l'anima in una tale abbondanza di pensieri, o d'immagini e sensazioni spirituali, ch'ella o non è capace di abbracciarle tutte, e pienamente ciascuna, o non ha tempo di restare in ozio, e priva di sensazioni'). What all these passages suggest is an element of the fantastic – not just as *an element* but something *fundamentally* fantastic and fabulous – about human thought.

The fantastical and the real are not opposed to one another because there is something fantastic at the heart of the real, and therefore of any science of it. Galileo, stimulated by his own readings of the fantastical author Ariosto, set us thinking seriously about this. Leopardi extends the meditations in this area enormously, often most signally when he is musing on, or influenced by, qualities in Galileo's habits of thought and writing. It is of great interest that Sigmund Freud defined scientific creativity in a letter to Sándor Ferenczi as the interplay between 'daringly playful fantasy and relentlessly realistic criticism.'[41] In modern times Calvino and Rushdie, among others, were to keep spinning this idea of an endless interplay between the fantastical and the real. It is a top of creative consciousness, which spins and spins, particularly in the control of writers such as these who have learned how to keep it going by arts of narration. By contrast, interconnecting links between the fantastical and the everyday (or 'relentlessly real') are precisely what hyperreal works, such as *The Venetian* in Las Vegas, are designed to paper over with gimcrack – in a word, to conceal.

When the inexistent knight Agilulfo in Calvino's 1959 text stresses that in relation to chains of command, 'I observe the dispositions strictly' (Mi attengo strettamente alle disposizioni), he indicates that his obsession is with orders, not with novelty, for there is no desire in him to do what has never been done before. We might say that he fears what might be the consequences in an ongoing and unknown future. In something like the same way, I would claim that Las Vegas domesticates both our past and our future by seeking to incorporate them both in a vast (not to forget, capitalistic) present. I have been concerned to outline another lineage of fantasy, which shows its concern with culture and history, not by minimalizing their importance, but on the contrary by stressing their and its own unboundedness.

3 Passion in the Operatic Repertoire

We are used to the cliché that Italian temperaments are operatically passionate. Is there anything more interesting to be said about this notion, either as to how it came to be perpetrated, or whether there are not scintillas of a more complex truth underlying it? Or is opera, so stylised as it has always been, scarcely representative of the lived experience of either its audiences or their surrounding contexts? In short, did certain kinds of passional expression evident in earlier phases of the Italian operatic tradition take on a life of its own that affected, or was in turn ongoingly affected by, the wider culture?

By raising such difficult questions I hope to advance the discussion in this under-researched area of sociocultural history – namely, the complex field of relations between what was for several hundred years a highly attended musical and dramatic art form in Italy, as elsewhere, and the rest of lived culture. The chapter addresses, for the most part, textual and contextual questions (rather than strictly musicological ones) as to how and why expressions of passional intensity had become a rich and varied aspect of Italian operatic tradition during the eighteenth and first decades of the nineteenth centuries. What kinds of passion had become possible and indeed expected within this art form? Can we go so far as to think in terms of a genealogy of feeling down through several historical generations of opera? If so, what were some of the major changes in type and quality of expression within such a lineage?

The excellent work that has been done of late on perceptions of passional 'southernness' can help us launch a similar enquiry into operatic passion. Critics such as Marta Petrusewicz, John Dickie, and Nelson Moe have explored ways in which 'southernness' came to be read as a feature of character, both in respect of Italy in relation to other cultures and, within Italy, in terms of divisions between different latitudes of its peninsula and islands.[1] Moe's recent study of the prejudices and anxieties surrounding northernness and southernness in Italy, *The View from Vesuvius: Italian Culture and the Southern Question*, explores the historical construction of the Italian South as backward, corrupt, and (perhaps above all) passionate in temperament. Notably, one early passage that Moe uses to exemplify his case about the cultural construction of a passional Italian southernness comes from Montesquieu's *De l'esprit des lois* (1748), in which he discusses climate in relation to temperament. What has not been so examined, however, is that in Montesquieu's explanation, opera – specifically its differing effect upon culturally different audiences – is the empirical proving ground:

> In cold countries, one will have little sensitivity to pleasures; one will have more of it in temperate countries; in hot countries, sensitivity will be extreme. As one distinguishes climates by degrees of latitude, one can also distinguish them by degrees of sensitivity, so to speak. I have seen operas in England and Italy; they are the same plays with the same actors: but the same music produces different effects in the people of the two nations that it seems inconceivable, the one so calm and the other so transported.[2]

> Dans les pays froids on aura peu de sensibilité pour les plaisirs; elle sera plus grande dans ley pays tempérés; dans les pays chauds, elle sera extrême. Comme on distingue les climats par les degrés de latitude, on pourrait les distinguer, pour ainsi dire, par les degrés de sensibilité. J'ai vu les opéras d'Angleterre et d'Italie: ce sont les mêmes pièces et les mêmes acteurs, mais la même musique produit des effets si différents sur les deux nations, l'une est si calme, et l'autre si transportée, que cela paraît inconcevable.[3]

The passage offers much to consider, but what is significant is that it is written from a point outside either the calm English or the transported Italian temperaments it seeks to contrast. In addition, it takes other matters for granted. Montesquieu's general reference to operatic works and singers leaves out the fact that both would have been Italian. Increasingly filling the bill of operatic performances across Europe by Montesquieu's time were works in the Italian language sung by native Italians. This matter of Italian opera having established itself in theatres, courts, and burgeoning opera houses across Europe in little more than a century since its inception is a sign of the fervent popularity of the art form beyond Italy alone. Allowance must be made, too, for the fact that

Italian audiences would have better understood the words of the libretti, and for that reason been more susceptible to being 'transported' by their meaning. In countries other than Italy the musical intensities, rather than any subtleties of the sung text, must have predominated.

Montesquieu implies that the temperature aspect of climate is of overriding importance where *sensibilité pour les plaisirs* is in question. However, I want to examine what he is discussing – passion in opera and its effect on audiences – from a somewhat different angle. Doing so will inevitably involve a shift from Montesquieu's point of analysis outside the cultural frame of his subject to a point significantly *within* the Italian language, its poetry, and what is expressed in dramatic, consequently operatic, form by means of it.

Consider a characteristic passage from a drama by Pietro Metastasio that was much used as a libretto for operas. In Metastasio's play *La clemenza di Tito* of 1734, which was later adapted and set to music by composers as various as Caldara, Hasse, Jomelli, Gluck, and Mozart, the situation of Sesto, Titus's right-hand man and closest friend, is problematized from the outset because of his love for Vitellia. She feels neglected by Titus in his selection of a possible empress, and she pressures her devoted Sesto to kill Titus in consequence. Early in the dramatic text, Sesto has this to say to Vitellia:

>   Before berating me
> At least allow that I explain to you my state.
> You ask vengeance of me;
> Titus wishes for loyalty. You spur me
> With offer of your hand; he restrains me
> By his kindnesses. For you love,
> For him duty speaks. If I turn to you,
> Always in your face I find
> Some new beauty; if to him,
> Always in his breast I discover
> Some new virtue. I wish to serve you;
> To betray him I do not wish. I cannot live
> If I lose you, my life; and if I win you,
> I become a thing of hatred to myself.
>
>   Pria di sgridarmi,
> Ch'io ti spiego il mio stato, almen concedi.
> Tu vendetta mi chiedi;

Tito vuol fedeltà. Tu di tua mano
Con l'offerta mi sproni; ei mi raffrena
Co' benefizi suoi. Per te l'amore,
Per lui parla il dover. Se a te ritorno,
Sempre ti trovo in volto
Qualche nuova beltà; se torno a lui,
Sempre gli scopro in seno
Qualche nuova virtù. Vorrei servirti;
Tradirlo non vorrei. Viver non posso,
Se ti perdo, mia vita; e se t'acquisto,
Vengo in odio a me stesso.[4]

What we have here is a characteristic contrasting of oppositional feelings in Metastasian drama. A modern formulation might be to say that Sesto's heart and his head are at variance. But that would be both a distortion and a simplification because his feelings for both Vitellia and for Titus are equally of the heart, and his head is simply acting as the analytical instrument of articulation. A host of intensely felt contrasts arise in the passage's closely woven and highly eloquent syntax. The contrasts concern the vengeance that Vitellia demands from Sesto and the faithfulness that Titus's nature inspires. Vitellia passionately spurs Sesto to violence against Titus by the promise of her hand, while thoughts of Titus's acts of generosity equivalently restrain him. And then there is Vitellia's outward beauty ('in volto') contrasted with Titus's inner virtues ('in seno'). Above all, if Sesto were to act chivalrously by serving Vitellia's wishes, this would constitute betrayal of his intimate friend, the emperor. Making progress in his love suit for Vitellia will involve treachery, and thus Sesto will incur self-hatred.

Sesto is driven by mutually exclusive extremes, towards new qualities of beauty that he ceaselessly discovers in Vitellia, on the one hand, and towards Titus's equally inexhaustible virtues, on the other. Furthermore, he is seeking to explain this *stato d'anima* – this knot of unresolved passion – to one of the subjects of the intense feelings. However, because Sesto cannot suppress his attraction towards the other, Vitellia goes on repelling him with anger and disdain. 'No, you do not merit, ungrateful one, / The honour of my angers.' ('No, non meriti, ingrato, / L'onor dell'ire mie.')

It becomes rather apparent how intrinsic qualities in the dramatic material itself differ from Montesquieu's attention to such external factors as how opera was received by different European cultures. Rather than avert our own attention from things within and expand on his kind of early sociology of reception, we might further note *opera seria*'s basis in neoclassical exemplification of the workings of power, friendship, and sexual drives upon the individual. Or we might draw attention to the fact that there is not just one vector of libidinal drive evidenced in this Metastasian instance, but rather a conflictual duality of forces operating within one and the same character. Instead of positing that this stands for some peculiar 'southernness' of temperament, I submit that the particular case represents complex and irreconcilable moral feelings that may congregate in *any* single *stato d'anima*. This is what links Metastasio to the greatest of all neoclassical dramatists, Jean Racine. Voltaire indeed had singled out *La Clemenza di Tito* as worthy of the earlier writer.[5]

In the preface to his tragedy *Phèdre*, Racine characterizes the protagonist precisely in terms of her inner passional conflict. In that play Phèdre's dilemma is more intense even than Sesto's, because she is driven on by gods, and is fraught with the additional self-horror at her incestuous desire for her stepson Hippolytus. She therefore suffers from a consciousness of her own unpardonable sinfulness, even as her passional drive for her stepson is insurmountable and forces her to further destruction, including eventually that of herself. 'She is committed by her destiny, and by the anger of the gods, to an illegitimate passion which she is the first to abominate,' Racine had said of her in the preface. The case is not dissimilar from the one painfully acknowledged by Sesto in *La clemenza di Tito*. For as Racine was to go on to say of his play, and we could validly claim the same for Metastasio and for much eighteenth-century *opera seria*, 'the passions are only portrayed to expose all the chaos of which they are the cause.'[6]

That, at any rate, is one side of the case – the chaos of the passions. In Racine's work there is chaos in play after play as each drama progresses ineluctably towards a tragic outcome. In Metastasio's later offerings, which were products of a more moralizing age, while important characters such as Sesto certainly display self-conflicted states of feeling, there is often one figure whose virtuous actions and purposes make him or her into a beacon of moral clarity. Here that figure is the Emperor Titus. The clemency he holds out to Sesto, after he has taken part in a failed uprising, and to a contrite Vitellia as well as all the other conspirators, never really falters. By this reckoning *opera seria* need not be tragic.

Indeed Metastasio's play, source libretto of many later operas, is not tragic. By contrast it seeks an almost equivalently difficult dramatic goal, that of moral uplift and example. David Kimbell, in his 1991 landmark study *Italian Opera*, points out that although a number of Metastasio's early works for an *opera seria* format were attempts at 'genuine operatic tragedy,' in his later plays 'Metastasio has shifted the aim of tragedy from "purgation" ... to edification.' Kimbell continues by defining a major effect of such a shift: in the subsequent history of *opera seria* form, so influenced by Metastasio's works, 'in place of tragedy audiences were offered a quality sometimes referred to as "sospensione," a tension that arose out of some conflict in the mind of the protagonist between virtue and passion; or duty and expediency.'[7] That tension is characteristically resolved in much *opera seria*. The eventual righting of imbalances of feeling means, in consequence, that there is frequently in opera of the Enlightenment period, from the time of Metastasio onwards, a happy ending, or *lieto fine*.

A few years after Montesquieu's theories on hot- and cold-climate temperaments in *De l'esprit des lois*, there appeared an important dissertation on Metastasio that claimed for his writings an especial strength, defined as his 'singular handling of passions' ('maneggio singolar di passioni') such as terror, compassion, love and pity' ('il terrore, la compassione, l'amore, la pietà'). This was the 'Dissertation by Ranieri de' Calzabigi of the Academy of Cortona, on the Dramatic Poems of Sig. Abate Pietro Metastasio,' in the first of ten volumes of Metastasio's *Poesie*, published in Turin in 1757. Calzabigi was something of a feather for different winds (others would not mince words, and simply call him a turncoat) since only a few years later he was responsible for the texts of Gluck's important reform operas, *Orfeo ed Euridice* (1762) and *Alceste* (1767). These sought to leave behind the existing, essentially Metastasian forms of *opera seria*.[8] In the printed score of *Alceste*, Gluck's dedication to Grand Duke Leopold of Tuscany was ghostwritten by none other than Calzabigi. This dedication constitutes an implicit repudiation of the qualities of Metastasio's dramas that he had earlier defended in his dissertation, for he now stresses that in the libretto of *Alceste* there are no 'flowery descriptions, superfluous similes,' or 'cold, sententious morals,' implying that these had been the typical vices of the earlier paradigm of *opera seria*.

Above all, at issue in Calzabigi's words concerning reform of operatic practice in Gluck's *Alceste* were contrasts between aria and recitative in the opera format. 'I decided not to stop an actor in the heat of the dialogue ... I did not feel obliged to hurry through the second part of an aria, though it was the more impassioned and significant, in order to be able to repeat four times the words of the first part, finishing the aria where perhaps the sense was left unfinished, all so the singer might have the leisure to show the many ways in which he can vary a passage at will'.[9] The traditional form of the embellished *da capo* aria was under attack. Traditionally, when the verses of an aria, normally in two parts, had been sung through once, the first part was repeated with embellishments that were often of the singer's own devising. In Metastasio's plays for operatic performance, separate passages in the form of lyric verse for sung arias constituted a break in dialogue. Such arias gave the opportunity for a break in dialogue, in order to sum up a situation or state of feeling, or articulate a moral. Calzabigi's case was that such *da capo* arias had become too much an excuse for virtuoso showiness. In his opinion the reforms he and Gluck were bringing to pass were against self-display on the part of singers, especially where it stood in the way of the onward development of 'more impassioned and significant' matters (note the collocation of these terms). The very definition of an aria and its place in operatic form was at stake. In 'reformed operatic' practice, according to these stated principles, the aria is never mere embellishment, nor even a pause in the onward momentum of the opera. It is a dramatic unfolding in its own right (no less than the recitative 'dialogue') of the 'impassioned and significant' in the action and human feelings represented.

We are already beginning to see that at each point in the historical development of opera different pragmatic balances were being reached between the importance of drama on the one hand and music on the other, in what was inevitably, on the performers' part, a struggle to hold the attention of audiences. With respect to Montesquieu's concern with effect on an audience, did arias as expressions of passion – although by Metastasio's reckoning essentially serving a 'non-dramatic or decoratife function'[10] – tend to transfix attention that had been lost in passages of recitative? Or did the relative stasis of dramatic unfolding during the outpourings of feeling constituted by arias, on the contrary, result in inattention? Put differently, does the art film *Farinelli* get the picture more or less right at the point where it portrays a specific aria as the composer's and solo castrato singer's prime opportunity for transfixing audience attention? Or is the performer/audience dynamic necessarily more complex than that popular modern portrayal of its workings?[11] And how, in any case, would the answer to such a question change over the space of approximately a century, in various operas of Handel, Mozart, and Rossini? Answering such questions is the business of the following argument.

In 1711, one year after George Frideric Handel first visited England (having spent several years already in Italy) and, likewise, one year before he settled in London, the poet and essayist Joseph Addison, later popularized by Pope for 'damning with faint praise,' did just that on the subject of opera. In his popular journal *The Spectator*, Addison wrote, 'An opera may be allowed to be extravagantly lavish in its Decorations, as its only Design is to gratify the Senses, and keep up an indolent Attention in the Audience.'[12] Thirty-two years later, Pope himself, in his newly written fourth book of *The Dunciad*, condemns outrightly (no 'faint praise' – or 'faint blame' either for that matter – ever passed forth from *this* satirist's pen) the habits and character of Italian opera, which enters his poem in the figure of 'a Harlot form soft sliding by.' But Pope makes an exception for the extraordinary music of that relatively anglicized (by this point) composer Handel. What had transpired since Addison's tart comment, especially given Pope's account here of Handel's career and of the Harlotries of Italian opera?

> When lo! a Harlot form soft sliding by,
> With mincing step, small voice, and languid eye;
> Foreign her air, her robe's discordant pride
> In patch-work flutt'ring, and her head aside:
> By singing Peers up-held on either hand,
> She tripp'd and laugh'd, too pretty much to stand;
> Cast on the prostrate Nine a scornful look,
> Then thus in quaint Recitativo spoke.
>   'O *Cara! Cara!* silence all that train:
> Joy to great Chaos! let Division reign:
> Chromatic tortures soon shall drive them hence,
> Break all their nerves, and fritter all their sense:
> One Trill shall harmonize joy, grief, and rage,
> Wake the dull Church, and lull the ranting Stage ...
> But soon, ah soon Rebellion will commence,
> If Music meanly borrows aid from Sense:
> Strong in new Arms, lo! Giant Handel stands,
> Like bold Briareus, with a hundred hands;
> To stir, to rouze, to shake the Soul he comes,
> And Jove's own Thunders follow Mars's Drums.
> Arrest him, Empress; or you sleep no more' –
> She heard, and drove him to th'Hibernian shore.
>   *The Dunciad* (1742), bk. IV, 45–70

Handel really did have 'new Arms' – more extended thunder and drums – by 1743. They were those of English oratorio. He had been transferring his creative attention to this other musical form since the late 1730s, though still composing occasional Italian operas, none of which were very successful. By comparison with earlier years, of the 1720s especially, his music in this period was relatively unappreciated in London. At an invitation from the Lord Lieutenant of Ireland, Handel had gone to Dublin, 'th'Hibernian shore,' in late 1741. He stayed there until August 1742, during which time Pope composed this section of the fourth book of *The Dunciad*. What Pope complains of here by way of 'Division' and 'Chromatic' trills in Italian opera had been part of the very essence of Handel's own great Royal Academy operas in Italian. The principal castrato singer, Senesino, had indeed been 'celebrated for his "divisions," i.e. breaking up each of a succession of long notes into a number of short ones, and so dwelling on a single syllable of the word he was singing.'[13] As for chromatic trills, in *Rodelinda* of 1725, one short aria by its chief male protagonist, Bertarido (a part that would originally have been sung by Senesino), demonstrates that it is not just chromatism and trills on the part of the singer that were used for their appeal and lyric intensity. Typical for Handel's writing in that earlier period, he also arranged an echo effect of chromaticism and trill in the orchestration to represent the streams and fountains, caverns and mountains, which empathetically respond to the husband singing of his separation from his wife:

Con rauco mormorio
Piangono al pianto mio
Ruscelli e fonti.
(With hoarse murmur in response to my crying cry streams and fountains.)
[At this point there is an echo response in the orchestration to the
   chromatic trilling of the singing by Bertarido.]

E in tronchi e mesti accenti
Fann'eco ai miei lamenti
E gli antri e i monti.
(And in broken and sad accents make echo to my laments both caves and
   mountains.)
[Echo effects in the orchestration naturally follow.]
                                        (Act 2, sc. 2, 'Luogo delizioso')

This is exceptional music, but *not* exceptional in terms of Handel's arias in the Italian operatic form. We find such echo effects also woven into duets. For instance, Bertarido, having doubted his wife Rodelinda's constancy, is disabused of his mistake and reconciled to her. But no sooner are they together than he is led off to prison by guards of the man usurping his Longobard dukedom, Grimoaldo. In the famous parting duet between husband and wife, 'Io t'abbraccio' ('I embrace thee' – first sung by Senesino and Francesca Cuzzoni), similar echo effects are used in the two voices, which weave about each other in the two-part patterning. The appoggiaturas and chromaticism of the balancing parts constitute a fine melodic display. Only Bach could match or surpass these rhythms of echoed human mutuality in ways suggesting stops and arrests of feelings, their relaunch, and the subsequent eventual loss of the beloved other being. But Bach would mainly use such patterning to stress themes of the 'Passion' in a religious sense.

So why did the Italian operatic format in London – as developed in particular by Handel – lose popularity in the 1730s, and why did Handel's own Italian operas suffer long subsequent inattention, not to be rediscovered fully until the early twentieth century? Hugo Meynell has stressed that in Handel's operas 'the emotions expressed can on the whole be reduced to a fairly small set of categories, such as love, melancholy, rage, jealousy, malice, joy and fear.' He goes on to point out that 'deviations from these general types ... are rare.'[14] In an age – the 1730s and 1740s – when people were capable of responding to the intricacies of tone and feeling in such satirical writing as we witness in the extract from Pope, the simplicities of the stronger passions in Handel's Italian operas were perhaps bound to lose their appeal. And this resulted in spite of what Meynell quite rightly claims was the 'almost limitless variety' with which each passional category among the few he names is expounded in the music.[15] If we ourselves were offered seasons on end of Handelian opera, as London had been in the 1720s and early 1730s, its passional simplicities, no matter how alluring the music, might wear on our spirits sooner than we would at the outset have predicted.

I have considered complexities of passion that are more common in Metastasian drama and operas based upon it than in these works by Handel. What differences do we encounter in a later period such as that of Da Ponte's collaborations with Mozart? The title page of their second collaboration reads, *Don Giovanni ossia il dissoluto punito* (*Don Giovanni or The Punished Dissolute*), a *dramma giocoso* (playful drama) by Lorenzo da Ponte, *con musica di* W.A. Mozart. Generations of critics have sought to determine what genre this magnificent creation belongs to, so mercurial are its modulations of tone and direction, right from its opening aria of class grievance sung by the manservant Leporello (encapsulated in the two lines 'Voglio far il gentiluomo, / E non voglio più servir'; 'I want to be a gentleman / And I don't want to serve any longer').

Two of the many things that this *dramma giocoso* hybridizes are the previous, and largely separate, forms of *opera seria* and *opera buffa*. For instance, there is dramatic *gioco* (or play) introduced almost immediately when, upon Don Giovanni's killing of Donna Anna's father the Commendatore in the first scene, Giovanni appears before his cowering manservant Leporello, who asks 'Who is dead – you or the old man?' Surely this is a way of habituating the audience early on to the idea that the dramatic interweave between serious and comic will be like nothing before in opera. It is very much a case of what Mary Hunter, in her book *The Culture of Opera Buffa in Mozart's Vienna*, has called 'the idea that ... operas "converse" with the conventions of the genre.'[16]

A moment earlier, in the trio sung by the master and servant, two baritones, and the dying Commendatore, a bass, the Commendatore laments his dying at the hands of an 'assassino,' and sings 'Sento l'anima partir' ('I feel my soul depart'). Giovanni, by contrast, is an onlooker at the same process: 'Veggo l'anima partir' ('I see his soul depart'). Leporello, by an even greater contrast, comments upon the terrified feeling within himself, using the same terminology, 'palpitating breast,' as did the other two. But in his case the motivating feeling is pure *spavento* (fear). 'Entro il sen dallo spavento / Palpitar il cor mi sento' ('In my breast from fear / I feel my heart to beat'). In terms of previous traditions of *opera seria* this is pure iconoclasm. For in Leporello, the words *seno*, *palpitare* and *sentire* are being used to constitute an entirely different sense from the same terms issuing forth from the dying, but also still singing, Commendatore. Indeed the Commendatore's expiring two lines use the same individual words as Leporello, not to express fear as in the manservant's case, but to mark his soul escaping from his breast, like breath never to be drawn again. 'E dal seno palpitante / Sento l'anima partir' ('And from my beating breast / I feel my soul depart'). In terms of the theme of passion in opera, we have a brazen contrast between dying – expressed by the very person undergoing it as a passional process – and cowardly fear in a servant, who is solely preoccupied with surviving the bloody situation. Leporello attests to what is going on emotionally within himself rather than in the spectacle before him, even if it *is* the spectacle that inspires this fear. Only five minutes after the end of its overture the work is already very definitely, in Hunter's terms, conversing with the conventions of the genre. Or rather, more literally, it is *simultaneously* singing back into, and out of, the prior conventions of both serious and comic opera, but in a way that renders them inextricable. By iconoclastically intertwining them thus, into what Rossini will later call, in another multiple-part aria from his opera *La cenerentola*, a *nodo aviluppato* (an inextricable knot), Da Ponte and Mozart create from the ancestral genealogies of opera one magnificent hybrid of a piece.

In his book *Either/Or*, the nineteenth-century Danish philosopher Søren Kierkegaard hints at how we might understand all this in passional terms, as a 'comic relationship' common in works from the Middle Ages onwards, 'where the one individual compensates for the disproportionate greatness of the other.'[17] Leporello has disproportionate greatness of two kinds before him, in the killer Giovanni and in the mortally wounded Commendatore, and both are singing the passion of their utterly differing situations in contrast to his comic terror of them. However, in order to understand the totality of the *concertato trio* as music and, at the same time, recognize its deep and passional totality in terms of unity of artistic presentation, we also have to consider Kierkegaard's subsequent notion of the 'speculative ear.' While indicating that Don Giovanni's irony and 'Elvira's essential passion' should be 'heard simultaneously,' Kierkegaard goes on to say, 'As the speculative eye sees things together, so the speculative ear should hear things together.'[18] That remark seems to me highly revelatory if applied to the situation of the trio I have been analysing. I do not simply mean the obvious, that a trained listener will hear all three parts, but rather wish to make a more philosophical point, that the extreme difference in positioning of the three characters emerges precisely from their being co-involved, dramatically and musically, in a unitary scene. Just as Giovanni's later mocking ironies will inform Elvira's passion of rage, so too here the very differences between the three singers' passions mutually inform the totality of the situation, making comic and tragic opera possible in the same instant, as never so intensely before or perhaps since. But the achievement depends on our hearing all this with that 'speculative ear' of which Kierkegaard spoke. And the supreme irony is that the tragic of *opera seria* and the comic aspects of its iconoclastic other, *opera buffa*, both operate in one and the same musical unfolding. Scarcely a librettist other than Da Ponte was inclined to blend such extremes, and certainly no composer apart from Mozart was able to hold them together musically.

One person with just such a speculative ear for *Don Giovanni* is the Italian-American scholar Robert Viscusi. His critique of the opera offers some additional *aperçus* about its radical nature. Viscusi characerizes it as an intertwined genealogy of different lineages of opera that have historically come before it: 'It is an opera about the history of opera. It subsumes all that is known to the art when it is written, and it dramatizes its own sudden awareness of this subsumption.'[19] Viscusi detects premonitions of Europe's own near future in this opera of 1787, 'as when the noble characters and the outlawed hero all together sing "Viva, viva la libertà," and one seems to see the old regime lean over to listen for the early rumblings of its own collapse.'[20] These rumblings had already been distinctively heard in Da Ponte's and Mozart's previous opera, *Le nozze di Figaro*. It is as though, by collaboratively subsuming much European social consciousness into their work, these operas had managed to inspect class conflict so intensively that, in historical terms, they had kept the dramatization running beyond the present, into presentiments of the forthcoming revolutionary times. Giovanni's downfall is imbued with rituals of transformation and mythologies of damnation as he is confronted by the statute (the unappeased spirit of the Commendatore) and pulled down into hell. But at a popular historical level, Don Giovanni's nemesis is also that of the oppressor classes of the ancien régime, whose figuration and representative he is.

The relationship that we have been following, between the particularities of opera and the generalities of culture, was considered in a wide variety of ways in the Romantic period, in particular by Stendhal, who was one of the keenest witnesses of both opera and Italy. Mathilde de la Mole, one of the two heroines in Stendhal's *Le rouge et le noir* (1830), has what Stendhal, in his earlier work *De l'amour*, had called a 'crystallization' of her feelings for the hero Julien Sorrel on hearing an aria at the Italian Opera in Paris. Her reactions to the 'cantilena worthy of Cimarosa' ('une mélodie digne de Cimarosa') – 'I must punish myself if I too much loved' ('Devo punirmi se troppi amai') – are indeed so intense that 'her ecstasy reached a point of passionate exaltation' ('son extase arriva à un état d'exaltation et de passion').[21] Mathilde's is only one specific case, as we consider representative moments in the production of and reaction to operatic arias, over the century and a bit leading up to this novel of 1830.

Throughout the previous century there had been evidence in much European literature that such moments of intensity in the unfolding art form of Italian opera acted as inspiration in producing passional feelings in audiences from Dublin to St Petersburg. As Stendhal himself was to say when he introduced the man he named as Napoleon's successor,

'Napoleon is dead; but a new conqueror has already shown himself to the world; and from Moscow to Naples, from London to Vienna, from Paris to Calcutta, his name is constantly on every tongue. The fame of this hero knows no bounds save those of civilization itself; and he is not yet thirty-two.' Stendhal's new hero was Italian rather than French, even though in other parts of Europe sung Italian would have been only slenderly understood, and its main intensities received via the music rather than the words. 'If the narrator of this epic may claim to deserve his reader's confidence, it is because he has lived for eight or ten years in those same towns and cities which Rossini was electrifying with his masterpieces.'[22] Stendhal's accounts of the effects of Rossini notwithstanding, he was one of our prime witnesses to the levels of audience *in*attention in the box system of most opera houses. By his report on La Scala in 1817, in a typical box 'every evening, one sees fifteen or twenty distinguished men sit themselves down one after another; and if the conversation ceases to be interesting one listens to the music.'[23]

What was it that so electrified Stendhal about this all-conquering composer, Rossini? Would anything like the limitations that I have hinted at in the historical appreciation of Handel also undermine any twenty-first-century attempt on our part to agree with Stendhal's excited responses to this newest (and for once native Italian) composer of Italian opera? Possibly not. Writing before much of Rossini's career had developed, Stendhal rated the early *opera seria*, *Tancredi*, above even the comic *Barbiere di Siviglia* and *La gazza ladra*. Let us examine a brief example of his appreciation, the part that most relates to Rossini's techniques in aria and orchestration in his portraying of human passions:

> Upon Tancredi's entry, the orchestration reaches a superb climax of *dramatic harmonization*. This is not (as it is foolishly believed in Germany) the art of employing clarinets, 'cellos and oboes to re-echo the emotions of the characters on stage; it is the much rarer art of using the instruments to voice nuances and overtones of emotion which the characters themselves would never dare to put into words [l'art bien plus rare de faire dire par les instruments la partie de ces sentiments que le personnage lui-même ne pourrait nous confier] ... Tancred *must* not speak; but while he is contained in a silence so perfectly expressive of the feelings raging within him, the sighing horns of the orchestra conjure up a new portrait of his spirit, and echo emotions which, perhaps, he hardly dare acknowledge to himself, and which certainly will never find form in words.[24]

This is a last-ditch stand of *prima la musica, poi le parole* (music first, then the words). But it is written in the very name of a more complex portrayal in musical orchestration of the nuances and overtones of passion, which, at this point in the given opera at any rate, Stendhal is claiming are beyond the very grasp and expression of the characters that experience them. This is not mysticism, but rather an argument that the human passions can sometimes be expressed in orchestral form with complexities that do not permit of verbal expression. With that remark we seem – in the matter of the expression of passions within Italian culture – to be leaving not simply the baroque, but also the classical age in music definitively behind and entering a very particular and subtly drawn sensibility of Romanticism.

It would be interesting to speculate, somewhat anachronistically, on how someone of Montesquieu's analytical temperament would have responded to Stendhal's argument. For although the subject – namely, extreme sensitivity in relation to the passional expressions of opera – is similar, Stendhal's case focuses the topic entirely differently. He has gone inside the music itself for the location of his analysis of the passions, and he has seen it as a prime determinant, more important even than words, and certainly more than climate, which has been quite left behind as a viable hypothesis. If he has been speaking about the inner feelings of the characters rather than the temperaments of an audience, he will go on to suggest in *Le rouge et le noir*, in his remarks on Mathilde de la Mole at the opera, that the effects of a character's aria in an opera by a composer such as Domenico Cimarosa can play directly into the sensibility of an individual audience member. This, too, is more a tenet of the Romantic ethnos from which he is writing in that novel than a conception that there are a priori factors that predetermine reactions, such as cold northern or hot southern temperaments, as Montesquieu had been arguing many decades earlier. Indeed, it had been Stendhal's opening argument in his book on Rossini that this composer had quite ironed out individual differences of (e.g., national) temperament, by the pervasiveness of his conquest of passions across the face of Europe.

Stendhal has been careful early in the same chapter on *Tancredi* to stress Rossini's limitations in this line, and to make him appear neither a Michelangelo or Beethoven in high-mettled conception nor a Haydn in force of strength, but always himself – eloquent and witty in orchestration, as much as in recitative and aria.

How ironic that the case he is making for musical expression seems almost an inversion of points expressed *against* operatic form by the very person from whose tragedy this work by Rossini had been drawn, namely Voltaire. In his 1748 *Essay on ancient and modern tragedy*, Voltaire had criticized opera as inimical to the deeper expression of tragedy, which in his opinion had to be conveyed through verbal rather than musical sense. Throwing theatrical concentration onto music is destructive, according to Voltaire, because it accustoms 'young people to know themselves through sound rather than spirit; to prefer the ear to the soul and trills to sublime thoughts; and to value the most insipid and worst written works when they are sustained by a few arias that please them.'[25]

In most of the arguments I have been examining, whatever the emphasis on music or on words, and whether the case is being made that they are complementary or, as in Voltaire, at loggerheads and disadvantaging of sense for the sake of sound, the most convincing advocacy has always been in favour not of simplistic passions, but of nuanced and complexly evolving ones. Where human passions are concerned, not all eighteenth- and early-nineteenth-century Italian opera managed to avoid being a mere musical decorating of simplicities. Indeed, sadly, the majority of it was often little more than that. But in those rare cases when something more extraordinary *was* being expressed, very different as the few examples offered from major composers have been, my implicit case throughout has been that the complexities are wasted if not heard with some such attunement on our parts as the 'speculative ear' of which Kierkegaard spoke. While not claiming that its cultivation is easy – When were complexly interrelated passions between individuals or within groups ever easy to understand? – I have attempted to spell out further implications of this philosophy of musical receptivity throughout the chapter.

4 Capital Contrasts: Naples and Turin a Century before Unification

The following critical meditation compares the cites of Turin and Naples as they existed well before Italian unification, in the last decades of the *ancien régime*. I want to consider these very different capitals of independent kingdoms within the total geographical space that would later became the one Kingdom of Italy. During that drawn-out phase of history, we see such states undergoing the ferment of Enlightenment thought and technological and institutional advances; however, deep structural changes had yet to be wrought in the old political and material dispensation of Europe, which was still in essence profoundly feudal. Later on in the chapter I will offer a comparative argument concerning reforms in either city. But I begin with a short series of meditations: on Giambattista Vico and his university post, on the adolescent Wolfgang Amadeus Mozart in Naples, and on Vittorio Alfieri's return to Turin, where he spent his youth. In these brief analyses, I am not so much presenting a case as seeking to understand through micro-study of scraps of statements by these three figures the cultural imaginary each deploys, and only then, by inference, the cities each suggests.

Insofar as possible I seek to answer some difficult questions about the eighteenth-century configurations of these two kingdoms, well before the incorporation by one of them in 1860 of most of the peninsula and all the major islands, the simultaneous cancellation of the other along with its Bourbon royal line, and the inclusion of the extensive realm that comprised it into the larger, 'Italian' entity.

Among the best historians of the period of Bourbon rule in Naples have certainly been Benedetto Croce (1866–1952) and Franco Venturi (1914–94). Venturi's studies in reformist thought of the Enlightenment period in Italy, but also in Europe generally, together with his work on nineteenth-century populist and socialist movements that formed the roots of the Russian revolution, make him so much more than an historian of individual ancien régime cultures. It is the very comparativism of his work, including writings on reform in Naples and in his native Piedmont – always placing them within a wider context – that is so worthy of emulation. Nonetheless, my own venture in this chapter will constitute a more freewheeling shuttle between the Neapolitan and the Piedmontese contexts than he may have felt prudent. Venturi's studies in the radiating and Europe-wide reformist movement showed not only greater clarity than those of anyone previously; but they were also models of patience and comprehensiveness. The present chapter is written largely in tribute to the groundwork Venturi laid in studies of reformist thought of the ancien régime period, both Italian and European.[1] My study weaves not just between two very different cities, but in and out of writings by or about figures associated with them, whether king, queen, philosopher, musician, tragedian, guidebook writer, political economist, architect, or novelist, as the case may be.

I am comparing these two different royal capitals during a period of relative peace – despite a disastrous year of famine such as 1764 in the Regno di Napoli – and politically speaking something of an Indian summer for both courts (if in many respects delusory) before the tumults of the revolutionary period. There are few references either to republican or direct French rule on the one hand, nor, on the other, to the later restoration period of 1815 and thereafter. My emphases are social and artistic, based on what can be known of the general cases from representative evidence. I am making no claims at comprehensive coverage of these years in the history of either city. Rather, I seek to evoke contexts from the writings of persons who experienced them intensively, to produce a kind of comparative imaginary of the two cities as a way of rescuing historical studies from what might otherwise prove to be an overpowering conformism.[2]

Quite apart from the work of major historians, one of my models in terms of the 'feel for context' that I am striving to achieve is Susan Sontag's evocation of Naples in her finest work, *The Volcano Lover: A Romance*, of 1992. Descriptions such as the following are as necessary to the way we practise history, as they are to the long-dominant genre of the novel:

> [Naples was] ... a place that for sheer volume of curiosities – historical, natural, social – could hardly be surpassed. It was bigger than Rome, it was

the wealthiest as well as the most populous city on the Italian peninsula and, after Paris, the second largest city on the European continent, it was the capital of natural disaster and it has the most indecorous, plebeian monarch, the best ices, the merriest loafers, the most vapid torpor, and, among the younger aristocrats, the largest number of future Jacobins ... It was the time when all ethical obligations were first put up for scrutiny, the beginning of the time we call modern.[3]

Sontag richly and precisely captures a particular time and place, while also relativizing that earlier moment in terms of the modern age that is in the process of being slowly and often painfully born. Her pages on the populace's abhorrent treatment of the overthrown republicans in 1799, and on Lord Nelson's and Emma Hamilton's part in the bloody reprisals against them on behalf of the Bourbons, constitute some of the most searing writing of the present era on inhumanities our species has perpetrated. (The royal couple, King Ferdinand and Queen Caroline, mainly kept in Palermo until the hanging of republicans was completed.) This is a very different touchstone of inhumanity than the more usual one of Nazi death camps. In the case of Nelson, it involves a man – the 'hero,' as Sontag's novel goes on calling him with mounting irony – whose reputation in Britain is to this day almost entirely positive. Indeed, he is one of few persons considered in a recent television series that sought to identify the greatest Englishman of all time. Needless to say, for Lord Nelson to figure in such a series at all, the program extolling him had to downplay his involvement in these assassinations, which, nearer to their time of occurrence, had in Stendhal's eyes made him the scandal of Europe.

Stendhal was aware of how an entire generation of thinkers had been hanged by the pro-Bourbon populace: 'Not seventeen years ago, supported by Nelson, they gave themselves up to the pleasure of hanging all there was by way of mind in Naples. What French admiral has ever played the role of this Nelson, of whom there is a column in Edinburgh, nation of *thought and of humanity*?' ('Il n'y a pas encore dix-sept ans que, appuyés par Nelson, ils se sont donné le plaisir de faire pendre tout ce qui avait de l'esprit à Naples. Quel amiral français a jamais joué le role de ce Nelson, qui a une colonne à Édinbourg, le pays *de la pensé et de l'humanité*?')[4] Sontag's pages on these events are exquisitely researched and morally intense, and in no respect do they flinch from seeking to understand and spell out the blame that needs to be attached historically to Nelson and to the Hamiltons, both husband and wife.

But our concerns in this chapter are essentially with earlier decades – years leading up to these revolutionary and counter-revolutionary events in Turin as in Naples, the latter of which Stendhal declared to be 'beyond all comparison the finest city in Europe.'[5] In terms of Naples we need to begin attempts at re-evocation shortly before the Bourbon era itself. There is no more interesting a figure around whom to seek to delineate at least some aspect of all that we might understand by imaginative history than Giambattista Vico (1668–1744).

Marta Petrusewicz cites Vico in her important work on the Kingdom of the Two Sicilies between 1815 and 1849, before the so-called 'southern' question had been constituted. Petrusewicz claimed that Vico was 'prescient in arguing for an approach to historical studies that took different societies on their own terms, rather than in terms of universalising categories like "human nature."'[6] This may seem a little misleading at first, since Vico nowhere studies different societies in any detailed way, but rather provides an ideal, and incidentally cyclic, schema for understanding the course of general human history. But what Petrusewicz may have had keenly in mind is one of Vico's great emphases, the kernel of which appears in his book on the *scienza nuova*. His claim is that there has been insufficient study by humans of the very thing it was in their power to know, namely what has been humanly (as opposed to divinely) created, the realm of nations and of civil society. Focused as he was on a philosophical plane of what could be known and what could not be known, Vico did indeed encourage what Petrusewicz has called historical studies. But he meant something different both from what passed for history in his own day or from anything we might nowadays intend, at least at a simple level, by such a term. In the *Scienza Nuova* he provides stages in an ideal history of mankind – ideal in the sense understood by Croce, in saying of Vico that he seeks out laws 'of the human spirit such as to explain the history of both past and future, applicable ... to an infinite number of worlds.'[7] Vico moves from an account of primitive men with 'very strong sensations and a strength of imagination such as civilized men can hardly understand,' through the 'heroic age' to the 'plebeian.'

These ideas anticipated – though they scarcely at all influenced – Romantic historicism of Herder and his followers.[8] The following sentence by Vico signals that philosophers have worn themselves out trying to grasp what God has created; namely nature – 'questo mondo naturale' – which he claims God alone can know, and we only see obscurely through a glass darkly, so to speak.

> Whoever reflects on this cannot but marvel that the philosophers should have bent all their energies to the study of the world of nature, which, since God made it, He alone knows; and that they should have neglected the study of the world of nations, or civil world, which, since men had made it, men could come to know.

> Dee recar maraviglia come tutti i filosofi seriosamente si studiarono di conseguire la scienza di questo mondo naturale, del quale, perché Iddio egli il fece, esso solo ne ha la scienza; e traccurarono di meditare su questo mondo delle nazioni, o sia mondo civile, del quale, perché l'avevano fatto gli uomini, ne potevano conseguire la scienza gli uomini.[9]

Rather than seek to emulate God's grasp of the world of nature, it should be our prime business to come to know ourselves more fully, through study of what we as humans have created. This indeed is the burden of Vico's other important point: 'But in the night of thick darkness enveloping the earliest antiquity, so remote from ourselves, there shines the eternal and never failing light of a truth beyond all question: that the world of civil society has certainly been made by men, and that its principles are therefore to be found within the modifications of our own human mind.' ('Ma, in tal densa notte di tenebre ond'è coverta la prima da noi lontanissima antichità, apparisce questo lume eterno, che non tramonta, di questa verità, la quale non si può a patto alcuno chiamar in dubbio: che questo mondo civile egli certamente è stato fatto dagli uomini, onde se ne possono, perché se ne devono, ritruovare i princìpi dentro le modificazioni della nostra medesima mente umana.')[10] Since this remark has been the subject of a profound, if unjustly neglected, exposition written by Erich Auerbach in 1937,[11] I will concentrate here on another, which has added relevance for the present chapter.

In Auerbach's 1949 study entitled 'Vico and Aesthetic Historicism,' he had established that in this area of his thinking Vico made claims for 'the predominance of the historical sciences, based on the certitude that men can understand men.' By reason of the very 'potentialities of the human mind ... we are capable of re-evoking human history from the depth of our own consciousness.' This, as Auerbach is quick to point out, is equally a 'theory of cognition' as of history, and he proceeds to demonstrate how Vico moves historically from concepts of primitive society to accounts of the first forms of animistic religion, then through philosophical theories of a second heroic age to a 'rationalistic and democratic period, where imagination and poetry have lost their creative power.'[12] Plainly, it is different from anything we are involved in by way of historical practice today.

But should it be? Perhaps at deeper levels there are pointers to be followed in our own practice. These two important ideas from Vico have just slightly different emphases. The first had suggested that we can derive our knowledge of the human through study of what has been created in the civil world – by which term I understand Vico to intend all that we have lately come to know as 'culture' in the widest sense. In the second idea, he stresses that precisely *because* we have made it, this world of the human is open to our knowledge and understanding (*scienza*). In combination, the two sentences suggest that we can trace ourselves even from times of antiquity because, although we are enveloped in darkness, there is a small light shining even from so far back in time. That light is the very *studiability* of the human world by ourselves as humans, down through history, by reason of sedimented constructions of our *mondo civile*, our civilization. Interestingly (and this is the difficult part), the sedimentation is posited by Vico as being not so much material as *mental*, as though in this thought he was anticipating Jung. We have the potential to become archaeologists, so to speak, of the human mind, which is understood generically as a continuum from the present back into darkest antiquity. In a much later age than that of Vico, Jung would claim that 'the conscious mind cannot be denied a history reaching back at least five thousand years,' and that the 'unconscious psyche ... moulds the human species and ... though ephemeral in the individual, is collectively of immense age.'[13]

What, then, is the relevance of all this for the subject in question? Simply, I wanted to demonstrate that at the very beginning of the period I am interested in, the greatest of Neapolitan philosophers stressed that we can come to know things about ourselves, specifically the 'nations' we have created and their civil (that is to say their political, social, economic and artistic) realities, even though he himself did not go very far down that road of closely focused historicism, but stayed in the idealist position of the one who points the way. That being so – and speaking now from the non-idealist position of the present – there is good reason for comparative study because nations are so intrinsically different. This is of particular interest when what is being compared are two kingdoms that are on a course – as could not have been foreseen from any stage in the eighteenth century itself – that will eventually bring them to political convergence (some would even claim the incorporation and domination of the larger and more important state by the smaller and lesser state), including all the additional political and social problems that ensued from Italian Unification, initially under the house of Savoy.

Of additional interest to our understanding of Naples at the time is that Vico writes as one of the earliest university professors in anything like a modern sense of the term. The first edition of the *Scienza Nuova* of 1725 had been 'reverently addressed' to no less a collectivity than 'the Academies of Europe.' In 'this enlightened age' as his dedicatory address defines it, Vico shows an expectation that those academies' '*cattedre*,' or professorial chairs such as his own, will be the locus of this 'new science of the nature of nations' ('una nuova scienza della natura delle nazioni').[14] The dedication is intended as a wake-up call from what he saw as their enslavement to strict Cartesian philosophy. Though he was a member of distinguished academies of Naples and of elsewhere, with a wonderful range of (often comic) names – the Accademia degli Uniti di Napoli, the Accademia Palatina, the Accademia dell'Arcadia, the Accademia degli Assorditi (deafened) di Urbino, the Accademia degli Oziosi (idle – even lazy, or leisurely)[15] – Vico was the impoverished scholar par excellence in his private existence. As Auerbach summarizes, he was at a mundane level a 'solitary old professor at the University of Naples who had taught Latin figures of speech all his life and written hyperbolical eulogies for the various Neapolitan viceroys and other important personalities.'[16]

These conditions never significantly changed in Vico's lifetime, even though his career as a university professor crossed the timelines between vice-regal rule from Spain, which had lasted slightly more than two centuries to 1707, Austrian domination from 1707 to 1734, and the inauguration of an independent lineage of Bourbon rulers, with the advent of Carlo di Borbone to the throne in 1734. We know from Vico's auto-biography, told in the third person, that he was forced to do his studies till late at night in the unfavourable conditions of a household with an illiterate wife and wailing children. The situation was all the more acute when he entered what would nowadays be called university 'concorsi,' or in other words, competitions for important academic position or advancement in Naples. As he said of one such application in his autobiographical narrative: 'He worked at it all the preceding night until five in the morning, while discussing with friends and amidst the screams of his children, as was always the context of his reading, writing and meditating.' ('Egli la pensò fino alle cinque ore della notte antecedente, in ragionando con amici e tra lo strepito de' suoi figliuoli, come ha uso di sempre o leggere o scrivere o meditare.')[17]

Considering today's extensive job application processes, some may find Vico a figure with whom they empathize intensely, especially as he was subjected to such exhausting applications at various points throughout his adult life. I would say that he seems in these respects a thoroughly modern figure; however, I then swiftly realize that I actually mean something almost the opposite of that term. For one need only witness the obsequiousness of his letters of application for royal favour in obtaining such posts – including the one he eventually wrote on his son's behalf in the hope that he might succeed him in an important Neapolitan chair of rhetoric – to discover how very feudal still were the structures of university office-holding, and the power wielded over it from on high. This flip in my perspective – feudalism as the counterface of Vico's apparent modernity in our eyes – perhaps hints at how dubiously or only partially modern we are in such matters ourselves. How much have conditions significantly changed for the better, away from the continuance of those same (or very similar) feudal structures, in the intimacies of our own age's deployments of academic power and of power over academies?

A quarter of a century later, in 1770, an utterly different sensibility was briefly present in Naples – that of the youthful Mozart, who was compulsively seeing *opera buffa* in the life around him because that was the musical form he was most immersed in during this second visit to Italy with his father Leopold. As a musical prodigy who would soon take Italian opera in utterly different directions, mainly by giving its external forms more intense inner life, Mozart, who was only fourteen at the time, watched the new and 'beautiful,' but already 'old-fashioned' Jomelli opera in the San Carlo theatre, which was built in 1737.

> The opera here is one of Jomelli's; it is beautiful, but too serious and old-fashioned for the theatre. De Amicis sings amazingly well and so does Aprile, who sang in Milan. The dances are wretchedly pompous. The theatre is beautiful. The King has had a rough Neapolitan upbringing and in the opera he always stands on a stool so as to look a little taller than the Queen. She is beautiful and gracious, and on the Molo (that is a drive) she

bowed to me in a most friendly manner at least six times. Every evening the nobles send us their carriages to drive out with them to the Molo.[18]

The opera house in question, as Susan Sontag affirms, was 'the biggest in Italy, [and] provided a continual ravishment of castrati, another local product of international renown.'[19] Mozart needed only to turn his attention from the stage to the audience to see in their royal box the comic king and queen of this southernmost state. Like the good-natured brother he was, he would later recount to his sister Nannerl in a dashed-off letter some of the local commonplaces about the royal pair. Whether he actually saw the king on the aforementioned stool is unimportant; what matters is that this is how he has been led by gossip to imagine the situation. It is indubitably a frozen moment of *buffa*, even if, positionally, the king and queen are actually part of the audience *watching* the opera: he is a 'rough Neapolitan' by upbringing, she is, by contrast, a 'beautiful and gracious' Austrian. To the sensibility of young Mozart, this king and queen are *representational* in their own right, much like any such royal figures in the operas that constituted so much of what he was absorbing of musical culture in Italy.

We should not forget that the distance between Naples and Salzburg, which we may tend to overestimate in physical and psychological terms, was by no means great. 'Write to me and do not be so lazy,' he joyfully teases his sister in German, and then follows up with banter that is quintessential Italian comic opera, with a lineage from *commedia dell'arte* slapstick: 'Otherwise I'll give you a real beating' ('Altrimenti avrete qualche bastonata da me'). In another letter sent to her a little later, once he and his father were back in Rome on their slow northward trajectory, he tried out typical fourteen-year-old scatalogical humour in poor Italian on her: 'goodbye, be well, and go shit in your bed such that it makes a loud noise' ('addio e statevi bene, e cacate [*sic*] nel letto che egli fà fracasso').[20]

Because of his boundless brio and lack of inhibition as a correspondent, Mozart is another good touchstone for reviewing some important social and cultural realities of Naples in this period. Precisely because such realities are being revealed by a visitor from a more northerly and much smaller European court culture, the comparisons he offers guarantee a certain authenticity, even when there is clearly little conscious striving for effect on the part of the correspondent. Much the same can be said of his father's letters, so much is their mission in Italy a joint one.

In the present instance, Mozart is only seeking to amuse and impress his sister. Like his father, if not quite so avidly, he wishes to establish to what degree they (who in Salzburg are court servants, something that only several years later would grate terribly upon Mozart the young man) are taken up by the nobility of the states they visit.

And so we see into that leisurely world of Neapolitan aristocracy, out in its caliches on the Molo, which a guidebook of the same years defines as the most frequented street of its day: 'for the great number of carriages which are continually seen there, as for the crowds of people who resort there for pleasure' ('per il gran numero di carrozze che di continuo vi si veggono, come per la gran frequenza di popolo, che per deliziarsi vi concorre').[21] Here for Mozart are obsequious interchanges with royalty itself. The queen bows to him, and not once but several times. Whether this bowing actually happened as described is not the issue. What was important was being sought as guests of the nobility in their social parading, in which royalty certainly participated in Naples, as it did in most other European states. (Interestingly, Queen Maria Carolina was only eighteen at this stage, a mere four years older than Mozart. So it is quite possible that she did take a rather heightened interest in this Austrian co-national, who in his status as a youthful prodigy was so different from the 'rough Neapolitan' royal to whom her life had been recently linked forever by dynastic marriage.) The queen is not presented as bowing in a general way to their carriage, nor even to son *and* father, but to Mozart himself. On the young man's part there is certainly a very robust sense of self-worth displayed in the phrasing of his letter, which comes as no surprise. For Naples, according to his father's reports, was a culture among the foremost they had visited in recognizing the artistic gifts of his son. Driven as the Mozarts were by their near obsession with the nobility in Naples (as elsewhere), and with receiving royal notice, it is of striking interest that when the boy describes the poor of the city he does so in terms of an inverse image of feudal, ancien régime culture: 'We saw the King and Queen at Mass in the court chapel at Portici and we have seen Vesuvius too. Naples is beautiful, but it is as crowded as Vienna and Paris. And of the two, London and Naples, I do not know whether Naples does not surpass London for the insolence of the people; for here the lazzaroni have their own general or chief, who receives twenty-five ducati d'argento from the King every month, solely for the purpose of keeping them in order.'[22] It is only 1770, and the correspondent is merely fourteen. But the cultural comparisons he makes impress us because we know with historical retrospect what he is on his way to becoming, namely, one of the greatest artists the world has ever known. At this age of fourteen there seems in him a distaste for the insolence of the populace. He offers the pejorative comment that it is only by means of a regular and targeted payment that the king keeps the *lazzaroni*, or beggars, in a feudal structuring of their own, with a 'general or chief' who is a kind of mirror inverse of the king's own relation to the nobility. All this the young man takes in, aware as he also is that the king himself is only of 'rough Neapolitan upbringing.'

What the boy artist cannot yet know is that in his comic operas of the 1780s, in collaboration with Lorenzo da Ponte, he will provide critique of an oppressive and cheating count, and have a chorus of both nobility and populace sing out the importance of 'libertà,' resulting from their anger at a womanizing Don. So far, in 1770, Mozart displays only a two-dimensional awareness, as it were, of the pressures bubbling up through feudal structures, which can still be suppressed in this Neapolitan society by direct and regular payments from the king to the beggar general.

The Mozarts are exquisitely dressed in rich-coloured moiré, trimmed with lace and lined with silk. 'We have left our fine cloth suits in Rome and have had to put on our two beautifully braided summer costumes. Wolfgang's is of rose-coloured moiré, but the colour is so peculiar that in Italy it is called colore di fuoco or flame-coloured; it is trimmed with silver lace and lined with sky-blue silk. My costume is of the colour of cinnamon and is made of piqued Florentine cloth with silver lace and is lined with apple green silk. They are two fine costumes, but, before we reach home, they will look like old maids.'[23] If we focus at an almost Geertzian level of 'thick description' on these two musicians from north of the Alps as they don their finest moiré silk costumes for this southern courtly society, we begin to grasp not merely the intent of the Mozarts, but also their assumptions about the culture of reception. As a result, we sense the calculated effect of their smart clothes upon a world where consumption, elegance, courtly address to important persons, and (of paramount importance) exceptional musical talents all count so strongly.

Knowingly or not, the Mozarts are in a kingdom whose own silk works at San Leuccio, near the capital, were only established in the previous reign of Charles. In the present reign of Ferdinand and Caroline, these silk works figure as the finest instance of royal, philanthropic, 'industrial' development. The pair show themselves in Naples in clothes not merely of striking colours – Wolfgang wrote to Nannerl, 'Yesterday we put on our new clothes and we were as beautiful as angels' – but made in part from the finest material that the kingdom itself is proud to manufacture. The two are therefore not just musically, but also culturally, attuned to modes of self-display among the nobility and artists of this society.

As though these special clothes were insufficient, Mozart's father soon orders from a tailor serving the nobility in Naples, 'with the assistance of M. Meurikofer' (Jean Georges Meuricoffre, a Swiss merchant friend they had first met in Lyons in their major European travels of 1764–5), another summer suit for each of them, every bit as colourful as the previous outfits.[24] It is questionable whether the apple-green shot moiré chosen this time for Wolfgang by his father would have appealed to the boy in view of his known dislike of green fabrics.[25] What matters here is that the letter detailing these additional outfits is sent to Mrs Mozart only a week after the previous one. In it, we recall, Leopold had also given her details of two brightly coloured summer outfits for them both, and at first expressed fear that they would have to wear them till they were threadbare. He seems now to be stressing to his wife in Salzburg how successful they have quickly become in noble Neapolitan society, and how much money they were taking in at Wolfgang's various concerts. The anxiety expressed in one letter – of arriving back in Salzburg in threadbare outfits – and the note of pride that shines through the next letter's details of yet another tailoring commission are two sides of the same coin of being an artist dependent on noble favour. Both Leopold and Wolfgang were to know forms of that artistic anxiety all their lives, whether here in Naples, back in Salzburg, or in the imperial court city of Vienna, to which Wolfgang transferred in the 1780s to the consternation of his father, from whose fussy protection the still-young man was finally able to establish some distance.

Interestingly, the only mature Mozart opera in the Italian language that is actually set in contemporary Italy, *Così fan tutte*, is located in Naples, and it even makes reference to Vesuvian levels of passion in act 2, when Dorabella sings to Guglielmo during a duet with him, 'I seem to have / a Vesuvius in my breast' ('Nel petto un Vesuvio / D'avere mi par'). It is worth pointing out how important is that 1790 *dramma giocoso*'s own presentation of two principal males who 'return' to their lovers in Naples in exotic 'Valecchian' or 'Turkish' disguises. 'Che sembianze! che vestiti! / Che figure!' ('What faces! what clothes! / What appearances') sings the servant Despina at the dashing figures of the disguised Guglielmo and Ferrando (act 1), much as ordinary folk witnessing the two Salzburg musicians might have exclaimed exactly twenty years earlier in *actual* rather than *representational* Naples. As with the male pair in the later opera, the *éclat* of the Mozarts' appearances was clearly intended.

There is no way that the mature Mozart would have set his opera in a small northern court city like Turin, with its population by that time of some 70,000, compared with Naples's more than 300,000, and which, interestingly, did not figure in the Mozarts' musical itineraries in Italy. In *Così* the two young women, Fiordiligi and Dorabella, are themselves from another court city, Ferrara. But with no explanation needed, as society belles they have simply established themselves as residents of the much grander culture of Naples. (As the previous quote from Mozart makes clear, the only relevant comparisons with Naples in terms of size and importance are the other major European capital cities that he already knows: London, Vienna, and Paris.)

In 1770 Leopold Mozart is not embarrassed by what may be revealed from a deeper (possibly unconscious) level in his notion that with heavy use Wolfgang's and his silk finery may look old-maidish. For the logical corollary of that statement is that in their freshly tailored state they turn themselves out with a certain youthful *femininity*. The South, luxury, and notions of 'effeminacy' go together in the late eighteenth century: such, at any rate, was a commonplace about southern cultures, with luxury often seen as the corrupting element. From what else is said in this phase of the Mozarts' correspondence, it is clear that Naples absorbs these two silken artists, these virtual birds of paradise, into the thick of its own display culture of opera-going, carriage rides along the Molo, classical sightseeing, and collecting. Indeed, the wife of the important English plenipotentiary and major collector of his day, William Hamilton, plays her new harpsichord, which was built by Burkat Tschudi, in the presence of this youth of trans-European fame; she trembles at displaying her own (apparently very considerable) talents in view of his stupendous ones.[26] And like eminent persons on the Grand Tour – though this is not what Mozart father and son are here for, theirs being fundamentally a commercial enterprise, one of displaying Wolfgang's musicality in important Italian cities – they visit Vesuvius, Pompeii, Paestum, Portici, and other classical sites in which the Campagna immediately surrounding Naples abounds. They and thousands of others.

In 1758, twelve years before the Mozarts had made their lengthy second journey to Italy, including that stay of several weeks in Naples, another boy (but this one of a minor aristocratic background) had transferred, at the age of nine and a half, from his native town of Asti in Piedmont to the nearby capital and court city of the Kingdom of Sardinia to attend its *Accademia di Torino* for several important years of schooling. In what follows I shall begin with Vittorio Alfieri's account in his autobiography, many years later, of one of his first impressions of Turin. I will then consider his remarks on the city based on a later visit, seeking to contextualize them either by comparative reflection upon other accounts of roughly the same period, or by means of modern studies. In 2002 a new *Storia di Torino* was published in several volumes, including, importantly, one offering extensive coverage of the ancien régime period, with essays by several authors, edited by Giuseppe Ricuperati.[27] This volume has been an invaluable resource and point of departure for much of what follows.

There exist also numerous travel accounts, which have sections on Turin from the eighteenth century itself. Another source I used was a 1753 guide for foreigners, *Guida de' forestieri per la real città di Torino*, one of the first 'pocket' guidebooks of any European city, with itemized walks that could be followed by a visiting tourist. It was written by a bookshop clerk and native of Turin, Giovanni Gaspare Craveri. The book is not without prejudicial spin, giving, as it does, a patriotic and royalist account of the material fabric and civic organization of Turin's various structures. As Maria Teresa Silvestrini has said, it is 'an image of Turin centred on its function as a capital and on its organization of urban space dominated by the edifices of political and ecclesiastical power, such as to exclude almost completely the economic, productive and commercial life of the city, or private existence.'[28] But as comparativists of eighteenth century city cultures seeking to grasp the imaginary of how a place such as Turin saw and understood itself, it behoves us more than ever to wander the city's streets and institutions following just such itineraries as those of this much-reprinted pocket guidebook, written for the kind of *forestieri* (outsiders) we more than ever are. (Even if we should happen to be modern citizens of Turin, we are 'strangers' to its mid-eighteenth century; 'visitors' in the sense of not living its *then* realities, but rather the modifications of them which have evolved over the intervening two hundred and fifty years.) By direct contrast with Craveri's guidebook of 1753, the Duke of Noja, in the south, had indicated an unknown or even unknowable quality to Naples in his remarks of 1750. He said, in effect, that the 'people had no clearer idea [of it] than they had of the cities of Japan or Tartary.' In Venturi's synopsis of Noja's points, 'while very fine maps existed of Petersburg and Moscow, there was no decent map of the "largest city in Italy."'[29]

Capital Contrasts: Naples and Turin a Century before Unification 117

At the outset we must recognize that in the case of Turin we are dealing with what was then a compact capital of some 158 hectares in area;[30] 'petit et bien bâti ... le plus beau village du monde,' as Montesquieu had described it with dainty wryness early in the century in 1728.[31] The city scarcely grew beyond its two miles of fortified perimeter walls until Napoleon decided to have them torn down. In part, though by no means entirely, for such reasons of space, Turin's population during the eighteenth century would never reach 100,000. As I treat these and further matters about the city, I wish to begin also serious comparisons with Naples, the sprawling capital city of the large southern kingdom, which had a population of well over 300,000 by the 1760s and 1770s, and was in excess of 400,000 by the end of the century. (In computing the number of beggars alone to be 50,000 to 60,000 in Naples during the time of his visit, Montesquieu was pronouncing a figure in excess of his estimation of the *total* population of Turin in 1728 at 40,000.)[32] Most serious scholarship of these ancien régime kingdoms focuses on them one at a time. But we now have such good histories of and sources for material information about both that a different kind of study is possible, at once synthetic *and* comparative. Only by means of such dualistic concentration on both cities in this early period, well before Unification, will the sheer scale of differences, which in their later manifestations were to be melded together into the same political entity, be appreciable.

Looking back from his mature years in 1790, Alfieri used the words *città anfibia* – amphibian city – as his first summation of the Turin he had gone to as a schoolboy in 1758.[33] He must have been seeking to focus the experience of many years into one epithet, and indeed it is a brilliant one. In the immediate context in which it occurs, Alfieri is hinting at the city's linguistic positioning between French and Italian. In its regionalism he sees it as neither fish nor fowl entirely, in spite of the constitutional status of Italian as the 'official' language, which was established much earlier in the century. A rather distant 'half-uncle' of his was Benedetto Alfieri, the major mid-century architect of Turin, who was responsible for such buildings as the beautiful Royal Theatre in the very environs of Alfieri's own academy. He was also responsible for further developing the rational planning of the city more generally. This uncle was the boy's closest relation in Turin, and the family member whom he saw most. What at first annoyed the young Alfieri about this uncle ('mi seccava di più') was the fact that he spoke a pure literary Italian (*toscano*), which he had acquired from his earlier stay in Rome:

Speaking Italian was rather contraband in the amphibian city of Turin. But such is the force of the beautiful and the true, that the very people who began by making fun of my Tuscanizing uncle upon his return, having realized after a while that he did, after all, speak a real language and they themselves stammered out only a barbarous jargon, all began trying in discoursing with him to muddle along in a Tuscan of their own; particularly those many high and mighty, who wanted to renovate their houses somewhat, and make them appear to be palaces.

La cosa che di esso mi seccava di più era il suo benedetto parlar toscano, ch'egli dal suo soggiorno di Roma in poi mai più non avea voluto smettere; ancorchè il parlare italiano sia un vero contrabbando in Torino, città anfibia. Ma tanta è però la forza del bello e del vero, che la gente stessa che al principio quando il mio zio rimpatriò, si burlava del di lui toscaneggiare, dopo alcun tempo avvistisi poi ch'egli veramente parlava una lingua, ed essi smozzicavano un barbaro gergo, tutti poi a prova favellando con lui andavano anch'essi balbettando il loro toscano; e massimamente quei tanti signori, che volevano rabberciare un poco le loro case e farle assomigliar dei palazzi.[34]

Today we would see Alfieri's observation as full of prejudicial thinking about the relative importance of different speech usages. Written years earlier, but representing the state of affairs only shortly before the situation Alfieri describes upon arrival in Turin as a boy, Craveri's guidebook for foreign visitors of 1753 had presented the language issues of Turin very differently. With great regional pride, this guidebook informs its readers that in the private theatre of the Prince of Carignano, in addition to productions of *opere buffe*, tragedies and comedies were presented in both French and Italian. Clearly for Craveri the use of the two major literary languages in the theatres of the nobility is being interpreted as a cultural positive, a sign of cosmopolitanism on Turin's part.

Nonetheless, Alfieri, in his much later writing – prejudiced though it may seem against dialects – had probably correctly spotted the prickly issue of class conflict in the matter of language usage in Turin. It would appear that for wealthy citizens, cutting *una bella figura* in such a society implied living in a town palazzo rather than a more modest 'house.' This, in turn, might mean employing Alfieri's well-spoken uncle to convert one's casa into a palazzo, and conversing with him in the process in attempts at a good literary Italian of one's own, rather than in the local dialect of one's 'inferior' class or regional upbringing. For the court,

French remained the official language. In his chapter on the problems of language of this period in Turin, Claudio Marazzini cites Carlo Denina's testimony that, in court and indeed in ordinary conversation, 'for every one time that Italian is spoken, twenty other times it will be French' ('per una volta che si parli Italiano, venti altre si parla Francese').[35] As Craveri had said of Turin's citizens in his general remarks on their civic customs and mores at the end of his 1753 guidebook, 'They delight in foreign languages, particularly French' ('Si dilettano delle Lingue straniere, particolarmente della Francese').[36] (But note that the guidebook itself is written in literary Italian and that, for an ordinary Turinese citizen such as Craveri in the 1750s, French still counts terminologically as a foreign tongue.) The one language that was more and more unacceptable to be found speaking at any level of good society, and that was frowned on generally when used from the pulpit (not just in villages but sometimes in Turin itself), was the local piedmontese dialect.[37] As though to underline the abiding amphibian character of this small state, when the communal tower on the island of San Massimo was rebuilt in 1781, there was debate about whether to decorate the clock face in the Italian or in the French style of indicating the hours. On a vote it was decided to have an Italian-style clock – but with an added sphere with French hours![38]

There was simply no way that Turin's 'amphibian' status – in between other larger and more significant cultures – could be denied. Indeed, for sheer survival's sake this was a reality to be ongoingly nurtured through diplomacy and, wherever possible, through appropriate dynastic alliance with the more major European powers. For instance, at signs of war in the region between France and Austria in 1733, the Marquis of Ormea held talks with both parties to the dispute, and surprised the other European powers (in particular the Venetian diplomat in Turin at that time) by getting the king to align with France.[39] This was just one of many strategies of fine calculation by Turin as a third party between forces opposed to one another. At different times the balances of such alignments would have to be altered, so as to conserve Turin's independence and to maintain her respect in the eyes of major European states.

In Turin there were elaborate symbolic displays in all celebrations of alliance with greater powers. Some of the most splendid ceremonials in the city occurred during times of dynastic marriage, as was the union of the hereditary prince Vittorio Amedeo and the Spanish Infanta in 1750. Although officially married in Madrid, the nuptial festivities upon the couple's return to Turin in May of that year have a magnificence to them that is quite out of the ordinary. The city's most important architect, that same Benedetto Alfieri, headed a team employed to design machinery for fireworks to celebrate the young couple, including a platform with papier maché sculptings of Cupid and a seascape of tritons, dolphins, and seashells.[40] A generation later, when King Carlo Emanuele III died, Vittorio Amedeo III (subject of those earlier festivities) and his wife Maria Antonia Fernanda of Spain ascended the throne. It was again time to marry the new hereditary prince. A further alliance with a Bourbon line was struck; this time, however, it was not with Spain but with Clothilde of France. For this marriage there seem to have been still more elaborate festivities and symbolic constructions than for the earlier one. A grand firework platform was erected, representing the Alps dividing the kingdom's own provinces from those of France, with two rivers of Piedmont and two of France issuing into magnificent water fountains, and other images alluding to communication routes between the two states. The marriage itself had taken place in Versailles in August of that year. (As in the former generation, the dynastic scions are formally wed in the larger and more important of the two states that are parties to the new blood alliance.) When the wedding party, including the king and queen, returned to Turin during these festivities of 1775, the King's carriage was formally greeted by its governor and mayor, each of whom – and even this is symbolically important – addressed the sovereign and his daughter-in-law, the new princess royal, with speeches in French.[41]

At other times, Turin resorted to quite different ways of maintaining peaceful relations and trade communications with significant Mediterranean states. For instance, in 1785, as part of complex shifts of emphasis in the small kingdom's alliances with the Bourbons and the Hapsburgs, it received a visit in a private capacity from another reigning couple, King Ferdinand IV and Queen Maria Carolina of the Kingdom of Naples. This couple constituted, in their own right, an existing Bourbon-Hapsburg marital nexus. Though the Neapolitan party came in private and under assumed names, the disguise was little more than a folksy ritual of this king with the 'rough Neapolitan upbringing.' He and his queen were soon being lavishly entertained by the court and city authorities in Turin, with balls, concerts, and firework displays. To cap it all (because Ferdinand's hearty sporting predilections were well known to the House of Savoy), there was a magnificently organized stag hunt. Naturally, the eventual killing of the beast was reserved for the privilege of the visiting Parthenopian sovereign, and after the kill the beast's symbolically important left hoof was cut off and offered to him as a trophy.[42] All this was lavish, unsubtle massaging of relations between one kingdom and another, the two courts of the capital cities of Turin and Naples.

Relations to the north and east could not be allowed to fester either. In 1785 – the same year the Neapolitan king and queen visited Turin – the princess Carola of Savoy became the chosen bride of Prince Antony of Saxony, in a phase during which the foreign secretary of the Kingdom of Sardinia, in an anti-Hapsburg caprice, considered transforming the small state into another Palatine electorate in league with German equivalents.[43] This transformation of the kingdom into a German electoral principality did not come to pass, and it is notable that upon the eve of revolutionary events in France, a highly pro-Hapsburg party again formed in Turin.[44] What is significant is that any movement in one direction almost always has to be balanced by an equivalent reaction in another direction in the total economy of diplomacy that keeps this kind of small state independent. If we look back momentarily, we may recall the pummelling siege that Turin had sustained at the very beginning of the century in 1706. The French forces of Louis XIV had sought over months to bring this much smaller kingdom under their rule, albeit unsuccessfully. This set a significant precedent to maintain Piedmont/Savoy's independence in the decades that followed. That historic military avoidance of domination by another power comes to symbolize for the people of this strategic gateway kingdom between France and Italy the maintenance (however precariously) of its independent sovereignty, which would survive the entire course of the century, right up until 1798. Many important art works of the years succeeding 1706 directly represent the Siege of Turin and its eventual victorious outcome. This fact helps us to grasp why all the later dynastic manipulations and symbolic displays have, as their raison d'être, Turin's and the kingdom's independence through alliances.

But what was it actually like to live in the smallish capital and court city of Turin, with its highly rational grid of streets and *piazze*, in the later decades of the eighteenth century? To answer this we would do well to refer back to Alfieri's autobiography, again filling in details from others to obtain something like an adequately complex impression. Upon his three-week return visit to Turin in 1784, more than seven years after he had ceased living there, Alfieri found not a few of his old friends and acquaintances disinclined to recognize him, seemingly because they could not stomach his successes: 'some because I had written tragedies, others for my having travelled so much, others again because now I had reappeared in town with too many horses' ('gli uni mi trattavano così perchè io aveva scritto tragedie; gli altri, perchè avea viaggiato tanto; gli altri, perchè ora io era ricomparito in paese con troppi cavalli').[45] Alfieri finds that the constrictions of a small society are such that it cannot easily tolerate success that has been earned in the larger world. This is confirmed in his dealings with his brother-in-law, a first gentleman of the chamber at court, and with the king's minister. Both these figures reinforce his intuition that, in having to attend court and wait upon the king, he will unquestionably find the latter 'offended with me for having tacitly rebuffed him by my permanent residence elsewhere' ('Un altro amarissimo boccone che mi convenne inghiottire in Torino, fu di dovermi indispensabilmente presentare al Re, il quale per certo si teneva offeso da me, per averlo io tacitamente rinnegato coll'espatriazione perpetua').[46]

The king's minister does indeed put pressure on Alfieri to take up residence again in Turin and assume a place at court. There is even an implication that although it may be Alfieri's literary works that have brought him recognition and made him a desirable asset to the Savoy monarch and his court, these works are not intrinsically valued alongside their notion of service to the state.

> He [the minister] added that literary productions were well and good, but that there were greater and more important occupations, that I must feel were well within my capability. I thanked him courteously, but persisted with my refusal; and I even had the moderation and generosity not to load pointless mortification on the good gentleman, even though he merited it, by leaving him to understand that their dispatches and diplomacy appeared to me, and were certainly, much less important and quite another thing than my own and certain other people's tragedies. But this kind of person is, and must perforce remain, unbending.

> Egli [il ministro] soggiunse: che le lettere erano belle e buone, ma che esistevano delle occupazioni più grandi e più importanti, di cui io era e mi dovea sentir ben capace. Ringraziai cortesemente, ma persistei nel no; ed ebbi anche la moderazione e la generosità di non dare a quel buon galantuomo l'inutile mortificazione, ch'egli si sarebbe pur meritata; di lasciargli cioè intendere, che i loro dispacci e diplomazie mi pareano, ed eran per certo, assai meno importante ed altra cosa che non le tragedie mie o le altrui. Ma questa specie di gente è, e dev'essere, inconvertibile.[47]

It is apparent from Alfieri's fine psychological reading of his dealings with courtiers that this was not a state in which a major writer could work

Capital Contrasts: Naples and Turin a Century before Unification 123

unhampered by court interference. He hints that he would be pestered by a host of petty expectations about how he ought to absolve his social responsibilities to the king and to his hierarchy.

Alfieri's own position is likewise unbending in a sense; he realizes well enough by the age of thirty-five that he has – beyond all gainsaying – 'embraced the realm of writing, and for better or worse would practice it for the rest of my life' ('avendo io abbracciata l'arte delle lettere, o bene o male la praticherei per tutto il rimanente di vita mia').[48] The court enticements to return to Turin, however warmly and sincerely held out by officialdom, indicate how beyond their conception it would be to place Alfieri's literary activity at the top of the agenda of what he would be expected to engage in upon such a return. This says a lot about cultural context.

Having put his subtle negative construction on the Turin court, Alfieri goes on, in what he recounts of his subsequent encounter with the king himself, to praise the progressive and enlightened status of this state compared with other more regressive monarchies of Europe. There is a twist in the ending of such praise, however, as Alfieri indicates that however enlightened, this is still despotism – thereby displaying his developed distaste for 'tyranny' even in its mildest forms. (We should remember that Alfieri's account, although *about* an encounter in 1784, is written in 1790, and in Paris furthermore, with all the fervour of change and of definitively casting aside ancien régime realities that were in the air by then.)

> Although I do not like Kings in general, and least of all the more arbitrary ones, I must ingenuously say that the line of these Princes of ours is the best of the bunch, above all upon comparing it with almost all the other current European lineages. And in the privacy of my own heart I felt affection rather than aversion for them; this King and equally his predecessor being full of the best intentions, of good, civilized and altogether exemplary natures, and who do more benefit than harm to their state. For all that, when one considers and vividly senses that doing good or ill depends on their absolute will, one cannot but tremble, and flee.

> Ancorchè io non ami punto i Re in genere, e meno i più arbitrari, debbo pur dire ingenuamente che la razza di questi nostri Principi è ottima sul totale, e massime paragonandola a quasi tutte l'altre presenti d'Europa. Ed io sentiva nell'intimo del cuore piuttosto affetto per essi, che non avversione; stante che sì questo Re che il di lui predecessore, sono di ottime

intenzioni, di buona e costumata ed esemplarissima indole e fanno al paese loro più bene che male. Con tutto ciò quando si pensa e vivamente si sente che il loro giovare o nuocere pendono dal loro assoluto volere, bisogna fremere, e fuggire.[49]

This is all part of what Franco Valsecchi saw over forty years ago as Alfieri's primary role in turning his back on the past and unveiling a different future. In terms of political thought, as Valsecchi accurately summarized,

> The most audacious ferment, which most presaged the future, had its greatest interpreter in Alfieri, in his open polemic against tradition, in his rebellion against 'Piedmontism,' in his negation of regional pride in the name of a more vast and lofty concept of Italianness ... In his 'Panegyric to Trajan,' his apology for liberty and the closing disquisition against absolute tyranny assume the significance of an act of accusation against the old Piedmontese state, now overtaken by events. Alfieri's panegyric is the signal of new times, in its sharp break with the inheritance of the past. The condemnation of the profession of arms pronounced by Alfieri and his affirmation of the superiority of the pacific arts of commerce and of agriculture were designed to wound to the quick the old warrior Piedmont, to strike the ancien régime's very foundations.

> I fermenti più audaci, che maggiormente precorrono l'avvenire, hanno il loro massimo interprete in Alfieri, nella sua aperta polemica contro la tradizione, nella sua ribellione al 'piemontesimo,' nella sua negazione dell'orgoglio regionale in nome di un più vasto ed altro concetto di italianità ... Nel suo Panegirico a Traiano, l'apologia della libertà, la requisitoria contro il despotismo assumono il significato di un atto d'accusa contro il vecchio Stato piemontese, ormai superato dagli eventi. Il Panegirico dell'Alfieri è il segnale dei tempi nuovi, nel distacco deciso dall'eredità del passato: la condanna del mestiere delle armi, pronunciata dall'Alfieri, l'affermata superiorità delle pacifiche arti del commercio e dell'agricoltura, venivano a ferire nel vivo il vecchio Piemonte guerriero, a colpire nelle sue stesse basi il vecchio regime.[50]

Valsecchi is describing Alfieri's 'Panegiric of Pliny to Trajan,' a work in which collapse of an old order is figured as something very near in time. Valsecchi is also suggesting something that we have witnessed in the autobiography, namely that Alfieri's writings can function metaphorically as a commentary on the destiny of Piedmont.

There had been across the entire eighteenth century strong traditions of description of the very different material beauties of Turin and Naples. In Naples' case what often drew praise was its overall climate, its perch from classical times beneath a sometimes smoking and sometimes more active volcano, and its sprawl all around a crescent bay. As Montesquieu pointed out, 'Nothing is more beautiful than the position of Naples on a gulf: it is an amphitheatre onto the sea, but a deep amphitheatre.' ('Rien n'est plus beau que la situation de Naples dans un golfe: elle est amphithéâtre sur la mer, mais un amphithéâtre profond.')[51]

In the case of Turin, by contrast, praise almost always began with the finely unified architecture, not much of it more than a century and a half old, or with comment upon the ongoing street-widening or piazza extensions and improvements. Indeed, we can assert that within its walls Turin was substantially an architectural and symmetrically designed ensemble with far fewer centuries of layering than Naples. Therefore, it seemed a more unified urban work of art than the southern capital, even though it might not be a good place for artists themselves to reside by Alfieri's reckoning. From approximately the early seventeenth century onwards, Turin's progressive layout and the realization of a rational ensemble of streets and buildings, on a very human scale and within a relatively small compass of fortified walls, made it a rare instance of composite architectural unity. In a sense, Alfieri's relative, Benedetto Alfieri, does not play nearly significant enough a role in Vittorio's autobiography. For as I have indicated, more than anyone else it was he who was responsible for the perfecting of this architectural and urbanistic ensemble.[52]

The view-painting traditions of the eighteenth century made much of Turin, notably in major works by Canaletto's nephew Bernardo Bellotto. But even the much smaller and artisanally produced *vedute* for the *mondi nuovi*, which I discussed in my first chapter, show many townscapes of Turin's rationally planned streets and piazzas, and are notable for their concentration on the symmetries of its architectural design.[53] (This is that '"mental cinema" ... even before the invention of the cinema,' as Calvino defined its pictorial imaginary in *Six Memos for the Next Millennium*.)[54] Craveri's 1753 pocket guidebook for foreigners does not really distinguish between the splendid lifestyle of Turin's citizens and the architectural context which contains and enhances it. The city has, he proclaims, no need to 'envy any of the cities of Europe, for to none of them does it cede place for the splendour and magnificence of its court, for the finery of its nobility, for the good manners of its citizens, for the sumptuousness of its manufacturing, for the streets which are almost all of a level, for its magnificent churches and its spacious and ornate piazzas' ('invidiare alcune delle Città dell'Europa, come a niuna di esse cede per lo splendore e magnificenza della Corte, per fasto della Nobiltà, per la gentilezza de'Cittadini, per la sontuosità delle fabriche, e delle Contrade, che sono quasi tutte tirate a livello, e per le magnifiche Chiese, e per le spaziose, ed ornatissime sue Piazze').[55]

By contrast, consider what Venturi has to say about the Duke of Noja's sense of the unplanned, confusing city of Naples in much the same mid-century moment. Noja thought that 'the city was "extremely badly constructed," without any plan or design, unlike Paris, Vienna or Rome. There were no "broad, straight" streets, no squares and it was totally unsuitable for carriages. There were no places to meet and take refreshments and the dwellings were distinguished in a way which, above all, was socially dangerous. "It is clear how much narrow winding streets contribute to making a people restless and quarrelsome."'[56]

Turin was becoming associated with enlightened planning, and therefore with equivalent lifestyle possibilities. At the same time, what for one may be the beauty of symmetry and a unified ensemble on a pleasingly human scale, may for another weary the eye. To Edward Gibbon, a visitor to Turin in 1764, eleven years after the first of several editions of Craveri's pocket guidebook, 'The architecture and government of Turin presented the same aspect of tame and tiresome uniformity.'[57] Even much earlier in the century, Montesquieu ran through a gamut of reactions during his relatively short stay. The city was at first a 'ville riante' to him,[58] but he seems to have experienced some of the same frisson of the closed-in nature of its society as Alfieri, stressing, not unlike the latter did more than sixty years later, that he would not 'for anything be a subject of one of these petty princes! They know all you are doing; have you always under their eyes; know your income to a nicety, and find ways of making you spend it.' ('Pour rien, ne voudrois être sujet de ces petits princes! Ils savent tout ce que vous faites; il vous ont toujours sous les yeux; ils savent vos revenus au juste; trouvent le moyen de vous les faire dépenser.')[59] Later again, he implies the place is full of spies. An isolated line in his travel narrative simply reads, 'Ici les murailles parlent.' ('Here walls speak.')[60] However, in the final analysis it is not so much, as in Alfieri's case, that he was spooked by presentiments of absolutism that forced Montesquieu to flee, but rather it was boredom. The same *ville riante* of the beginning of his account became a 'ville assez ennuyeuse' by the end of his relatively short stay.[61] To offset this rather negative account by Montesquieu, another French visitor, Charles de Brosses, who was president of the Burgundian Parliament, uttered an unequivocally positive response. Only twelve years after Montesquieu's visit, de Brosses found Turin 'the most beautiful city of Italy, and perhaps of Europe, for the straightness of its streets, the regularity of its buildings and the beauty of its piazze ... Here nothing is outstandingly beautiful, but all equally so, and nothing mediocre; it forms an ensemble, small yes, because the city is small, but fascinating.'[62]

What may be considered highly indicative of a society's assumptions about itself, and therefore its identity, are its institutions for coping with the marginalized elements of its population. What can be said, in this regard, of some of Turin's institutions, and how do they compare historically with those in Naples? As far as surveillance and control of vice in the city are concerned, in 1753 Craveri spoke in revealing ways about the *Ricovero di Donne Forzate* in Turin, or literally, Refuge for Forced Women. As Craveri explains, 'The refuge workhouse for Forced Women, so called for their being badly inclined and scandalous women, and therefore brought here by force, as to a house of correction, the youngest and most attractive and most given over to vice being always preferred because those, in sum, might be the greatest impediment to the innocence of others. This shelter was founded in 1750 by the goodwill of Riccardo Veken, tailor to His Majesty, under the patron Saint of Mary Magdalen and under direct Royal protection.' ('Ricovero di Donne forzate, così dette, per esser Donne mal inclinate, e scandalose, quivi a forza condotte, come in casa di correzione, e sono sempre prescielte le più giovani, e le più avvenenti, e fra queste le più scandalose, le quali ponno per conseguenza esser di maggior inciampo all' altrui innocenza. Fu fondato quello ricovero nel 1750 dalla carità di Riccardo Veken, Sarto di S.M, sotto il patrocinio di Santa Maria Maddalena, e sotto l'immediata Regia protezione.')[63]

The 'Rules' for this workhouse are divided into a general and a particular section. In the 'General Rules' it was specified that into the establishment 'are to be taken women of bad behaviour, public equally as private prostitutes, [such as are] obstinate in vice, of whatsoever city, place and condition they may be, provided they are native or inhabiting in the states of His Majesty' ('debbano in essa [Istituzione dell'Opera] venir ritirate tutte le Donne di mala vita, e così tanto le pubblicamente, che privatamente prostituite, e pertinaci nella loro disonestà, di qualunque città, luogo, e condizione siano esse, purchè native, o abitanti ne' stati di S.M.').[64] Places in the shelter are in fact to be accorded by preference to the youngest, most comely and attractive, to those of best family, especially if from Turin itself, and to those living most scandalously. And there is one more stipulation of preference: places go to those best able to pay, either all or part of their board and lodgings. So although the women might be 'forced' into this establishment, one of the deciding factors inclining the authorities to take them in would have been their ability to be less of a financial burden than others!

With regard to the more 'Particular Rules' of the establishment, we find that 'the women shut up in this workhouse are to be equally treated, in food and drink as in all the rest, without any distinction, even in respect of those who pay for their keep.' ('Le Donne racchiuse in quest'Opera saranno tutte egualmente trattate, tanto nel mangiare, e bere, che in tutto il rimanente, senza veruna distinzione, anche rispetto a quelle, le quali pagheranno qualche pensione.') To regain their freedom and be released from the hard work and dreadful surveillance of this correctional establishment, these young Magdalens had to display a total change in attitude by the reckoning of the authorities who oversaw them. Normally, however, a woman would not transfer from this facility back into society, but rather into a vacant place in an only slightly less severe institution, that of the Opera of the Converted. ('Quando poi alcuna di de[tte] Donne dasse segni d'una vera, e stabile converzione, in tal caso ... si potrà la med[esim]a trasferire, sendovi posto vacante all'Opera delle Convertite.')[66]

Just how degrading the situation back at the Refuge for Forced Women could be is indicated by another of the particular rules, which stipulated, 'She amongst the women who does the reading at table must be given in addition a slice of cheese, such that by this means all the others will be encouraged to learn to read.' ('A quella poi delle Donne, che farà la lettura durante la tavola, se le dovrà anco dare una fetta di formaggio, per andarle, con questo mezzo, tutte invitando ad abilitarsi alla lettura.')[67] The work that the women were often assigned was the spinning of linen. Additional rigorous rules were set for their conduct in chapel, in confession, in the *parlatorio* (parlour for visitors), and at their work.

In particular, the Mother of the establishment, who had to be a 'virtuous widow' and one whose whole attention was to 'bringing back to God the women shut up in this House,' was to see that no theft of the raw materials distributed for spinning occurred: 'She will weigh the said [linen for spinning], and then the thread that comes back to her, to know that the work has been done without deceit.' ('Peserà prima il medesimo [lino da filare], e poscia il filo che le verrà consegnato, per riconoscere se il lavoro si sarà fatto senza frode.')[68]

The worst note of all, as far as surveillance and punishment of these women is concerned, is struck in the matter of their spiritual devotions in chapel. The rules stipulate that 'they must all comport themselves in chapel with devotion, in rigorous silence, on their knees, or in other sedate posture in the case of someone being unable to remain permanently on her knees, under pain otherwise of rigorous punishment.' ('Dovranno pur tutte star in Capella con divozione, e con rigoroso silenzio, in ginocchio, ò in altra composta positura, quallor alcuna non potesse star sempre in ginocchio, sotto pena in caso contrario, di rigoroso castigo.')[69]

Such an institution clearly acted as a deterrent to the illicit sexual conduct in the city by monitoring public behaviour of members of the female sex, and by incarcerating 'by force' those who were deemed 'scandalous.' There was also a Hospital for the Insane (*Ospedale dei pazzerelli*). Very interestingly, too, once Jesuits had been banished early in the reign of Vittorio Amedeo III, it was their chapel that in 1785, some ten years after their expulsion, was taken over by the *Ritiro degli Oziosi, e dei Vagabondi* – that is, the retreat 'for the lazy and for vagabonds.' Such taking of control over the secular existences of specific categories of people in the very location where, before the ban on them, Jesuits had sought dominion over mind and body through religious exercises, is perhaps indicative of trends towards greater dominion over private existence on the part of the state. An earlier institution in the 1770s normally goes by the name of House of Correction on balance sheets and accounts. The overall philosophy of correction is laid down most clearly in a document of 9 April 1789; that is to say, very late in the period, and in the face of clamour in different parts of Europe for an entire overhaul of aspects of the ancien régime itself. The text in question is a memo of Senator Ghiliossi, 'on the matter of Arts and Trades to be ... exercised in the projected Houses of Correction that are to be set up in the City of Turin' ('circo quelle Arti, e Mestieri che poteano essere ... esercitati nelle Case di Correzione che erano per stabilirsi nella Città di Torino'):

> The public Workhouses must be places in which are taught arts and trades that unite in bringing advantage to the *Opera* and to the public, and that can be exercised by the detained even after their regaining of liberty. Women of bad morals, idlers, wilful vagabonds, those who have been subject to Inquisition, and all those condemned for certain specified crimes, shall be shut away in these houses ... The prime moving law over the detained is to shake them from their former life. Fear of punishment and the certainty of some

advantage [to them] are two invincible means of extracting profit from those who, upon their first entering the houses of correction, will become accustomed to harsh conditions, sobriety, obedience, patience, vigilance, and to methodical and periodic toil.

Le pubbliche Case devono essere ritiri, nei quali si insegnino arti, e mestieri, che uniscano in se il vantaggio dell'Opera, e del pubblico, e possano esercitarsi dai Trattenuti anche dopo il riacquisto della propria libertà. Le Donne di mala vita, i poltroni, e i vagabondi volontari, gli Inquisiti, e i condannati per certi generi di delitti, sono quelli, che saranno per essere rinchiusi in esse case ... La prima legge motrice di questi Trattenuti è di scuoterli dalla loro precedente vita: Il timore della pena e la sicurezza di un qualche vantaggio sono due invincibili mezzi per trarre profitto da' medesimi, i quali al loro primo ingresso nelle case di correzione veranno avezzati alla durezza, alla sobrietà, alla obbedienza, alla pazienza, alla vigilanza, ed alla fatica metódica, e periodica.[70]

Altogether the categorizing of marginal, socially obstreperous, and generally demonized persons of the city and incarcerating them in institutions according to the term with which they were being branded ('scandalose,' 'oziosi,' 'vagabondi,' etc.) was a powerful means of policing the habits and private lives of the resident population. As Alfieri well saw and subsequently defined, this was not a society in which to step out of line or live by 'alternative' values as a free spirit – not even as a dedicated man of letters. The city's relatively small size meant that one could not go unnoticed.

It was indeed a society where a certain Enlightenment form of systematicity – most evident in the nascent science of statistics – prevailed. Already by the 1750s, 'peace allowed for a major focus on internal realities, as is shown by concentration in the capital on statistical data furnished by the intendants, on demand of the exchequer, allowing for an extremely precise measure not only of taxation, but also of political economy in sectors such as agriculture and industry.'[71] Franco Valsecchi gives us an exact account of how, beginning already with a provision of 1742, instituting an annual census and tally of produce, including indications of which lands had been cultivated and which remained uncultivated, the kingdom became one where statistics were used with impressive degrees of precision and success. Over a relatively short period, fiscal accounting became such in Turin that, by the reign of Vittorio Amedeo III, it was organized within a chamber of accounts, under the office of a controller general. This was, in short, 'the first state in Europe to use regular and itemized balance sheets, based on accounting with certain fixed norms' ('il primo Stato, in Europa, a dar l'esempio di un bilancio regolare e particolareggiato, di una contabilità con norme certe e fisse').[72]

Such a use of statistical science in the realm of political economy, however much it may have been wished for by Genovesi and other social thinkers who followed him, was an unrealizable dream in the far more chaotic and complex conditions of poverty that prevailed in the Kingdom of Naples, which also suffered from disastrous imbalances between its urban and its rural economies. And yet, for all that, Genovesi's chair at the University of Naples was the first such in the named discipline of political economy and commerce.[73] What we can say is, that in this matter Turin was already beginning to *practice* a 'science' of economic control for political ends that Neapolitan thinkers were only able to *conceptualize*, and never put into action with full or lasting success.

Naples is 'a place,' according to Sontag, 'that for sheer volume of curiosities – historical, natural, social – could hardly be surpassed.' The main institution of care and correction in *that* city, already substantially built (like the even earlier San Carlo opera house) in the realm of the first Bourbon monarch of the Regno di Napoli, Charles III, was the huge – even this word hardly suffices – *Albergo dei Poveri*, or Hotel of the Poor. Over its three-door entrance was the Latin inscription, *REGIUM TOTIUS REGNI PAUPERUM HOSPITIUM*, indicating its grand function as a poorhouse for the peninsular part of the entire kingdom, not just for the city of Naples.

This 'Hotel of the Poor' was begun in 1751, and although it was soon put to use, construction was not finally completed until the 1820s. Designed by Ferdinando Fuga, a Florentine architect who had served the Pope in Rome, it was to cover an area greater than any other edifice in the south of the Italian peninsula. Though certainly built with laudable reformist intentions, the initial construction costs came to 900,000 ducats, while in the same period 6,133,808 ducats were spent on the Royal Palace under construction at Caserta by Fuga's rival, Luigi Vanvitelli.[74] Clearly, this is some indication that even the urgency of housing under one roof all the poor of the kingdom was not in the same league of importance as housing the royal family in a fabulous new residence.

Designed to be more than 600 metres long and over 150 metres wide, the hospice was to include five courtyards, but two were never built. Its three in-line courtyards, nonetheless, make for a building more than a third of a kilometre in length. Fuga's harmonious but austere classicism is well on its way to achieving an ideal of Enlightenment functionalism. It is, indeed, those very functions that it is to serve that are so interesting – and almost frightening in the degree of regimentation of minds and bodies that they were to put into effect. Upon entrance to the institution there are baths in the area of the first courtyard, for cleaning of newly arrived paupers and their clothes. But it is what is then to occur by way of architected segregation that is truly stupefying. Fuga designed chambers to separate men into the left side of the building and women into the right. But in each case a further segregation is effectuated, of mature males from boys, and of women from girls. As a result, there were four groups of inmates, held by a 'bulkhead' system of architectonics, which prevented the groups from coming into contact with each other. Each of the four categories of the poor were to have separate dormitories on the first or second floors, with access to the ground floor of the edifice by means of individual staircases. Courtyards were separated from any of the other three categories, as were refectories, workshops, and even the naves in the centralized chapel of the building. The patrons, who were behind grill-screens in the chapel, were cut off from the public worshippers and from the other three groupings of the poor, and they were only able to catch glimpses of persons in the other categories.[76] What is surprising is that in the institution that is the main forerunner of the *Albergo dei Poveri*, the system of segregation, although strict, had one important category of paupers that was suppressed in the plans for the new building. The large San Gennaro Outside the Walls, a church erected in 788, modified as a Benedictine convent in 1476, then enlarged and destined to accommodate paupers in the 1650s and 1660s onwards, had five categories of indigents; men, boys, women, girls, and, significantly, married couples.[77] Allowing marital partners to live together seems a kindlier measure than the stricter separations of the later institution.

Naples, it should be stressed, had insurmountable problems of poverty to overcome. The poor and, at the extremes, the enormous numbers of *lazzaroni* were everywhere in this southern capital and throughout the kingdom. Furthermore, the city was not and could never become, for any amount of reformist wishful thinking, 'rationally' structured in the manner of Turin, which had largely been built over the space of only two centuries, on flat terrain and in accordance with a grid plan. Rather, Naples was an unparalleled example, as Paolo Giordano has put it, of 'an urban anthology, or city of the heterotopic fragment, of the multiple analogy, characterized by the co-presence of many superimposed urbanistic and architectonic models, interwoven and interactive, both in terms of one another, but also in relation to the complex geophysical nature of the site.' ('Napoli è un'antologia urbana, ovvero la città del frammento eterotopico, dell'analogia multipla, caratterizzata cioè dalla comprenza di più modelli urbanistici ed architettonici sovrapposti, intrecciati e coagenti tra di loro, tra questi e la complessa natura geo-orografica del sito di appartenenza.')[78]

And yet in a burst of reformist zeal, Carlo di Borbone had Ferdinando Fuga build in Naples an *Albergo dei Poveri* which was intended to be, if anything, even more severely constraining in principles of surveillance and control than any of the Enlightenment rationalism we have encountered in Turin. In conception the building had disturbing levels of segregation, as well as an intention not merely to house the poor, but also to teach them skills and make them productive. In the process, it would order and control their eating, their exercise, and their religious observance. Such principles are, indeed, the very essence of the key design features of this 'mastodontic' building, to use an adjective more common in Italian. My question is, Why? At the same time as the Bourbon monarchs of this state are having built at Caserta their challenge to the French royal achievement of Versailles, why erect this huge hospice for the poor?

Keeping men apart from women betrays, on the surface, an intention to control their morals. As such, this was an architectural edifice for mass purification, 'perfected from the functional point of view and unprecedented typologically' ('perfetta dal punto di vista funzionale e inedita dal punto di vista tipologico'),[79] as Giordano has affirmed, even though it is also true that most public institutions such as hospitals and schools would have had considerable, if not total, segregation by gender in this period. Such moral intentions of purification signify something at once deeper and also more pragmatic than purity itself. The distaste for 'overbreeding' in classes, races, or people different from one's own is a well known and all too common prejudice. I cannot avoid the hypothesis that there is a 'political unconscious' on the part of the authorities in their commissioning from Fuga such a well-designed separation of sexes. It would seem nothing less than a desire to inhibit reproductivity in the pauper classes housed therein. If the hypothesis is correct, the distaste in this instance is clearly one of class, and determines in the very architectonics of this building a stark absence of any possibility of family life within the institution. The uninspected implication (also perhaps unconscious) on the part of the governing authorities – the king and his chief minister Tanucci – is that the problem is the poor themselves, more than their *condition* of poverty. Or at the very least, it is in the sheer scale of their numbers that the problem lies, and any measure that will curb such numbers is already a relief.

Actually a similar distinction, between poverty as a condition and the poor as its victims, is used critically in the analysis of the architect of the building by his first biographer Francesco Milizia. Milizia is interesting because he remarks on the authorities' failure to see the difference between poverty and the poor. In an expanded edition of Milizia's *Memorials of Architects Ancient and Modern* of 1786, in the section on Fuga, he very acutely asks a rhetorical question about the cost of the grand endeavour in relation to its perceived failure to cope with the problem it sought to staunch: 'Who knows when it will be finished? The building has been under construction for almost thirty years. With less expense and in a shorter space of time all poverty might have been eradicated from the richly plentiful Kingdom of Naples. It is a constant experience that hospices such as these do not make the poor disappear. But this is not a consideration for the architect; rather it pertains to Good Government.' ('Chi sa quando si finirà; e sono quasi trent'anni, che si lavora a quest'opera. Con minore spesa, e in più breve tempo si sarebbe tolta per sempre ogni povertà dall'abbondantissimo regno di Napoli. È una sperienza costante, che per questi ospizi non si tolgono i poveri. Ma questo non è affare dell'architetto, ma del buon Governo.') The thinking here is quite subtle. Milizia's clause, which includes the verb 'disappear' in Italian – 'per questi ospizi non si tolgono i poveri' – more literally translates as 'by means of these hospices one doesn't take away the poor.' An expanded subtext to this remark might run roughly as follows: Yes, you can take on these elaborate projects. (Milizia has just denominated this one a 'great Reclusorium, the vastest Hospice in Europe,' 'il gran Reculsorio, il più vasto degli Ospizi che sieno in Europa.') You can even subdivide the eight thousand persons it was planned for (a number never reached) into your 'four categories, that is men, women, boys and girls, with no communication between them' ('quattro ceti, cioè di uomini, di donne, di ragazzi, e di ragazze, senza alcuna communicazione tra loro'). Any yet, even though by such means you do stop them from multiplying and keep *these* poor from the streets, others will replace them in those same streets because it is the social conditions which reproduce poverty, not merely the already poor. As we have seen, Milizia was well persuaded that quite other methods in the amelioration of social conditions for the poor were possible in this 'abbondantissimo regno di Napoli' (cf. 'the wealthiest as well as the most populous city on the Italian peninsula' – Sontag). 'Good government' in the kingdom should be seeing to it that such wiser and also (by his reckoning) less expensive expedients were followed.[80]

Just as the numbers of the poor were proving irreducibly high, so the kingdom's levels of productivity in most manufacturing remained perennially low. An analogy from the production of agricultural manure is used to explain the function that the *Albergo dei Poveri* would assume in instilling useful trades in its inmates. 'There was a wish to transform the refuse that was encumbering Naples, just as filth sticking to the feet, once gathered up and over time macerated and trodden becomes finest manure for the fields and ... nourishment of the soil' ('Voleasi fare del pattume che allora ingombrava Napoli come delle immondezze, le quali lordano i piedi, ma over sian poi raccolte e col tempo fatte macere e trite riesconto ottimo ingrasso pe' campi e ... succhio per la terra').[81] The training in trades afforded in this enormous hospice would thus be an attempt to winch up manufacturing levels by turning members of what is perceived to be an otherwise non-productive 'refuse' class into models of satisfactorily apprenticed productivity, that is to say finest manure ('ottimo ingrasso'). This motive of boosting productivity in such poorhouses and houses of correction was common across Europe, even if not expressed elsewhere in such pejorative and depersonalizing terms. My point here is not solely about Naples. There is even evidence, for instance, that while this Neapolitan *Albergo dei Poveri* was in a phase of projection, Turin was being studied for inspiration. A record suggests that Fuga was told 'for the planning of the building to have an eye to the hospice in Turin' ('Per la disposizione della fabbrica si gli dicea aver occhio all'ospedale di Torino').[82] The latter city's successes in artisanal training of the poor within similar institutions were noted as a precedent for Naples by no less a figure than the pioneer of a new and 'enlightened,' Italian-wide historicism, Ludovico Antonio Muratori, as early as 1749.[83]

Perhaps the most disturbing aspect of symbolic representation in the architectural program of Fuga is the way it sought to enhance the reputation of its royal founders as enlightened rulers. On pedestals in niches alongside the central portal entry to the grand edifice, the architect planned to have marble statues of Carlo, on the left, and of his queen, Amalia of Saxony, on the right. All too obviously, as Giordano clinches the point, 'the two statues indicate to the respective genders, male and female, the two different lateral entrances by which they were to reach the areas assigned to them.' ('Entrambe le statue indicano ai rispettivi sessi, maschi e femmine, i due diversi ingressi laterali per raggiunger i reparti loro assegnati.')[84] The statues never filled such niches. Twelve ducats were paid, however, to Nicola Fornaro in 1762 for gilded frames for portraits of the king and queen by Salvator Rosa.[85]

What are we to make of such intended symbolism? Plainly, the founding royal couple were keen to denote their role in the 'enlightened' social charity dispensed, even though it included disquieting levels of force and exploitation of the underclass it thus institutionalized. We must remember that the *Albergo dei Poveri* was directly facing onto an approach road into Naples from the northeast. This approach connected with the Via Appia from Rome, and relatively early in the construction of the edifice, in 1766, was newly made into a main carriageway, as the Duke of Noja's posthumous *Topographical Map of the City of Naples and of its Surroundings* (1775) clearly indicates. Fuga's project was therefore the first major building one would encounter in coming down into Naples by the main land route from the north. Stendhal well describes the descent in 1826: 'Grandiose entry: one descends for an hour towards the walls by means of a road carved out of the soft rock on which the city is built. Solid walls. The first building to come into view is the Hotel of the Poor, more striking by far than that much vaunted chocolate box in Rome that they call the People's Gateway' ('Entrée grandiose: on descend une heure vers la mer par une large route creusée dans le roc tendre sur lequel la ville est bâtie. Solidité des murs. *Albergo de' Poveri*, premier edifice. Cela est bien autrement frappant que cette bonbonnière si vantée, qu'on appelle à Rome la Porte du Peuple').[86] And as we have noted, it was intended that the arriving visitor see not just the enormous building, but also upon approaching nearer, the statued forms of the royal couple responsible for it. Nevertheless, the chances of seeing this pair in the flesh were now diminished because of their having a more splendid residence than ever at Caserta.

It is not an exaggeration on a symbolic level to say that the intention was for the royal couple to be in two places at once. In statuary form, they were to stand before their royal hospice, as its benefactors, its moral guardians, and as exemplary figures on separate sides of the public entrance, indicating (if only subliminally) the 'enlightened' segregation of the institution. But all the while, in their actual social and court selves, they were leading quite another life.

Rounding up the kingdom's paupers, insofar as possible, and accommodating them in this gigantic 'Hotel,' with its multiple gender and age segregations,[87] was the king's and his ministers' best solution for coping with poverty. What, by contrast, did Neapolitan historical and economic thinkers, from Genovesi to Palmieri and beyond, have to say about fundamental problems of state? To summarize their many and complex theories would take at the very least a long chapter in its own right. What is more, this intricate scholarship has been already conducted by Franco Venturi in a way that will not soon be surpassed. Nonetheless, some revealing examples are useful.

In general, it is crucial to establish to what extent the Neapolitan economic thinkers looked to England (more than to Spain and France) for an example of a seafaring nation that had successfully adopted a relatively free-market, post-feudal mercantilism.[88] Antonio Genovesi himself, in his 'Discourse on Commerce,' which serves as an introductory essay to a 1757 Italian translation of John Cary's *History of Trade of Great Britain*, opens his address to the reader with an important general statement about the English model. For Genovesi it is not a mere matter of chance or of the times, nor the character of the English, and not even the location of that island nation or its climate that are the main contributing factors to its economic successes. Rather it is the 'singular art and diligence deployed there in promoting the foundations of commerce and trade.' The entire cast of Neapolitan economic thought in the years that follow practices, as Genovesi does here, a kind of cultural comparativism.

On the one hand, for Neapolitan Enlightenment thinkers, there is the scale of their own problem, which they do not tend to underestimate. Theirs is a weak and poor home nation with a sluggish economy mired in endemic feudalism in both its agricultural and its commercial practices. On the other hand, there are more modern, inherently post-feudal, commercial and trade practices that might be followed – certain rules to be known and a skill to be adopted ('quelle regole conosciute e quell'arte adoperata') – along such lines as the successes of Britain in recent decades.[89] (A much smaller Italian state such as Piedmont did not figure in such comparisons between nations that emerged from Neapolitan economic thinkers of the period.)

Also – and in this the Neapolitans closely resemble certain Scottish thinkers – 'backwardness' in the home nation tends to be likened to that of exotic peoples, supposedly at earlier stages in what is today called (especially in writings on the Scottish Enlightenment) a 'stadial theory' of human development.[90] Therefore, we have the famous likening of primitivism and poverty in the Neapolitan kingdom to that of Hottentots.[91]

Highlanders and islanders in Scotland (especially after the defeat of Jacobites at Culloden) were said by some Scottish Enlightenment thinkers to resemble, precisely, 'native' peoples of relatively newly discovered or conquered cultures. Later in the century, Giuseppe Palmieri would say in reference to the peoples of the Neapolitan Kingdom, 'may the foreigners at least stop short of treating us like Indians' ('si contentino gli stranieri di non trattarci come gl'Indiani').[92] The remark reveals his larger concern that the Neapolitan kingdom was falling steadily in thrall economically to stronger nations to its north and west, much as other, farther-flung parts of the New World had been (and went on being) colonized by those same European superpowers. The fear is not just one of colonial domination by others, but of conditions of 'backwardness' in the home nation that may seem to invite such domination in the first place. For Palmieri seems already to have known a piece of up-to-date 'colonial discourse theory': namely, that the imputation of backwardness in another nation becomes the best alibi – that of a *civilizing mission* – on the part of its potential conquerors.

Francesco Mario Pagano interprets the Calabrian earthquake of 1783 symbolically as a catastrophe revealing something more deeply amiss in society itself.[93] Interestingly, for the considerations of the present chapter, the earthquake for him is a kind of climacteric of a long feudal period. For all the destruction unleashed on Calabria on 5 February 1783 ('day of sadness ... of mourning and bitterness,' 'giorno di tristezza ... di lutto e di amarezza,')[94] he wants to see it as a leveller and destroyer of feudal hierarchies from which the poor of the kingdom have too long suffered. Feeling themselves now on a par with the rich and powerful, and with a look and tone of voice as if 'relieved of an oppressive weight' ('sgravato di un opprimente peso'), 'the peasants and poor of Calabria ... broke out into a feeling of joy,' which in turn gave way to shouts that, with our benefit of hindsight, we would interpret as nothing short of revolutionary: 'We are now equal and level, nobles and plebeians, rich and poor' ('i villani e i poveri delle Calabrie ... proruppero in un sentimento di gioa, cominciarono a gridare: "Ed eccoci omai tutti uguali e pari, nobili e plebei, ricchi e poveri"').[95]

Pagano's way of theorizing all this is to suggest, in the spirit of Vico writing on the different ages of human history, that just as after the age of floods and catastrophes came the Age of Saturn, with its hallmarks of equality, friendship, and liberty, so after any great time of natural disaster, such as this Calabrian one, political inequality founders *along with* the destruction of societies and the annulment of civil intercourse. The consequence is that humans can then be compared with one another simply because they belong to the same species and no longer in terms of rank.

But Pagano sees more than just a revolutionary levelling of society down to primary conditions of equality. ('Always extremes meet and touch,' 'Gli estremi son vicini e si toccano ognora.')[96] In his depiction of the unrestrained happiness and often dissolute licentiousness that followed the disaster, he mixes reference to both the Old World of classical Mediterranean myth, and the New World of Pacific Island promise. Most poignantly, a sense of hopelessness and loss also imbues the descriptions of merrymaking: 'After the quakes, Calabria seems converted into the Isle of Cyprus or of Tahiti. Venus seems to have transferred her palace and throne there. Licence, pleasure and dissoluteness prevail in cottages where those left destitute after the shocks are treated, and in the countryside where the poorest of people wander dispersed.' ('Dopo i tremuoti le Calabrie sembrano convertite nell'Isola di Cipro o de' Taiti. Venere ivi par che abbia trasferita la sua reggia e il trono. La licenza, il piacere, la dissolutezza scorre per le capanne, ove si sono ricoverati que' miseri avanzi de' tremuoti, e per le campagne ove la più bassa gente erra dispersa.')[97]

Pagano sees a causal connection between natural disaster and the origin of fables, indeed, the entire realm of mythopoeia. At the level of ideas this clearly owes much to Vico, of whom he is constantly aware in his writings that touch on the philosophy of history. However, at the level of reality – that is to say, of what he has himself borne witness to in 1783 – the particularities of the Calabrian tragedy are detailed by him in the additional spirit of a local historian, quite unlike any writings by his predecessor: 'that stunned condition [taken together with] the damage suffered by the organ of thought, that confusion and darkening of ideas, [together constitute] an ample source of fables, as is here demonstrated' ('quello sbalordimento, quell'offesa dell'organo di pensare, quella confusione ed oscurità dell'idee, ampio fonte di favole, secondoché si è ivi dimostrato').[98]

Pagano's *Saggi politici* are subtitled *Civil Progress of Nations, or Principles, Progress and Decadence of Societies.*[99] We do indeed recognize in the terms of that subtitle more than faint echoes of Vico. Like many other eighteenth-century Neapolitan political or historical writers, Pagano looks back to Vico as a great philosophical forebear. In line with my own contention that Vico did not go far down the road he was pointing to, of close historical focus on different nations, but instead stayed in the more idealist position of the one who points, Pagano suggests that Vico established a philosophical basis for exact histories of nations, but that he did not really engage such empirical study in his own practice. Pagano's way of putting this case about Vico is as follows:

> Before going further it behoves us to pay due praise to our fellow citizen, Giambattista Vico. This gentleman, who honoured his country every bit as much as, by contrast, it was ungrateful and failed to recognise such great merit, was the first to tread the new and unexplored pathway of extracting philosophy from history. Thucidides, Tacitus and Machiavelli had all written before him in a philosophizing spirit: but none had formulated a philosophy of history. However, Vico showed us more how we ought to proceed than he thus proceeded himself. He tried out rather than achieved. His *Scienza nuova* is a light obfuscated by dense clouds, his thoughts lightning flashes in the murky horror of foggy night.

> Or senza andar più oltre, qui è dovere di render la dovuta lode ad un nostro concittadino, Giambattista Vico. Questo valentuomo, che onorò tanto la sua patria, quanto ella fu ingrata e sconoscente a si gran merito, il primo a tentare si fu tal nuovo e sconosciuto sentiero di ridurre a filosofia la storia. Tucidide, Tacito, Macchiavelli l'aveano prima di lui filosofando scritta: ma niuno avea della storia formata una filosofia. Vico però ci ha mostrato più ciò che si debba fare, che non ha fatto. Ha più tentato ch'eseguito. La sua Scienza nuova è una luce offuscata di dense nubi. I suoi pensieri son lampi nel fosco orrore di caliginosa notte.[100]

Pagano sees Vico as achieving a grand philosophical schema but, in the main, stopping short of demonstrating its usefulness in the mapping of particular national histories. Pagano's own essays, while continuously indebted to Vico's 'idealism' – with titles like 'Poetry is a genre of history, or rather a universal history,' or 'Unfolding of the human spirit, and origin of religion' – gradually turn towards a more empirical social and political history of Europe, with an eventual focus on Naples. He outlines the various periods of Longobard, Norman, Angiovine, Swabian, and Aragonese rule, spicing his accounts with negative generalizations: 'How could government be strong, when its forces were so precarious, depending as they did on the arbitrariness of feudatories?' ('Come poteva essere potente il governo, quando erano precarie le sue forze, quando esse dall'arbitrio de' feudatari dipendevano?') Or he points out the endemic sluggishness of past economic systems: 'Such is a portrait of a kingdom where trades, agriculture, and commerce have languished.' ('Ecco il ritratto di un regno, ove le arti, l'agricoltura e il commercio languivano affatto.')[101]

Pagano's final chapter of the *Saggi politici* pulls back, however, from the abyss of negativism, and becomes a panegyric of enlightened Bourbon rule of his own times under Charles III and Ferdinand IV. Of the latter he says as part of a fine peroration:

> This immortal prince, supported by his august and wise consort, is now entirely intent on destroying the formless edifice that is the work of barbarous times, founded on error, prejudice, and ignorance. His great aims are directed at the reform of legislation, finances, and the protection of trades and commerce. In this age we once again lay claim to arts and sciences in which we once led Europe.

> Cotesto immortale principe secondato dall'augusta e saggia consorte è tutto ormai intento a distruggere quell'informe edifizio, opra de' barbari tempi, sugli errori, pregiudizi e sull'ignoranza fondato. Le sue grandi mire sono dirette alla riforma della legislazione, delle finanze, alla protezione delle arti e del commercio. Le scienze, e le arti, delle quali noi fummo all'Europa maestri, in questo secolo si rivendicano da noi.[102]

What Pagano has seen, in his attempt to name (still following Vico) and outline the new science of the philosophy of history, is the delivery of the Neapolitan state under the rule of Ferdinand and Caroline to a great age of enlightened reforms. According to this last panegyric, if not everything necessary has been accomplished, at least the 'great aims' of the right course have been set. This was a public text in 1783, and perhaps Pagano could not pursue critical remarks on the Kingdom of Naples to the point of including the current Bourbon ruler and his parental predecessor in his assessment of barbarous and feudal practices. He does not, for instance, point again to the devastation left by the Calabrian earthquake as something the King of Naples and his consort would have to do their utmost to ameliorate. His peroration to these long *Saggi*, in other words, fails to connect back to the urgent topicality of their opening, hundreds of pages earlier. Like Vico before him, Pagano had to make his personal way within hierarchies of power, at the apex of which particular rulers were to go on reigning supreme for quite some while longer.

It comes as something of a surprise, therefore, to find two years before this, in 1781, a thinker altogether more radical and scathing in his criticism of the age in question. Admittedly, the ideas of Gaetano Filangieri, with which I shall now conclude the present chapter, come from a private letter that was not published until 1962. But its stand against feudal practices that the mild reforms of these first two Bourbon monarchs, Charles and Ferdinand, had in no fundamental ways even begun to remove – and which would not finally be legislatively abolished until the later period of French rule – is unflinching and trenchant. It is a stand all the more interesting for being one directed, first and foremost, against *all* great capitals that feudally repress the provinces which feed and sustain them, and only secondarily against Naples in particular.

> I have always looked with horror on great capitals. Goaded on by their princes, these monstrous *colossi*, which oppress by their weight the miserable provinces of their states, are the prop of despotism and the intimate cause of the evils that oppress nations. The five hundred thousand inhabitants who share in the pleasures and vices of my native city are the unerring signs of the misery and languor of our provinces. May God see to it that this truth reaches the ears of my king. I have enunciated it with courage in my book, but the spirit of reading is not the spirit of our amiable sovereign ... In this third volume feudalism will be attacked frontally. The persecutions of certain monsters, who call themselves barons, far from frightening me, have hardened my resolve. I shall demonstrate that the rights they hold to are incompatible with private security and civil liberty. The reform of criminal procedure has administered me the opportune occasion to give a last shake to the tottering feudal system ... This undertaking will call down on me the hatred of men of my class, but render me dear to those who think as you do.

> Io ho guardato sempre con orrore le gran capitali. Questi colossi mostruosi, che i principi incensano, e che opprimono col loro peso le misere provincie degli stati, sono il sostegno del despotismo e la causa prossima de' mali che opprimono le nazioni. I 500 mila abitanti, che si dividono i piaceri e i vizi della mia patria, sono i segni infallibili della miseria e del languore delle nostre provincie. Faccia Iddio che questa verità pervenga fino all'orecchia del mio re. Io l'ho enunciata con coraggio nel mio libro, ma lo spirito di lettura non è lo spirito del nostro amabile sovrano ... In questo terzo tomo la feudalità sarà urtata di fronte. Le persecuzioni di alcuni mostri, che si chiamano baroni, in vece di scoraggiarmi, mi hanno inasprito. Io mostrerò che i loro pretesi dritti sono incompatibili colla sicurezza privata e colla

civile libertà. La riforma della criminale procedura mi ha somministrata l'occasione opportuna per dare quest'ultima scossa al vacillante sistema de' feudi ... Questa intrapresa mi richiamerà l'odio degli uomini della mia classe, ma mi renderà caro a coloro che pensano come voi.[103]

Filangieri's letter was sent to a provincial reformist, Domenico Pepe, who was from one of the major families of the town of Mola in the province of Bari. Pepe had preceded with a letter of his own, counselling Filangieri not to be disheartened by the lack of notable response in Naples to his major work, the *Scienza della legislazione*: 'In consequence of the vortex of pleasure and dissipation in capitals and big cities, public evils are not noticed there, or not cured, or they do not suffice to staunch the torrent of distractions. In the country, yes, in the country one feels things ever so much more closely. There it will be read, there admired and prized.' ('I mali pubblici nelle capitali e nelle città grandi per i continui vortici del piacere e della dissipazione o non si sentono o non si curano, o non bastono a frenare il torrente delle distrazzioni. In provincia, in provincia si fanno più da vicino sentire. Colà sarà letta, sarà ammirata, sarà l'opera prezzata.')[104]

By this reckoning, Naples tended to impoverish its hinterland, with inevitable consequences to its own order, well-being, and viability as a capital city. If in this kingdom the city and the country operated by quite different rhythms, and if, indeed, the former was parasitic on the perennially inadequate productivity of the latter, the same vicious circle of economic dependency cannot be said to pertain in the case of the enormously smaller realm of Turin – not, at any rate, to anything like the same degree, over the course of the later decades of the ancien régime that I have been dealing with in this chapter. In the cases of both kingdoms, it took a period of French rule for remnants of absolutism and of feudal agrarian and trade practices to be legislatively abolished (never entirely successfully in the case of the Kingdom of Naples and the Two Sicilies). But the steady gradualism of reforms in Turin, even before it first came under direct French control in 1798, were readying it (with hindsight we can say this) to fulfil the later destiny of a modern state, including in that very notion the ambitious agglomeration of other, less-advanced Italian powers. As the nineteenth century progressed, the political efficiency deriving in large measure from its far smaller and more manageable size made it the natural focus for the Risorgimento movement, with its eventual outcome in Unification.

5 Justice and the Individual, Torture and the State

When one examines the traditions of justice in the theory and, to a more limited extent, practice of Italian law, sometimes the obverse face of injustice becomes the one most on view. The effects of justice or injustice on wider public feeling and perception in Italy must also be taken into account as I seek to define an Italian lineage of writing on this subject since the Enlightenment. In 1964, two important figures in such a tradition were examined by A.P. d'Entrèves in thematic terms that I should like to reassess. D'Entrèves presented outstanding texts by Cesare Beccaria and by his maternal grandson Alessandro Manzoni – *Of Crimes and Punishments* (1764) and *The Column of Infamy* (1842) respectively – to a public that had fairly recently witnessed the injustices of the Second World War in Europe.[1] In doing so, he managed to put elements of Enlightenment and Romantic thinking about great injustices into a larger historical crucible of reckoning that included the more recent Fascist epoch.

But other major texts have enriched the same lineage of Italian thought. In particular I should like to include some reflection on key points of the 1948 Italian Constitution and an analysis of Leonardo Sciascia's fierce investigation of injustice in *Death of the Inquisitor* (1964),[2] which consciously owes much to Manzoni in both method and content. Leonardo Sciascia found *The Column of Infamy* to be so profoundly human that he several times pointed to it as foundational in his own narrative writings on injustice, whether in fiction or non-fiction. In particular, the Manzonian text was highly influential in Sciascia's use of 'investigative' (*racconto inchiesta*) procedures in dealing with historic injustices from times such as those of the Inquisition in Sicily. *Death of the Inquisitor* not only makes mention of the earlier Manzonian text, but also becomes crucially intertextual with it. Sciascia shows a determination to further Manzoni's fervid lines of thinking on justice and injustice.

As anyone used to reading Italian newspapers will have realized, the public's interest in criminal investigation and legal process ranks high in communal consciousness. Luciano Violante has gone so far as to affirm (exaggeratingly, but his point is instructive) that 'connections between public prosecutors of the Republic and the media are woven ever closer: the majority of Italian news is news of court proceedings.' ('Si intrecciano sempre piú strettamente le relazioni tra procure della Republica e mezzi di informazione; la cronaca italiana è in larga maggioranza cronaca giudiziaria').[3] Certainly, Italians are sophisticated readers of newspaper reportage on criminal investigations. They are not, for instance, bamboozled as I was at first by a sentence such as the following (chosen almost at random from coverage of the killing of an eleven-year-old boy, Samuele Lorenzo):

> After the storm of the last few days, the command for presiding attorney Maria Del Savio Bonaudo is Stop the Quarreling! Above all, that which has broken out at a distance between this presiding attorney and the judge of preliminary investigations, Fabrizio Gandini, who signed the cautionary custodial order concerning Anna Maria Franzoni, a step then disapproved of by the review tribunal of Turin

> Dopo la bufera dei giorni scorsi, per il procuratore capo Maria Del Savio Bonaudo la parola d'ordine è stop alle polemiche, soprattutto quella a distanza scoppiata tra il procuratore capo e il giudice per le indagini preliminari Fabrizio Gandini che ha firmato l'ordinanza di custodia cautelare per Anna Maria Franzoni, provvedimento poi sconfessato dal Tribunale del Riesame di Torino.[4]

There is a fundamental difference between an *investigative* legal system, such as that of Italy, and the *trial by jury* system in operation for important cases in Britain and the United States. Looked at from a culture with quite different structures and traditions of legal process from those of Italy, such a newspaper remark will at first seem opaque. What is at issue in the quotation is a highly sophisticated layering of dealings between preliminary investigation by an individual judge, a presiding attorney, and, separate from either of these, a review tribunal. The last has to be convinced that a criminal enquiry may proceed to a next stage, but the judge and attorney may be locked in ongoing contention, as these seem to have been, even as the tribunal attends to its role of review. All three bodies are normally at different geographical locations in the nation to prevent collusion. Furthermore, they are usually not based close to the scene of the crime itself, a dispersal thought to minimize pressure from members of the public involved in the case, or close to those who might be. What is referred to here as a 'storm' of polemics over the particular judicial investigation is all exciting grist to a genre in Italian journalism based on criminal proceedings. The reading public is certainly smart enough to follow the intricacies of this genre, or articles wouldn't take the complex forms they do. Legal cases, in other words, are widely reported in the Italian press and on television, sustaining the public's developed taste for, and skills in, examining various real life *gialli* (detective mysteries) in modern Italy. One thing that can be said of such Italian journalistic procedures is that they succeed in keeping issues of justice well to the fore in public consciousness.

Modern journalistic uses of the investigative genre in Italy can rely, it seems to me, on a newspaper or television public that is familiar with intricate legal procedures and technicalities. In this they differ somewhat from Manzoni's scrutiny of a case from the more distant past, or from Sciascia, who was consciously writing in Manzoni's wake about operations of the Spanish Inquisition in Sicily a little later in the seventeenth century. (Like Manzoni before him, Sciascia had to explicate some of the techniques and procedures of the Inquisition for his readership, even while decrying their unjust usage.) My running hypothesis is that it is partly because of such texts as *The Column of Infamy* by Manzoni and *Death of an Inquisitor* by Sciascia that a honing in Italian culture of what constitutes justice has occurred. The point will perhaps carry more conviction if put as a generalization about more than just these two exemplary texts. I would submit that because of a powerful tradition of writings on justice and injustice in Italy, the modern Italian public has an acute awareness of the legal issues at stake in specific cases.

Manzoni's and Sciascia's texts are certainly important works in the tradition. But writings by the likes of Beccaria and Pietro Verri nearer to its inception, or Judge Giovanni Falcone in his modern prosecution of the mafia (in particular his opening statements in maxi-trial documents of incrimination), should not be left out of consideration. These constitute only a few of the writers in a major lineage of Italian thinking about justice, so much of which has fed into modern newspaper or televisual journalism. This is not to claim that journalists and the reading public are keenly aware of such a lineage, or that the earlier works that I shall be dealing with are much known nowadays. Indeed, I intend to demonstrate what has gone into the making of an Italian sensibility about issues of justice and injustice, however scanty may be the awareness displayed by most modern Italians (including even some judges and lawyers) of those positive earlier influences on public legal culture.

Such earlier uses of the *inchiesta* narrative genre by Manzoni and Sciascia and the passionate concern with justice displayed in them have by now been deeply absorbed by Italians and become distinctive features of national character, beyond anything remotely similar in the United Kingdom or the United States. Overall, this is something strikingly positive in Italy, which has to be set in the balance when the finger is being pointed at cases of corruption, injustice, and statist interference in relation to individuals or social groupings of the nation.

The three major texts – from the eighteenth, nineteenth, and twentieth centuries respectively – that I mainly comment upon in this chapter constitute profound critiques of older legal codes. They can help us to see how such codes were practised, and whether they still affect contemporary usages or thinking. The texts are also evidence of individually inflected passion for justice in all three writers. Crucially, they are interlinked. For example, Manzoni makes specific reference to Beccaria's text in his discussion of the evils of torture. Sciascia links his meditations on justice and injustice to Manzoni's text in his attempt to understand the intensity with which the Inquisition in Sicily focuses those issues for him. My point is that we don't need to laboriously make the case for these texts constituting an unbroken tradition of thought, or to trace this lineage by means of a painstaking academicism. Rather, deliberate retrospective linkage is there in the texts themselves.

More in need of consideration, however, is what keeps this tradition of thinking about justice so vibrant in present Italian culture? Although answers to this last question are somewhat beyond the scope of the present study, I shall go on hinting at the urgency of seeking them, if we are to attain to deeper understanding of contemporary Italian preoccupation with justice and injustice. One major text that enshrines a particular and important moment of thought in this tradition, since it follows on some of the worst excesses of the Fascist era (in particular, the infamous race laws of 1938), is the 1948 Constitution of the new Republic.[5] The first great problem that had to be faced in drawing up the Constitution was its relationship with the past, in particular, the recent past. A middle course had to be charted between consigning to the dustbin of history the Fascist legacy and the need to maintain cultural continuity.[6]

Very few cultural lineages can be traced with absolute finality to just one source. But Italian thinking about justice and injustice can be said to have attained perceptible new momentum with the publication and subsequent wide diffusion of a specific text during the Enlightenment. I refer to Cesare Beccaria's meditations on rights and freedoms from cruel punishment in law in his 1764 tract *Dei delitti e delle pene* (*Of Crimes and Punishments*).[7] In presenting his edition of the work in 1965, the greatest Italian historian of Enlightenment culture, Franco Venturi, saw this text as something excitingly new in its day. In identifying its innovations, Venturi generalizes about moments when specific cultural lineages originate because of the advent of some new element. Furthermore, he confesses, with a touch of personal fervour, that 'to seize the moment in which a new element enters a culture and begins to change and transform it is perhaps the most thrilling thing an historian can seek to do' ('Cogliere il momento in cui un elemento nuovo entra a far parte d'una civiltà e comincia a mutarla e trasformarla è forse la cosa piú appassionante che uno storico possa tentar di fare,' p. vii).

It is Venturi's edition of the original Italian text that teaches us most clearly the strength of both positive and negative feelings that Beccaria's work stirred across the face of Europe. For example, as well as being acclaimed and published immediately in many languages, Beccaria's text incurred antagonism from conservative and ecclesiastical circles that interpreted it as a work of social and religious heresy. Almost the first person to react publicly, Ferdinando Facchinei, in Venice early in 1765 (i.e., shortly after the work itself had appeared), was so incensed at this 'Italian Rousseau' that he fulminated against Beccaria as one of the prejudiced 'socialists' of the day. Facchinei is very early with his use of both terms, *socialista* and *socialismo*, in his scathing attack on a work that he saw as undermining traditional Italian states and their ancien régime rulership.[8]

By contrast with that early horrified reaction, A.P. d'Entrèves' implicit case in re-introducing Beccaria's text in English to a postwar public in 1964 was that the treatise had done for the Enlightenment a task again necessary in Italy's period of re-emergence from Fascism. That task had been, in Beccaria's own words from the text, an examining and overturning of 'the cruelty of punishments, and the irregularity of criminal procedure, a part of legislation so fundamental and so neglected' (p. 12) ('la crudeltà delle pene e l'irregolarità delle procedure criminali, parte di legislazione cosí principale e cosí trascurata,' p. 10). D'Entrèves argues that Beccaria was not above recasting the old edifice of Roman law, just as Italians after the war had needed to correct many of the abuses of Fascism. He further claims that 'most of the changes which Beccaria advocated are now law in all civilized countries.' The most important changes, in d'Entrèves' listing of them, are 'the "certainty" of law, the respect of the principle *nulla poena sine lege*, the adoption of clear and simple rules of procedure ... [and] the very notion of punishment as a measure of safety and prevention, not of expiation and revenge' (pp. x–xi). D'Entrèves stresses how works of this calibre bring to bear reformist pressure on a society. Beccaria's treatise would merit reinspection for that reason alone, even if there were not, as there certainly are, other grounds for its examination.

Beccaria's book begins with thinking about how the legal codes of Europe are themselves in large measure regrettable residues of a Roman judiciary lineage, codified under the Emperor Justinian in the *Corpus Iuris*. The corpus of law in question – a 'debris of barbarous times,' ('uno scolo de' secoli i piú barbari') according to Beccaria – arrives in his age with accreted dross of prejudicial commentaries from more recent centuries.

> Certain residues of the laws of a race of conquerors in times long past, compiled by order of an emperor who ruled in Constantinople twelve centuries ago, later intermingled with Lombard usages, and eventually gathered into ill-digested tomes by obscure commentators who spoke only for themselves – such forms the body of traditional opinion which passes for law in the greater part of Europe today. (p. 6)

> Alcuni avanzi di leggi di un antico popolo conquistatore fatte compilare da un principe che dodici secoli fa regnava in Constantinopoli, frammischiate poscia co' riti longobardi, e involte in farraginosi volumi di privati ed oscuri interpreti formano quella tradizione di opinioni che da una gran parte dell'Europa ha tuttavia il nome di leggi. (p. 3)

The clearest modern synopsis of the several centuries of legal residue and accretion in question is offered by Perry Anderson, who states that 'the dense overgrowth of customary law had never completely suppressed the memory and practice of Roman civil law in the peninsula where its tradition was longest, Italy.' He continues:

It was in Bologna that Irnerius, the 'lamp of the law,' had started the systematic study of Justinian's codifications once again, in the early 12th century. The school of Glossators founded by him methodically reconstituted and classified the legacy of the Roman jurists over the next hundred years. They were followed, in the 14th and 15th centuries, by 'Commentators' more concerned with contemporary application of Roman legal norms, than with scholarly analysis of their theoretical principles; and in the process of adapting Roman law to the drastically altered conditions of the time, they both corrupted its pristine form and cleansed it of particularist contents. The very infidelity of their transpositions of Latin jurisprudence paradoxically 'universalized' it, by removing the large portions of Roman civil law that were strictly related to the historical conditions of Antiquity (for example, of course, its comprehensive treatment of slavery).[9]

Anderson reminds us in a footnote that it was Weber who had seen that the medieval modifiers of a code coming to them from Antiquity had given to the revamped lineage what logic it possessed. Weber had seen continuities up to and including the early twentieth century. In a text of 1914 he had stressed that the 'conception of law which still prevails today and which sees in law a logically consistent and gapless complex of "norms" waiting to be "applied" became the decisive conception for legal thought' in the earlier centuries of glossators and commentators.[10]

Already in his text of 1764, Beccaria attempted to criticize that continuous lineage and interrupt its smooth continuance. He promises to examine these legal traditions and their accretions, and in doing so, to produce reasons for reforming them on enlightened principles. According to him, old inheritances from Roman law must be seen as the bad practices they often are. He stresses that he can only 'draw the attention of those charged with public welfare to the confusion of such laws' ('i disordini di quelle [cioè delle leggi] si osa esporli a' direttori della pubblica felicità') because of the wise government under which he himself works. 'The open-minded search for truth, the independence from popular opinion with which this book is written, are results of the gentle and enlightened government under which the author lives' (p. 6). ('Quella ingenua indagazione della verità, quella indipendenza delle opinioni volgari con cui è scritta quest'opera è un effetto del dolce e illuminato governo sotto cui vive l'autore,' p. 3.) In case we are in danger of turning Beccaria into an entirely 'modern' thinker, it needs to be said straight away that throughout the text he praises the kind of enlightened rulership that he saw himself living under in Milan, and that he claims for some other parts of Europe. These were years of reformist Habsburg rule by the empress Maria Theresa and then by Joseph II, co-ruler and emperor from 1765 (the year after first publication of Beccaria's text in a Leghorn edition).[11] As d'Entrèves points out, 'the government in Vienna could count on the loyal and even enthusiastic support of the intellectual élite in Milan, which had among its members such men as Pietro and Alessandro Verri, Gianrinaldo Carli, Paolo Frisi, Cesare Beccaria' (p. ix).

Beccaria is adamant that although 'Divine justice and natural justice are of their essence immutable' ('La giustizia divina e la giustizia naturale sono per essenza loro immutabile e costanti'), 'human justice ... being no more than a relationship between the actions and variations of society, can vary in proportion as those actions become useful or necessary to society' (p. 8) ('la giustizia umana ... non essendo che una relazione fra l'azione e lo stato vario della società, può variare a misura che diventa necessaria o utile alla società quell'azione,' pp. 5–6). This nod in the direction of utilitarianism is important. In his introduction to the postwar English edition, d'Entrèves stresses Beccaria's grounding in the principle 'discovered in Helvétius and in turn handed over to Bentham' – 'the greatest happiness of the greatest number' (p. x) (la massima felicità divisa nel maggior numero, p. 9). Beccaria's implied offer on the opening pages of his text is to 'analyse the complicated and very changeable interconnexions of civic interests' (p. 8) ('analizz[are] i complicati e mutabilisssimi rapporti delle civili combinazioni,' p. 6), at stake in the adjudication of appropriate punishments for specific crimes.

Giuseppe Ricuperati has pointed out that already before Beccaria there had been gathering 'discussion of the legal system in the early eighteenth century both in Italy and the rest of Europe ... [T]he ruling classes and governments were aware of the need to bring order to the chaos of a legal system which on one side was based on Roman law and on the other relied on a confused inheritance of customs and precedents.'[12] Ricuperati also tries to turn away attention from the more traditional areas of critical concern with Beccaria's text, namely its dealings with torture and the death penalty. By contrast, I concentrate my own argument in precisely those traditional areas because they seem to me to hold the crux of Beccaria's philosophy of what it is to be human and, more specifically, an individual in relation to the legal sovereignty of society. But it is important also to acknowledge the other areas where, in Ricuperati's opinion, Beccaria's text broke new ground. 'What stood accused was the social system itself and its profound inequality. The discussion of the nobility, honour, duelling and aristocratic injustice was just one side of the argument. On the other was the strong awareness that crime was born of the unequal distribution of wealth. Poverty which went hand in hand with ignorance was a breeding ground for crime. Therefore it was futile to use the machinery of justice to contain a malaise that went much deeper and was created by the system itself.'[13] Ricuperati is certainly right to remind us here that there is a lot more in this text than its dealings with torture and capital punishment; although I happen to believe that Beccaria remains more concerned with that 'machinery of justice' throughout his text than Ricuperati acknowledges. What is valuable in Ricuperati's de-emphasizing of arguments over torture and capital punishment is the way he thereby reminds us to read between the lines of Beccaria's *entire* text, for its substantial and abiding concerns with all classes of society.

Nonetheless, as Beccaria's relatively brief text unfolds, we note that the most important of its several criticisms of the law as practised throughout much of Europe is indeed his concern with its resort to torture, and furthermore, with codification of procedures of torment allowed to be applied to the accused. We see not just how barbarously cruel he found the continued use of torture, but also how pointless and counterproductive in the service of truth. A cardinal point in his argument, detached from most of the closer reasoning of his case – although itself a point about the need for close reasoning – is that 'Violence confounds and obliterates those minute differences between things which enable us at times to know truth from falsehood' (p. 33). ('Ogni azione violenta confonde e fa sparire le minime differenze degli oggetti per cui si distingue talora il vero dal falso,' p. 42.)

To see how he arrived at that generalization about the confounding effects of violence, we must follow in detail a couple of Beccaria's best arguments. Possibly the most subtle, and therefore persuasive, is his perception of how torture splits its victim's identity in two:

> Requiring a man to be accused and accuser at one and the same time, and requiring pain to be the crucible of truth as if truth could be judged in the nerves and muscles of some poor wretch, reveals only a desire to confound the known relationship of things ... The law which ordains torture is a law which says: 'Man, resist pain; and if nature has created in you an inextinguishable self-love, if she has given you an inalienable right of self-preservation, I now create in you a totally opposite emotion: an heroic hatred of yourself; and I command you to incriminate yourself by telling the truth even while they tear your muscles and dislocate your bones.' (p. 32)

> ... egli è un voler confondere tutt'i rapporti l'esigere che un uomo sia nello stesso tempo accusatore ed accusato, che il dolore divenga il crociuolo della verità, quasi che il criterio di essa risieda nei muscoli e nelle fibre di un miserabile ... La legge che comanda la tortura è una legge che dice: *Uomini, resistete il dolore, e se la natura ha creato in voi uno inestinguibile amor proprio, se vi ha dato un inalienabile diritto alla vostra difesa, io creo in voi un affetto tutto contrario, cioè un eroico odio di voi stessi, e vi comando di accusare voi medesimi, dicendo la verità anche fra gli strappamenti dei muscoli e gli slogamenti delle ossa.* (pp. 38, 43–4)[14]

It is in no way assured that truth will come forth from pain. Admittedly, you can make the accuser accuse himself, by tearing his muscles and dislocating his bones. But the self-accusation you have forced from him by violence can in no way be guaranteed. Because 'an inalienable right of self-preservation' in the victim will have been brought into play by the torture itself. In splitting his identity in two by violence – making him accuser and accused, with both identities in contradictory conjunction in the one body that is being put through terrible duress – you have made the statements he comes out with not the revelations of truth, but the attempted evasions of further pain.

Always implied and sometimes directly stated by Beccaria is a further point, namely, that such logic about the fruitlessness of torture in producing assured truth is automatic in a judge, and that therefore all torture down through human history has been practiced in bad faith by its perpetrators. Indeed, the code that allows for torture and purportedly finesses its permissible usages is itself bad, and, since knowingly so on the part of generations of judges who have used it to justify their cruelties, also *barbarous*. Again and again, Beccaria's text stresses that in their hearts and minds judges have always secretly known the injustice of torture. Therefore, its ancient codification in Justinian, as well as its retention and variation down through long centuries, has been part, not of a system of justice, but of a lineage of *injustice* privately acknowledged in their consciences to be so by centuries of judges.

Or, to take a subtly different line of Beccaria's argument:

> Of two men equally innocent or equally guilty, the one who is robust and physically brave will be acquitted, the one who is feeble and fearful will be condemned, in virtue precisely of this train of reasoning: 'As judge I had to find you guilty of such and such a crime; you, the stronger one, have been able to withstand the pain, so I acquit you; you, the weaker one, have given way to pain, so I condemn you. I feel that the confession wrung from you by

torture has little force, but I shall torture you again if you do not confirm what you have now admitted.' (p. 33)

Di due uomini ugualmente innocenti o ugualmente rei, il robusto ed il coraggioso sarà assoluto, il fiacco ed il timido condannato in vigore di questo esatto raziocinio: *Io giudice dovea trovarvi rei di un tal delitto; tu vigoroso hai saputo resistere al dolore, e però ti assolvo; tu debole vi hai ceduto, e però ti condanno. Sento che la confessione strappatavi fra i tormenti non avrebbe alcuna forza, ma io vi tormenterò di nuovo se non confermerete ciò che avete confessato.* (p. 43)

The latter part of the argument just adduced relates to the common code, which stipulated that a confession wrung from a victim by torture had to be repeated while it was no longer being applied, even though the penalty for not confirming the original confession was resubmission to torture. The process could go on until the second confession had followed the first, although, as Beccaria says, 'Some doctors of law – and some countries – allow the infamous *petitio principii* to be repeated only three times; other countries and authorities leave it to the judge's discretion' (p. 34). ('Alcuni dottori ed alcune nazioni non permettono questa infame petizione di principio che per tre volte; altre nazioni ed altri dottori la lasciano ad arbitrio del giudice,' p. 43.)

Beccaria continually stresses that it is impossible that judges could ever have believed that this was an effective way of reaching the truth. On the contrary, judges feel bound to produce a guilty party, 'as if the law and the bench were interested not in searching out the truth, but merely in discovering a crime' (p. 40) ('quassiché le leggi e il giudice abbiano interesse non di cercare la verità, ma di provare il delitto,' p. 75). Under that pressure, they will wring, by means of torture, confessions that they know are unsound. Beccaria parodies a sequence of illogical steps in the judge's mind, each reason being weaker and more unjust than the previous one: 'the law tortures you, because you are guilty, because you may be guilty, and because I want you to be guilty' (p. 35) ('*le leggi ti tormentano, perché sei reo, perché puoi esser reo, perché voglio che tu sii reo,*' p. 44). In this parody, Beccaria approaches a modern perspective by situating the reason for determining guilt not in the realm of justice and truth, but in the personal imperatives of the accusing judge. For according to Beccaria, proper reasoning on the part of judges would inform them that 'the signs that generally reveal the truth despite a man have all ... been altered by pain and convulsion' (p. 33). ('Le convulsioni del dolore alterano tutti i segni, per i quali dal volto della maggior parte degli uomini traspira qualche volta, loro malgrado, la verità,' p. 42.) Therefore, instead of increasing the real detection rate of crimes, torture is bound to diminish it.

Beccaria is also against capital punishment, with reasons often quite dissimilar to ones adduced nowadays. One of the strongest is that the pains of a cruel life sentence (and he stresses that life means life, and a ghastly one at that) act as a greater disincentive to potential wrongdoers than summary death. What is impressive again, however, is the sheer subtlety of his logic, as though he were performing a kind of canny moral calculus.

> By what right do men take it upon themselves to slaughter other men? Certainly it cannot be that right which gives birth to sovereignty and law; which are nothing but the sum of the smallest portions of each man's personal liberty, representing the public will, which is the aggregate of the individual wills. But who has ever been willing to give other men authority to kill him? How can the least possible sacrifice of each individual's liberty ever involve sacrifice of the greatest good of all, life itself? And were it possible, how would it accord with that other principle, that a man is not master of his own life and death? Which he must be, if he has been able to give that right to others, or to the whole of society. (p. 45)[15]

> Qual può essere il diritto che si attribuiscono gli uomini di trucidare i loro simili? Non certamente quello da cui risulta la sovranità e le leggi. Esse non sono che una somma di minime porzioni della privata libertà di ciascuno; esse rappresentano la volontà generale, che è l'aggregato delle particolari. Chi è mai colui che abbia voluto lasciare ad altri uomini l'arbitrio di ucciderlo? Come mai nel minimo sacrificio della libertà di ciascuno vi può essere quello del massimo tra tutti i beni, la vita? E se ciò fu fatto, come si accorda un tal principio coll'altro, che l'uomo non è padrone di uccidersi, e doveva esserlo se ha potuto dare altrui questo diritto o alla società intera? (p. 62)

These sentences begin with outright doubt about the justice of capital punishment, that is to say, doubt about society's judicial right to kill its own members. The thinking proceeds with a calculation that the 'public will' (la volontà generale), upon which sovereignty is based, is an aggregate of small portions of each individual's personal liberty. Beccaria is adamant that no one wills over to others authority to kill him. There then follows the greatest leap of all, the idea that the portions of liberty sacrificed by all, which in composite form make up the sovereignty of the law, could never be sufficient to justify a further sacrifice of the ultimate good, which is human life itself.

Even supposing that it were possible to will to others the right to put one to death, that would contravene the great interdiction against suicide. Precisely from its being the greatest good of all, life should be inalienable on our parts, either through willed suicide or by execution. D'Entrèves had hinted that 'there is an anticipation of Kant' in Beccaria (p. xiii). I think we find it in that argument about the greatest of all good things being life itself. Interestingly, d'Entrèves' example lay in another pronouncement in the text: 'Liberty vanishes whenever the law, in certain cases, allows a man to cease to be a *person*, and to become a *thing*' (p. 67). ('Non vi è libertà ogni qual volta le leggi permettono che in alcuni eventi l'uomo cessi de esser *persona* e diventi *cosa*,' p. 50.) In both textual instances we sense a premium on human life that is indeed Kantian – a little before the fact.

Beccaria's best piece of argumentation against capital punishment is by his own confession somewhat counter-intuitive. 'That very few societies, and only for a very brief time, have forborne to inflict death, is more favourable than contrary to my case; since it accords with the fate of all great truths, which endure for no longer than a flash, compared with that long dark night in which mankind is enveloped' (p. 51). ('Che alcune poche società, e per poco tempo solamente, si sieno astenute dal dare la morte, ciò mi è piuttosto favorevole che contrario, perché ciò è conforme alla fortuna delle grandi verità, la durata delle quali non è che un lampo, in paragone della lunga e tenebrosa notte che involge gli uomini,' p. 69.) Here we see ignorance as the perduring darkness of an unending night, which is something of a cultural lineage in its own right. Truth, by contrast, never manages to sustain itself as a tradition, or even during the passing of an epoch, however short. It is a mere flash of light in that enduring night of ignorance. This is a strange pronouncement coming from someone who elsewhere in his text proclaimed the times – and most especially 'the government under which the author lives' – enlightened. Possibly, however, a special kind of rhetoric was being adopted in the case of his reasoning against capital punishment. He needed to make his case for dispensing with capital punishment seem to have a positive rarity factor, of truth amidst predominant ignorance. If contrasts of light and darkness could serve to strengthen his argument, he would use them, no matter if they ran counter to other judgments on the times that he had offered. He was, as it were, trying to spell out a *universal* case about the relation of truth to ignorance, even if it should contradict a *particular* case about his own age, and the good government from which he claimed to have benefited. (On my own part, this last sentence may seem a case of devil's advocacy in his favour, since Beccaria would have been the first to claim that truth cannot be split into two ways like that, particularly not if mutually contradictory.)

A sad revelation about Beccaria's own career as a state bureaucrat in Milan thirty years later, towards the end of his life, is that he could not persuade other reformers to adopt by majority a suppression of capital punishment in the revised legal code for Lombardy that they were drafting. If capital punishment had itself been in disuse, although still on the statutes, the case would not have mattered as much as it did. But as Adriano Cavanna's work on the subject has made clear, the years beforehand had witnessed in Austrian-held Lombardy some of the most horrendous public spectacles of capital slaughter imaginable. Cavanna cites from a *Register of Condemned Persons* that recorded death sentences in the State of Milan over three centuries and that specified varieties of cruel supplementary tortures still in use in Austrian Lombardy in the latter part of the eighteenth century. The middle years of the century had frequently seen

> dragging of the condemned to the gallows *ad caudam equi*, red-hot pincers applied *in itinere* to the scaffold, breaking of bones on the wheel, quartering, and the exposing of the severed head in an iron cage 'at the site where the crime had been committed.' Above all, the torture of the wheel, reserved in general for *latrones viarum*, seems used with terrifying frequency: as late as 1785 this instrument was being additionally set ablaze, with all the ferocious innocence of persons passing judgment with rigid respect for the *Novae Constitutiones*.

> In una miriade di sentenze troviamo prescritto, in pieno Settecento, lo strascinamento al patibolo *ad caudam equi*, i colpi di tenaglia rovente inferti al reo *in itinere* verso la forca, lo schiantamento delle ossa sulla ruota, lo squartamento, l'esposizione del capo mozzo nella gabbia di ferro 'al sito del commesso delitto.' Soprattuto il supplizio della ruota, riservato in genere ai *latrones viarum*, appare praticato con frequenza impressionante: l'abbiamo d'altronde visto irrogare, con la feroce innocenza di chi giudicava nel rigido rispetto delle *Novae Constitutiones*, ancora nel 1785.[16]

A comparable passionate concern with truth and justice was evident in Beccaria's maternal grandson, Alessandro Manzoni. *The Column of Infamy*, Manzoni's appendage to *I promessi sposi*, is a burning enquiry into how specific injustices could have been perpetrated in the seventeenth century in the persecution of so-called *untori* – persons who, it was claimed, had smeared plague on walls in Manzoni's own city of Milan. Ever since the definitive form it took in 1840 (subsequently published as an appendage to the final 1842 revision of the novel), *The Column of Infamy* has tended to be presented and read separately from *I promessi sposi*. Scholars and students often study it as a free-standing text, as indeed I am doing here, in spite of Manzoni's express desire that the two texts complement one another.

The investigative genre as developed by Manzoni in *The Column of Infamy* was a historical attempt to comment upon the proceedings of a 1630 legal enquiry into who and what had caused the plague to spread. In effect, Manzoni was playing the entire role of a review tribunal at a much later point in time. (We cannot say his was a 'preliminary' investigation, since he was following, move by move, how legal minds had arbitrated the original case two centuries previously.) Manzoni frequently has to gloss for his readers certain legal procedures of the earlier age, and only then, as a separate analytical stage, note whether the judges had followed the letter of the law in their prosecution of the case. His overall position is that not only are the tortures the authorities resorted to for extracting confessions abhorrent to the sensibilities of his age, but they also did not even apply them according to the strict legal constraints of their own day.

Manzoni notes that the frequency and duration of any tortures used were prescribed in law in the seventeenth century, and that there were also limitations on the status to be accorded the confessions extracted by means of them. Even by these criteria (however dubious as a measure of justice they may appear to a later age), the judges were terribly at fault in their application of the law. In this matter, therefore, Manzoni's argument embodies a sophisticated cultural relativism. It says that it is one thing to *judge these judges* of an earlier age by our standards. But it is another thing entirely to judge them by standards of their own times. Manzoni proceeds to say that *even* by their age's own cruel allowance of specified usages of torture, the seventeenth-century judges grossly erred in their prosecution of the defendants that they were demonizing as *untori*.

Manzoni's intertextual enlistment of Beccaria's text in his cause is an interesting point at which to move into further analysis of *The Column of Infamy*. Manzoni is in the process of explaining what subtleties comprised the allowable usages of torture in the seventeenth century. These were all vain attempts, he says, to reconcile certainty with doubt, to avoid torturing the innocent or extorting false confessions, while yet using torture as an instrument precisely to discover if someone were innocent or not. The way his grandfather's treatise is mentioned is as follows:

> The logical consequence of the underlying intention would have been to say outright that torture was absurd and unjust: but against this stood the barrier of a blind reverence for antiquity and the Roman law. That little book *Dei delitti e delle pene*, which played a notable part not only in the abolition of torture but in the reform of all our criminal legislation, opened with these words: 'Certain residues of the laws of a race of conquerors'; a phrase which at the time seemed (as indeed it was) audacious, the bold stroke of a brilliant mind; but a century earlier it would have seemed ... extravagance. (pp. 134–5)

> La conseguenza logica sarebbe stata di dichiarare assurda e ingiusta la tortura; ma a questo ostava l'ossequio cieco all'antichità e al diritto romano. Quel libriccino *Dei delitti e delle pene*, che promosse, non solo l'abolizion della tortura, ma la riforma di tutta la legislazion criminale, cominciò con le parole: 'Alcuni avanzi di leggi d'un antico popolo conquistatore.' E parve, com'era, ardire d'un grand'ingegno: un secolo prima sarebbe parsa stravaganza.[17]

Manzoni does not mention Beccaria by name, which seems almost a point of family modesty on his part. He is attributing to a relatively short text (a *libriccino*) the consequence of having shaped European opinion, and thereby changing the course of history for the better. But he is also suggesting that there is an appropriate moment for great truths to have their gestation and birth. In an earlier age Beccaria's work, rather than influencing change in legal codes throughout Europe, would have registered as a mere 'extravagance.'

In other words, the history of legalized uses of torture may not have turned out thus positively with their overthrow. It was one of Manzoni's fundamental beliefs that profound change is rare, because people do not have the audacity or brilliance to effectuate it. The last words of *The Column of Infamy* state this point most explicitly: 'It happens quite often; good reasons come to the aid of bad ones, and then the combined effect of both is that a truth which has taken a long while to come to birth has still to remain for a while concealed' (p. 212). ('È avvenuto più volte, che anche le buone ragioni abbian dato aiuto alle cattive, e che, per la forza dell'une e dell'altre, una verità, dopo aver tardato un bel pezzo a nascere, abbia dovuto rimanere per un altro pezzo nascosta,' p. 99.) This, too, seems like a repetition – certainly more than an echo – of the already quoted passage from his grandfather's *libriccino* on the fate of great truths, illumination from which 'lasts as a mere lightning flash, in comparison with the long and dark night which envelops humans.'

Very interestingly, in terms of Sciascia's drawing heavily on the *inchiesta* genre of this shortish piece by Manzoni (and perhaps more heavily still on its morality), *The Column of Infamy* is a work sometimes overlooked when Manzoni's place in Italian, or indeed European, literature is being reviewed. Sciascia himself was to describe it in an essay as 'this small great book ... amongst the least known in Italian literature' ('questo piccolo grande libro ... tra i meno conosciuti della letteratura italiana').[18] First, it established a methodology, pressing to the limits of what could be known from old and mostly neglected archives about remarkable instances of 'ordinary people' standing up to those in power, and eventually paying with their lives rather than abandon their principles. Both Manzoni and Sciascia unravel each musty archival detail of the two seventeenth-century cases they study, analyzing to the full what they can be made to reveal. The patchy evidence of Inquisition procedures that Sciascia pores over – and Manzoni's discoveries in the Milanese archives before him – show much, including in both cases the actual recorded screams of agony and the words exchanged between the accused and their tormentors while tortures were being inflicted. (Spanish authorities in Milan and the Inquisition in Palermo clearly had able scribes to record verbatim much of the grisly verbal and even non-verbal details.)

But in each case, what becomes evident is that there can be no definitive account of the deepest thoughts and the bedrock beliefs of persons engaged in great struggles against the injustices of those in power in earlier centuries. There can only be speculation, from the point of view of the present. Perhaps the greatest service that Manzoni and Sciascia render in their respective works is a demonstration that our grasp on the morality of human justice must be founded on precisely such speculation about the past. Both writers are left in puzzled admiration, unable finally to penetrate the minds of their protagonists during the moments of their ultimate acts of defiance. For each of the main historical victims studied in these two texts refuses a last offer to recant and, as a result, places the judges themselves on trial – a trial of their procedures and, even more, of the ethical beliefs underpinning them. The protagonists of both *The Column of Infamy* and *Death of an Inquisitor*, having already faced almost unbearable pains, go, pathetically struggling but in an important sense morally undefeated, through the further torments of death sentences imposed on them.

Manzoni's narrative in the *The Column of Infamy* rests on a topic still not considered in his times as 'a proper subject for history,' namely 'the sentences of criminal courts' and 'the fate of the poor (taken a few at a time)' (p. 205). ('I giudizi criminali, e la povera gente, quand'è poca, non si riguardano come materia propriamente della storia,' p. 92.)[19] This feeling for the poor and the making of them a new province of concern for history is comparable in certain respects with the work of Charles Dickens, which appeared slightly later. Instead of writing accounts of the poor of his own age, however, as Dickens was frequently to do in succeeding decades, Manzoni attempts to fathom strange and (partly from the lapse in time since their occurrence) well nigh inscrutable instances from an earlier history of great injustice. This search to understand better the nature of oppression of the weak by the powerful is undertaken not merely in homage to the victims of past oppression, but also to shed light on injustice as a general phenomenon, not least within his own nineteenth century Italy.

An important aspect of the texts by Beccaria, Manzoni, and Sciascia, and their linked concerns with justice (in a lineage that I believe includes the 1948 Constitution) is *periodization* in their treatment of the individual in relation to community, and therefore, to the sovereignty of the state. One of the most interesting sentences of Manzoni's text is a complex one about periodization that comes in the penultimate paragraph. He has just been claiming that in the period of which he writes, an esprit de corps – literally a *spirito di corpo* – ensured that judges and explicators, rather than indicating where their predecessors had failed (sometimes knowingly) to uphold justice, often tended to buttress such earlier wrongs with renewed false reasoning, thereby making the injustices their own.

Manzoni goes on to suggest that in more recent times the earlier *esprit de corps* has been broken, and for the better in the specific case of torture. His important sentence, because the most radical, defines what he sees as a major change in *geist*, from an essentially corporative to an individualistically based society. 'Questo spirito' – he is referring to continuities in esprit de corps that had pertained up to and including the seventeenth century, and then on into the eighteenth – 'è combattuto e indebolito più che mai dallo spirito d'individualità: l'*io* si crede troppo ricco per accattar dal *noi*. E in questa parte, è un rimedio; Dio ci liberi di dire: in tutto' (p. 99). (Kenelm Foster translated the passage: 'such institutional loyalty is, now more than ever before, resisted and undermined by individualism: the "I" thinks itself too rich to beg from a "We." And in this respect individualism is beneficial; God forbid I should say in every respect,' p. 212.) It is this important sense of arrival into modernity, defined as an age where the 'I' believes itself too rich to beg from the communal 'We,' that I want to dwell on. For Manzoni is specifying difference between the age *in* which he writes, the nineteenth century, an age of the 'I,' and the earlier age that furnishes his subject matter, an age of the communal 'We.'

In Manzoni's text the so-called *untori* are luckless devils caught up in a maelstrom of anxiety about the plague and of urgent need – felt at various public levels – to find scapegoats for its spread. As commoners, the suspected *untori* are seized on almost at random for having been seen near points of notable outbreak of the disease, or else they are persons falsely incriminated under torture by those who were first arrested. All the suspects are investigated and tried by means of horrendous and, even for those days, illegitimately applied torture, so determined are the authorities to repose in ignorance rather than admit to enduring uncertainty over the causes of the plague. The authorities eventually sentence the scapegoats to still more horrendous judicial execution, although they also find ways of exonerating a co-accused member of their own class of Spanish dignitaries.

Importantly, Manzoni's sense of the key scapegoats from the humbler classes is of their utterly bewildered 'ordinary unheroic innocence,' as he calls it, in the face of torture tactics determined to force them to incriminate themselves. Throughout, Manzoni focuses on two figures whom the authorities torment – Piazza, who is very much a man of the people in spite of his official status as commissioner of heath, and the barber Mora, whom Piazza names under torture as a collaborator in smearing the plague. Both show themselves ill prepared for defending an individual *io* or 'I.' Thinking in the terms of Manzoni's hypothesis about change in *geist*, these two tortured spirits would not have been used to experiencing richly constituted individual identity, as Manzoni's contemporaries had become. For they lived instead in an age of greater apprehension of reality in terms of a communal *noi* or 'We.'

But here we encounter an interesting problem. Already with his text of

1764, Beccaria had made the individual one of the foundational principles in his case against the death penalty by means of an argument that we have already considered: 'Who has ever been willing to give other men authority to kill him? How can the least possible sacrifice of each individual's liberty ever include sacrifice of the greatest good of all, life itself?' Elsewhere in Beccaria's text we have seen that he represents the primacy of the individual's body and conscience: 'requiring a man to be accused and accuser at one and the same time, and requiring pain to be the crucible of truth as if truth could be judged in the nerves and muscles of some poor wretch, reveals only a desire to confound the known relationship of things.' So for Beccaria the individual is morally indivisible: truth can in no way be wrested assuredly from the muscles and fibres of a being undergoing torture. How far are we already advanced towards the *io* Manzoni notes of *his* age, and shedding in Beccaria's text a logic of the communal *noi*, which may have existed formerly at the expense of individual rights? A long way, would be my answer to this question.

More fundamentally, have we not already reached in Beccaria a sense of the *primacy* of individual life? We do not have to recur to Kant in order to situate Manzoni's *io* in the prior period. Close study of Beccaria's text has shown a sense of foundational value in the individual life and its necessary freedom from either torture or execution by a communal *noi*, however legitimately constituted that corporate 'We' may in other respects seem. Nor can the *noi* appeal to *precedent* with impunity. For according to Beccaria in 1764, to seek to justify injustice by means of what has prevailed through the ages may well be simply to perpetuate the long night of judicial ignorance, instead of using truth's single flash to shed new light.

Nevertheless, we can go further still in our periodization of individualism. For Sciascia, the individual – admittedly, *only* his protagonist and not those by whom he is surrounded – is already of overriding significance, in what transpires from his reading of documents from seventeenth-century Sicily (i.e., an earlier age than Beccaria's, and closer in time to that which Manzoni was investigating in his *Column of Infamy*). Sciascia's protagonist in *Death of an Inquisitor*, Fra Diego La Matina, a priest from his own town of Racalmuto, was someone who, by all the available evidence of his reactions under Inquisition, displayed wellsprings of a strong and specifically modern form of grand doubt in man's and even God's justice.

As Sciascia studies the case, he finds that others have written later accounts of Fra Diego's defiance. From a novel written in 1923 by Luigi Natoli entitled *Fra' Diego la Matina,* Sciascia is stirred to the hypothesis, for lack of firm evidence, that Fra Diego was occupied by the problem of justice in a world and during a time that was fundamentally unjust. 'From the particular private case Fra Diego does approach a broader vision of the state of things: a feeling of aversion for the Spanish rule responsible for the Inquisition, and the understanding that the people's revolt is just and necessary' (p. 170). ('Dal caso particolare, privato, egli in qualche modo perviene a una più lata visione delle cose: a un sentimento di avversione contro il dominio spagnolo di cui l'Inquisizione è un portato, alla coscienza che la rivolta del popolo è giusta e necessaria,' p. 45.)

Fra Diego La Matina thus becomes for Sciascia a kind of *grand revolté*. Sciascia even suggests that a single word in one of the archives of the case reveals a 'unique gap' ('unica smagliatura' – my sense is that he means a kind of extraordinary historical window) 'that allows us to catch a glimpse of Fra Diego's heresy, and to hazard the hypothesis that he was debating the problem of justice in the world, during a wholly unjust period. And that explains the silence of his contemporaries, and their horror' (p. 200) ('l'unica smagliatura che ci permette di intravedere l'eresia di fra Diego, di azzardare l'ipotesi che egli agitò il problema della giustizia nel mondo in un tempo sommamente ingiusto. E ciò spiega il silenzio dei suoi contemporanei, e l'orrore,' p. 94). In his tendency to raise problems inconceivable and also horrifying to his contemporaries, Fra Diego, in Sciascia's presentation of him, reads the world against the entire grain of others' experience and mental habits.

What is significant in Sciascia's suggestions at this point is that he seems to glimpse this *grand revolté* as already enshrining, during an age still dominated by a communal 'We,' something like what Manzoni must have meant by that spirit of rich individualism of the 'I.' Elsewhere, in summing up what writing *Death of an Inquisitor* has meant to him, Sciascia likens Fra Diego to other 'heretics not before religion ... but before life.'

> Besides the chronicles, reports and studies cited here, I have read, or presume to have read, everything there is to read on the Inquisition in Sicily; and I may say that I have worked on this study more, and with more dedication and passion, than on any other of my books ... And memories have been with me, too – of persons loved and esteemed, of my family and of my town, who are gone now. Men, as Matranga would say, of 'tenacious conception': stubborn, inflexible, capable of standing up under enormous

sufferings and of self-sacrifice. And I have written of Fra Diego as of one of them: heretics not before religion (which in their own way they observed or did not observe), but before life. (p. 211)

> Oltre le cronache, le relazioni, gli studi qui citati, ho letto (o presumo di aver letto) tutto quel che c'era da leggere relativamente all'Inquisizione di Sicilia: e posso dire di aver lavorato a questo saggio più, e con più impegno e passione, che a ogni altro mio libro ... E mi hanno accompagnato i ricordi: di persone amate e stimate, della mia famiglia e del mio paese, che ora non sono più. Uomini, direbbe il Matranga, di *tenace concetto*: testardi, inflessibili, capaci di sopportare enorme quantità di sofferenza, di sacrificio. Ed ho scritto di fra Diego come di uno di loro: eretici non di fronte alla religione (che a loro modo osservano o non osservano) ma di fronte alla vita. (pp. 116–17)

All such other 'heretics ... before life,' as Sciascia considers them, are from more modern times, people he himself has met, even if now dead. Because Fra Diego is from the same town, he is offered in the text as their typological antecedent. And this, too, is part of the extraordinariness of Fra Diego La Mattina for Sciascia, that he is an anachronistic individual, even as he bears characteristics of tenacious stubbornness of mind (in harbouring difficult concepts) that prefigure those of the townspeople whom Sciascia has directly known. None of Manzoni's harrowed commoners in *The Column of Infamy* quite reach that pitch. On the contrary, Manzoni is concerned to go on pointing out that the main reason why the condemned so easily implicated themselves and others is that they were just common people; not *grands révoltés* such as Fra Diego.

Sciascia's sense, from studying as many earlier documents as were available, is that even from motives of self-interest the forces of the Inquisition would not have harried Fra Diego if there had not been another and grander aversion or doubt in him, indeed a kind of *strong* heresy. The following passage in which Sciascia speculates on the form which that heresy may have taken, if heresy it was, can serve a double purpose, since, in being the passage in Sciascia's text that mentions Manzoni's, it conveniently delivers us back to the concerns with justice raised in *The Column of Infamy*:

> And it seems easy enough to formulate the hypothesis that his revolt against social injustice, against iniquity, against the usurpation of property and of rights, led him to the point – at the moment when he saw his own defeat without remedy and without hope, and identifying his own destiny with the

destiny of man, his own tragedy with the tragedy of existence – of indicting God. Not to deny his existence, but to accuse him. And this recalls the passage in Manzoni's *Storia della colonna infame*, where the author says that 'searching for a guilty party justifiably to despise, the mind shudders to find itself led to choose between two blasphemies, which are two aberrations: to negate Divine Providence, or accuse it.' And consider that the reality which Manzoni was contemplating in the records of the trial of the plague spreaders had been suffered by Fra Diego in his flesh and in his mind for years on end. (p. 200)

E par facile poter formulare l'ipotesi che dalla rivolta contro l'ingiustizia sociale, contro l'iniquità, contro l'usurpazione dei beni e dei diritti, egli sia pervenuto, nel momento in cui vedeva irrimediabile e senza speranza la propria sconfitta, e identificando il proprio destino con il destino dell'uomo, la propria tragedia con la tragedia dell'esistenza, ad accusare Dio. Non a negarlo, ma ad accusarlo. E vien fatto di ricordare quel passo della *Storia della colonna infame* in cui Manzoni dice che *cercando un colpevole contro cui sdegnarsi a ragione, il pensiero si trova con raccapriccio condotto a esitare tra due bestemmie, che son due deliri: negar la Provvidenza, o accusarla*. E si consideri che quella realtà che Manzoni stava scrutando nelle carte del processo agli untori fra Diego l'aveva sofferta nella carne e nella mente, per anni. (p. 93)

This progressing in both texts to a hypothetical stage where there was, on the part of the tormented, a possible questioning or even accusing of God stands as a kind of last-minute, Christ-like 'Why hast thou forsaken me?' (Elsewhere, in a separate essay on Manzoni's *Column of Infamy*, Sciascia was to stress that the earlier author reaches this pitch in his text where his moral sense is deeper than, and puts to rout, his otherwise self-defining Catholicism.)[20] By enrolling Manzoni's text in his own narrative in this way, Sciascia is perhaps wilfully lowering one real threshold of difference between his own agnosticism and Manzoni's deep-seated religious beliefs. It appears that Sciascia fails to take in the fullness of Manzoni's further argument at this point of *The Column of Infamy*. For that argument turns away from any fleeting thought that this may have been God's injustice, to the proofs Manzoni brings forth that it was a specifically human injustice on the part of the judges.

By this stage, Sciascia's reading of the documentary evidence on Fra Diego's exclamations and silences during acute torture has led him to see this priest from his own town as a thoroughly tragic figure of the mid-seventeenth century. He is someone whom Sciascia interprets as progressing from revolt against social injustice, to revolt against God for the very *universality* of injustice. In the process this has given Sciascia a lot of scope for his own thinking, not only about the particular case of injustice studied, but also about the forms it may take during any period of great and violent repression. The more recent age of Fascism, for instance, provides certain cultural comparisons in the text.

Sciascia's quotation from Manzoni comes from the introduction to *The Column of Infamy*. Manzoni's whole line of argument, which he proceeds with in the very next sentence – significantly not quoted by Sciascia – is *not* to lay the blame for injustice upon God, but to place it firmly in the hands of humans. It is quite significant that, having indeed reached the brink of a choice between disbelief in God or apostasy concerning His actions (as Sciascia's quote from him suggests), Manzoni's next word, beyond the point where Sciascia finishes quoting, is 'Ma' (But).

> Our mind, seeking the true culprit, the right object for its revulsion, is dismayed to find itself hesitating between two alternatives, equally blasphemous and insane: a denial, or an indictment, of Providence. But if, on a closer examination of the facts, we are able to discern an injustice that those who committed it could themselves have recognized; a violation of rules that they themselves accepted; an acting in clean contradiction to principles not only admitted in that age but also evidently respected, in similar circumstances, by the very men who acted in this way – then we can with relief conclude that if these men did not know what they were doing it was because they did not choose to know, and that theirs was the kind of ignorance that men adopt and discard as they please; not an excuse for crime, but itself a crime; and that such things as they did may indeed be suffered, but not done, under compulsion. (Manzoni, *Column*, p. 107)

> Cercando un colpevole contro cui sdegnarsi a ragione, il pensiero si trova con raccapriccio condotto a esitare tra due bestemmie, che son due deliri: negar la Provvidenza, o accusarla. Ma quando, nel guardar più attentamente a que' fatti, ci si scopre un'ingiustizia che poteva esser veduta da quelli stessi che la commettavano, un trasgredir le regole ammesse anche da loro, dell'azioni opposte ai lumi che non solo c'erano al loro tempo, ma che essi medesimi, in circostanze simili, mostraron d'avere, è un sollievo il pensare che, se non seppero quello che facevano, fu per non volerlo sapere, fu per quell'ignoranza che l'uomo assume e perde a suo piacere, e non è una scusa, ma una colpa; e che di tali fatti si può bensì esser forzatamente vittime, ma non autori. (Manzoni, *Storia*, p. 6)

This is possibly the greatest passage of moral thinking about human behaviour in all Manzoni. It forms the best argument I know against the defence put forward by perpetrators of crimes against humanity, that what they did was 'under compulsion'; 'just carrying out orders' as the saying in English goes. Sciascia wishes to make Manzoni more agnostic in his religious beliefs than he is, more like Sciascia himself. A careful look at the sequential logic of the passage will show that Manzoni's approach to heresy against God's providence is scarcely more than a rhetorical ploy in order to blame immediately afterwards and vehemently the hearts and minds of human authors of misdeeds, which they were in no way providentially forced to commit.

Sciascia is the successor to Manzoni, but he is also someone who, in full acknowledgment of his moral and intellectual debt to the earlier writer, seeks to add to a genre that has already been used, in *The Column of Infamy*, to trace limit conditions reached by persons suffering in a past epoch. Each of the two writers shows an awareness that his investigations are into events from a crucial phase of European history, and that he himself lives at a lattermost edge of that history's many complexities. Sciascia's 'edge' is that much later than Manzoni's, and therefore the achievement of the earlier author is part of what Sciascia's gaze includes as he seeks to extend the powers of the *racconto inchiesta* genre such that it express the fullest critical history of which he is capable. *Death of the Inquisitor*, Sciascia's history of the humble priest Fra Diego from Racalmuto, who stands up to the Inquisition's might and in a flash of pure revolt kills the Inquisitor General of Sicily, traces what would otherwise be another of the lost annals of the poor.

Manzoni and Sciascia are both concerned to extract lessons for the present from their respective narratives. Indeed, in writing about Manzoni's earlier piece, Sciascia defended it staunchly from others' attempts to consign it to the realm of the dead letter. What he has to say in an essay on *The Column of Infamy* in his collection of critical writings, *Cruciverba*, develops into a highly principled stance about how the order of history achieved in Manzoni's text continues to have bearing on the charged historical present. Sciascia's fundamental point here is that 'we can verify Manzoni's vision of justice by establishing an analogy between the Nazi concentration camps and the trials against the *untori*, their torments and death.' ('La giustezza della visione manzoniana possiamo verificarla stabilendo una analogia tra i campi di sterminio nazisti e i processi contro gli untori, i supplizi, la morte.')[21]

Sciascia enunciates the enduring moral and historical values he saw worked out in Manzoni's piece. He defends them against latter day attack. For instance, some earlier twentieth-century criticism had claimed that since mental benightedness and institutions of torture were a feature of the seventeenth century, it had been a mistake for Manzoni to take men of that earlier age to task. According to such criticism, Manzoni's quarrel with the past had been as pointless as fighting a fact of nature such as an earthquake or a flood. Sciascia defends both Manzoni's record and that of his Enlightenment predecessor, Pietro Verri, against such historical pedantry that refuses to be judgmental about errors of an earlier age. It had been Verri who first called into question the justice of the seventeenth-century Spanish authorities in Milan, and decried the column as commemorative of their acts of torture and execution:

> Niccolini takes no account of the fact that Verri was waging a battle; a battle which today also must be fought: against men like these, against institutions like these. Because the past, its error, its evil, is not in the past: and we must continually live it and judge it in the present, if we wish to be indeed historians. That past which no longer exists – torture as an abolished institution, Fascism as a passing fever from a vaccination – belongs to a historicism of profound bad faith, if not of profound stupidity. Torture still exists. And Fascism always.

> Non tiene per nulla in conto, il Niccolini, che il Verri faceva una battaglia; una battaglia che ancora oggi va combattuta: contro uomini come quelli, contro istituzioni come quelle. Poiché il passato, il suo errore, il suo male, non è mai passato: e dobbiamo continuamente viverlo e giudicarlo nel presente, se vogliamo essere davvero storicisti. Il passato che non c'è piú – l'istituto della tortura abolito, il fascismo come passeggera febbre di vaccinazione – s'appartiene a uno storicismo di profonda malafede se non di profonda stupidità. La tortura c'è ancora. E il fascismo c'è sempre.[22]

What is perhaps so interesting about Sciascia's defence of Manzoni's kind of history, and of the illuminist Verri's before him, is that it reads very like another rehearsal of what Nietzsche had meant by 'critical history,' a kind of perpetual moral reckoning of the present in relation to the past. The need to cling to some such critical history is felt to be paramount because it is the means by which fundamentals of human morality are preserved, refined over time, and at any given moment adequately understood. As Walter Benjamin put it in dark days of 1940, shortly before his death, 'Every image of the past that is not recognized by the present as one of its own concerns threatens to disappear irretrievably.'[23] Such disappearance is not good if it means that moral lessons cannot be learned for lack of key points of historical purchase.

It is clear from other aspects of his emulation of Manzoni's particular development of the *racconto inchiesta* genre in *The Column of Infamy* that Sciascia believed the importance of Manzoni's work had never been adequately recognized by Italians. More than that, it transpires that he felt his own use of the legalistic *inchiesta* genre in *Death of the Inquisitor* had met with similarly unjustified neglect. 'There has been nothing similar [to *The Column of Infamy*] in Italy. And when someone, more than a century later, tries to take up the "genre" (since Manzoni, exactly as Negri says, prefigures the "genre" of the present-day investigative narrative with legal ambience), "le silence s'est fait": just like then.' ('Non c'era mai stato niente di simile, in Italia; e quando qualcuno, piú di un secolo dopo, si atenterà a riprendere il "genere" [poiché Manzoni, come esattamente dice il Negri, prefigura il "genere" dell'odierno racconto-inchiesta di ambiente giudiziario], "le silence s'est fait": come allora.')[24]

If we have managed to predate aspects of Manzoni's sense of the modern 'I' to Beccaria's text, and even seen Sciascia glimpsing a kind of grand (if anomalous and anachronistic) individual in the mid-seventeenth century, what historical *afterlife* does that 'spirit of individualism' have?

In some ways a communal 'We' is reconstructed during years of the Risorgimento, especially during and after 1848. Chief exponents of the way a sense of common identity is fostered and defined in Italy are Count Camillo Benso di Cavour and Giuseppe Mazzini in politics, Giuseppe Verdi in the realm of music and spectacle, and Giuseppe Garibaldi on the battlefield. But as the closing chapter on lifestyles will make clear, the decades after Italian unification reveal how profoundly *disunified* in social and economic terms the nation remained. There was not a sustained and effective Italian 'We' in the late decades of the nineteenth century or the early decades of the twentieth century. Too many different groupings of the multiply divided nation contended for supremacy or simply for adequate conditions for their own survival. With the additional suffering resulting from the First World War, possibilities for a communal 'We' were weakened still further, such that a relatively easy way was left open for the Fascist takeover and for its unfolding project of the following two decades and slightly more; the so-called *ventennio*. This is not the place for an extensive discussion of the years of Fascism, treated so much more thoroughly by others. What I should like to claim, merely, is that Manzoni's age of rich selfhood – so rich indeed that the communal '"We" is resisted and weakened' thereby – seems decidedly like a lost ideal during the *ventennio*, with its ethos of conformity to certain binding ideals of labour, power, and conquest. The 'I' becomes progressively weaker under Fascism, and very much begs what small legitimacy it still possesses from, precisely, a corporate and statist 'We,' symbolized in the fasces. The liberal notion of valuing the individual is replaced by a different and pervasive philosophy; what Silvio Trentin defined in 1930 as a subjugation of the individual citizen ('asservimento del cittadino').[25] The conquering, generic hero of Fascist myth, often the Duce himself, stands in the place of the lost 'I' of the Romantic age's 'spirito d'individualità' that Manzoni had felt he was witnessing in its prime.

In so far as there is a remnant of the private individual with an inner life and drives in Fascist Italy, the situation is rather like the one described by Theodor Adorno under Nazism. Indeed, there are few more perceptive comments on the *asservimento* – worse than that, the *avvilimento* – of the individual in this period than the following: 'The only responsible course is to deny oneself the ideological misuse of one's own existence,' suggests Adorno, 'and for the rest to conduct oneself in private as modestly, unobtrusively and unpretentiously as is required, no longer by good upbringing, but by the shame of still having air to breathe, in hell.'[26] This is all that one can do for justice: simply not serve injustice by retreating from an 'ideological misuse' of one's existence in the bad causes of the times. It is pathetically little. (As long as histories are written, many will go on thinking that it is not nearly *enough*; it is so much easier to imagine oneself acting more honourably in past situations than those who were caught up in them. For it is hard, when one lives in much better times, not to make an equation between *avvvilimento* and *vigliaccheria* – humiliation of the spirit and outright baseness.)

According to this statement by Adorno, the private citizen even puts his vestigial spirit of individuality – as something noted by others – to the task of self-erasure, out of guilt that their hell may be worse than one's own. For theirs may be 'airless,' with all the awful meanings such a thought implies for the times in question. Adorno discusses some of those further meanings (notably, total war and death camps) in his notebook *Minima Moralia: Reflections from Damaged Life*. The 'Damaged

Life' in question is a long way from Manzoni's rich spirit of individualism of a century earlier, which is cockily at liberty even to deny the bonds of our plural existence.

Be that all as it may, my own interest now turns in conclusion towards rebirth in more modern times of justice in relation to the individual, which requires that we look at the immediate postwar period. One of the things that is so interesting after the fall of Fascism and during the postwar reconstruction of Italy as a republic is that the new Constitution of 1948 was as punctilious about recuperating and protecting rights of the individual as it was in defining a necessary community between persons for their mutual fulfilment. It was a case of prioritizing both the 'I' and the 'We.' These dual preoccupations were already promulgated in the Constituent Assembly as early as 1946 in an 'order of the day' presented by Giuseppe Dossetti, who argued how the Constitution should be framed:

> The only condition which the new Italian democratic Statute must satisfy, and that truly respects the historic exigencies, should be a) that it recognize the substantial priority of the human individual before that of the State. Not only should the individual's material but also spiritual values and needs be understood; the State's purpose lying in service to the same. b) It should recognize at the same time the social needs of persons, who are destined to satisfy and fulfil themselves in mutual ways, through reciprocal economic and spiritual solidarity, above all in various intermediary groupings disposed in a natural progression (communities of family, territory, profession, church, etc). Therefore, in whatever ways these communities prove insufficient, the State should make good. c) It should therefore affirm the existence of both fundamental rights of individuals as well as rights of the community, before any concession be made on the part of the State.

> La sola impostazione veramente conforme alle esigenze storiche, cui il nuovo Statuto dell'Italia democratica deve soddisfare, è quella che: a) riconosca la precedenza sostanziale della persona umana (intesa nella completezza dei suoi valori e dei suoi bisogni non solo materiali, ma anche spirituali) rispetto allo Stato e la destinazione di questo a servizio di quella; b) riconosca ad un tempo la necessaria socialità di tutte le persone, le quali sono destinate a completarsi e perfezionarsi a vicenda, mediante una reciproca solidarietà economica e spirituale: anzitutto in varie comunità intermedie disposte secondo una naturale gradualità (comunità familiari,

territoriali, professionali, religiose, ecc.), e quindi, per tutto ciò in cui quelle comunità non bastino, nello Stato; c) che perció affermi l'esistenza sia dei diritti fondamentali delle persone, sia dei diritti delle comunità anteriormente ad ogni concessione da parte dello Stato.[27]

These are lofty ideals, and many will claim they have been multiply reneged on. But constitutions are foundational, and they can be returned to for reference in later times. Palmiro Togliatti, a founding member of the Italian Communist Party who had remained outside Italy for most of the Fascist period, spoke in this immediate postwar moment of a 'unity necessary in making the Constitution – not that of one or other party, nor of one or other ideology, but the Constitution of all Italian workers, of the whole nation' ('quell'unità che è necessaria per poter fare la Costituzione non dell'uno o dell'altro partito, non dell'una o dell'altra ideologia, ma la Costituzione di tutti i lavoratori italiani, di tutta la nazione').[28] Togliatti's 'workerist' terminology is hardly surprising in the leading communist figure of the day. It is preserved in part in the wording of the subsequent constitution itself. In fact, the very first sentence of the document, in Article 1, asserts that Italy 'is a democratic Republic *founded on work*' (my italics) ('una Repubblica democratica fondata sul lavoro').[29]

Dossetti's sense that the individual's rights should precede those of the state, and that the constitution would otherwise entirely miss its intended purpose, is realized in the fully drafted work. As for the state not existing for its own sake, but to serve the individual and society, it had been a fundamental premise of Karl Marx in his maturity: 'Freedom consists in the conversion of the State from an organ superimposed on society into one completely subordinated to it.'[30] Although some of those involved in drafting the constitution (e.g., former partisans) may have held to the further Marxist ideal of abolition of the state altogether, they would have been among those pressing hardest in this initial phase for its subordinated role.

There is a fascinatingly mixed notion under definition in Article 2, of the necessary provisions for personal development on the one hand but within a binding sociality on the other. 'The Republic recognises and guarantees the inviolable rights of man, whether as an individual or within social formations where personality is developed, and requires the fulfilment of political, economic and social solidarity' ('La Repubblica garantisce e riconosce i diritti inviolabili dell'uomo, sia come singolo sia nelle formazioni sociali ove si svolge la sua personalità, e richiede l'adempimento dei doveri inderogabili di solidarietà politica, economica e sociale.')[31]

What is significant about the wording here, in the light of the issues of this chapter, is that we are not revisiting the 'spirit of individualism' of the kind mentioned by Manzoni. Although Manzoni had welcomed that spirit in the given instance – 'in this respect individualism is beneficial' – we may recall that he specifically ends the same sentence by pronouncing, 'God forbid I should say in every respect.' What we seem to see under definition in the wording of the second article of the Italian Constitution is a real sense of the mutual interdependence of individualism and social solidarity – the *io* as well as, and sometimes in terms of the *noi*. Subtextually, Manzoni seemed to be hinting that such a mutuality of the *io* and of the *noi* would be preferable to the hegemony of either. Certainly his 'I' that deems itself too rich to beg from the communal 'We' is in the long run a displeasing personification of the individual pronoun's mental attitude of self sufficiency. All this the Italian Constitution seems unconsciously to know, possibly because of the terrible experiences of Fascism leading to war, and eventually in turn to *civil* war in Italy, which had so recently and for so long divided the nation. Those previous years had disrupted 'work' of the kind possible in peacetime and, in more spiritual senses, personal and social fulfilment. All these priorities of peace are now being made much of in the Italian Constitution's opening articles.

I shall close with some simple remarks about the wording of Article 3, which treats the social dignity of all and equality before the law. This article seems to have been developed through reflection on injustices and inequalities in Fascist ideology and practice. The equality under definition here is specifically in terms of 'gender, race, language, religion, political opinions, and social and personal circumstances' ('senza distinzione di sesso, di razza, di lingua, di religione, di opinioni politiche, di condizioni personali e sociali').[32] Several of these categories had been sites of tyranny, which became progressively more totalitarian under Fascism. I have already mentioned the Race Laws of 1938, after the passing of which the situation for Jews became so much more perilous and in many cases fatal. Equality of 'political opinions' before the law was another area in which the Fascist record had been a squalid one from its earliest years.

What is most noteworthy in a general respect is that reflection on the lessons of the past, if done well in the drafting of a constitution, can act as a safeguard for the uncertain future. For instance, it was to be several decades before there were notable increases in the numbers of persons of other races in Italy, which occurred with the rather new phenomenon of immigration from the 1980s onwards. The specific wording in the Constitution against inequality on grounds of race had been drafted with the recent history of terrible mistreatment of Italian Jews probably uppermost in mind. But it can serve a somewhat different purpose in our own times. The experiences undergone by specific immigrants and migrant groups in Italy during the past fifteen years approximately have often been unjust, sometimes extremely so. But it is certainly better to have a document with constitutional status warning of such dangers as those of racism, sexism, and discrimination on grounds of language, religion, or politics. It defines a culture's ideal standards of justice, thereby making the outright abrogation of any one of them not only more difficult in any given historic conjuncture, but also more readily *perceived as unjust* by ordinary decent people when it occurs. Indeed, a part of what has made for their 'ordinary decency' is precisely the social and political lineage that links them back to that earlier historical moment of the drafting of the constitutional document itself. That moment of emergence from Fascism is widely studied now in schools and universities, much written about, and, above all, preserved in the text of the constitution itself, which is the foundational principle of the nation's present legal framework.

6 Italy's Romantic Reputation

The arrival of the age of individuality, where the 'I' believes itself richer in spirit than the communal 'We,' is an all-important issue in light of the much-debated construction of what we have seen Alessandro Manzoni call the difficult 'We' of Italians – *la costruzione del difficile 'noi' degli italiani*. It was Manzoni's sense that this difficult 'We,' rather than being a communal spirit in the process of formation, is something largely of the past, increasingly lost to the individualism (*spirito d'individualità*) of the present age. Of equal importance is his gloss that the 'I' of individualism is confident in, and proud of, its own richness of spirit, and by no means feels diminished by, or isolated in consequence of, its distinction from a plural 'we.' Indeed, it displays a superiority complex in relation to that broken down and weakened *spirito di corpo* of the historic 'We.' Do we have to depend on Manzoni's testimony for this felt richness of individuality in the Romantic period in Italy, or is there testimony of other kinds?

My intention in this chapter is to reconsider some of the primary configurations of Italy's Romantic age, in particular, notions of Italy and of Italianness promulgated mainly by key writers in the French language, and opinions held by Italians themselves. The Romantics generally (by no means the French and Italians only) establish contours for Italy's enduring reputation, in particular among other peoples and cultures. Many of these contours do not change in their essentials down to our own times. Romanticism, in other words, largely bequeaths to us what is still felt to be romantic about Italian life, art, landscape, and history. We are perhaps overly used to interpretation of Italy based on English poets or travel writings. In 1957 C.P. Brand mapped this terrain in his seminal volume *Italy and the English Romantics*. Brand covered everything from the appeal of travel, to studying the Italian language, to the interest in

Italian literature and its influence on English Romantic writers. He also studied the English interest in Italian arts and landscape, and the romance of Italian history, politics, and religion. His study reminds us how far the flamboyant generation of Byron and Shelley disseminated memorable accounts of Italy and its people. Perhaps even more important, however, Brand displays something we may have forgotten in the work of William Wordsworth, something evident, for example, in lines about Italy from the sixth book of *The Prelude* that are less often recorded, but are worthy of scrutiny for their meditative qualities:

> Ye have left
> Your beauty with me, a serene accord
> Of forms and colours, passive, yet endowed
> In their submissiveness with power.[1]

In these lines the enduring beauties of the Italian landscape, and the power that they hold over the imagination of the young poet-traveller Wordsworth, seem to be subtextually contrasted with a former *political* power of Italy. If anything, the earlier political power of Italy, now 'passive,' is felt to hibernate (so to speak) within those natural beauties, during its long period of 'submissiveness' to foreign domination.

However, it is vital to recall that not just the English, but Germans, French, and indeed many others – Scandinavians, Swiss, and Russians for instance – had figured among important grand tourists during the age of neoclassicism and after. Such travels, though largely curtailed during the period of the Napoleonic wars in Europe, resumed still more avidly afterwards. Some French citizens had gone on experiencing Italy during the revolutionary and Napoleonic periods, either because for reasons of class they were in exile for their own safety or in consequence of military campaigns by Napoleon's armies. Others were supporters in the setting up and administration of satellite revolutionary republics, or else were involved in puppet kingdoms in which members of Napoleon's own family were enthroned dynastically across southern Europe during the crucial years of his empire.

A classic and detailed study of Italy's reputation throughout the Enlightenment and Romantic periods is available in Franco Venturi's lengthy section, 'L'Italia fuori d'Italia' ('Italy outside Italy') in the third volume of the *History of Italy*.[2] I am reliant upon Venturi for the larger story. His work makes possible the sort of focus I will adopt in examining how the ideas of four key writers (three who wrote in the French language, De Staël, Sismondi, and Stendhal, and one who wrote in Italian, Leopardi) correlate or differ. Of the two novelists, De Staël wrote about Italy in *Corinne, ou l'Italie* fairly early in the Romantic era (1807), and in ways that suggest some debilitating weaknesses in the character of her people. Stendhal, on the other hand, recorded multifarious impressions of Italy in travel books and journals throughout the several decades of his career as a writer, until his death in 1842. Late in the Romantic period proper, he produced a challenging and, in the main, positive account of Italian mores in his novel *La chartreuse de Parme* of 1839. I will chart the wide gamut of reactions to Italy offered by these two writers, both in contrast with each other and in relation to the non-fiction analysts Sismondi and Leopardi.

The great reversions and restorations of the years 1814 and 1815 led to a renewal of leisured travel by the moneyed classes in Europe. Leopardi was to say, for instance, some ten years after the fall of Napoleon, that never before had there been such a spate of travel literature by writers of many different nationalities than in the age in question. 'Amongst all of which there are infinite publications of foreigners about things to do with Italy, which has become a universal object of curiosity and of travel, more indeed than any other specific country ... It is certain ... that in these recent years, from *Corinne* onwards there have been published in Europe more works favourable to Italy than all such publications of former times, and therein more good is said about us than we have even said of ourselves.' (Fra' quali sono anche infiniti quelli pubblicati dagli stranieri e che si pubblicano tutto giorno sopra le cose d'Italia, fatta oggetto di curiosità universale e di viaggi, molto più che ella non fu in altro tempo, e molto più generalmente, e più ancora che alcun altro paese ... Certo è... che in questi ultimi anni si sono divulgate in Europa dalla Corinna in poi più opere favorevoli all'Italia, che non sono tutte insieme quelle publicate negli altri tempi, e nelle quali si dice di noi più bene che mai non fu detto appena da noi medesimi.')[3]

Not simply Manzoni, by 1842, but several years earlier Leopardi, in the just quoted *Discorso sopra lo stato presente dei costumi degl'Italiani* (*Discourse on the Present State of Morality of the Italians*), had borne witness to the breakdown of the Italian 'We' into an increasingly isolated and asocial 'I.' Indeed, Leopardi had given here the most shocking account of isolated individualism in Italy, even if the shock in question was not available to others until the eventual publication of this work in 1906, and then was not really taken up by Italian political commentators and intellectuals till the 1970s and 1980s. In Leopardi's eyes there was no longer in Italy any such real thing as society, nor spirit of connection between people. Yet how can so positive a foreign reputation of Italy and of Italians as Leopardi mentions coexist with a sense of breakdown within Italy (the country) of all political and social cohesiveness in public life – in short, with a fragmentation of the former communal 'We' into the individual and often isolated 'I'? And does the individuality that is seen as largely replacing community tarnish Italians' own appreciation of Italy? These are some of the questions of this chapter.

My argument stretches between two mooring points: the interpretation of a work mentioned by Leopardi, De Staël's novel-cum-travel-narration, *Corinne, ou l'Italie* of 1807, and a contrasting analysis of the last novel by someone initially greatly influenced by De Staël's seemingly definitive grasp of Italy. I refer to Stendhal's *La Chartreuse de Parme* of 1839, which moved into different Romantic terrain than that covered in the earlier work by De Staël. Stendhal's novel is more sceptical about character and motive, but also more passionate in all the complexities of its great love for Italy. Such passion had had decades to mature in its author, since he first journeyed there with the French Republican army in 1800. The novel more or less begins with that earlier period (actually Napoleon's first Italian campaign of 1796) and covers much of the time span during which Stendhal himself had witnessed the evolution of Italian mores and lifestyles. Not only does Stendhal's *La Chartreuse de Parme* turn some of De Staël's Romantic theses about Italy curiously inside out, showing that what seemed full of meaning in them may be relatively empty, and what empty, full. It is from the outset a more difficult work to interpret that hers, especially as to its fundamental positions about the nature of Italian lifestyles and politics.

Apart from De Staël, Stendhal, and Leopardi, another author who must be included in any account of Italy's Romantic reputation is the Swiss Protestant historian of Italy's greatness from the age of its medieval republics forward, J.C.L. Simonde de Sismondi. He produces for the Romantic age influential theories of Italy's decline in the sixteenth, seventeenth, and eighteenth centuries, offering an all-enveloping account of the degree to which 'the character of Italians from youth to old age had been nurtured on corrupting poisons, how their energy had been destroyed with care, their spirit condemned to laziness, their pride humbled and their sincerity corrupted' ('ils sont abreuvés, dès leur enfance jusqu'à leur extrême vieillesse, de poisons corrupteurs; comment leur énergie a été détruite avec soin, leur esprit condamné à la paresse, leur fierté humiliée, leur sincérité corrompue').[4]

Sismondi and De Staël were firm friends in the years preceding the publication in 1807 of her novel about Italy and of the first two volumes (of an eventual sixteen) of his *History of the Italian Republics of the Middle Ages*. He had been a frequenter of her literary salon during her roving exile from France in earlier Napoleonic years. Their versions of contemporary Italy's shortcomings by contrast with its former greatness have interesting affinities, in part from having been worked out collaboratively during the authors' times spent together, not least on Italian soil.[5]

In the beginning of *Corinne* we note that positives in the interpretation of Italy mainly exist in isolated individuals, who stand out within a surrounding context mainly composed of negatives, which tend to be concentrated in the collectivity or mass of contemporary Italian society. Within the character of Corinne, De Staël has sought to distil not just the natural and artistic beauties of Italy, but also its expressive powers. Corinne is hence in her own right both creation and creator. She is also uniquely female, although she incorporates male strengths of personality that are not a little problematical for her repressed English lover Lord Nelvil, who expects timid submissiveness in his ideal woman, which he eventually finds in Corinne's English half-sister.[6] Corinne, although essentially a symbol (especially early in the novel) for an ongoing Italian greatness of soul and creativity, is portrayed by De Staël as also a mere individual and, furthermore, one increasingly isolated. She takes her strength largely from an Italian past, without significant additional sustenance from contemporary Italian society. When that rich past largely fails to meet her present need to bridge the cultural divide between herself and her lover, she is left tragically disempowered. Her attempt at a cross-cultural pairing with the gloomy Lord Nelvil snags on his final unwillingness to marry outside his cultural frame of origin. This inward-turning British aristocrat is haunted by the legacies of a puritanical background, as vividly portrayed in late portions of the novel dealing with English-Scottish border regions. Lord Nelvil's behaviour in staving off marriage to Corinne and eventually instead marrying her half-sister is reinforced furthermore from beyond the grave by his north-country father. In consequence, death becomes De Staël's only possible outcome for Corinne.

Switching temporarily to Sismondi's history, we find it above all important, not for what it says of the greatness of an earlier Italy over more than fifteen volumes, but for the thesis about decline marshalled in its final volume of 1818. This thesis is most pronounced in the very last chapter, entitled 'The causes which have changed the character of Italians, since the enslavement of their republics' (vol. 16, chap. cxxvii, 'Quelles sont les causes qui ont changé le charactère des Italiens, depuis l'asservissement de leur républiques,' pp. 407–60). There Italy's religion, education system, legislation, and morality of honour are each closely inspected, and the causes of her decline found in them. Although the descendent of a Tuscan family, Sismondi was a Protestant of Geneva, unsparing in his account of how, after the Council of Trent, there had been change for the worse in the Catholic church in Italy, initially during the pontificate of Paul IV, with disastrous ongoing consequences. A succession of popes, according to him, took the side of rulers of the various states in Italy, rather than of the people ruled. Instead of concentrating on a true morality of individual conscience, as Protestantism in more northern parts of Europe had done, the Catholic church, according to Sismondi, had substituted the study of casuists. It went on trafficking in indulgences, in spite of attempts by the Council of Trent to put an end to such practices. Regularity of church devotion rather than genuine virtue was prioritized. In sum, religion in Italy taught her people to play tricks with their consciences, rather than obey them.

Educational practices in Italy were scarcely better by Sismondi's reckoning, intimately linked as they were with the bad influences of her religion. He saw education as having been wrested from the hands of independent philosopher figures and handed over to the clergy during the sixteenth century. The great works of the ancients were still taught, but as a lore of facts and authorities, rather than an ongoing stimulus to thought. Rote learning and tautologous prayer made for spiritual inertia and distraction, and became the breeding ground of something still worse, namely wide-scale hypocrisy.

Legislation too, Sismondi's third great fallen pillar of Italy's greatness, had, like religion and education, become in his view a matter of blind and implicit obedience on the part of a cowering and largely downtrodden people. The rise of absolutist princes had led to the crushing of legality and justice, and to the primacy of mere privilege. Legal process, potentially the very groundwork and foundation of public morality, being so often cloaked now in secrecy, had given justice itself a bad name. More and more frequently an accused was not even informed of a charge, and so could not mount an adequate self-defence. Bad justice itself had led, accordingly, to habits of dissimulation and of flattery. As if that were not evil enough, violence was fostered by the frequent spectacles of state-sanctioned torture. In addition, the law of primogeniture led to a diminution of liberty. The younger siblings of privileged inheritors were reduced to hopeless inactivity and base resentment. Surviving mothers too, in cases where their sons received all the inheritance and they nothing, were left with only want and envy. Finally, with the exponential growth of legal cases, chicanery among lawyers thrived.

In some ways what Sismondi says about change in the morality of honour, although professedly the least important of his four categories, is the most striking. Here he comes close, literally and in spirit, to the psychological readings of Italian national temperament undertaken in the sixth book of De Staël's novel, 'Moeurs et caractère des Italiens' ('Italian Customs and Character'). For Sismondi, punctilios of honour had become the equivalent of national institutions in Italy. Very importantly, moreover, there had developed an exaggerated delicacy over female chastity, which had led to women over succeeding centuries losing the honourable free will of action they had possessed in the great former age of Italian republics, and to their coming under greater control of their husbands. The latter even felt obliged sometimes to undo the training in matters of individual conscience instilled in their wives by their convent educations, as somehow inapposite to family well-being. In addition, there was an exaggerated importance now attached to male valour, possibly in reaction to its lack during the age of the republics. Sixteenth-century wars drawing Italians to arms had fostered in them almost Castilian codes of honour. But with the decline of the military in the seventeenth century, the nobility fell back into sloth and ease, which led, in the eighteenth century, to Italians shamelessly admitting their lack of courage.

Revenge against personal offence had become a code of honour, with poison and the dagger coming to the defense of outraged self-esteem. Although such violent and barbarous practices had declined in more recent times, Sismondi believed that a diffuse legacy of perfidiousness remained in the character of Italians. In an earlier chapter Sismondi had tackled another issue of character in relation to family honour, namely, the rapid rise and development of a widespread tradition of women taking *cavalieri serventi* or *cicisbei* in addition to husbands. In some respects he talks about this strange custom with a more moralizing negative attitude than about any other. But because De Staël had also tackled the phenomenon in her novel of some eleven years earlier,[7] I defer discussion of his attitudes about it until we have seen hers more clearly, and can make the contrast more pertinently.

One would suppose that with so lengthy a list of vices Sismondi had nothing left to say in Italy's favour. But he ends his sixteenth volume, and with it the entire *Histoire*, by stressing her remaining and natural virtues, and suggesting that the past itself has left seeds of greatness. The implication is that under the right conditions, or with appropriate methods of nurture, there might still be cultural regrowth in Italy.

In *Corinne, ou l'Italie*, De Staël had been at pains to review Italy's qualities. Because the protagonist Corinne enshrines many of these qualities symbolically, they function as fundamental attributes that her lover, the Scottish Lord Nelvil, must understand. More generically, what gets said about Italy, especially in the opening books of the novel, functions as De Staël's distillation of the complex reputation this nation had come to hold, both for herself and for the Romantic age during, and on behalf of which, she was writing. Italy's achievements are for De Staël, as for her friend Sismondi, mostly in the past: 'Italians are much more outstanding for what they have been and by what they might be than by what they are now.' ('Les Italiens sont bien plus remarquables par ce qu'ils ont été, et par ce qu'ils pourraient être, que par ce qu'ils sont maintenant.') Italy constitutes a 'mystery which has to be understood by the imagination rather than by the critical intellect which is particularly developed through English education'[8] ('mystère qu'il faut comprendre par l'imagination plutôt que par cet esprit de jugement qui est particulièrement développé dans l'éducation anglaise').[9] The overall implication is that Italy must be *re*imagined from all that it has been, rather than solely judged on the basis of what it is now. As we might gather from the novel's title, which links character and nation, Corinne in her own right is De Staël's venture in understanding Italy imaginatively. But De Staël creates her hero Lord Nelvil as someone unendowed with the necessary imagination and, rather *over*-endowed with precisely the critical intellect so counter-productive (according to De Staël's theory) in understanding such a mystery as Corinne represents.

Early on Corinne is singled out, in a laudatory speech by an Italian prince, as a surviving image of what Italy once was, and of what it would be still, were it not for 'the ignorance, the envy, the discord, and the indolence to which our fate has condemned us' (p. 27) ('elle est ce que nous serions sans l'ignorance, l'envie, la discorde et l'indolence auxquelles notre sort nous a condamnés,' p. 57). Corinne is, according to this prince, 'an admirable product of our climate and of our arts, as an offshoot of the past, as a harbinger of the future. And when foreigners talk ill of this land which gave birth to the great minds that have enlightened Europe, when they have no pity for our failings which arise from our misfortunes, we say to them: "Look at Corinne"' (p. 27) ('une admirable production de notre climat, de nos beaux-arts, comme un rejeton du passé, comme une prophétie de l'avenir; et quand les étrangers insultent à ce pays d'où sont sorties les lumières qui ont éclairé l'Europe; quand ils sont sans pitié pour nos torts qui naissent de nos malheurs, nous leur disons: – regardez Corinne,' pp. 57–8).

De Staël proceeds to develop the idea that the best of Italian character has taken on in the present an internalized and specifically feminine poetic form. 'Yes, we would follow her in her footsteps, we would be men as she is a woman, if men could, like women, make a world for themselves in their own hearts, and if the fire of our genius, compelled to be dependent on social relationships and external circumstances, could be fully set alight by the torch of poetry alone' (p. 27) ('Oui, nous suivrions ses traces, nous serions hommes comme elle est femme, si les hommes pouvaient comme les femmes se créer un monde dans leur propre coeur, et si notre génie, nécessairement dépendant des relations sociales et des circonstances extérieures, pouvait s'allumer tout entier au seul flambeau de la poésie,' p. 58).

It is highly notable that De Staël's best-case exemplar of Italy only exists in present times in individuated and female form. Lord Nelvil's initial negative prejudices against Italian women, before they undergo a radical transformation in Corinne's inspiring presence, are quickly spoken in De Staël's text: 'he thought they were passionate but fickle, incapable of experiencing deep, permanent affection' (p. 35) ('il les croyait passionées, mais mobiles, mais incapables d'éprouver des affections profondes et durables' (p. 69). We need to hang on to this feminized image of Romantic Italy, asking whether and to what degree it is common to other authors in this chapter's study. Also, how does it relate to the masculinized notion of Italy's earlier, Renaissance age?

Called upon by the ceremony of her installation as poet laureate to improvise on the topic of 'The Glory and Happiness of Italy,' Corinne says a lot about Italy's past achievements. She is explicitly and implicitly critical of the present: perhaps nowhere more than in what she has to say about Dante: 'Italy, at the height of its power, lives again to the full in Dante's work. Animated by the spirit of the republics, a warrior as well as a poet, he fans the flames of action amongst the dead, and his shades are more vibrantly alive than those living today. Memories of earth still pursue them; their aimless passions claw at their hearts; they agonize over the past, which to them seems less irrevocable than their eternal future' (p. 29)[10] ('L'Italie, au temps de sa puissance, revit tout entière dans Le Dante. Animé par l'esprit des républiques, guerrier aussi-bien que poëte, il souffle la flame des actions parmi les morts, et ses ombres ont une vie plus forte que les vivants d'aujourd'hui. Les souvenirs de la terre les poursuivent encore; leurs passions sans but s'acharnent à leur coeur; elles s'agitent sur le passé, qui leur semble encore moins irrévocable que leur éternel avenir,' pp. 60–1).

The oddity of this profound judgment on Dante's shades of the dead is that, *mutatis mutandis*, it seems to work by and large as a judgment by Mme De Staël on Italy too. For Dante's shades, the past seems less incomplete than the present. For them the past is even where some as-yet-unfulfilled greatness of soul lies *in potentio*. Though by definition already past, it is paradoxically 'less irrevocable' than the compromised future, in which these shades must forever expiate their sins. Dante is its poet, the republican communes are its political form, and memory and passion are its dominant conceptual modes. It is precisely in the narrative encounters between Dante himself and the dead in the *Commedia* that topoi of Italy's former glory and happiness (Corinne's topic too, remember) are frequently located and defined. Corinne is in the line of poetic greatness stretching from Dante through Petrarch and later Tasso to the present. Tasso was, like Corinne, to have been proclaimed poet laureate in Rome, the very walls of which he loved, but he died the very day before the ceremony. In a somewhat earlier age Petrarch, 'like Dante,' was the 'courageous poet of Italian independence. In other lands all that is known of him is his love, but here more austere memories honour his name for ever and his native land inspired him better than Laura herself' (p. 30) ('Pétrarque fut aussi comme Le Dante, le poëte valeureux de l'indépendence italienne. Ailleurs on ne connaît de lui que ses amours, ici des souvenirs plus sévères honorent à jamais son nom; et la patrie l'inspira mieux que Laure elle-même,' p. 62). All such statements tend to link Corinne not simply with the past but with a line of great poetic individuals.

Most scenes in the novel displaying corporate social temper in contemporary Italy suggest the worst. We meet this in the dramatic scene of a fire in Ancona early in the novel, in which the townspeople seem so helpless, whereas the outsider Lord Nelvil plays a heroic role in the saving of lives. Anconan bystanders are even portrayed here as wishing that the city's Jews and the inhabitants of its madhouse die in the flames, a severe indictment indeed on the author's part, and for us in a later age eerily prescient of the worst excesses of Fascism/Nazism. In some ways De Staël's most extensive case about Italians of her day lies in that sixth book, 'Italian Customs and Character' ('Les moeurs et le caractère des italiens'). In her own voice she soon pronounces that there is a fundamental lack of social bonding or agreement among Italians (her French word is *commérage*). They make decisions and act on the basis of outright egoism (translation, p. 88; original French, p. 144). We thereafter receive highly gendered accounts of imbalances in the Italian temperament, admittedly some of them in words of the culturally biased character Oswald (Lord Nelvil). His case against Italian men is that they have little strength of character and no seriousness of purpose or action, because they have come under the domination of stronger-willed women. Indeed, he goes so far as to suggest that women have come to play in this society the role of the sultan, with their men folk subject to them – just as, inversely, women are to all-powerful males in eastern seraglios or harems (p. 97; p. 157).

Mozart, among several other composers of opera, had already shown Europeans entrammelled in an Eastern seraglio (in *Die Entführung aus dem Serail*), and Rossini was shortly to make comic play of differences between Islamic and Italian societies, in both *L'italiana in Algeri* and *Il Turco in Italia*. But even Oswald's colourfully inverse comparison here of gender relations in Italy with those of more eastern societies does not do full justice to De Staël's own case, which had been rendered slightly earlier. Her main account of social and sexual relations among Italians makes them appear utterly strange and culturally very foreign. Above all, what is at issue is the custom of the *cavaliere servente* or *cicisbeo*. Because on this issue Sismondi and Stendhal also have a lot to say, I shall deal first with De Staël's account of the phenomenon in the following quotation, which is of necessity somewhat lengthy:

> People were going for supper and every *cavaliere servente* hastened to sit down beside his lady. A lady visitor came in and could not find a seat; no one, except Lord Nelvil and Count d'Erfeuil, offered her his own. It was not out of discourtesy, nor selfishness, that no Roman had got up. But the great Roman nobleman's idea of honour and duty is not to leave his lady's side even for a moment. Some who could not find seats stood behind their ladies, ready to attend to their slightest needs. The ladies spoke only to their escorts; gentlemen visitors wandered in vain around the circle; no one had anything to say to them. Women in Italy do not know what coquetry is, what in love is only satisfied pride. They want to please only the man they love; there is no seduction of the mind before that of the heart and eyes; the most sudden beginnings are sometimes followed by sincere devotion and even by a long faithful

attachment. In Italy, infidelity is more severely blamed in a man than in a woman. Three or four men with different functions follow the same lady, who, sometimes without even taking the trouble to mention their names to her host, takes them with her; one is the favourite, another is the man who aspires to be so, the third is called the sufferer (*il patito*). He is completely scorned; but he is allowed to play the part of ardent admirer; and all these rivals live peacefully together. Only the lower classes have still retained the custom of using daggers. In this country, there is a strange mixture of simplicity and corruption, of deceit and truth, of good nature and vengeance, of weakness and strength, which can be explained by careful observation. The fact that nothing is done out of vanity explains the good qualities, and the bad ones develop because a great deal is done out of self-interest, be it concerned with love, ambition, or wealth. (pp. 92–3)

On allait souper, et chaque *cavaliere servente* se hâtait de s'asseoir à côté de sa dame. Une étrangère arriva, et, ne trouvant plus de place, aucun homme, excepté lord Nelvil et le comte d'Erfeuil, ne lui offrit la sienne: ce n'était ni par impolitesse, ni par égoïsme, qu'aucun Romain ne s'était levé; mais l'idée que les grands seigneurs de Rome ont de l'honneur et du devoir, c'est de ne pas quitter d'un pas ni d'un instant leur dame. Quelques-uns n'ayant pas pu s'asseoir se tenaient derrière la chaise de leurs belles, prêts à les servir au moindre signe. Les dames ne parlaient qu'à leurs cavaliers; les étrangers erraient en vain autour de ce cercle, où personne n'avait rien à leur dire; car les femmes ne savent pas en Italie ce que c'est que la coquetterie, ce que c'est en amour qu'un succès d'amour-propre; elles n'ont envie de plaire qu'à celui qu'elles aiment; il n'y a point de séduction d'esprit avant celle du coeur ou des yeux; les commencements les plus rapides sont suivis quelquefois par un sincère dévouement, et même une très longue constance. L'infidélité est en Italie blâmée plus sévèrement dans un homme que dans une femme. Trois ou quatre hommes, sous des titres différents, suivent la même femme, qui les mène avec elle, sans se donner quelquefois même la peine de dire leur nom au maître de la maison qui les reçoit; l'un est le préféré, l'autre celui qui aspire à l'être, un troisième s'appelle le souffrant (*il patito*); celui-là est tout-à-fait dédaigné, mais on lui permet cependant de faire le service d'adorateur; et tous ces rivaux vivent paisiblement ensemble. Les gens du peuple seuls ont encore conservé la coutume des coups de poignard. Il y a dans ce pays un bizarre mélange de simplicité et de corruption, de dissimulation et de vérité, de bonhomie et de vengeance, de faiblesse et de force, qui s'explique par une observation constante; c'est que les bonnes qualités viennent de ce qu'on n'y fait rien pour la vanité, et les mauvaises, de ce qu'on y fait beaucoup pour l'intérêt, soit que cet intérêt tienne à l'amour, à l'ambition ou à la fortune. (pp. 150–1)

This cultural critique, which in a later age would qualify as fully fledged anthropological reportage, and can certainly be described as already *proto*-anthropological in kind, covers outward behaviour and inner feeling, as well as the linkage between the two. The manifestations noted in contemporary Roman society by De Staël are culturally marked and highly gendered. Her passage also hints (historically) at cultural evolution, out of and away from the violent practices of an earlier age. In saying that 'the custom of using daggers' remains only among lower classes (in the original, *les gens du peuple*), her implication is that in the upper echelons of society such violence has been 'bred out,' to be replaced by a weird conviviality among sexual rivals. Indeed, there is not much in the entire passage suggesting social interaction among groups of more than two, except in the case of male sexual rivals: all significant relations between the sexes in Italy, she seems to be claiming, are conducted in person-to-person intensities – *à deux*.

What is of interest, especially if one goes on thinking of this as a form of proto-anthropological writing, is the positivism of the act of analysis itself. No matter how complex the mixture of opposites that are deemed to prevail in Italy – simplicity and corruption, deceit and truth, good nature and vengeance, weakness and strength – the claim is that all such complexities, although culturally strange to any foreign beholder, are susceptible to explanation by *une observation constante*. I focus on this because in a sense this novel only *superficially* conforms to the genre of the novel. It also aspires to the status of another genre of De Staël's day, that of travel writing. (We saw that Leopardi casually mentioned *Corinne* in the mid-1820s as his sole and definitional instance of books of this other genre.) De Staël's work documents the *moeurs et charactère* of both Italian and British peoples. It has been deliberately constructed by De Staël such that Corinne and Oswald, its main figures, respectively originate from Italy and Britain, travel between and extensively *within* the two nations, and have characters that symbolically represent a great deal of the two cultures as she sees them.

This is a work that, by blending the contemporary genre of the novel with that of travel writing, seeks primarily to function as an analysis of comparative cultural specificities. Interestingly, in the French original of the passage quoted, the key terms deployed act as a sophisticated set of filters in the analysis being undertaken. Not only are they a relatively extensive set of abstract (mainly behavioural) concepts: to wit, *impolitesse, égoïsme, honneur, devoir, étranger, coquetterie, amour, amour-propre, dévouement, constance, infidélité, simplicité, corruption, dissimulation, vérité, bonhomie, vengeance, faiblesse, force, vanité, intérêt*; they furthermore only receive their present concrete meaning in context, from their positioning in the syntactic structures of the overall account. Each of the terms is handled in a way that suggests that, if used of some other culture, it would have a different valency and stand as a descriptor of different vectors of behaviour and feeling.

Taking only the first of these terms, it is obvious that De Staël is saying that what in the countries of origin of Lord Nelvil and Count d'Erfeuil (Britain and France) would be shocking *impolitesse*, here in Roman society is nothing of the kind. Once we see how the terminology is being used, as an analytical (and frequently comparative) cultural grid, our simplest notions of Saussurean linguistics will remind us that all such words acquire accretions or changes in meaning through use, and over extended time. Any particular use deploys such meaning as the terminology has acquired up to the given moment, but with new syntactic purpose. Here, for instance, terminologies in the language of French culture are being used to describe behaviour and feeling in an adjacent and (by this reckoning) dramatically different one, that of Italy. More than a hint of what the same terminological grid, if used to analyse Parisian or indeed Edinburgh society, might produce is subtextually (or indeed directly) implied, in De Staël's portrayal of this particular scene in Rome.

We need only compare De Staël's attempt at an objective and non-judgmental accounting for the Italian phenomenon of *cavalieri serventi* with that of her friend Sismondi, to see – in stark contrast with what I have called her proto-anthropological method – how moralizing a cast of history his is. Sismondi's account comes years later, in the third-last chapter of the final volume of his *Histoire*, published in 1818, as part of his description of the revolutions of the seventeenth century. As we shall see later, Stendhal derives from Sismondi the idea that 'the more one advances, the more one becomes convinced that the history not simply of its individual republics, but of the Italian nation itself ended with the year 1530' ('Plus on avance et plus on demeure convaincu que l'histoire, non point des républiques seulement, mais de la nation italienne elle-même, a fini avec l'année 1530'; vol. 16, p. 220). Sismondi sees that in this 'end of history' some very profound suffering was driven *within*, lodging in the breasts of individual Italians. Each man (the account hereabouts is written from the perspective of the male gender) suffered in silence, 'in his family, as a man, and not as a citizen' ('dans sa famille, comme homme, et non comme citoyen,' p. 221). There follows the most harrowing account of private relations being poisoned, hopes being destroyed, and fortunes crushed, in a general calamity, but one that was always suffered at the level of the *individual* conscience, accusing *itself* of culpability.

And what is 'the most universal private suffering in all Italian families' ('la plus universelle des souffrances privées de toutes les familles italiennes,' pp. 221–2)? Why, none other than 'the attack on the sacredness of marriage by another avowed bond, considered honourable, and which foreigners note always in Italy with the same surprise without being able to understand it, namely, the custom of *cicisbei* or *cavalieri serventi*' ('l'atteinte portée au lien sacré du mariage, par un autre lien avoué, con-sideré comme honorable, et que les étrangers voient toujours en Italie avec une égale surprise, sans pouvoir le comprendre, celui des *cicisbei* ou *cavalieri serventi*,' p. 222). Italian courts were the first to spread the custom, but by Sismondi's reckoning the practice soon devolved downwards through the classes, such that family peace was banished throughout Italy. 'No husband could any longer look on his wife as a faithful companion, linked intimately to his existence; none could any longer find in her undoubting counsel, a prop in adversity, a saviour in danger, a consolation against despair; no father dared assure himself that the children who bore his name were his own; none felt tied to them by nature; and pride in conserving reputation, replacing as it did sweeter and more noble sentiments, poisoned all domestic relations' ('Aucun mari ne regarda plus sa femme comme une compagne fidèle, associée à toute son existence; aucun ne trouva plus en elle un conseil sans doute, un soutien dans l'adversité, un sauveur dans le danger, un consolateur dans le désespoir; aucun père n'osa s'assurer que les enfans qui portoient son nom étoient à lui; aucun ne se sentit lié à eux par la nature; et l'orgueil de conserver sa maison, mis à la place du plus doux et du plus noble des sentimens, empoisonna tous les rapports domestiques,' p. 222).

Sismondi goes into the complex nature of *cicisbeism* as a practice, and describes some of its powers and attributes as an institution. It calmed the unquiet spirits of a people too recently subjugated by foreign powers, damping down those whose mettle remained 'too masculine' ('trop mâles') by effeminizing both nobles and citizens impatient of the yoke and forcing them to forget the liberty they had lost (pp. 222–3). It was likewise a sexual outlet for younger brothers, who (as we saw in our earlier account of Sismondi's social analyses) were excluded from inheritance and hence from any hope of marrying well. This group in particular, according to Sismondi, was the one around and on behalf of whom the bizarre rights and duties of the *cicisbei* were invented. 'These were founded entirely on two laws that the *beau monde* imposed; no woman could with decency appear alone in public; and no husband could without ridicule accompany his wife' ('On les fonda tout entiers sur deux lois que s'imposa le beau monde; aucune femme ne put plus avec décence paroître seule en public; aucun mari ne put sans ridicule accompagner sa femme,' p. 224). The grand result – social breakdown.

> Laws, custom, example, religion itself in the manner in which it was practiced, tended in everything to substitute egoism in place of every more noble incitement. But while men were forced to answer for everything in themselves, they were at the same time stripped of all private joys that they might have experienced. The father of a family – married to a woman he had not chosen, did not love, and by whom he was not loved; surrounded by children of whom he didn't know whether he was the father, whose education he did not follow, and from whom he obtained no love; embarrassed ceaselessly within the family by the presence of the gallant of his wife; separated from a number of his brothers and sisters who had been shut up early in religious institutions; wearied by the uselessness of the others, for whom, as an established practice, he was obliged to lay a place at table – was not considered by them all except as administrator of the family patrimony. He alone was responsible for its budget, whereas all the others, brothers, sisters, wife, and children, had entered into a secret league, so as to siphon off for themselves as much as they could of the common incomings, to enjoy themselves, and to obtain for themselves a state of ease, without a care for the exigency in which their family head might find himself.

> Les lois, les moeurs, l'exemple, la religion même, telle qu'elle étoit pratiquée, tendoient à substituer en toute chose l'égoïsme à tout mobile plus noble. Mais tandis qu'on forçoit les hommes à tout rapporter à eux-mêmes, on les privoit en même temps de toutes les jouissances qu'ils auroient pu trouver en eux-mêmes. Le père de famille, marié à une femme qu'il n'avoit point choisie, qu'il n'aimoit point, dont il n'étoit point aimé; entouré d'enfans dont il ne savoit point s'il étoit père, dont il ne suivoit point l'éducation, dont il n'obtenoit point l'amour, gêné sans cesse dans sa famille par la présence de l'ami de sa femme, séparé d'une partie de ses frères et de ses

soeurs, qu'on avoit enfermés de bonne heure dans des couvens; fatigué de l'inutilité des autres, auxquels, pour tout établissement, il étoit obligé de donner toujours un couvert à sa table, n'étoit regardé par eux tous que comme l'administrateur du patrimonie de la famille. Il étoit seul responsible de son économie, tandis que tous les autres, frères, soeurs, femme et enfans, étoient entrés dans une ligue secrète, pour détourner à leur profit le plus qu'ils pourroient du revenu commun, pour jouir, pour se mettre eux-mêmes dans l'aisance, sans se soucier de la gêne où pouvoit se trouver leur chef. (vol. 16, pp. 227–8)

Sismondi charts a nexus of social and sexual ills within Italian history of the period. The greatness of the account is as a representation. We should not, I believe, be exclusively interested in the truth or otherwise of Sismondi's diagnosis. What we can see straight away is that it is a discourse with a particular, patriarchal bias. As such, it is social breakdown seen from only one (however intense) point of view. One could, for instance, imagine a very different account of the phenomena in question, as provided by wives in this society, or else by younger sons or convent-sacrificed sisters. But given the obvious biases of its unitary perspective – from the patriarchal apex of a generalized Italian family – the passage's account of a fallen moral state of Italy, based in the decline of all family feeling, is magnificent. While clearly very influential in its day, the classic status of this analysis of family breakdown and internal estrangement has been little recognized in modern times. Many accounts of the seventeenth and eighteenth centuries in Italy that emerge after Sismondi's great summation of decline, published in 1818, clearly derive (directly or indirectly) a lot of their power to shock from this primary account of the phenomenon of *cicibeismo*.

Consider only the middle sentence of the paragraph quoted. 'The father ... was not considered by them all except as administrator of the family patrimony.' In between subject and main clause comes the terrible vision of that miasma of ill-willed family members. We should remember here that in the overall *Histoire*, Sismondi's main point in these closing chapters is not even that Italians such as the ones portrayed in these sentences are bad in their inner natures. They themselves are mere pawns of the forces of history, *once liberty has been lost in the Italian peninsular to outsiders*. Many another commentator was to put the case less forcibly. Sismondi in passages such as the one quoted here raises historical writing to a standing alongside other major literary genres.

Sismondi is judgmental to the point of seeing national tragedy in a custom that De Staël had treated as merely something bizarre in Italian customs, not to be judged morally, and that she did not see in historical terms of cause and effect, as he does. I now wish to highlight in *Corinne* a set of sentences almost immediately following the ones that I last quoted, as a bridge to consideration of the other main writers in this chapter, Leopardi and Stendhal. De Staël had been suggesting in the earlier passage that opposites in the Italian temperament are open to analysis, but only through careful observation. She goes on to be still more cautious, in her warnings against over-hasty judgment in the face of bewildering opposites in the Italian character:

> Idleness together with the most tireless activity is yet another of the contrasts in their characters. In everything they are people you must be wary of judging at first sight, for the most contradictory virtues and vices are to be found in them. If at one moment you see them acting prudently, it is possible that in another they may turn out to be the most daring of men. If they are idle, it is because they are resting after doing something or are preparing to act again. In a word, they lose no spiritual strength in society, but gather it all up within them for crucial situations. (p. 93)

> C'est encore un des contrastes de leur caractère, que la paresse, unie à l'activité la plus infatigable; ce sont en tout des hommes qu'il faut se garder de juger au premier coup-d'oeil: car les qualités, comme les défauts les plus opposés, se trouvent en eux; si vous les voyez prudents dans tel instant, il se peut que, dans un autre, ils se montrent les plus audacieux des hommes; s'ils sont indolents, c'est peut-être qu'ils se reposent d'avoir agi, ou se préparent pour agir encore; enfin, ils ne perdent aucune force de l'âme dans la société, et toutes s'amassent en eux pour les circonstances décisives. (p. 151)

De Staël is at the utmost stretch of positivism in her speculations here. We see here her caution against over-hasty judgment. And yet, however diffident she shows herself over moral censure of Italians, she persists in describing their inner contrasts as something she presumes to have understood in fundamental ways. It is hard to fathom her abiding confidence that such *contrastes de leur caractère*, such *qualités, comme les défauts les plus opposés*, do remain open to analysis, and furthermore of a non-judgmental kind. In a sense she teeters on the brink of a contrary belief, namely, that the complexities in question defy full understanding or explanation. Had she proceeded beyond this point, and turned her back (if only partially) on analytical positivism, she might have developed into a figure more like the late-period Stendhal, as I seek to present him in what follows. For in Stendhal there is always a sense in his treatment of Italian temperament of elements of character that surpass explanation in their mysteriousness.

In De Staël's final sentence quoted there is, whatever else, an element of self-consistency with her earlier positions about the strength of individualism and weakness of communal or social existence in Italy. This is, furthermore, the aspect of her account of Italy and Italians that is most carried over into figures such as Leopardi and Stendhal. Leopardi will suggest that there is no longer society as such in Italy. Stendhal will show an ostensible Italian society of the Restoration period, but one that is really no such thing in any fully fledged sense – more a series of shock encounters and of interlocking adventurism between the otherwise tangential individualisms driving characters separately along. Behind De Staël's last sentence would seem to lie a notion of Italians preserving their libidinal energies for momentous events, a notion partially captured in the well-known French saying, *reculer pour mieux sauter* (to draw back in order to leap further). According to De Staël, what Italians hold back their *force de l'âme* from is *société* – by which we may extrapolate that she means the very possibility of a social existence that is of consequence and gratifying. They do so, according to this account, in order to concentrate energy for their leaps when *circonstances décisives* require. Mme De Staël's own novel rarely lives up in excitement to this insight embedded in it. Still, the sentence, with its sense of *force de l'âme* first preparing itself for, then launching daringly during, *circonstances décisives*, seems quintessentially insightful applied to Stendhal's *La Chartreuse de Parme*.

One thing that the writer of *La Chartreuse de Parme* appears to be is without illusions. He is almost entirely sceptical about people's behaviour and motivations; except, that is, for those of his young protagonists Fabrice del Dongo and Clélia Conti, at such times as they behave out of an appealing innocence from not having yet grasped all that is selfish and malevolent in others. One might suppose that Stendhal's groundwork of scepticism would make his novel harshly critical about Italy. Instead, the paradox is that even as he moves towards outright cynicism, his novel's fondness for Italian persons and contexts appears only the more intense on each successive page. *La Chartreuse* is the last and most complex of my exemplary Romantic texts, the one in which Italy most seems a vibrant living context, even though it does not admit of the analytical positivism of a Sismondi or a De Staël. (It would, for instance, be hard to summarize the novel's positions about Italy as I have done in the case of the historian Sismondi.) Importantly, the very subtleties of *La Chartreuse de Parme*, in its intricately combined positivity and negativity, make it more apt for comparison *forward* in history, with the myriad-natured Italy of modern times. Stendhal always did strongly believe he was writing for the 'happy few' who could understand him in his own times, but otherwise for a readership of a later age, when all that was unclear or only potential in what he wrote about the present had been more fully revealed.

In fundamental respects Giacomo Leopardi had reached before Stendhal certain equivalent or even greater depths of scepticism about Italy and Italians. In his 'Discorso sopra lo stato presente dei costumi degl'Italiani,' written some time between 1824 and 1827,[11] he had put forth a series of very radical propositions. Before even specifying Italy as the focus of his analysis, Leopardi had indicated what he saw as a 'universal dissolution of social principles' ('universale dissoluzione dei principii sociali') of the entire age, leading to a form of 'chaos truly frightening to the heart of a philosopher' ('caos che veramente spaventa il cuor di un filosofo,' p. 448). The only remaining aspect of civilized manners (*buoni costumi*) was, by his reckoning, the outward appearance of 'good form' (*buon tuono*). By this account, where even good form is lacking only force prevails (p. 452). There is a decline of civilization into the equivalent of a Hobbesian war of all against all.

More specifically, in dealing with Italy and Italians, Leopardi's case is that 'the nation having no centre, there is truly no Italian public sphere' ('la nazione non avendo centro, non havvi veramente un publico italiano'). Indeed there is no 'social bond'; which in turn means that all honour has gone missing ('non v'ha onore dove non v'ha società stretta,' pp. 453–4). Life is a kind of empty and meaningless vacuum ('la vita non ha in Italia ... sostanza e verità alcuna,' p. 456).

By this point, Leopardi has attributed so much scepticism to Italians – more indeed than scepticism, 'an open and continual cynicism of spirit, in thought, character, habits, opinions, words, and actions' ('un pieno e continuo cinismo d'animo, di pensiero, di carattere, di costumi, d'opinione, di parole e d'azioni') – that he suggests they have insight into 'the vanity and misery of existence and the perversity of humans' ('la vanità e la miseria della vita e la mala natura degli uomini,' p. 461), such as is given to no other people to the same degree. They are more philosophical than any foreigner about all that is bad in the world. This might seem to be a positive, were it not that Leopardi quickly disillusions us still further in proceeding directly to propound the view that from this philosophical insight/cynicism flows the greatest harm possible. We reach a worst-case scenario about Italians at this point in Leopardi's text. 'Like desperation, so too disgust and an inner feeling of life's emptiness are the enemies of all good action, and beget evil and immorality, from which dispositions is born the most radical, profound and efficacious indifference towards both self and others.' ('Come la disperazione, così nè più nè meno il disprezzo e l'intimo sentimento della vanità della vita, sono i maggiori nemici del bene operare, e autori del male e della immoralità. Nasce da quelle disposizioni la indifferenza profonda, radicata ed efficacissima verso se stessi e verso gli altri,' p. 461).

We shall see that what in Leopardi is this groundwork for utter despair becomes, in Stendhal's no less philosophically bleak vision of the nature of Italy and of Italians, the basis for inner richnesses of selfhood in main characters. Passion – on the part of extraordinary individuals for extraordinary others – becomes an ultimate. Stendhal's last novel suggests that in an age when society itself is an empty form, *only* individualism – in its highest expression, passional feeling for another (hopefully reciprocated) – has a chance. So rare is such passion, however, that the isolated individuals capable of it seem elitist in their ability to dismiss the rest of human kind, other than those who are the objects of their desires. This exclusivity in the characters in turn constitutes elitism on the part of the writer who has authored them.

There is a last main overriding position in Leopardi's 'Discorso' that we must also carry over into our critique of Stendhal's novel: the notion that, since no such thing as society in any recognizable sense exists in Italy, there is in consequence very little real communication ('conversazione,' in the widest sense) between humans. And what little there is, is noxious. 'There being no other than a pure and continual war without truce, without treaties ... over things of no substance ... it is manifest how far it must disunite and alienate spirits ... always offended in their self esteem ... Therein consist precisely the moral evil, the perversity of custom, and the moral turpitude of action and character' ('Quel poco ... che v'ha in Italia di conversazione, essendo non altro che una pura e continua guerra senza tregua, senza trattati ... sopra cose di niuna sostanza, ... è manifesto quanto ella debba disunire e alienare gli animi ... sempre offesi nel amor proprio ... nelle quali cose precisamente consiste il male morale e la perversità de' costumi e la malvagità morale delle azioni e de' caratteri,' p. 465).

Society elsewhere too is largely an illusion by Leopardi's reckoning, but at least one that admits of imagination, and hence creativity, among peoples suffering from such illusion. This is bleak philosophical terrain indeed; a vision of a more inwardly corrosive temper than anything Sismondi had diagnosed in his accounts of the fallen state of Italy and Italians. Because it was not published until the next century, Leopardi's 'Discorso' could not have read by Stendhal. But he had wide experience of the same Italy from which its analysis emerged. How far did Stendhal share Leopardi's lack of belief in human communication, and the Romantic angst that is a necessary consequence of this diagnosis of the Italian soul? Very little, is my main answer. But we need to be clear why he did not.

Stendhal's novel cannot be approached from a cold start. Some idea of the sort of person who could write it and, comparatively, of the place of Italy amidst his wider experience of Europe, is necessary. We also need to grasp at the outset that, as deeply as Stendhal believed in pleasure, such belief coexisted in intimate liaison with a knowledge of how precarious and awful life could be. For all his attention to every nuance of happiness, in other words, Stendhal never mistook the hypocrisies of the varying murderous ages he had lived through for the good faith that was publicly proclaimed during them as official policy. Two brief extracts from a work written in 1817 in the wake of Napoleon's fall, but then published in very different form in 1826, drive home the point. Both depict nightmare aspects of the preceding years. I quote from the 1826 text. The first is a negative reflection on Britain's Admiral Nelson, aider and abettor of the reinstalled Bourbons in Naples, in their policy of speedily exterminating the forces that had briefly ousted them:

> I'm told by Mme Belmonte that there exists in Naples a particular philosophical school. But I should hold a pitiful opinion of any person of lively intellect in Naples now who published a metaphysical explication of man and nature. Because others have got in first, and declared their own explication *official*, persons with the power to despatch to the gallows our latter-day Neapolitan philosopher. Why, it is scarcely seventeen years ago that, supported by Nelson, they offered themselves the pleasure of hanging all the best minds in Naples. What French admiral has ever played the role of such as Nelson, of whom there is now a column in Edinburgh, land *of thought and humanity*? People of the North admire beyond measure virtue that exposes its life, the only kind not inclined to hypocrisy, and also the only kind that all understand.

> On trouve à Naples, à ce que m'a dit Mme Belmonte, une école particulière de philosophie. Mais j'aurais une pauvre idée d'un homme d'esprit habitant Naples et qui ferait imprimer une explication métaphysique de l'homme et de la nature. Il y a des gens qui ont pris les devants; ils ont fait déclarer *officielle* leur explication et pourraient bien envoyer à la potence le philosophe napolitain. Il n'y a pas encore dix-sept ans que, appuyés par Nelson, ils se sont donné le plaisir de faire pendre tout ce qui avait de l'esprit à Naples. Quel amiral français a jamais joué le rôle de ce Nelson, qui a une colonne à Édimbourg, le pays *de la pensée et de l'humanité*? Les peuples du Nord admirent, outre mesure, la vertu d'exposer sa vie, la seule qui ne soit pas susceptible d'hypocrisie, et la seule que tous comprennent.[12]

I present this passage at the outset, lest one derive a false impression later on, from the opening pages of *La Chartreuse de Parme*, that Stendhal saw everything in Italy in roseate terms. He is declaring that actions such as the hanging of a generation of 'all the best minds in Naples' render ridiculous the idea that there should be so soon afterwards a 'new' school of philosophy there. His point, as I take it, is that what any philosophy would have above all else to account for is how and why the recent age's philosophers, artists, and statesmen had been wiped out. Logically, therefore, it could not really be *new*, but something grounded in a terrible recent history. 'Be serious,' he seems to be saying, because in such chattering as that of Mme Belmonte there is an insufficient understanding of human history, without which there can be no meaningful philosophy. He is also pointing at Britain, ostensibly famed for seriousness, and saying that the fact that it can erect monuments to such as Nelson utterly compromises its reputation for 'thought and humanity.'

Although written as part of his same account of Italy in 1817, my other instance of Stendhal's apprehension of history as fundamentally constituted by crisis is his memory of Napoleon's Russian campaign, and of the terrible experiences of Moscow and Smolyensk in late 1812. Like hundreds of thousands of other Frenchmen, Stendhal had been on the fateful march back from Moscow. As a supply intendant he had been under impossible orders to find food for vastly more mouths than he or any person could feed in the increasingly cold conditions of retreat. This particular memory from succeeding years is interesting, precisely for the way it surfaces in the midst of an idyllic description of an Italian landscape – the distant perspectives visible from the walls of his favourite of all cities, Milan. Like the former quotation from the same travel book,

Rome, Naples and Florence, it is presented in the form of a journal entry for autumn 1816:

> The trees still have all their leaves today, the 10th November. There are shades of magnificent red and bistre. The view of the Alps from Porta Nova as far as Marengo is sublime. This is just one of the fine views I have experienced in Milan. I had pointed out to me the *Resegon di Lec* [the eleven-peaked mountain over Lecco] and Mount Rosa. These mountains, seen thus rising over a fertile plain, are of a striking beauty, but *reassuring*, like Greek architecture. The mountains of Switzerland, by contrast, remind me always of the weakness of man and of the poor devil of a traveller caught by an avalanche. Such feelings are probably personal. The Russian campaign repulsed me in the matter of snow, not because of any peril to myself, but from the hideous spectacle of awful suffering and the lack of pity. At Wilna, holes in the walls of the hospital were staunched with piecemeal limbs of frozen cadavers. So how could I, with such a memory, find pleasure in seeing snow?
>
> Les arbres ont encore toutes leurs feuilles aujourd'hui 10 novembre. Il y a des teintes de rouge et de bistre magnifiques. La vue des Alpes, à partir du bastion *di porta Nova* jusqu'à la porte de Marengo, est sublime. C'est un des plus beaux spectacles dont j'aie joui à Milan. On m'a fait distinguer le *Resegon di Lec* et le mont Rosa. Ces montagnes, vues ainsi par-dessus une plaine fertile, sont d'une beauté frappante, mais *rassurante* comme l'architecture grecque. Les montagnes de la Suisse, au contraire, me rappellent toujours la faiblesse de l'homme et le pauvre diable de voyageur emporté par une avalanche. Ces sentiments sont probablement personnels. La campagne de Russie m'a brouillé avec la neige, non à cause de mes périls, mais par le spectacle hideux de l'horrible souffrance et du manque de pitié. À Wilna, on bouchait les trous dans le mur de l'hôpital avec des morceaux de cadavres gelés. Comment, avec ce souvenir, trouver du plaisir à voir la neige.[13]

This passage has the convenience of introducing those wide gamuts of feeling between polar opposites that mark Stendhal's oeuvre, most particularly *La Chartreuse*, a novel similarly set in a part of Italy with views of the Alps from its higher towers. Stendhal freely admits, in this passage from a travel book, that even the most beautiful of sensations may coexist with awful personal memories. Life in that respect is a balance of beauty and terror. The further point, however – never made over-explicit – is that experience of Italy is often the assuaging factor in this combination of the uplifting and the terrible.

Usually Stendhal's touchstones for the outrightly terrible come to his mind from some other theatre of recent European history. Sometimes, however, Italy itself is the context of both the sublime and the terrible. For example, although the many rapscallion human motives that we witness in Stendhal's last novel are never so horrific as those frozen cadavers at Wilna that he remembers, nonetheless the portrayal there of humans at their worst is strong, and contrasts with a Romantic idyll of life (and in a sense of Italy) also on offer in this rich work. Perpetually in the novel there is contrast between, on the one hand, lives driven by passion and forceful imagination and, on the other, persons of great venality incapable of altruistic projection beyond self.

Another instance in Stendhal where a less favourable Europe is contrasted with something far finer in recent Italian culture comes from an actual journal entry from Moscow in 1812. Written partially in Italian, it concerns a reality he seems to have been deliberately musing over in order to take his mind off nearer horrors: a jotted explanation of his consuming love of the compositions of Cimarosa, who vied in his mind with Mozart and Rossini for favourite status. 'I believe,' he writes, 'that my love for Cimarosa comes from the fact that he causes to arise sensations such as I hope to inspire one day. That combination of happiness and tenderness of the *Matrimonio* [*segreto* – Cimarosa's opera buffa *The Secret Marriage*] is deeply congenial to my temper.'[14] Happiness and tenderness: 'quel misto d'allegria e tenerezza' is the wording of Stendhal's original Italian. I submit that there is no more heartrendingly simple formulation of what Stendhal was searching to experience and in turn inspire, right up to the final years of creativity from which *La Chartreuse* comes. His distillation in this journal entry is objectified and rationally calm, coming though it does from out of the context of the conflagration of Moscow, a city that, even in flames, he can recognize as, materially speaking, one of the greatest of Europe, but now being destroyed. 'This city was unknown in the rest of Europe', he remarks. 'It had six to eight hundred street mansions [*palais*] such as do not exist in Paris. Everything was devised for the purest form of sensual living. There were stuccos and colours of the freshest and most beautiful; English furniture, the most elegant statuary, charming beds, sofas of a thousand ingenious forms.' ('Cette ville était inconnue en Europe: il y avait six à huit cents palais tels qu'il n'y en a pas un à Paris. Tout y était arrangé pour la volupté la plus pure. C'étaient les stucs et les couleurs les plus fraîches, les plus beaux meubles d'Angleterre, les psychés les plus élégantes, des lits charmants, des canapés de mille formes ingénieuses.') And now 'the spectacle of this charming city, one of the most beautiful temples of sensuality, changed into black and malodorous ruins, in the midst of which strayed unfortunate dogs and a few women, searching for something to eat' ('le spectacle de cette ville charmante, un des plus beaux temples de la volupté, changée en ruines noires et puantes au milieu desquelles erraient quelques malheureux chiens et quelques femmes cherchant quelque nourriture').[15] This is the very context in which, for steadying and objectifying purposes, he dwells on the earlier pleasures of Italy and of Cimarosa.

Only days before Stendhal died, in his fourth-last journal entry of 8 March 1842, he had addressed himself with the instruction, 'Ton affaire est de faire des comédies sans fin,' 'Your job is to write an endless string of comedies' (another translation might read 'comedies without endings').[16] In this he was being consistent with the ambitions of his earlier self: for instance, the young man who, when he first arrived in Paris in 1800 from the provincial town of Grenoble at age sixteen, had the ambition of becoming over time another Molière. That specific arrival had been three days after Napoleon's coup of the Eighteenth Brumaire. Within short months Stendhal was enlisted in the young commander's French army, in its new Italian campaign. (This period in European history is passed in review towards the end of his life in the opening pages of *La Chartreuse de Parme*.)

What is significant is that Stendhal spends the next fourteen years in and out of Napoleon's various campaigns, demobilizing himself intermittently to spend time in Italy or Paris. During such breaks from army campaigns in which he served as an administrator of supply, he feasted in Paris and throughout Italy on the previous fifty years of European culture, much of it musical, and specifically Italian opera. From almost his last journal entry we can go back, for instance, to his first letter of recorded date, to his younger sister Pauline, still in Grenoble (18th ventôse year 8, 9 March 1800), where he is found drawing up a program for the cultural education of his sister, which significantly includes, among much else by way of private reading and courses of instruction, counselled attendance at some good comic operas: they will develop in her 'a taste for music' ('du goût pour la musique') but also bring her 'infinite pleasure' ('un plaisir infini').[17] Pulses of feeling as represented even in other rapidly advancing art forms, such as the novel, could now often best be defined in terms of analogies from the genre of opera. But since the times were not naive, either artistically or politically, but rather constituted 'this age of cant,' as Stendhal (consciously quoting another favourite of his, Byron) never ceased to demonstrate,[18] it was not merely the sublimity of sensation that opera brought with it that mattered, but something by way of its twinned opposite, namely comic perspectives, that might allow for objective distance even *from* such sublimities.

I want to transfer now, without modulation, to *realpolitik*. In late 1830 Stendhal was turned down for the French consulship in Trieste, after representation by Austrian censors (of which we have documented records) had finally been made to no less a person than Metternich himself, to the effect that this dangerous person should not be confirmed in a post that he had, as it happened, already briefly and improperly assumed. Stendhal was not overly troubled about being thrown out of an Austrian-controlled area of Italy. It had happened to him before, from Milan, as the new tirades against him by Austrian officials scrutinizing his case did not cease to point out. He certainly sensed he could gain a replacement posting to a more exciting part of Italy from the new French government of the so-called July Monarchy. So he jauntily requested the southernmost consulship in the whole of Italy, that of Palermo, asking powerfully placed friends in Paris to lobby for it on his behalf, all in comically turned letters. He *was* transferred, but to a plague-infested backwater, Civitavecchia, which he came to loathe even more than, probably, he would have done Trieste over time. However, with his known penchant for capturing happiness against the odds, he spent much of the twelve-year Civitavecchia posting leagues away in Rome, or on still farther furlough in Paris, writing during the remainder of his life most of his best work (with the exception of the just-published *Le rouge et le noir*, 1830).

In tribute to just *how* politically offensive Stendhal could appear to some people – but also in order to understand radical features in his art of novel writing – consider the words of the Austrian prefect of police in Vienna, justifying to the chancellor of state, Prince Metternich, why this 'doubly suspect being, Henri Beyle,' should be halted in his tracks, and certainly not confirmed in the Trieste consulship. Interestingly, the document reads very like the voice of highly conservative officialdom in the state of Parma, as it is imagined in Stendhal's last novel. And the person defined by the prefect of police as a subversive malefactor seems not unlike Stendhal's hero of that novel, Fabrice del Dongo:

> Your Highness will wish to see the attached report by the director general of police in Milan ... to the effect that the Frenchman Henri Beyle, who in 1828 was evicted from Milan and all Austrian states as author of many revolutionary pamphlets written under the apocryphal name of one Baron de Stendhal and directed above all against Austria, recently turned up again in Milan en route for Trieste, in order to assume the functions of Consul General there bestowed on him by the present royal government of France. In spite of the fact that his passport was not stamped with a visa by our Austrian embassy in Paris, he continued his journey to Trieste with the consent merely of Lombardy's governor. In order to illustrate both the degree of hostility this Frenchman is animated by against the Austrian government and the dangerous character of his political principles ... permit me to communicate to Your Highness the pieces of advice given by our censor on three of his works: *The History of Painting in Italy*, Paris, 1817, Didot; *Rome, Naples and Florence*, Paris, 1826, Delaunay; and *Promenades in Rome*, Paris, 1829. I take the liberty to suppose that Your Highness will purely and simply refuse confirmation in the position of Consul General at Trieste, if the French government persists in demanding it for a doubly suspect being such as Henri Beyle.[19]

To turn the nature of the prefect's argument on its head, I submit that it is precisely on account of Stendhal's multiply subversive qualities – as a writer I now mean – that we should confirm him in a kind of posthumous 'consulship' in matters of heart, mind, and action. Our reason for doing so becomes clear after only a few pages of *La Chartreuse de Parme*, about which it is time now to speak more directly.

In some ways the closest analogy for quickly coming to terms with the opening of Stendhal's novel is the fairy tale of Sleeping Beauty. 'The miracles of gallantry and genius of which Italy was a witness in the space of a few months aroused a slumbering people.' ('Les miracles de hardiesse et de génie dont l'Italie fut témoin en quelques mois réveillèrent un people endormi.')[20] The French Republican army under General Bonaparte in 1796 awakens the peoples in the Italian north, under Austrian rule until this moment, from a sleep of befuddlement that had prevented their living out their true natures. In earlier accounts that Stendhal had been in the habit of giving, the 'sleep' in question dated from well before Austrian rule. He had long been in the habit of defining dramatic – even *melo*dramatic – changes in the communal Italian soul. For example, some twenty years before composing *La Chartreuse* he had basically followed Sismondi (though affecting to find his

History 'mediocre') in seeing that with the end of republics in Italy, and the fall of its powers to foreign domination in 1530, a great age had passed. 'They had liberty, but in 1530 they lost it ... A people of giants died in 1530 and were replaced by pygmies.' ('Ils avaient la liberté, en 1530 ils perdirent la liberté ... Un peuple de géants est mort en 1530 et a été remplacé par un people de pygmées.')[21] While calling Sismondi on these very pages 'unreadable,' Stendhal clearly buys deeply into his thesis about the greatness of the Italian Renaissance republics. Much later, in the opening pages of *La Chartreuse* it is specifically *republican* French forces that in 1796 stir the Italians from slumber. So the reawakening holds also the promise of a return to an earlier and better political paradigm.

From the point of view of where we left off with Mme De Staël and later with Sismondi, Stendhal sees the effeminate ridiculousness to which the Italian people had stooped in the preceding age as quintessentially concentrated in the custom of women having *cavalieri serventi* or *cicisbei*.

> Two or three years after that great event in her life [a noble marriage], the young lady in question used to engage a devoted admirer: sometimes the name of the *cicisbeo* chosen by the husband's family occupied an honourable place in the marriage contract. It was a far cry from these effeminate ways to the profound emotions aroused by the unexpected arrival of the French army. Presently there sprang up a new and passionate way of life. A whole people discovered on the 15th May, 1796, that everything which until then it had respected was supremely ridiculous, if not actually hateful. The departure of the last Austrian regiment marked the collapse of the old ideas: to risk one's life became the fashion. People saw that, in order to be really happy, after centuries of cloying sensations, it was necessary to love one's country with a real love and to seek out heroic actions. (vol. 1, pp. 3–4)

> Deux ou trois ans après cette grande époque de sa vie, cette jeune fille prenait un chevalier servant: quelquefois le nom du sigisbée choisi par la famille du mari occupait une place honorable dans le contrat de marriage. Il y avait loin de ces moeurs efféminées aux émotions profondes que donna l'arrivée imprévue de l'armée française. Bientôt surgirent des moeurs nouvelles et passionnées. Un peuple tout entier s'aperçut, le 15 mai 1796, que tout ce qu'il avait respecté jusque-là était souverainement ridicule et quelquefois odieux. Le départ du dernier régiment de l'Autriche marqua la chute des idées anciennes: exposer sa vie devint à la mode; on vit que pour

être heureux après des siècles de sensations affadissantes, il fallait aimer la patrie d'un amour réel et chercher les actions héroïques. (pp. 5–6)

The nonchalant, tongue-in-cheek wit is deceptive, but deeply characteristic of Stendhal. It may at first obscure from us the fact that most of his deepest life values are evinced in these sentences. Indeed, much of the rest of the novel will be about what comes up here in generalized form: namely, passionate lifestyles and living by new ideas rather than age-old 'cloying sensations.' Of utmost importance during an age of revolutionary renewal is love of country and almost any and all heroic action. Like De Staël, Stendhal is discussing the *moeurs* of Italy. He is full of mockery for its former staid and unimpassioned period of *ancien régime* effeminacy in the noble classes. The idea that, with the connivance even of her husband and his family, a woman might be licensed to have named gallants (*cicisbei*), far from being seen by him as an opportunity for passion, is presented as the very opposite – a recipe for a mediocre lifestyle dominated by codification and paperwork.

Stendhal writes differently about *cicisbeismo* than did either De Staël or Sismondi before him. De Staël, we recall, had been a *cultural comparativist* in treating the Italian custom of *cavalieri serventi*, and keen to ward off over-hasty moral judgment about it, or indeed about any other oddities of Italian lifestyle. Sismondi had moralized over this custom's undermining of family values in Italy. Stendhal, by contrast, provides satirical persiflage about Italian noblewomen and their *cisisbei*, but, more crucially, sees the custom itself not as timeless, but as having a historical before and after, which contrast starkly with it. Writing as he was towards the end of his life, and late in the Romantic period, Stendhal had the advantage of longer perspectives about Italy than Mme De Staël, who by 1807 had had opportunity to study the nation only as an intelligent outsider. Stendhal, though equally born into French *ancien régime* culture, had seen the successive revolutionary and then Napoleonic periods from the inside, including during periods with the army in Italy in 1800 and 1801. He 'considered his own first entry into Milan as his true birth' ('considérait son entrée dans Milan comme sa vraie naissance').[22] He had subsequently travelled as a private individual in Italy in 1811 and early 1812, before going with Napoleon's army on the Russian campaign. With the Restoration he spent parts of whole years in Italy, at first mainly in Milan but then, with the advent of the July Monarchy in 1830, in his consulship at Civitavecchia or in nearby Rome. He had by then devoted to Italian subject matter literally thousands of pages of travel books, journals, accounts of composers, or novellas in the form of his *Chroniques italiennes*. Thus, if by late 1838, rather than attempting culturally objective positivism of De Staël's kind or moralizing history *à la* Sismondi, he was instead writing of Italy with a host of intermingled ironies and appreciations, he at least did so deliberately.

According to Stendhal the Italian peoples 'had been plunged in the darkest night by the continuation of the jealous despotism of Charles V and Phillip II; they overturned these monarchs' statues and immediately found themselves flooded with daylight' (vol. 1, p. 4) ('On était plongé dans une nuit profonde par la continuation du despotisme jaloux de Charles Quint et de Philippe II; on renversa leurs statues, et tout à coup l'on se trouva inondé de lumière,' p. 6). We note two things in this account. By an exaggeration of Sismondian history, night is seen to have begun historically for Italy by reason of foreign domination in the sixteenth century. Daylight, by contrast, results from a different foreign invasion, that of the revolutionary and republican French of 1796. We know from other texts by him that Stendhal was not ignorant that Italy had had Enlightenment thinkers of her own, such as Pietro Verri and Cesare Beccaria in Milan itself, in the decades of Austrian domination before the French invasion. But he is using novelistic hyperbolae here, so as to accentuate polar extremes in lifestyle before and after change. It suits these techniques of comic exaggeration – as in the Italian *opera buffa* form so dear to him – to indicate that darkness prevailed in Italy during the period of the Enlightenment, and that the values of the latter only reached it with this 1796 French invasion. 'For the last half-century, as the *Encyclopaedia* and Voltaire gained ground in France, the monks had been dinning into the ears of the good people of Milan that to learn to read, or for that matter to learn anything at all was a great waste of labour' (vol. 1, p. 4) ('Depuis une cinquantaine d'années, et à mesure que l'*Encyclopédie* et Voltaire éclataient en France, les moines criaient au bon people de Milan, qu'apprendre à lire ou quelque chose au monde était une peine fort inutile,' p. 6).

We should always bear in mind that the novel begins with this revolutionary *interim* in Italy, between two separate periods, the *ancien régime* and the Restoration, during both of which forces of conservatism prevailed. It is about a small group of people who persist in living largely by the passional and heroic ethic of these brief interim years, and on into their aftermath. As Michel Crouzet has said, 'This prelude, evoking an absolute age of gold, might from contrast make all that follows seem like a human desert. But from the point of view of passion there is no going back: all the characters are born in one way or another with this sprightliness of energy; the entire novel *descends* thus from 1796.' ('Le prélude, évoquant un âge d'or absolu, ferait par opposition de toute la suite un désert human. Mail il n'y a pas de retour en arrière du point de vue de la passion: tous les personnages sont nés d'une manière ou d'une autre avec cette jouvence de l'énergie; le roman tout entier *descend* de 1796.')[23] Most of *La Chartreuse de Parme* is set in the Restoration period, after Napoleon's loss of the battle of Waterloo. Indeed, the protagonist Fabrice has witnessed and 'risked his life' – 'heroically' – in this great battle that reseals the fate of Europe. Though uncertain ever afterwards if he has truly been at the battle, so bewildering are his personal experiences of it, he is for the rest of the novel Stendhal's most uncompromising exemplar of the energies and passions that have had their Italian *re*birth (as Fabrice himself has been literally begotten) in 1796.

There are subtle hints here and later in the novel that Fabrice is in fact the offspring of an affair between his noble Italian mother and a dashing but distressingly ragged officer in the French army, a certain Lieutenant Robert, who is billeted in the Milanese palazzo of the Marchesa del Dongo. Certainly he is not in character the son of his 'official' father, the Marquis del Dongo. But in a sense Stendhal is correct never to clarify this matter. For he is in part playing with conventions of the novel in order to write all the more pointedly his history of the times. In terms of such novelistic conventions, Fabrice the character is born of the carnivalesque spirit unleashed in Milan by the inhabitants' reception of the French, the chief instancing of which, for purposes of the narrative, is certainly the meeting between the classical Italian beauty, the Marchesa del Dongo, and Lieutenant Robert.

The latter is from the outset defined as 'assez leste' (p. 8), 'not overburdened with scruples' (vol. 1, p. 6), in his scratching together a ragged uniform from the battlefield dead. This he does in order to present himself at dinner with the Marchesa del Dongo and 'her husband's sister, who was afterwards that charming Contessa Pietranera' whom 'no one, in posterity, surpassed ... in gaiety and sweetness of temper, just as no one surpassed her in courage and serenity of soul when fortune turned against her' (vol. 1, p. 8) ('soeur de son mari, qui fut depuis cette charmante comtesse Pietranera: personne dans la prospérité ne la surpassa par la gaieté et l'esprit aimable, comme personne ne la surpassa par le courage et la sérénité d'âme dans la fortune contraire,' p. 9). Thus, casually, is the main female character first introduced to us, in terms of chronicle-like generalizations of all that she will later, novelistically, become. The sentences' extravagant praise is straight out of a seventeenth-century *récit*, such as the opening of Mme de Lafayette's *Princesse de Clèves* – for example, that text's similar introduction of the main female character in terms of unsurpassed beauty and spirit.

Onto this earlier cultural layering Stendhal will build specific nineteenth-century detail. For the moment he has to go on creating *combinations* of a mythical any-and-all time with detail specifying *this* particular historical moment. The blending of mythical and real is handled most subtly of all perhaps in the account the lieutenant gives of his meeting with the two women:

> He and his orderly spent the two hours that divided him from this fatal dinner in trying to patch up the tunic a little and in dyeing black, with ink, those wretched strings round his shoes. At last the dread moment arrived. 'Never in my life did I feel more ill at ease,' Lieutenant Robert told me; 'the ladies expected that I would terrify them, and I was trembling far more than they were. I looked down at my shoes and did not know how to walk gracefully. The Marchesa del Dongo,' he went on, 'was then in the full bloom of her beauty: you have seen her for yourself, with those lovely eyes of an angelic sweetness, and the dusky gold of her hair which made such a perfect frame of the oval of that charming face. I had in my room a *Herodias* by Leonardo da Vinci, which might have been her portrait. Mercifully, I was so overcome by her supernatural beauty that I forgot all about my clothes. For the last two years I had seen nothing that was not ugly and wretched, in the mountains behind Genoa.' (vol. 1, p. 7)

> Son voltigeur et lui passèrent les deux heures qui les séparaient de ce fatal dîner à tâcher de recoudre un peu l'habit et à teindre en noir avec de l'encre les malheureuses ficelles des souliers. Enfin le moment terrible arriva. 'De la vie je ne fus plus mal à mon aise, me disait le lieutenant Robert; ces dames pensaient que j'allais leur faire peur, et moi j'étais plus tremblant qu'elles. Je regardais mes souliers et ne savais comment marcher avec grâce. La marquise del Dongo, ajoutait-il, était alors dans tout l'éclat de sa beauté: vous l'avez connue avec ses yeux si beaux et d'une douceur angélique, et ses jolis cheveux d'un blond foncé qui dessinaient si bien l'ovale de cette figure charmante. J'avais dans ma chamber une Hérodiade de Léonard de Vinci, qui semblait son portrait. Dieu voulut que je fusse tellement saisi de cette beauté surnaturelle que j'en oubliai mon costume. Depuis deux ans je ne voyais que des choses laides et misérables dans les montagnes du pays du Gênes.' (pp. 8–9)

The graceless tatterdemalion that is the time-bound lieutenant straight from battles meets the timeless grace of the Marchesa, herself straight out of a Leonardo da Vinci painting. The Marchesa and her sister-in-law Gina are introduced by means of a purported conversation in later years (presumably in France) between Robert and the author, who is reminded that he too has seen the elder of these two beauties in her full younger glory. The comedy and embarrassment of 'shoes ... made out of pieces of soldiers' caps, ... picked up on the field of battle, somewhere beyond the Bridge of Lodi' (vol. 1, p. 6) ('les semelles ... en morceaux de chapeau ... pris sur le champ de bataille, au-delà du pont de Lodi,' p. 8) is allowed its place in the description, but then forgotten and swept aside in the speed and ease of narration, with the succeeding vision of 'supernatural beauty.'

I want to make four main points based on this passage before closing this chapter. First, the description of the Marchesa as being like a Herodias by da Vinci takes us back to a previous great Italian age, the time between having been as it were erased. The Marchesa thus becomes in this moment the reincarnation of something lost in that intervening time. That something is specifically Italian. Sismondi's theories had been based on politics and religion, education and manners. Stendhal's innovation is to suggest that there may be an important further category, Italian female beauty. The Marchesa is like a reincarnation of the finest form of beauty of the former great age. In being so, she can stand symbolically as a guarantee of the return within the present – at least in rare individuals – of all that was best in that former age.

Second, it is well known that Napoleon's armies over the years of their campaigns gathered up many Italian art treasures of the Renaissance, which now reside mainly in the French national collections of the Louvre. We might connect Lieutenant Robert's appreciation of the (living) beauty of the Marchesa del Dongo, and his likening of her to a Herodias in his room by da Vinci, with the historic French appreciation, and hence their subsequent *appropriation*, of so many beautiful artistic treasures of Italy. (Over the years there is a factor in Stendhal's own love of Italy that is nakedly and irrepressibly appropriative.)

Third, Stendhal was in any case interested in superimposing the High Renaissance upon this time of revolutionary renewal in Italy. He says in his 'Avertissement' to the novel that he wished to retell this story in imitation of Italy's own sixteenth-century storyteller of perversity, corruption, and horror, Matteo Bandello. In the introduction to the 1973 Garnier edition of the novel, Antoine Adam points out that at the beginning of 1833 Stendhal, already involved in writing his series of

Chroniques italiennes, had brought together a collection of histories relating to events of the sixteenth and seventeenth centuries in Italy. In one of them, which recounted the origins of the Farnese family's greatness, he found material decidedly different from what he frequently referred to as the flatness of modern or 'American' society, where one might indeed be virtuous, but where, in his words, 'one is overcome by yawning' (l'on bâille à tout rompre').[24] The history of Fabrice had originally begun as one such novella about events of that earlier age. The work that eventually became *La Chartreuse de Parme* had, in other words, initially been conceived as a chronicle history of a Renaissance pope, Alessandro Farnese, in the years of his daring and amoral climb to the top of the greasy pole of power.

Fourth, however, and most interestingly of all, Alessandro Farnese had become Pope Paul III shortly after that watershed year of 1530 (in 1539 to be precise).[25] Stendhal's interest in him was therefore not, like Sismondi's, in the greatness of those times *before* the beginning of Italy's moral decline. It was specifically an interest in someone living in a succeeding corrupt age, who debauched himself in climbing over others to the top. Likewise, Stendhal's explicit interest in Bandello's *novelle* and his choice of other plots for the *Chroniques italiennes* show more than a hint of fascination with an age of horrors immediately *following* the artistic and political glories of the earlier Renaissance. In eventually removing the time-setting of his novel to the end of the eighteenth century and first decades of the nineteenth, Stendhal has put it on the cusp of a similar historical juncture, between one great age, the Napoleonic, and the squalid times that follow. Stendhal is, in short, specifically interested in the exciting individualisms of his characters, and in what besets them in the context of venal practices of the society surrounding them. It serves his purpose better therefore that most of the novel is set *after* 1814/15, just as his own interest in earlier centuries had been more in the corrupt times *following* 1530 than in the age of achievement before that juncture. This is an important parting of the ways between himself and Sismondi. And it is of a kind that helps us differentiate his case markedly from Leopardi's too, or the earlier De Staël's. He thrills to the drama of individualism pitted against pervasive corruption.

Corruption or simply *tedium vitae*. Part of what makes Stendhal's small grouping of three main characters (four if we count Clélia) important in this novel is that they have a passionate interestingness that intrigues the rest of society, and that it cannot do without. We may muse as to why Stendhal has settled not for the Italy of great cities and fine culture, but for a small principality that seems (in representation) to be a throwback to earlier forms of tyranny: 'What a lamentable piece of stupidity to come and live at the court of an Absolute Prince! A tyrant who knows all his victims; every look they give him he interprets as a defiance of his power' (vol. 2, p. 47). ('Quelle funeste étourderie! venir habiter la cour d'un prince absolu! un tyran qui connaît toutes ses victims! chacun de leurs regards lui semble une bravade pour son pouvoir,' p. 296.) These are the thoughts of Gina Pietranera on realizing that the Prince of Parma, Erneste IV, has double-crossed her and imprisoned her nephew Fabrice for murder of the actor Giletti, when she had seemingly bested him by threatening to leave his court forever if he did any such thing.

However, there is wider significance in Stendhal's settling for precisely such a small and corrupt Restoration court as his main setting. To understand why he does so we must follow the main characters' own life choice to stay on in Parma. Gina's threat throughout, whenever sickened by the ennui or by the corrupt intrigue of a small princedom, is that she will remove to one of the great cultural capitals that Stendhal himself had so appreciated over preceding decades: basically Naples or Milan. In the interview between the Prince and Gina two chapters earlier than the preceding quote, the drama (from the Prince's point of view) is between holding this beauty in his own court or losing her forever to Naples. His desire to hang onto her is based on the intensity of her attractiveness, accentuated as it is by her very threat of leaving his court. 'Never had the Duchess been so gay or so pretty; she did not seem five-and-twenty' (vol. 2, p. 4). ('Jamais la duchesse n'avait été aussi leste et aussi jolie; elle n'avait pas vingt-cinq ans,' p. 259.)

Before the interview the prince savours the thought of the duchess appealing to him for clemency: 'She was, really, too insupportable with her little airs of independence! Those speaking eyes seemed always to be saying to me, when the slightest thing offended her: "Naples or Milan would have very different attractions as a residence from your little town of Parma"' (vol. 2, p. 3). ('Elle était aussi trop insupportable avec ses petits airs d'indépendance! Ces yeux si parlants semblaient toujours me dire, à la moindre chose qui choquait: "Naples ou Milan seraient un séjour bien autrement aimable que votre petite ville de Parme,"' pp. 258–9.) With exquisitely good manners she in fact turns the tables on the prince, indicating that precisely because he is going to ensure that her nephew (still at large) is condemned to death in his absence, she has decided to leave the court of Parma forever.

The gradations of psychological duelling between the two are some of the finest in literature. For instance, the duchess prefaces her explicit condemnation of the prince's court, later in the interview, with gratitude that is almost teasingly saccharine: '"I am going to take advantage of the cool night air to travel by post," went on the Duchessa, "and as my absence may be of some duration, I have not wished to leave the States of His Serene Highness without thanking him for all the kindnesses which, in the last five years, he has deigned to show me"' (vol. 2, p. 5). ('Je vais profiter de la fraîcheur de la nuit pour courir la poste, reprit la duchesse, et, comme mon absence peut être de quelque durée, je n'ai point voulu sortir des états de son altesse sérénissime sans la remercier de toutes les bontés que depuis cinq années elle a daigné avoir pour moi,' p. 260.) Very different in tone is the explicit and un-ironic way she will offend the prince later in the interview. 'It was with an expression of the most violent anger, and indeed of contempt that she said to the Prince, dwelling on every word: '"I am leaving the States of Your Serene Highness for ever, so as never to hear the names of the Fiscal Rassi and of the other infamous assassins who have condemned my nephew and so many others to death"' (vol. 2, p. 6). ('Ce fut avec l'expression de la colère la plus vive et même du mépris, qu'elle dit au prince en pesant sur tous les mots: "Je quitte à jamais les états de votre altesse sérénissime, pour ne jamais entendre parler du fiscal Rassi, et des autres infâmes assassins qui ont condamné à mort mon neveu et tant d'autres,"' p. 261.)

This chapter is about Italy's Romantic reputation. What is at stake here is a kind of timeless image of individuals showing contempt for repressive and tyrannical Italian states, or simply boring backwaters, and a desire to be in its very different cultural capitals. Stendhal knew this syndrome well, having spent very few of the years of his diplomatic posting actually in Civitavecchia, and on the contrary taking lengthy absences in Rome, or even more extensive furloughs in Paris (years at a time in certain instances, on dubious grounds of health). It is of further note that in his 'Discorso' of the 1820s Leopardi is categorical that his nightmare of social *anomie* and malevolence is realized at its worst in small towns (his own long-term residence in his natal Recanati being an obvious case in point). For Leopardi, the 'cynicism of mind, thought, character, manners, opinion, words, and action' ('cinismo d'animo, di pensiero, di carattere, di costumi, d'opinione, di parole e d'azioni,' p. 461), the 'moral ill and perversity of customs' ('il male morale e la perversità de' costumi,' p. 465) – all reminiscent of the colourfully awful Italian world Stendhal is portraying some ten to twelve years later – is felt less in the great capital cities.

There are better or at any rate less ill manners in the capitals and major cities of Italy than in the provinces, secondary cities, and towns. The reason is that in the former one has a little more society, therefore a little more care for public opinion, and a little more real existence of such public opinion, hence more study and following of honour, of concern with individual reputation, more need to care for conformity to others, more altogether of customs, which for that reason tend to be good rather than bad. In contrast to what might seem the case, small cities and provinces in Italy have manners and principles much worse and more unregulated than the capitals and major cities, which may seem to be more corrupt, and are indeed always considered so, generally even nowadays, but wrongly.

V'ha migliori o men cattivi costumi nelle capitali e città grandi d'Italia, che nelle provincie, e nelle città secondarie e piccole. La ragione si è che in quelle v'ha un poco più di società, quindi un poco più di cura dell'opinion pubblica, e un poco più di esistenza reale di questa opinione, quindi un poco più di studio e spirito di onore, e gelosia della propria fama, un poco più di necessità e di cura di esser conforme agli altri, un poco più di costume, e quindi di buono o men cattivo costume. Al contrario di quello che può sembrar verisimile, le città piccole e le provincie d'Italia sono di costumi e di principii assai peggiori e più sfrenati che le capitali e città grandi, che sembrerebbero dover essere le più corrotte, e per tali sono state sempre considerate, e si considerano generalmente anche oggi, ma a torto. (Leopardi, 'Discorso,' p. 473).

This passage accords very closely with Stendhal's line of thought in *La Chartreuse*. Indeed, we first meet the senior male character, Count Mosca, principal minister of the tiny principality of Parma, avoiding its pitfalls and social snake pits while on pleasurable furlough in Milan. Spending his nights at La Scala opera, he has fallen in love there with Gina Pietranera (later, by an arranged marriage of his own devising, Gina Sanseverina). As his lover she removes to Parma and becomes its leading socialite. But at every advent of trouble – and notably during their lovers' quarrels – peace of mind is restored by the mere mention of their removal to one of the great operatic centres, Milan or Naples, even without much money to live on. As the count says philosophically to the duchess late in the novel, 'After all, neither you nor I have any need of luxury. If you give me, at Naples, a seat in a box at the San Carlo and a horse, I am more than satisfied; it will never be the amount of luxury with which we live that will give you and me our position, it is the pleasure which the intelligent people of the place may perhaps find in coming to take a dish of tea with you' (vol. 2, p. 220). ('Au fond, ni vous ni moi n'avons besoin de luxe. Si vous me donnez à Naples une place dans une loge à San Carlo et un cheval, je suis plus que satisfait; ce ne sera jamais le plus ou moins de luxe qui nous donnera un rang à vous et à moi, c'est le plaisir que les gens d'esprit du pays pourront trouver peut-être à venir prendre une tasse de thé chez vous,' p. 444.) It is interesting, given the close parallels that I am developing between Leopardi's vision of Italy in the 1820s and Stendhal's novel, set by the time of this speech in the same decade, that Leopardi himself moved for the last years of his life from his small natal town of Recanati that had so often felt like a prison to him: first to Florence in 1830 and then, for the last four years of his life, to Naples and its vicinity.

Clearly, Stendhal could not have made an exciting novel out of that daydream on Count Mosca's part, of happy tea parties between intelligent and companionable persons. And admittedly his travel books on Italy and his journals *had* dealt extensively with the salon and opera worlds of Milan, Naples, and other places. But when it came to writing this novel, he was more attracted to a world such as Leopardi describes, in the latter's horrific vision of an Italy still only minimally touched by a reborn civilization of Enlightenment values, after the darker ages of barbarism:

> The great and undeniable benefit of reborn civilization and of the rise of the Enlightenment is to have liberated us from that state as far from culture as from nature, properly of the dark times, that is the utterly corrupt times; from that state neither civilized nor natural, of in other words literally and simply barbarous, ... from horrible disorder in government, or rather no government, no law, no constant form of republic and administration, uncertainty of justice, of rights, of laws, of institutions and regulations, all in the power and at the discretion and pleasure of force, and this latter for the most part possessed and used without courage, and such courage as there was never for country, or for perils encountered on its behalf, but for low ambitions and passions, or for superstitions and prejudices, vices not hidden by any mask, the sins not thought to merit any excuse, outrageously infamous customs attaching to the greatest and especially to those who made profession of the most holy life and character, wars of religion, religious intolerance, inquisition, poisons, horrible torments for true or supposed criminals, or one's enemies, no rights of the people, torture, burning of persons, and such like things.

> Il grandissimo e incontrastabile beneficio della rinata civiltà e del risorgimento de' lumi si è di averci liberato da quello stato egualmente lontano dalla coltura e dalla natura proprio de' tempi bassi, cioè di tempi corrottissimi; da quello stato che non era nè civile nè naturale, cioè propriamente e semplicemente barbaro, ... dai disordini orribili nel governo, anzi dal niun governo, niuna legge, niuna forma costante di repubblica e amministrazione, incertezza della giustizia, de' diritti, delle leggi, degl'instituti e regolamenti, tutto in potestà e a discrezione e piacere della forza, e questa per lo più posseduta e usata senza coraggio, e il coraggio non mai per la patria e i pericoli non mai incontrati per lei, nè per la gloria, ma per danari, per vendetta, per odio, per basse ambizioni e passioni, o per superstizioni e pregiudizi, i vizi non coperti d'alcun colore, le colpe non curanti di giustificazione alcuna, i costumi sfacciatamente infami anche ne' più grandi e in quelli eziandio che facean professione di vita e carattere più santo, guerre di religione, intolleranza religiosa, inquisizione, veleni, supplizi orribili verso i rei veri o pretesi, o i nemici, niun diritto delle genti, tortura, prove del fuoco, e cose tali. (Leopardi, 'Discorso,' pp. 469–70)

Leopardi's entire sentence at this point in his 'Discorso,' only a small portion of which I have quoted, is a full page long – 366 words! My claim is not that Stendhal filled out in his novel every detail of this nightmare vision of Leopardi, the original of which, we recall, he could not in any case have known. Rather, the Restoration age after 1815 in the petty states of Italy seemed to Stendhal like a return to the exciting corruption and false values of the sixteenth century. Leopardi would seem to have been speaking of a time after 1530 but before the advent of the Enlightenment. Nonetheless, even he goes on to say that there are plenty of conservative thinkers in Italy who would efface Enlightenment values and, out of a bizarre and indefensible love of the past, return Italy to the *tempi bassi* of this vision. Stendhal's novel is very much about just such a court world, one that wishes to deny the Enlightenment or repress its positive legacies. If that world of which Stendhal writes in *La Chartreuse* is without wars of religion, the Inquisition, and some of the worst excesses of torture, it has much else that is written of here by Leopardi.

What is more, in his portrayal of Parma Stendhal is clearly fired by excitement at the exquisite horrors of a state as equally untouched by the greatness of Renaissance or Napoleonic times as by the Enlightenment, and in which many of the horrors of the sixteenth century, as we have seen both Leopardi and Sismondi define them, have endured or been reborn in the present. His quartet of two older and two younger protagonists are fighting against such corruption, even though the older couple, Mosca and Gina, are much more inclined to play along with it, in order to stay ahead of and continue to outwit those who are truly mired therein.

As far as Italy's own Romantic reputation is concerned, Stendhal is really the only one among the four main writers considered here who appreciates the full drama of individuals making their destinies in a corrupt age. Sometimes they win out by an almost perversely creative innocence, as frequently in the case of Fabrice and his beloved Clélia Conti. Youthful innocence in Leopardi's poems or in De Staël's *Corinne* always seemed more doomed than this, and not so likely, furthermore, to enjoy exciting adventures in the course of that doom. Sometimes Stendhal's characters, such as his mature heroine Gina Sanseverina, get the better of rogues through the sheer superiority of beauty over all else, or beauty combined with scheming and with passion for another (in her case passion for her nephew Fabrice, rather more than for her lover Count Mosca).

In short, in Stendhal's novel positive forces win out over the very negatives of corruption that a cultural analyst such as Sismondi had in other respects convinced us were dominant in the case of a latter-day, post-Renaissance Italy. Stendhal's corrupt prince of the novel, Ranuccio-Ernesto IV, is straight out of the worst of Sismondi's scenarios of what has made for Italy's decline. But the manner in which he is constantly baulked in his designs not merely by Fabrice – who tends to win out by happenstance rather more than by design – but also by Gina and Mosca, who usually outwit him by superior political manoeuvring, is part of the ongoing triumph of the book.

In sum, this is *triumph over* the worst aspects of Italy's Romantic reputation. Stendhal is highly aware of the negative cases that can be – and that in his own times (and slightly earlier) were being – put. Indeed, he sets them up with consummate irony, as a series of bogeys to be outfaced. In *La Chartreuse de Parme* he wrote a novel that shows how much he was in love with Italy, for all its acknowledged faults. He builds those faults deep into the fabric of what his work acknowledges about the condition of Italy, seeming by so doing to have thoroughly absorbed the lessons of some of those very contemporaries whom I have devoted much of this chapter to analysing. And he says again and again in this beautiful and moving novel that there is another and positive Italy, perpetually at war with decadence, squalor, and corruption. However precariously, in this novel it goes on winning that battle.

I contend that most people in modern times who are wise to both the negative and the positive sides of Italy's reputation enjoy thinking of how, through thick and thin, the second of these might maintain dominance over the first. For several centuries the contest has been a fine one to witness.

7 Lifestyles High and Low in Changing Post-Unification Urbanism

In this, my last chapter, I deal with Italian urbanism of the mid- and late nineteenth century, and tackle altered and expanding urban contexts, as well as novel commercial paradigms and industrial structures. In its closing section I enquire how changed urban lifestyles were represented visually, in paintings and later (retrospectively) in historical films. In doing so I seek all the while to account for evolutions in urban Italian lifestyles that such rapid changes in built context brought about by way of opportunity for the well-to-do, or by way of further impoverishment on those already vulnerable. Not for nothing have I utilized those simple, old-fashioned social descriptors – high and low – in my chapter title. Unification is itself a major issue, bringing to an end as it did the independence of whole states of the former terrain, not least one large southern kingdom whose capital city, Naples, was in 1861 (and well on into the modern era) the most populous in Italy.[1]

In accounting for the rapidly changing major cities of post-Unification Italy – and consequently for the ways in which different people and classes lived within them – I am consciously striving to emulate the expressive and analytic intensities of Walter Benjamin in his many writings about Paris of the nineteenth century. For just as in earlier chapters, my project here, as Benjamin's was throughout his writings, is one of 'distilling the present, as inmost essence of what has been.'[2] In what follows architecture and lifestyle are not to be understood as separate – the one as matter and the other spirit – for as Benjamin himself brilliantly quotes from Hugo von Hofmannsthal, the city should be understood as nothing less than 'a landscape built of pure life.'[3] This closing chapter hence seeks ambitiously to capture at least some of the poetics of late-nineteenth-century Italian urban culture, sometimes appealing, sometimes terrible, but always no less compelling than that which Benjamin revealed in its complex Parisian counterpart. Indeed, the cultural paradigms that urban Italians took abroad with them, in their migrations to the Americas and elsewhere, were arguably even more important for the unfolding modern age than were those of the French *métropole*.

For convenience sake I shall take as my main contrasting cities Naples in the south and Florence and Milan in the north, with several examples from others where they are most revelatory. All the important cities of Italy grew rapidly after Unification, though some of them – Milan and Turin pre-eminently – with a commercial and industrial dynamic that was over time to show up that of others, principally Naples, as languishing by comparison. The main cities were also materially altered in their existing structures. With what looks to us nowadays like an overweening confidence, older medieval and Renaissance walls and quarters were cavalierly knocked down in order to 'open out' the cities, as Baron Haussmann was similarly doing in Paris between 1858 and 1870. To an extent Haussmann's work acted as incitement to Italian planners, many of whose bold alterations were undertaken with the French example already largely complete, or at least impressively unfolding.[4] Such planners considered the Parisian example from the distance of a neighbouring, newly unified European 'nation,' with a great past but an as yet largely uncertain present and future. Achieving in their own monumental tamperings with urban context a late-nineteenth-century aesthetic of grandeur seems to have been the least these planners felt they could do to promote their individual cities' self-images, and Italian nation-building in the process.

In an earlier book I mapped out some of the ideological implications detectable in the razing of older areas of Florence for the erection of grand monumental centrepieces such as the Piazza Vittorio Emanuele II (now Piazza della Repubblica).[5] In justification of the urban 'renovation' in question, the inscription on a huge 1895 archway portal to that piazza actually includes the term 'vita nuova' (new life), in what has to be a conscious verbal allusion to Dante's work of that title. The entire inscription reads: 'L'ANTICO CENTRO DELLA CITTA / DA SECOLARE SQUALLORE / A VITA NUOVA RESTITUITO' ('The ancient centre of the city / from centuries-old squalor / to new life restored'). However subliminal to persons in city governance the boastful overconfidence of their post-Unification age may have been, the wording of such an inscription involves something of a historical paradox. With the term 'vita nuova' the greatness of Dante is implicitly appealed to. Furthermore, we might say that the exiled Dante himself, as well as his fiercely held belief that there had been a terrible decline in Florence's morals and lifestyles in his own day, are being recuperated in this explicit *fin de siècle* boast about a clean-up of the city. Records of council meetings from as early as November 1864 show that the old centre was being spoken of as an 'agglomeration of obscure and disgusting alleyways' ('agglomerato di vicoli oscuri e schifosi').[6] In the following year, on 18 May, the newspaper *L'Avvenire* reminded its readers that Florence's central market piazza was also known as the 'cloaca massima' or *sewer maximus*![7]

Roughly speaking, the major Florentine alterations carried out in successive waves between 1865 and 1895 demolished what were felt to be outdated or 'squalid' buildings and structures, mainly dating from the twelfth through to the fifteenth centuries. These efforts included removal of most of the city's last set of defensive walls (1284–1333) on the northern side of the Arno River, as well as a clearing away of the central old market and surrounding streets dating from Dante's own age. In other words, what got flattened was surviving urban fabric from the long period that was acknowledged (even by the nineteenth century that was doing the knocking down!) to be the city's greatest prior age, that of the Commune and the ensuing Republic of Florence.[8] A newspaper account in the conservative publication *L'Opinione* of 13 March 1866 captured the conflicting issues in play. While calling this, in its editorial voice, 'the finest opportunity that has been had for creating in Florence all the best imaginable by way of modern building' ('la più bella occasione che si abbia avuto per fare in Firenze quello che di meglio può immaginare l'edilizia moderna'), the article goes on immediately to enact Florentine recoil at the desecration involved: 'But alas. There are the usual memories of ancestors.' ('Ma ahimè! Vi sono le solite memorie degli avi.')[9]

As we shall see from other cities, the confidence with which Florence – even in the face of enduring sentimental regret among its leaders and ordinary citizens alike – set about razing considerable portions of its acknowledged earlier greatness, to create a city that monumentalized Unification under Victor Emmanuel, was not unique. The significant and overriding fact is that the planners responsible for these bold destroy-and-rebuild policies seem to have felt they were producing as an outcome a vital renewal, 'vita nuova' no less. One of the challenges of this chapter is to discover how much good as well as bad came of these various 'renewals' of the major Italian cities after Unification. For it would be pointless to say that for the sake of history the old should never be cleanly knocked down to make way for the new, just as pointless as to think that the new will inevitably constitute a better living context than what preceded it.

It is interesting to see a balance sheet between the old and the new, drawn up in 1897 by Guido Carocci in his book *Firenze scomparsa: Ricordi storico-artistici*.[10] Nearing the end of the century Carocci could look back to a time, about thirty years earlier, when the 'destructive hammer had barely begun its work of transformation.' ('Trent'anni addietro, a Firenze, il martello demolitore aveva appena iniziata la sua opera di trasformazione,' p. 9.) His entire book is an attempt to re-evoke in the memory, sometimes street by street and building by building, the fabric of an earlier city, 'still preserving its emphatically original character – that air of gay simplicity, coupled with a certain medieval pride' ('quel suo carattere così originale, quell'aria di gaia semplicità accoppiata a quel certo che di medioevale fierezza,' p. 10). Carocci's nostalgia constitutes nothing less than a politics of regret, full of implied recrimination over the less than half a century that had turned an essentially medieval city, whose material fabric constituted an intact history of its own past, into a bustling modern metropolis, in which so much of that fabric of historical layering has been destroyed. He reports on a remembered city, bristling with ancient towers of the *consorterie*, or family groupings; threaded with unwidened alleyways and *Lungarni*; ringing with cries from sellers in the as-yet-undemolished central market area; and, perhaps above all, encircled still by its imposing third set of city walls, built between 1284 and 1333, but by 1897 largely cleared away for the new inner-ring system of *viali* – wide carriageways between the *centro storico*, the boundary of which they still defined, and the expanding *periferie*.

More than a century after Carocci, let us too attempt something of a balance sheet in our critical thinking about this example of Florence during its period of fiercely speculative rebuilding as Italy's capital between 1865 and 1871, and on into its aftermath of bankruptcy once capital status was abruptly removed to Rome upon the latter's assumption into the new Italian state. This disturbing history, told blow by blow in Silvano Fei's book on the birth and development of Florence as a 'modern' bourgeois city, *Nascita e sviluppo di Firenze città borghese* (1971), reveals a great deal about the hopes and expectations of Italy's wealthier classes after Unification. More clearly perhaps than happened in other cities, the conflicting pressures exerted by the members of Florence's Consiglio Communale and by speculators including British and Scottish companies that initially won big building contracts there, reveal to us the unfolding ideologies of class in nineteenth-century Italy. Yet much of the abiding significance of the story lies in how the urban proletariat were treated. For they were the prime subjects of eviction in many rebuilding schemes, and then were taxed heavily for years afterwards on items of consumption to pay off the city's huge debts accruing from the mistakes made by councillors and speculators during the boom years.

What is heart-rending is evidence of the goodwill that had led Florentines to destroy so much of their earlier city. Under intense time constraints, many of them exerted by parliamentarians and administrators transferring from Turin (which had briefly been the first capital city of the unified nation), Florence was altered in ways that were meant to make it grand and adequately imposing for its enhanced national status. The chosen main city architect, Poggi, was full of patriotic zeal in his hopes. In a frenzied rush, and with myriad consequent oversights, Florentines underwent the trauma of trying to please the nation, only to see the prestige capital-city status wrenched from them. By then much of the damage to the city's previous urban fabric was irremediable, and the huge and spiralling debts already incurred. In a document of 1878, in which the city councillors appeal to the Senate in Rome for financial relief, we witness the pathos of the psychological pressures that had led to the financial – one might also say the spiritual – crash in the city's fortunes:

> We ourselves, praying to be of help to the city of Florence in terms of justice, specifically hope that many of the nation's senators will recall how small this former capital of a small Grand Duchy seemed for the capital of the Realm; the impatience of all who lamented its defects; the general solicitude to make it not just larger but also more commodious; the regret of its citizens in seeing such bitter discontent; and therewith a febrile anxiety to please, a haste, a recurring to expedients such that, remembering these infelicitous events, the excess that was accidentally the outcome in that which then seemed necessary, and certain errors that were deemed to be mixed in with the useful provisions, we hope that the case will be judged by you by means of an accounting that is not only numerically exact, but that is based as well on equity and goodwill.
>
> The vote in Parliament will thereby be dictated by the persuasion and high sentiment that inspired the words of the Minister: 'Let it not be said that the Nation did damage to so eminent a city.'

> E noi, pregando di aiutare nei confini della giustizia il Comune di Firenze, singolarmente speriamo che molti fra i (Senatori) Rappresentanti della

Nazione ricordino, come testimoni, quanto piccola sembrasse per Capitale del Regno la già Capitale d'un piccolo Granducato, le impazienze di quelli che ne lamentavano i disagi, la sollecitudine generale, a renderla, non che più vasta più comoda, il rammarico dei cittadini nel vedere sì acerba scontentezza, e indi una febbrile ansietà di contentare, una fretta, un ricorrere ad espedienti, sicché rammentate queste non felici congiunture, il troppo che taluno per avventura riuscisse a scoprire in ciò che allora parve necessario, e qualche errore, che altri opiniasse frammisto agli utili provvedimenti, sarà, speriamo, giudicato da Voi, non solo coll'aritmetica buona dei numeri, ma coll'altra non meno buona dell'equità e dell'affetto.

Il voto del Parlamento sarà dunque dettato dalla persuasione e dall'alto sentimento che ispirò le parole del Ministro: 'Non si possa dire che la Nazione danneggiò una sì egregia Città.'[11]

The letter is full of a retrospective pathos at the possible excesses and errors committed in the earlier period, and certainly bears witness to a financial indebtedness that the signatories are hoping may be reduced through state subsidies voted from the Senate. But the document seems troubled by the possibility of 'damage to so eminent a city' of a more than financial kind. Subtextually, we seem to sense in the signatories a fear not only that there has been such damage, but that it may be irreparable. Such is the awful historical balance sheet that these nine councillors are probing their way towards defining. Some of them, including Mayor Ubaldino Peruzzi and the Marquis Giuseppe Garzolini, were long-serving members from the period before the rebuilding, and hence presumably are fraught with a sense of their co-responsibility for the situation. Clearly, they are in part trying to salve their consciences, and perhaps also those of Florentines more generally, by rehearsing what had been the national and municipal mood some twelve or thirteen years earlier, in 1865 and 1866.

Part of the force of their appeal to the Senate is the reminder of how externally produced (at the level of the new nation itself) had been the pressures exerted on the particular city of Florence. Eduardo Detti reminds us that Mayor Peruzzi himself had in fact been against the original transfer of capital status from Turin to Florence, prescient of the great disequilibrium it might produce in the life of the city: like others amongst the grouping of Tuscan 'moderates,' he had only lent himself to the rebuilding projects in earnest when the edict of transfer was a fait accompli.[12] Before that even, as Gramsci attests, these 'reactionary' moderates had not wanted the Grand Duchy of Tuscany to be wound up in the first place, but rather that it form part of an Italian 'federation.' ('I moderati toscani non volevano la fine del granducato, erano federalisti reazionari.')[13] In Gramsci's reading of them, the moderates had long constituted a political class timorous of social change, as first evidenced in their reactions to what they interpreted as the fearful 'excesses' of 1849.[14] Once the Risorgimento achieved its major aim of Unification, which they had opposed, they were obliged to adapt to new realities, none of which were substantially of their own choosing. When the latest link in the chain, the decision to remove the capital to Rome, had betrayed the moderates, the world that some of them, such as Peruzzi, had not desired anyway only grew worse. These moderates were largely at the helm of the Consiglio Communale during the years of upheaval and the rebuilding of Florence. No wonder, then, that the 1878 letter to the Senate by a group that included some of these original moderates reads, between the lines, like a forlorn wish that Florence had never been seduced into the great epoch of over-expensive renewal in the first place. The letter forcefully recalls those earlier pressures of the 1860s. Let us view here what some of them were, including what they led to by way of grand projects, and of social fallout.

Speculators in those earlier years 'found in the new capital a suitable humus for massive investments' ('trovarono nella nuova capitale l'humus adatto per massicci investimenti').[15] In 1865 prefabricated houses made of iron and wood were bought at considerable expense from the London firm Curbit to rehouse in more peripheral areas of the city some of the Florentine proletariat whose inner-city dwellings were being expropriated and demolished for redevelopment.[16] Rents in the properties left standing reached levels no longer affordable by the less well off, and so they too had to move to the prefabs, with the result that their former dwellings were taken over by a wealthier class of person.[17] This displacing of the poor from the *centro storico* of Florence, and their replacement (by and large) with a different class, is a story repeated in other Italian cities during their phases of *risanamento*.

Fei points out clearly that local voices such as that of the clerical publication *Il Firenze* were desolated by the seemingly indiscriminate destruction of so many monuments of fundamental interest to an understanding of Florentine culture. But these were countered by an external press, especially that of Turin, unmoved by the conscience-stricken Florentines. To add insult to injury, a newspaper such as the sub-alpine leftist *Il Diritto* could mockingly submit that 'Florentines cry like eagles when there is a single house to be demolished, a window to be relocated, or a nail to be moved, because they believe the memory of their ancient greatness is being profaned thereby.' ('I fiorentini gridono come aquile quando si tratta di demolire una casa, spostare una finestra, di muovere un chiodo poiché credono di profanare la memoria della loro antica grandezza.)'[18]

Perhaps the one factor that most assuaged the consciences of Florentines was that the remodelling of their city was to follow a grand Haussmann-like plan made by an excellent architect, Giuseppe Poggi, that had been published in 1865. Though not comprehensive, it seemed to promise a widening and straightening of streets, grand *viali* (somewhat along the lines of Paris's new boulevards) where the previous city walls had been, and an emphasizing of many of Florence's major landmarks and monuments. What was not so clearly realized at the time was that the substantial clearance around such monuments often left them devoid of their contemporary context. In the process they tended to become isolated heritage items of an earlier city, reset in a kind of nineteenth-century urban aspic formed by a notably different architectural aesthetic.

What was good in the scheme included the erection for ordinary citizens of entire new suburbs that often were not a great distance from the centre. A company such as the Società Anonima Edificatrice must be credited with the enormously positive step of being 'the first to build in Florence a type of habitation for ordinary rather than outrightly poor classes' ('d'intraprendere per prima in Firenze un tipo d'abitazione popolare e non dichiaratamente per indigenti').[19] But alongside this must be set the profiteering of the early years, undertaken by Florentines as well as outsiders, who by reason of their old aristocratic or newer bourgeois backgrounds were able to put up the speculative capital that made the large-scale changes possible. Some of these people had their fingers burned when their speculations miscarried in later years. But the poor and labouring classes bore proportionately greater burdens, and unlike those of the speculators, theirs began in the first phase of the boom. For the well-to-do that early period was an almost obscenely profitable time. Fei's words encapsulate all such times in the nineteenth century when the old established or newly wealthy classes were winners in economic processes not only in Florence, or Italy, but across the face of Europe:

> For the land-owning expropriators – a very restricted number in respect of the 145–150 thousand inhabitants of Florence, and most of them patricians

of old Florentine families – had arrived the period of the fatted calves. Nobles of ancient stock, wealthy entrepreneurs, professionals, and speculators found themselves submerged in a rain of wealth, unimaginable till then ... That in this kind of speculation there was participation, direct or indirect, by members of the municipal administration should not cause surprise; they all belonged to that 'caste' that held de facto economic power in the city.

Per i proprietari espropriandi, numero assai ristretto rispetto ai 145–150 mila abitanti di Firenze, nella miglior parte patrizi delle antiche casate fiorentine, era giunto il periodo delle vacche grasse. Nobili d'antica schiatta, imprenditori economici, professionisti e speculatori, si trovarono sommersi da una pioggia di danaro, inimmaginabile fino ad allora ... Che in questo genere di speculazioni ci fosse la partecipazione diretta o indiretta dei membri dell'Amministrazione municipale, non deve suscitare meraviglia: costoro appartenevano tutti a quella 'casta' che di fatto deteneva il potere economico e politico della città.[20]

Edoardo Detti has pointed out that those in charge in Florence 'were in the main rulers from the earlier period of the Grand Duchy, an aristocratic oligarchy for the most part of landowners, among whom however were increasingly asserting themselves numbers of rich townspeople, bankers, and lawyers.' ('Si trattava in sostanza della classe dirigente granducale, un'oligarchia nobiliare in prevalenza di proprietari terrieri, nella quale venivano però sempre più affermandosi esponenti borghesi, avvocati e banchieri.')[21]

It would be too easy to see in this story only good and bad people. The fact is that persons of all classes were in some real sense conned, here as elsewhere, by the grandiose promises consequent upon Unification. In Florence those promises had a very specific ephemerality, because of its capital-city status that was no sooner bequeathed in 1864 than all too soon withdrawn in 1871. We need to see, with impartiality, certain factors of undeniable appeal in the initial plans for grand-scale changes to the city. Poggi himself saw his appointment as an opportunity to 'put the breaks on' unplanned development – 'new buildings constructed in the city itself or along tortuous old suburban roads, with irregular but almost always scarce open spaces' ('porre un freno al modo con cui si costruivano presso la città, e lungo le vecchie strade suburbane, le nuove fabbriche, lasciando le communicazioni sempre con andamento tortuoso, con larghezze irregolari e quasi sempre scarse')[22] – and, instead of such extensions of the medieval city, to achieve by rational planning a city worthy of the modern lifestyles it now needed to accommodate.

That such a plan appealed more to a specific class than to those below it in the social scale is undeniable. 'Overall the plan of the Hausmannian Poggi remains a courageous document, conforming for the most part with politico-military, economic, and aesthetic exigencies felt by European bourgeois society.' ('Il piano dell'haussmanniano Poggi, nel suo insieme, rimane un documento coraggioso e conforme in gran parte alle esigenze politico-militari, economiche, estetiche, sentite dalla società borghese europea.')[23] Many of the changes carried out were undertaken with benefit of the few utmost in mind. The central area of the city 'was to be completely given over as a residential encampment for the new bourgeoisie' ('stava ormai per essere completamente saturata come campo residenziale per la nuova borghesia').[24] Admittedly, over time some of the nineteenth-century changes have worn well and become an inheritance shared by the entire world because of Florence's international standing. However, because of the bust that so quickly followed the boom, some of the best things that were planned were never built.

To me the most beautiful of these never realized marvels is found in other plans than Poggi's: a project for changing the central market area of Florence. Throughout these decades of urban transformation in Florence, it was always clear that the centuries-old central market area would eventually have to be demolished and replaced by *something*. So it seems a terrible shame that instead of the Piazza Vittorio Emanuele that was finally constructed, so pompous and inhuman in scale, the following 1869 plan for an entirely glass-arcaded crossroad of streets was not attempted:

> Construction of a crystal gallery over the Via di Pelicceria between Porta Rossa and the centre of the new piazza; intersecting with another gallery over the crossroad described in point no. 3. The central point of this intersection to be covered by a cupola also in glass, 20 metres in diameter and no less than 39 metres above the ground, not including its crown.
>
> Costruzione d'una galleria a cristalli lungo la via di Pelliceria tra Porta Rossa e il centro della nuova piazza; incrociata con altra galleria lungo la via descritta al n. 3. Il centro o crocicchio della medesima sarà coperto da una cupola pure in cristalli del diametro di metri 20 e alta da terra non meno di metri 39 non compreso l'incoronamento.[25]

Unquestionably such a glazed arcade with cupola over thoroughfares of the central area had the potential to rival the finest Milanese and Neapolitan arcades of the century, the aesthetic and use of which I will soon discuss. Being along streets, rather than immediately adjacent to them, it would have been remarkably different from what was achieved in those other two cities. After all, Europe had by now the recent example of what might be achieved in glass, in the form of London's Crystal Palace of the Great Exhibition of 1851.

But 'the action' essentially moved elsewhere, to Rome. There is a chilling but highly revealing justification offered by government finance minister Seismid-Doda in Rome in June 1878 as to why Florence's creditors should be sacrificed and the bankruptcy of the city accepted. He is appealing to the nation to concern itself no longer with the already decided fate of Florence, but with that of Rome, which is still being built and concerns all. 'In material comforts of life, and increase in everything that constitutes the lustre and decorum of civic union, may the Realm's capital prove worthy of the Italian nation. And may it rise to that level of intrinsic amenity that the municipality of Rome, short as it is of financial means, by its own powers could never achieve.' ('Negli agi materiali della vita, e nell'incremento di tutto quello che costituisce il lustro e il decoro del cittadino consorzio, la capitale del Regno sia degna della nazione italiana e possa salire a quel grado d'interna comodità a cui il municipio di Roma, scarso com'è di mezzi pecuniari, con le proprie forze non giungerebbe mai.')[26]

Seismid-Doda's arguments for the provision of amenities in Rome worthy of its new status offer us a quintessentially bourgeois vocabulary of values. In the original Italian he speaks of 'agi materiali della vita,' of 'il lustro e il decoro del cittadino consorzio,' and of an 'interna comodità' – all bespeaking a material substance deemed necessary in the realization of this high bourgeois ideal of Rome. Most arresting, however, is that this is a virtually identical 'value' vocabulary as had been employed to stimulate and justify the *earlier makeover* of the *earlier capital*, Florence: a city now not only physically abandoned by the government, but about to be left largely to fend for itself financially too. What is possibly revealed above all is that at the heart of urban bourgeois values in nineteenth-century Italy (and maybe elsewhere) lay a dangerous *anti*-value, or black hole, capable of sucking individual and corporate speculators down to their ruin. I am referring to financial infidelity: the implicit promise, such as that made to Florence, that with capital-city status would come uninterrupted prosperity, which is cancelled out entirely when the premise – capital-city status – is itself taken away. Within just three years of the transfer of the capital to Rome, Florence's population went down by 28,000 inhabitants, so large were the numbers of court, government, and civil service personnel who left it during the very time when rebuilding had reached fever pitch.[27] Florence and its people, under Mayor Ubaldino Peruzzi, had lived through the acute differences of two epochs: one of effervescent, but as it had turned out hollow, promise, the other of ruinous bankruptcy that adversely affected life in the city, including that of thousands of its poorest families, for decades.[28]

I wish to draw some further parameters for the highs as well as the lows in social experience in all that is to follow. A good way of doing so, it would seem, so far as highs are first concerned, is to look at two phases of the building in Milan of *gallerie* (grand-scale commercial arcades precisely), with some supplementary analysis of the Neapolitan ones that followed along similar lines. For representing lows in lifestyle there are reasons for first considering literary descriptions of poverty, such as those of the author Matilde Serao in her famous treatment *Il ventre di Napoli* (*The Belly of Naples*, 1894; 2nd rev. ed. 1906), followed by more official accounts by a well-trained technocrat of the period, Francesco Saverio Nitti, and only subsequently reaching out towards pictorial representation.

The famous arcade in Milan between its cathedral and opera piazzas, the Galleria Vittorio Emanuele, is even today a highpoint of social gathering and display, and sometimes indeed is referenced as the meeting point of the city's smart set. Almost as gleaming as when it was built, this arcade is a fine example of what Benjamin, in writing of the arcade as an architectural and cultural paradigm, called a 'primordial landscape of consumption.'[29] But although it is the grandest and most famous arcade in Italy, the Galleria Vittorio Emanuele was not the first to have been built, even in Milan. A forerunner from as early as the 1830s, the Galleria De Cristoforis, pulled down in 1920, merits initial inclusion in our study of urban lifestyles, for this earlier construction's architectural forms, and the ways people first reacted to its appearance, more or less define the ongoing social functions and typology of grand-arcade culture in Italy.

In the evidence of those initial reactions we witness something important: a high bourgeois culture that partly aligns itself with, but partly also displaces, an older aristocratic order. That newer culture establishes itself in Italy across the course of the nineteenth century in forms that will not be notably displaced in the twentieth. Lucio Gambi and Maria

Cristina Gozzoli, in their excellent account of the growth and development of Milan, are surely right to suggest that this Galleria De Cristoforis symbolically came to represent 'economic and social progress of the city.'[30] In a Milan that, in the words of Silvia Franchini, was taking on rapidly the status of 'cultural capital of Italy,' this arcade's particular significance was as a focus of civilized elegance. A materials shop, a fine men's clothier, a perfumery, and two shops for crystal, porcelain, and silverware were just some of the outlets bidding to make this the equal of the most spectacular Parisian arcades of the day.[31] (The extensive Galerie des Panoramas had first been constructed in Paris in the year 1800.)

Indeed, continuing with French comparisons (such as Italians of the times were themselves increasingly making), we could see this Galleria De Cristoforis as a paradigm of what Balzac, in his *Traité de la vie élégante* (1830), had seen as an indissoluble link between fashion, industry, and progress.[32] One of Balzac's principal claims in that sardonic treatise on fashion was that the old aristocracy and the arriviste bourgeoisie were in the process of forming a pact. Although he is principally thinking of Parisian society, Balzac's point has some importance for Italy too, in particular for Milan, a city about to take off in terms of social and industrial development:

> The aristocracy and the bourgeoisie are about to put in common, the one its traditions of elegance, taste, and high politics, the other its prodigious conquests in the arts and sciences. Then both, leading the people, will drag them along the route of civilization and enlightenment. But the princes of thought, of power, and of industry that form this enlarged caste will experience no less an unconquerable itch to make public, as nobles formerly did, their degree of power; and now, as before, social man will wear down his genius in discovering hierarchies.

> L'aristocratie et la bourgeoisie vont mettre en commun, l'une ses traditions d'élégance, de bon goût et de haute politique, l'autre ses conquêtes prodigieuses dans les arts et les sciences; puis toutes deux, à la tête du people, elles l'entraîneront dans une voie de civilisation et de lumière. Mais les princes de la pensée, du pouvoir ou de l'industrie, qui forment cette caste agrandie, n'en éprouveront pas moins une invincible démangeaison de publier, comme les nobles d'autrefois, leur degrée de puissance, et aujourd'hui encore, l'homme social fatiguera son génie à trouver des distinctions.[33]

Clearly, there is heavy irony here in Balzac's notion of progress, when he predicts that the new social alignments he envisages as coming to pass will behave with the same itch for social hierarchies as did the nobility of the *ancien régime*. And just as in that former age, the implication is that *le peuple* will be the real losers, in this melding of power, fashionableness, and know-how of the two dominant classes. Balzac's is an 1830 French scenario of the immediate future. But we would do well to hang onto his tart predictions in our thinking about urban Italy of the succeeding decades. It is apposite for us to remember, for instance, that even in the rapidly industrializing and, in that sense, most 'advanced' Italian city of Milan, by 1878 there were still, according to the affirmation of one former police official, some 8000 homeless.[34]

Gambi and Gozzoli reproduce an engraving of the De Cristoforis Arcade that appeared in a famous series edited by Luigi Valeriano Pozzi between 1835 and 1838 of ancient and modern urban topoi in Milan. The authors note how interesting it is that such a recent and prevalently commercial structure could gain immediate representation in an eminent series of plates of notable locations in the city.[35] As further evidence of the importance of the arcade they quote from a contemporary account by Giuseppe Sacchi, a frequent writer in different fashion journals of the day, detailing the reactions of people to its more amazing features, and their behaviour in the presence of them. Although Gambi and Gozzoli rather leave it to speak for itself, I should like to look at this passage more closely. For it seems from its period, the 1830s, to have more symbolic significance for the contemporary and ensuing high bourgeois age than they note, a significance worthy of being spelled out more fully.

Here, first, is the quotation they offer us from Sacchi:

> When towards the end of September of last year there opened for the first time in Milan the new De Cristoforis Arcade, it was one of those festive days that one notes on account of its civic solemnity in the minutiae of municipal history. To discover in a single family the enterprising courage to devote its own fortune in erecting a work of public accommodation as well as of ornament, and to run up this work in the brief space of a single year, spending on it the enormous sum of one and a half million lire, and devoting to it a daily labour force of more than four hundred workers, was for the city of Milan a subject of marvel and, I should almost say, of vainglory ... As though drawn to it by a wave, a confluence of people moved

towards the splendidly decorated and illumined gallery. It no longer seemed a place consecrated to industry and commerce, but a theatre space. Quite apart from the usual lamps hanging from the glass vaulting, *doppieri* were lit all around in beautiful bunches, and from the open shops spilled forth torrents of light. Such splendid display was marvellously repeated by the imposing mirrors, which constituted the walls of the café at the heart of the arcade. In them was disclosed to view a further scene, reproducing an illusion of reality. At intervals in the octagonal *piazzaletto* in front of the café, a band sent forth delightful harmonies to enliven the festive spirit, and steadied the steps, now quick, now slow, of the concourse of people. The seventy shops of the arcade were converted into salons for conversation, and the ones more encircled by an elegant parapet diminished to a role of tiers in a theatre.

Allorché sul finire del settembre dello scorso anno, s'apriva per la prima volta in Milano la nuova galleria De Cristoforis fu uno di que' giorni festosi che si notano nella storia minuta d'un municipio, come una civica solennità. L'aver trovato in una sola famiglia l'intraprendente coraggio di consacrare la propria fortuna ad un'opera eretta al pubblico comodo e ornato, l'aver improvvisato quest'opera nel breve periodo di un anno, spendendovi l'ingente soma di un milione e mezzo di lire, e prestando quotidiano lavoro a più di quattrocento operai, era per la città di Milano un soggetto di meraviglia e direi quasi di vanagloria ... Quell'affluire di gente s'avviava come travolto da un flutto verso la galleria splendidamente decorata e illuminata. Non la pareva più questa un luogo consacrato all'industria e al commercio, ma un'aula da teatro. Oltre le lampade consuete che pendono alla vôlta vetriata, le correvano in giro accesi doppieri disposti a bei gruppi, e dalle aperte botteghe uscivano de' torrenti di luce. Questo splendido prestigio era mirabilmente ripetuto dai grandiosi specchi che coprivano le pareti del caffè posto a capo della galleria: ivi schiudevasi una nuova scena che riproduceva l'illusione del vero. Nel piazzaletto ottagono che sta innanzi al caffè, una banda musicale mandava a intervalli liete armonie che avvivavano l'aura della festa, e reggevano i passi ora agitati, ora lenti di quel popoloso concorso. Le settanta botteghe della galleria erano convertite in sale da conversazione, e le più precinte da un parapetto elegante erano ridotte all'uso de' palchetti da teatro.[36]

We move rapidly here through key topics: the importance of the new *galleria* to a history of the city; the nature of public financing of such projects by private families acting as latter-day Croesuses; and notions of the arcade as theatre. Of these, the last is the most crucial for a reckoning of emergent high bourgeois culture, and becomes in a sense the justification for the other two.

For what is evident from this description, and is corroborated by even a brief perusal of the 1830s engraving of this arcade,[37] is that emergent styles of decorative architecture used for contemporary theatres – columns, parapets, and architraves – are being redeployed in a hybridized form here. For instance, at the four corners created by the intersecting axes of the arcade are columned entry spaces giving onto the two walkways themselves. We are told in the Sacchi passage that each of the arcade's seventy boutiques constituted a social focus, nothing less than a *sala da conversazione* in its own right. There are other shops too above, at parapet level, that are more suited for onlooking, and which therefore reproduce the function served in an actual theatre by a grand tier. Above all, instead of a stage there is a café, with a band playing in front of it, in ways that seem to dictate the rhythms of the steps of passers-by.

Another prose description, that of Giuseppe Reina in the third edition of his guidebook to Milan of 1845, will also draw attention to the café, which it claims 'seems almost an atrium in which the walkway terminates, and is encircled at the first floor by loggias' ('pare quasi un atrio con cui termina la via, ed ha al primo piano alcune logge in giro').[38] What is strange, but all-important, is that if we ask ourselves exactly who forms the audience and who the actors, in terms of the theatrical analogy deployed by Sacchi, we are flummoxed for an exact answer. Clearly, in an approximate sense the band fulfils the role that in a real theatre is played by the orchestra. But it is very much on view in its own right here in the commercial arcade. And passers-by – people at one level ogling the overall scene – to all appearances have the rhythm of their footfalls determined by the music being played. So from the vantage point of those seated in the café, or above at parapet level, the passers-by are not onlookers but 'dancers'; in other words, an integral part of the overall spectacle.

No sooner have we got that sorted out, however, than we realize that the café itself is walled with mirrors, in which what is reproduced is a representation in its own right, a *reflection* of reality. Quite apart from the café being a reality, and a key point of the arcade, it thus becomes understood in another sense as *representation*, something able to be looked at indirectly by means of extensive mirroring. Once again, therefore, those whom we might understand at one level as onlookers are, in another mirrored plane, an *illusione del vero* rather than *il vero* (reality) itself. It is this 'uncertaintizing' – if I may be permitted a neologism – of the viewer and the viewed, and likewise of the real and the illusion of the real, that seems to me to be all important in the emergence of high bourgeois culture. All are capable of impressing and so all are on display, in a kind of illusionist representation of their real selves. Apart from being mere onlookers, they are also *those viewed* in their own right. In short, everybody is at one and the same time the gazer and the gazed at. It is uncanny how deeply this corresponds to our contemporary sense of what high bourgeois display is like and about. What is important for our analysis is that a sense of this reflexivity of the high bourgeois gaze, and interchangeability of the real and the illusionistic within the culture in question, is given in a mere journal report of the 1830s. It can only be so because the new arcade certainly organized architectural space in just such premonitory ways.

Further, the matters at stake consist of more than just an 'uncertaintized' but all-pervasive theatricality. Take what else Sacchi writes about the shops. These boutiques are at one level so many small drawing rooms (*sale*) for conversation. At another they are sources of intense light. Here an older seventeenth- and eighteenth-century social phenomenon – the *salotto* culture – is being hybridized with notions of the creative origins of light, so as to add immeasurably to the shops' attraction in terms of what they fundamentally are in emergent bourgeois culture, namely, locations of commerce. The point is confirmed in a prose description of the more famous Galleria Vittorio Emanuele from several decades later. No less a writer than Luigi Capuana praises fulsomely the material delights on offer there – 'We feel more at ease under those airy porticos, before such magnificent shops with their varied decorations, under the glass vaulting that criss-crosses in a sea of light the fine knots of its dorsal iron spine' ('Ci sentiamo più a nostr' agio sotto quei portico ariosi, rimpetto quelle magnifiche botteghe svariamente addobbate, sotto quella volta di cristallo che intreccia in mezz' a un mare di luce gli esilissimi modi della sua spina dorsale di ferro') – and then concludes that the sensation was 'not the invading and disturbing feeling of artistic elevation ... but a satisfaction of material well-being, which appeases the eye even as it fulfils utilitarian exigencies' ('Non è un sentimento di elevazione artistica che c'invade e ci turba ... ma una soddisfazione di benessere materiale che appaga l'occhio e sazia le esigenze utilitarie').[39] Note here that, much as in Sacchi's earlier description of the Galleria De Cristoforis, material display is usurping the place of art, on something like, but in fact subtly different from, art's own terms. The total experience is not 'invading' and 'disturbing' in the manner of art, but satisfying and appeasing. This distinction between the disturbances of art and the gratifications of a lived bourgeois world merits attention for our larger subject of how cultural lineages develop and function. In both passages emphasis is being thrown off any vulgarity that might otherwise have been noted in the arcades' commercial status.

Vulgarity there may be – to be precise, 'vainglory' in the instance of the De Critoforis Arcade – but its origins are easily traceable back to the benefactor family. And there is a counterbalancing positive – 'wonderment' – that offsets it. Sacchi's passage holds firmly to these two balanced values. Taken all in all – the huge private donation, the novel building it financed, and, once built, the sensations induced in people upon its inauguration – the *galleria* 'was for the city of Milan a subject of marvel and, I should almost say, of vainglory.' This shifting of blame back to origins beyond the self and, equally, this balancing of such blame with a positive to be derived from the same set of phenomena, are prototypical of the high bourgeois culture that ensues. Wonderment at the building acts as sufficient exculpation for anything else that may be being signalled in the word vainglory. In Capuana's later passage the Galleria Vittorio Emanuele, in other respects so replete with artistic form, has as its main condition something that is posited as an *alternative* to artistic experience. From here to an understanding of how shopping usurps the place of art in much high bourgeois culture, by replacing the former's invading disturbances with the latter's intense material gratifications, the path is easy. Capuana has already constructed the logic for us.

Though not an example from Arcade culture as such, Augusta Pieragostini's silk shop, opened in 1843 on the Piazza di Spagna in Rome, is a perfect example of the degree to which the *bottega* could replace the functions of the social *salotto* of the preceding age. No one has captured this shift more precisely than Jonathan Morris in a fine chapter on fashion and shopping in the recently published *Annali* volume on *La moda*, in the great Einaudi *Storia d'Italia* series:

> All good salottos have need of a hostess, who puts her guests at their ease and encourages them to enter into the spirit of the occasion. Augusta Pieragostini was a woman of this type. In 1843 she founded a silk shop in the Piazza di Spagna, where she sold multicoloured scarves and elegant mantles in silk waste, with varicoloured folds (*rigature*). The shop was arrayed with rosewood *boiseries*, with a bench propped on lions' paw feet. It drew clients both from the Roman aristocracy and passing tourists. The latter were

attracted by the English shop signs and advertising, which boasted prizes won in Paris and Rome. They would have been relieved to find polyglot serving women, who sold at fixed prices. In the back of the shop were a *salotto* with eighteenth-century gilt furniture and a marquetry table depicting the Battle of Lutzen. Here Donna Augusta entertained the most important female members of the Roman aristocracy, as well as ladies on a brief stay, such as the queen of Sweden. Elegant, endowed with the best education, and with her 'majestic and ironical visage,' Donna Augusta put at ease her foreign guests with her command of English and French. Donna Augusta constituted a key element in all that her fashion shop explicitly offered its clientele, embodying its personal, made-to-measure service quite as much as did the merchandise itself.

Tutti i buoni salotti hanno bisogno di una padrona di casa, che metta gli ospiti a loro agio e li spinga a entrare nello spirito dell'occasione. Augusta Pieragostini era una donna di questo tipo: nel 1843 fondò una seteria in piazza di Spagna, dove vendeva sciarpe multicolori ed eleganti coperte di cascami di seta dalle rigature variopinte. Il negozio era arredato con *boiseries* di palissandro, con il bancone appoggiato su piedi a forma di zampe di leone, e attirava clienti sia tra l'aristocrazia romana che tra i turisti di passaggio. Questi ultimi erano richiamati dalle insegne e dalle pubblicità in inglese, che vantavano medaglie vinte a Parigi e a Roma, e sarebbero stati sollevati nel trovare commesse poliglotte che vendevano a prezzi fissi. Nel retro del negozio c'era un salotto con mobili dorati settecenteschi e un tavolo intarsiato con la battaglia di Lutzen. Era qui che donna Augusta intratteneva i membri femminili piú importanti dell'aristocrazia romana, come pure le *dame di passaggio,* tipo la regina di Svezia. Elegante e fornita di un'ottima educazione, con un 'aspetto maestoso e ironico,' faceva sentire a proprio agio i suoi ospiti stranieri grazie alla padronanza dell'inglese e del francese. Donna Augusta constituiva un elemento chiave della proposta al cliente sviluppata dalla sua bottega di moda, incarnando quel servizio personale che veniva cucito su misura del singolo cliente, come la merce stessa.[40]

How fascinatingly gradual, this description shows us, could be the passage from one social setting, the eighteenth-century *salotto,* to another, the nineteenth-century fashionable boutique. Note that the actual drawing room at the rear of the shop has furnishings from the earlier period, making this lineage from eighteenth into nineteenth century all the more crafted and seamless, to borrow terms from Donna Augusta's own tailoring trade. Also important is a certain polyglot spanning of fashionable European cultures of the day, achieved not only by the *padrona di casa*, but even by the accomplished shop assistants or *commesse*.

Can we add Naples to what has been discussed above in regard to new elegances in Milan and Rome? At the two opposite ends of the large southern city's most fashionable street, the Via Toledo, were built, first from 1876 to 1883 the Galleria Principe di Napoli (Prince of Naples Arcade), and then, between 1885 and 1892 the Galleria Umberto I. The second of these was erected at the very heart of the city, between the San Carlo Theatre and the Piazza del Municipio. We need to comment on the obvious at this point, for it reveals some of the subtext of high bourgeois culture in these two cities. The Galleria Vittorio Emanuele in Milan, and this new one in Naples borrowing inspiration from it (and similarly named after the reigning king, son of the said Victor Emmanuel), were close by the two greatest opera houses in Italy, the Teatro alla Scala and the Teatro San Carlo. The proximity of these imposing *gallerie* to the historic seats of unfolding Italian operatic culture is no accident. It is indeed more than mere proximity, it is interconnection. One moves from opera house to *galleria* and vice versa. The confluence of people in the *galleria* is drawn there very much in wonderment and, as Sacchi had stated of the earlier De Cristoforis Arcade, as though carried there by a wave and not by their own willpower merely. (We hardly need an Adorno to remind us of this connection between the high moment of the European bourgeoisie and operatic culture. Nonetheless, he puts the point in an arresting way: 'In opera ..., a self-assured bourgeoisie could celebrate and enjoy itself for a long time. On the musical stage the symbols of its power and material ascent combined with the rituals of the fading, but arch-bourgeois, idea of liberated nature.')[41]

And no matter if in a work by the greatest Italian composer of the day there existed a cogent criticism of the 'populous desert' ('popoloso deserto,' words from Piave's libretto of *La traviata*) that a great European city – in point of fact Paris – was felt to have become. In spite of all such criticism, the Arcade, as virtually the polar opposite of those words from Verdi's opera, namely a 'populous concourse' (Sacchi's formulation), is from the time of the Galleria De Cristoforis in 1830s Milan established as an absolute. Such arcades are for fashionable *passeggiate* in a high bourgeois, commercial (but also cultural) epicentre. After all, by now in Italian history the *haute bourgeoisie* as an economic class controls these and other *centri storici*, even if small individual shopkeepers and artisans still have a precarious place in them. The gathering movement to clear away smaller-scale urban fabric from earlier centuries, so as to make way for an architecture of grandeur in Italy's cities, is largely the sign of this new proprietorial hold by the rich and powerful of the day. And the fault lies not in opera nor, certainly, in these beautiful arcades *in themselves* – for they are exquisite examples of the best such grandeur – but in those of their patrons who as a class had by now attained all the significant levers of power.

Both of the arcades built in Naples were attempts to bring new luxury to a city where poverty continued to be a perennial issue. The building of the second was contemporaneous with the beginnings of a long-wished-for *Risanamento* (Revitalization) project for the entire city. But it is interesting that this Umberto Arcade, the pinnacle of late-nineteenth-century class and fashionable display in Naples, was constructed in far fewer years than the overall *Risanamento* project lasted. Indeed, the *Risanamento* proved incapable of achieving radical amelioration in either built context or attendant living conditions, especially in poorer quarters of the city, which continued to receive the least money and were the last to be tackled – not the first, as was the case with the Galleria Umberto I.[42] City planners not only lacked sufficient political will; any conception of how poverty might actually be overcome was possibly as remote as it had been during the building of the *Albergo dei Poveri* from 1753 onwards (an earlier project to solve the problem of vast numbers of the poor in Naples and its realm, discussed in chapter 4 above, pages 131–6).

Let us then look more at the poverty in question, now that we have witnessed distinctly Italian forms of its opposite, in buildings of theatricalized commercialism that promoted luxurious gratification, hard by opera houses that were delivering the preferred high bourgeois art form of the period.

Bad cholera struck Naples in 1884–5 and was a catalyst in legislation finally coming forward for a project to restructure and revitalize the city. It was a city that according to one account of 1879 by Rocco De Zerbi, entitled simply 'La miseria di Napoli,' was starkly divided between the well-to-do and the poor. Indeed, De Zerbi puts the case still more graphically, suggesting an upper crust of a mere 3000 genuinely rich persons; below them 7000 fashionable monkeys (*scimmie mondane* – a grouping of unproductive bourgeois flunkeys, so to speak); and then a multitude of some 450,000 human 'animals,' mired in poverty. These latter 'do not read newspapers, are not bothered by elections, go but very rarely to the theatre, are not seen by the other seven thousand on their fashionable walks, and have different habits, beliefs, and tastes, even a different inflexion of speech' ('non leggono giornali, non s'occupano di elezioni, non vanno che rarissimamente a teatro, non si fanno vedere alle passeggiate dagli altri 7 mila, hanno altre abitudini, altre credenze, altri gusti, altra inflessione di voce').[43] Among much else, De Zerbi ascribes the causes for the stark conditions of the poor to a decline of agriculture in the former kingdom, and to imbalances of population density between rural and urban sectors.

Indeed, De Zerbi declares there to be two different Naples. Rich Naples had its perimeter only one hundred metres to the west of an axis stretching between the museum at the top of Via Toledo and, at the other extreme, the Riviera di Chiaia in the former royal area of the city. On the eastern side of this axis it stopped abruptly at Monteoliveto and San Giuseppe. Such a perimeter also marked the limits of those fashionable *passeggiate* referred to by De Zerbi, and mentioned in the previous section. Impoverished Naples by contrast consisted of most of the rest of the city: agglomerations of old and dark lanes, and the shoreline slums (the *fondaci* and *portici*) of labouring and indigent families. It was 'an aggregate of houses encrusted to the small centre, but that has nothing more in common with the latter than an oyster's life has with the rock to which it clings.' ('Tutto il resto è un aggregato di casali incrostati sulla piccola città, ma che nulla hanno in comune con questa, come nulla ha di comune la vita dell'ostrica con quella dello scoglio al quale è attacata.')[44]

An entire book with almost the same title as De Zerbi's piece, *La miseria in Napoli*, had appeared in 1877 from the hand of an English writer and journalist with a social conscience, Jessie White Mario, married to an Italian of Garibaldian background and sympathies, and hence not new to Italy. The crux of this book was a relatively objective and accurate, but certainly also intense, description of the Naples of the plebeian slums. It confirmed – if any confirmation were needed – that since its 'annexation' by the larger Italian state at the point of Unification, things had only gone backwards for the city.[45] White Mario's various chapters deal with contrasts between London and Neapolitan poverty, 'trogloditic' lifestyles of Naples's slum dwellers, prostitution, divisions between the lives of *lazzaroni* on the one hand and the class of so-called *galantuomini* on the other, charitable institutions including the continued, large-scale use of the Albergo dei Poveri (discussed earlier in chapter 4), and, in a final section, 'Proposals and attempts already undertaken to improve the conditions in Naples' ('Proposte e tentativi fatti per migliorare le condizioni di Napoli'). White Mario displays her enduring Garibaldian sympathies throughout the book, and an anticlericalism typical of some social meliorists of the times. At one point she contrasts contemporary Naples with its former splendour in a passage rare for its descriptive emphases in her otherwise spare and factual prose:

> Once Naples was held to be one of the most salubrious resorts of Europe. Today foreigners avoid it as a place of infection, and in the best known guidebook to Rome, the one by Murray, one reads that the climate of Rome is maligned, because most so-called Roman fevers are in fact imported by travellers coming from Naples. This is certainly an exaggeration; but nobody can visit the poor quarters of Naples without marvelling, not indeed that so many fall sick, but that all do not die; that cholera and typhus do not entirely wipe out the population of the shacks, the dives, the underground dwellings, and especially the inns. The survival of the greater number cannot be explained any other way than in the words of the old woman who, when it was pointed out to her that her skinning eels alive must really torture them, replied, 'They're used to it.'

> Una volta Napoli fu ritenuta uno dei più salubri soggiorni di Europa. Oggi gli stranieri la evitano come luogo infetto, e nella più celebre 'Guida di Roma' – quella di Murray – si legge che il clima di Roma è calunniato, che la maggior parte delle febbri dette romane sono importate dai viaggiatori provenienti da Napoli. Questa è certo un'esagerazione; ma nessuno può visitare i quartieri popolosi della città di Napoli senza maravigliarsi, non già che molti si ammalino ma che tutti non muoiano – che il colèra e il tifo non facciano tavola rasa nei fondaci, nei bassi, nei sotterranei e specialmente nelle locande; e non si può spiegare il sopravvivere del maggior numero che al modo di quella vecchia, la quale, a chi osservava che deve fare male alle anguille l'essere spellate vive: 'ci sono abituate,' – rispondeva.[46]

These and other accounts of slum conditions, including those in the legislation for the *Risanamento* project itself, were a prelude to the most important single work on the subject, Matilde Serao's *Il ventre di Napoli* (*The Belly of Naples*), published in its original version in 1884. There are other European and Italian precedents for the kind of scandalized exposure of a given city's misery that Serao attempts in this volume. Henry Mayhew's four volumes of shocking and controversial articles from 1849 to 1852 on London's conditions of poverty were collected and eventually published in 1861 as *London Labour and the London Poor*. Émile Zola had brought out the second volume of his Rougon Macquart series of novels in 1873, titled *Le ventre de Paris* and set mainly in Les Halles. In order that, among Italians, Naples might not steal the limelight of revelations, shortly after the first edition of Serao's volume there was published a book entitled *Il ventre di Milano: Fisiologia della capitale morale* (1988), assembled by a society of *letterati*. But this volume on Milan took mocking exception to what it saw as a stereotypical *nostalgie de la boue* in writings on other cities. Although *Il ventre di Milano* does describe insalubrious areas of that city, this is not its main stock-in-trade: more important and noticeable is the way it shows pride in traditional customs of the working *popolo*, especially culinary festivities, and in the splendours of the city's well-to-do quarters, monuments, and public buildings. There is, in other words, a distinct bourgeois bias to the 'moral physiology' undertaken of this particular city's 'belly,' as perhaps is not surprising given the accelerating power and wealth by the 1880s of Milan in comparison with Naples.

Serao's book, by contrast, had been a gathering together at the very heart of the 1884 cholera crisis in Naples of various shorter newspaper articles on the living conditions of the poor that she had produced over three months since its outbreak. And there was an updated and enlarged second edition of her work in 1906, which she prefaces by declaring herself to be 'less trusting' than when the book first appeared, 'and more sceptical that a better social and civil future might ever be assured the Neapolitan people' ('più sfiduciato, più scettico che un miglior av-venire sociale e civile possa esser mai assicurato al popolo napoletano').[47]

Let us look more closely at *Il ventre di Napoli*. The first article in the series of several that were subsequently published as Serao's book had appeared in September 1884 in the Roman journal *Capitan Fracasso* (*Captain Clamour*).[48] It had been entitled 'Sventrare Napoli' ('Gutting of Naples'), a quotation from the prime minister of the day, Agostino Depretis. After visiting Naples in the company of King Umberto I and the Duke of Aosta, Depretis, witness to the city's dire poverty for the first time in his life, had said that nothing less than the tearing down of her slums was called for: 'Naples must be gutted' ('bisogna sventrare Napoli').

Serao's critique is the immediate reply of a Neapolitan of plebeian sympathies. We could skip a few of its opening pages, and go directly to her moving and explicit descriptions of the conditions in which the poor live. But that would be to miss what is so politically devastating in the initial rhetoric of her response to Depretis's turning up in Naples and so magisterially pronouncing on its ills. 'You did not know, honourable Depretis, the belly of Naples. And you were wrong not to, for you are the government and the government should know everything.' ('Voi non lo conoscevate, onorevole Depretis, il ventre di Napoli. Avevate torto, perché voi siete il Governo e il Governo deve saper tutto,' p. 41.) Serao proceeds on her first page to mock a pretentious Neapolitan literature that does not acknowledge the abject, poverty-striken side of the city, but that speaks instead only in terms of the deep blue sea and cobalt skies, of enchanting women, of the gulf and the flowering hills that overlook it.[49] This facile literature does not wish to be bothered by the real miseries of Naples, but to concentrate on localities (the Via Caracciolo, for instance) of an inspiringly salubrious kind. Serao implies that the rhetorical velleities of such writings reveal a great deal about the well-to-do classes of Naples and their absolute neglect of the poor. Theirs is a literature 'that serves that part of the public which doesn't wish to be annoyed by stories of poverty' ('serve per quella parte di pubblico che non vuole essere seccata con racconti di miserie,' p. 41). Note the attestation here of there being two Naples, as De Zerbi had earlier declared.

The truly culpable party is the government, which has demonstrated by its inaction an equivalent neglect of real national ills when it should, by very definition, have taken responsibility for and set about ameliorating them:

> The government should have known this other truth; the government which receives the statistics on mortality and on crimes; the government which receives reports from the prefects, the judges, the inspectors of police and from parliamentary delegates; the government which hears from directors of prisons; the government that knows everything: how much meat is consumed in a day and how much wine is drunk in a year in a locality; how many fallen women, let us call them that, there are, and how far their sweethearts have been admonished; how many beggars are unable to be admitted to hospices; and the numbers of the homeless who sleep in the street ... This other truth, this belly of Naples, if the government does not know it, who should? And if all these employees high and low, this immense bureaucratic engine that costs so much, do not tell you everything about it, of what use are they?

> Il governo doveva sapere l'*altra parte*; il governo a cui arriva la statistica della mortalità e quella dei delitti; il governo a cui arrivano i rapporti dei prefetti, dei questori, degli ispettori di polizia, dei delegati; il governo a cui arrivano i rapporti dei direttori delle carceri; il governo che sa tutto: quanta

carne si consuma in un giorno e quanto vino si beve in un anno, in un paese; quante femmine disgraziate, diciamo così, vi esistano, e quanti ammoniti siano i loro amanti di cuore; quanti mendichi non possano entrare nelle opera pie e quanti vagabondi dormano in istrada ... Quest'altra parte, questo ventre di Napoli, se non lo conosce il Governo, chi lo deve conoscere? E se non servono a dirvi tutto, a che sono buoni tutti questi impiegati alti e bassi, a che questo immenso ingranaggio burocratico che ci costa tanto? (pp. 41–2)

Several points are worth making here. Above all, Serao names a contradiction at the heart of public service. The machinery for knowledge of the nation's ills exists, and a government is in place that should (in theory) receive such knowledge from its bureaucratic structures and act upon it. But because of the (heavily implied) laissez-faire attitudes of those in rule, none of this raison d'être of the government and bureaucracy actually functions as it ought. Only when the prime minister sees with his own eyes a tiny fraction of the grievous reality is there uttered a succinct pronouncement. And then, for all the reasons of prior state neglect, as well as because of the inevitably inadequate perception of this one minister, he comes out with an inanity. The inanity provides the starting point and title for Serao's book and at the same time reveals the urgent need that she write it. This she does, in the *J'accuse* mode for which it is famous.

Note that Serao is addressing a dual audience: at one level she writes a journalistic letter to Depretis, head of the government in question, and hence the representative figure in the rhetorical 'you' that she adopts. But there is at the same time an implied reaching out to a larger political public – of Naples, and of Italy more generally – to whom, by means of her sarcasm, Serao all the while reveals how complacent and ineffectual are these (co-responsible and interlinked) political and bureaucratic classes. She is involved in disclosing what it is that they refuse to see in full, or only act upon in part. And her example is an important one, for Serao's voice of protest will be imitated many times until the present; whenever contradictions in Italy between what should be known and acted upon by its political classes, on the one hand, and their actual laissez-faire complacency, on the other, grow shockingly far apart.

Consider, for instance, the following rhetorical structure in her argument. By suggesting how little Depretis and his party have actually seen of Naples, Serao constructs in the prose itself a strategy for taking her readers on a fuller exploration of the Via de' Mercanti than these politicos were willing – or encouraged by those leading them – to undertake:

> You must have been shown one, two, three streets of the lower quarters and you were horrified at them. But you didn't see everything; the Neapolitans themselves who conducted you around do not know all the low quarters. The Via dei Mercanti, did you go all the way along it?

> Vi avranno fatto vedere una, due, tre strade dei quartieri bassi e ne avrete avuto orrore. Ma non avete visto tutto; i napoletani istessi che vi conducevano, non conoscono *tutti* i quartieri bassi. La via dei Mercanti, l'avete percorsa tutta? (p. 42)

Serao's very next paragraphs (and we are still only on the second page) consist of an exploration of the slum in question, which the national politicians scarcely began to see, because of their prior mindset and, equally, the mindset of the Neapolitan bureaucrats leading them. Two important functions – that of incriminating Italy's political classes, but also that of revealing the dark reality they wilfully neglected – are accomplished by one and the same rhetorical strategy in Serao's prose.

For example, in this slum 'all the filth of an African village seems concentrated' ('pare raccolta tutta la immondizia di un villaggio africano,' p. 43). (Serao is not free from cultural and racist stereotyping of other peoples, frequent during the age in which she writes.) On each side of the Santa Barbara Steps 'live fallen women who have made this their dominion. From laziness caused by their unhappy daytime unemployment, or from a dark hatred against man, they throw from windows fig and cucumber scraps, refuse or cornstalks, onto whoever passes by. And the situation remains unchanging on these steps, such that polite society no longer dares to come this way.' ('Da una parte e dall'altra abitano femmine disgraziate, che ne hanno fatto un loro dominio, e, per ozio di infelici disoccupate, nel giorno, e per cupo odio contro l'uomo, buttano dalla finestra, su chi passa, buccie di fichi, di cocomero, spazzatura, torsoli di spighe: e tutto resta, su questi gradini, così che la gente pulita non osa passarvi più,' p. 43.) Two terrible divisions are revealed in the sentence, one of class and one of gender, both of them underpinned by an endemic poverty. Indeed, the condition of being a 'fallen' woman, among the many other such *disgraziate*, seems always already to have come to pass and the large grouping in question to have constituted a subclass apart, from time immemorial, on these steps. If this is a description of their man-hating daytime states of unemployment, their nighttime employment by contrast is scarcely even implied, but is left to the reader to imagine. Our only guideline is a troubled sense that if the male sex is so generally hated by these *disgraziate*, the various reasons must lie rooted in terrible individual life histories. Altogether, Serao's sentences here form an indictment of predatory sexual relations in Naples's worst quarters. The victims of male exploitation of whom she writes constitute a female subclass of the tormented poor. A very few lines of description on her part is all it has taken to conjure in our minds their intensely distressed lifestyle.

Other analyses of Serao's intricate revelations could be attempted, but let the present example stand for many. Like so much else in this and other books devoted to revealing terrible truths about Naples, or indeed the slums of other Italian cities, there is another point being made: namely, that polite society (*la gente pulita* in this passage) no longer sets foot in such quarters. The physical divisions based on class (along with the gender twist that this particular example has revealed) have become absolute.

Among the only transgressions of these boundaries between rich and poor are representations in writing, painting, or photography. But to Serao's mind, many of the attempts to treat the subject artistically seek to make such poverty 'picturesque.' 'Painters have treated it,' she writes, 'and it has been made beautiful and almost elegant, with a tavern host who seems a shepherd from Watteau. In the collection of Neapolitan photographs that the English buy, along with the "convent nun," the "handkerchief thief," and the "flea-bitten family," there is also "the maccaroni man's stall"' ('dei pittori lo hanno dipinto, ed è stato da essi reso lindo e quasi elegante, con l'oste che sembra un pastorello di Watteau; e nella collezione di fotografie napoletane, che gl'inglesi comprano, accanto alla *monaca di casa*, al *ladruncolo di fazzoletti*, alla *famiglia di pidocchiosi*, vi è anche il *banco del maccaronaro*,' p. 55). Serao would seem to resent all such genres as make class suffering into a new 'picturesque,' something the leisured can own in the form of art, even as they shun its manifestations in real life.

Serao can never be content with the picturesque as a narratorial or pictorial mode, because it is a savouring of things in their status quo. She cries out in her writings for radically changed conditions, above all fighting against the perception of the poor as somehow inhuman. 'Those who live in these four popular quarters, without air, without light, without hygiene, bathing in black streams, rummaging in mountains of filth, breathing stenches, and drinking stale water, are not bestial, savage, or lazy. They are not stubborn in terms of faith, nor mired in vice, nor choleric from misfortune.' ('La gente che abita in questi quattro quartieri popolari, senz'aria, senza luce, senza igiene, diguazzando nei ruscelli neri, scavalcando monti d'immondizie, respirando miasmi e bevendo un'acqua corrotta, non è una gente bestiale, selvaggia, oziosa; non è tetra nella fede, non è cupa nel vizio, non è collerica nella sventura,' p. 47.) In rendering their sufferings acutely, and giving them back their human face through her descriptions, Serao's is a piercing political message.

She declares that we should not infer from the conditions in which people have been forced to live that theirs is a *natural* state: for 'this is not thereby a race of animals that is content with the mud. Nor is it thereby an inferior race that chooses the horrible from all that is ugly, and searches wilfully for filth. It does not merit the fate that has been imposed on it. It could appreciate refinement, given that the little it has been granted it has immediately assimilated. It is worthy of happiness.' (Non è dunque una razza di animali, che si compiace del suo fango; non è dunque una razza inferiore che presceglie l'orrido fra il brutto e cerca volenterosa il sudiciume; non si merita la sorte che le cose gl'impongono; saprebbe apprezzare la civiltà, visto che quella pochina elargitagli se l'ha subito assimilata; meriterebbe di esser felice,' p. 48.) This is an important staging post in the representation of lows in the social scale of late-nineteenth-century Italy. Serao's prose not only travels the streets of Naples, it goes inside and renders the lifestyles of the city's poorest inhabitants from within, as a *psychological terrain.*

Nonetheless, Serao's and other writers' vivid perceptions in the 1870s and 1880s of the depths to which Naples and some other places had sunk since Unification were lacking when it came to specific proposals for amelioration. To initiate the beginnings of interventive action by the state a different kind of writing was needed, one that would more effectively appeal to the consciences of parliamentarians. It came half a generation later from a young social and economic thinker, Francesco Saverio Nitti, at a moment in the history of Naples when the *Risanamento* project had already ripped apart, rebuilt, and extended much of the former city, but largely without providing it with new wealth-producing infrastructures. These it drastically needed, as Nitti made clear, initially in writings about the entire South in the 1890s, then in lengthy socio-economic analyses of Naples in 1902, followed in 1903 by his influential synthesis *Napoli e la questione meridionale* (*Naples and the Southern*

Question).⁵⁰ At this early stage in his career – before becoming a statesman in the Giolittian government and, briefly, a centrist prime minister (1919–20) – Nitti ensured that his political and socio-economic analysis of Naples's problems was accompanied by arguments that offered solutions.

Nitti for the most part eschews first-hand descriptions, preferring instead arguments based on objectifiable 'scientific' evidence. From the outset his text on Naples and the southern question constitutes a pejorative account of those who have simply claimed, however colourfully, that something should be done to solve Naples's many problems. Indeed, he gives such people the undignified one-word title of *qualchecosisti* (p. 114), after their mantra that 'something' (*qualche cosa*) should be done – what in particular rarely being specified or, if specified, then poorly judged according to Nitti. It is rather curious therefore that Nitti argues heatedly against particular schemes proposed by others that, exactly a century later, would appear to have been sensible and well founded.

For instance, he is against economic concessions to enhance the port of Naples as a link with points farther east. Likewise, he spends more than a chapter picking to pieces and abusing the arguments of those who wished for a direct train link between Rome and Naples. To us the fact that all the major northern cities of Italy were directly interlinked by train as far south as Rome, but not onwards to Naples, seems like a probable factor in the ongoing immiseration of the latter. Not to Nitti, however. On this point we can judge his ideas on the South in relation to those of the later, and far more radical, left-wing thinker Antonio Gramsci.

One of Gramsci's most famous analogies for explaining the enduring differences between Italy's already industrialized northern cities, Milan and Turin, and the largely unindustrialized Rome and Naples is that of a 'railway train of history.' 'The first of these forces [the urban and industrialized North] retains its function of "locomotive" in any case; what is needed, therefore, is an examination of the various "most advantageous" combinations for building a "train" to move forward through history as fast as possible.'⁵¹ In this 1934 passage in his *Prison Notebooks* (first worked on in 1929–30) Gramsci, like Nitti at one level, is considering how to overcome the comparative industrial backwardness of southern Italian cities; his idea is to make sure they are well hitched to the 'locomotive' North. I realize that Nitti in 1903 was discussing the *actual* railway network of Italy, whereas Gramsci some thirty years later is using the *analogy* of a railway train. Nonetheless, the very fact that Gramsci recurs to such an analogy at all for its explicatory potential indicates how inconceivable to him would have been Nitti's acceptance of Naples continuing not to be included in the main north–south rail network. But then, for Nitti it was not only unimportant, it was misconceived to press for large centralized state investment in making Naples at least a 'carriage' (in terms of Gramsci's analogy) of the train of Italian cities moving rapidly through history. The less direct routing of Rome–Naples rail travel via Gaeta was good enough, in his opinion.

Nitti's own favoured schemes for Naples's development, by contrast, formed an interlinked pair: utilization of the considerable Appenine water sources above Naples for hydroelectric power and major deployment of such power in new, or at any rate enhanced, metal foundries. In the latter instance he called for the kind of state subsidization that had already financed the development of a major metal production industry at Terni in Umbria. His arguments in favour of these choices for Naples were sound. But their realization was hobbled in succeeding years by the same forces of reaction, stagnation, and, worse still, parliamentary corruption, that no one was better than he at analysing and decrying. Effectively, what impeded achievement of his two forceful plans for Naples's industrial development was what he had concisely called, when only twenty-five, 'a species of parliamentary leprosy' ('una specie di lebbra parlamentare').[52]

Fundamentally, Nitti parted company with most prior writers, including Serao, who had been so much stronger in describing the hell that Naples had become than in making suggestions for retrieving it from the abyss into which it had fallen. Unlike Serao's, Nitti's prose does not wend its way along particular streets or up dubious steps of the demoralized city. For him the problems needed stating in a different way, and so his accounts of Naples's decline since Unification are largely based on comparisons, often statistical, both with the city's own levels of pre-1860 economic activity (e.g., production, supply, and consumption) and, perhaps more searingly, with the rapid post-1860 advances of Italy's northern cities.

For example, Nitti lays down the challenge to northerners, specifically to those in government, that since Unification Naples has been turned by them from its former status as 'colony of supply' ('colonia di contibuzione') into something still worse, a 'colony of consumption' ('colonia di consumo,' p. 60).[53] He was not the only person in these years to talk in terms of colonization of the South by the North. And once again Gramsci, in the early 1920s, will turn this worked-over formula into a plank in his own accounts of the southern question, in his claim that 'the bourgeoisie of the North has subjected southern Italy and the Islands and reduced them to the state of exploited colonies.'[54] Gramsci's nuancing – particularly his idea of a plurality of colonies, rather than just one – is an interesting later development of the argument. Still, Nitti's accounts of colonization are highly interesting in their own right, both because they emerge from a great age of European colonialism and because Nitti works out factors in the specific colonization of Italy's South differently than Gramsci.

There are moments in Nitti's text when he accuses Italy's ruling classes of having had northern enrichment at the South's expense as a *deliberate if largely undeclared* policy. Indeed, a kind of conspiracy theory is at the heart of his denomination of Naples as a colony of the north. Thinking along such lines gives rise to a generalization by him that, if true, will determine a continuation into the future of the Mezzogiorno's un-industrialized and tributary status. 'Northern Italy views with profound antipathy any attempt at an industrial reawakening of the South: not because of insufficient patriotism, but because no metropolitan power ever willingly envisaged the economic emancipation of a large colony.' ('L'Italia del Nord vede in generale con profonda antipatia ogni tentativo di risveglio industriale del Sud: non per poco patriottismo, ma perché nessuna metropoli vide mai volentieri l'emancipazione economica di una sua grande colonia,' p. 118.)

Implicitly we have a different division here between rich and poor than I have been tending to concentrate on so far in this chapter. For it is now a division not of different classes within one and the same urban context, but at the heart of the nation qua nation. Italy now incorporates, by this reckoning, both rich *metropoli* – a generalization for its industrialized North – and an extensive southern *colonia* kept in poverty.[55] 'Levels of consumption in Milan and Turin by comparison with those of Naples did not differ substantially thirty years ago. Now they differ as much as those of an English city by contrast with those of one of its colonial cities.' ('I consumi di Milano e di Torino in paragone di quelli di Napoli non differivano notevolmente trenta anni or sono; differiscono ora quanto quelli di una città inglese di fronte a quelli di una città coloniale,' p. 85.) Nitti indeed demonstrates that Naples has been forced to import from the north many of the foodstuffs and other necessities that it formerly produced. But a worse statistic emerges from these revelations, namely, that in spite of increases in Naples's population (though nothing like as great as those of the dynamically industrializing powerhouses of the north), there has been an overall diminution in goods consumed. In short, there is in Naples, decade by decade, as Nitti's tables and statistics prove (pp. 83–4), significantly less intake per person of foodstuffs vital to health and well-being, with the consequence that its population is rendered more vulnerable to the diseases by which it has indeed been ravaged.

Like Serao, Nitti shows some prejudices of the times, particularly in his use of comparisons with other cultures. He speaks of Neapolitans 'often eating no better than Indians' ('i suoi abitanti non mangiano spesso molto meglio degli indiani'), as though it might be expected that Indians should eat poorly, but hardly an Italian people. In much the same breath he excuses the 'oriental somnolence' ('la sonnolenza orientale') of her people and their 'strange southern laziness' ('l'ozio fantasioso dei meridionali') as resulting almost always from 'insufficient nutrition' ('una nutrizione insufficiente,' p. 85). Although at first sight he may seem to be slighting the other cultures conjured up in such analogies, Nitti is in fact making an effective point. His deployment of stock prejudices against the orient and against so-called southern laziness is integral to his demonstration. For what he seems to be trying to convey by these other-cultural notions is that Naples has at one and the same time been 'orientalized' and 'southernized' by northern minds, through processes of colonization. It is the colonization itself, he claims, that has resulted in the 'insufficient nutrition' and that is the real cause of the impoverished lifestyles evident in her population, not some ahistorical or *ab initio* factor.

In deploying such comparisons Nitti is working at his key concept of the South as a particular kind of colony of the North. Although he implies that even before Unification the South had been a 'colony of supply,' its latest immiseration by the North is graver than anything that had occurred before 1860, when the Kingdom of the Two Sicilies had at least been an important and independent state. To accentuate his case about the new form that the South's colonization by the North has taken, Nitti reminds us by contrast of its capital city's former glory. 'Naples had the richest court in Italy, by marriage interrelated with the greatest courts in Europe: it was the sojourn of princes and princesses, and its theatrical seasons were of European renown.' ('Avea Napoli la più ricca corte d'Italia, imparentata con le più grandi corti d'Europa: era soggiorno di principi e di principesse e avea stagioni teatrali che godevano rinomanza europea,' p. 54.)

The later Gramsci will not deploy stock prejudices about the South at all, not even with the rhetorical knowingness that they are mere prejudices that Nitti (a southerner himself) seems to have displayed in the preceding remarks. Rather, Gramsci will name them as something more pernicious even than prejudice. By his reckoning they constitute an entire 'ideology ... propagated through the multifarious forms of bourgeois propaganda among the masses of the North.' Such propaganda holds that 'the South is a lead weight which impedes a more rapid civil development of Italy; the southerners are biologically inferior beings, semi-barbarians or complete barbarians by natural destiny; if the South is backward, the fault is not to be found in the capitalist system or in any other historical cause, but is the fault of nature which has made the southerner lazy, incapable, criminal, barbarous' etc.[56]

Nitti should be half excused for any prejudices he displayed, because in his 1903 text he was at least locating the causes of the South's comparative backwardness in the divisive capitalist system of this entire period in Italy, with its internal colonialism of one sector of the nation by another. Nonetheless, it is Gramsci who shines the more brightly in the comparison between the two. He exposes as mere propagandistic constructs (ones, furthermore, used for class and political purposes) many of the notions that go on being propagated in our own times by politicians of the Northern League and others. And his remarks hold good at the general level for more than the specific Italian culture in terms of which they were couched: many modern social, historical, and economic analyses use his perceptions as cardinal to the way different cultures represent one another. (For example, the specific Gramscian case about pervasive ideologies in the representation of other cultures lies at the heart of Edward Said's *Orientalism*, as has often been realized.)

Nitti's outright distaste for colonialism as such is evident in his asseveration that funding the vast public works programs necessary in Italy's Mezzogiorno will be impossible for as long as, at the national level, 'military expenses' ('le spese militari') in the cause of 'useless or fantastical colonial adventures' ('inutili o fantastiche avventure coloniali') persist (p. 26). His reference here is to Italy's recent costly and unsuccessful attempt in Ethiopia to join the club of European nations carving up Africa. Nitti hints that the colonialism in question is not only an attempt at depredation of another people; it is based in a yet more vile, because pointless, national compulsion to display military power on the world stage. As events had proved, Italy did not even have the power it supposed before the specific colonial adventurism began. Hence the bitter, treble twist in the irony of Nitti's remarks on this point: first, the Italian government cannot refinance the South because it spends such moneys on colonial adventurism; but, second, the colonial adventurism is itself unsuccessful; which leads, third, by a vicious circle back to the financial compulsion to colonize all the more deeply its own South, so as to staunch any haemorrhaging of the national budget.

Nitti is at his own most colourful – and least scientific – when describing Italy's rulers. Early in the text his critique of them is almost mild by comparison with what it will become. 'Italian politicians are in general men of fairly mediocre worth. They do not appreciate annoyances and even the best among them are incapable of facing up to important problems. Hence, from its government as currently constituted and operational there is little or nothing to be hoped for by way of revitalization of the South. By the necessity of things, or out of ignorance of them, and so as to maintain a quiet life, the government reinforces the ills or at least does not combat them.' ('I politici italiani sono in generale uomini di assai mediocre valore: non amano noie e anche i migliori fra di essi sono incapaci di affrontare i problemi di larga importanza. Onde dal Governo così com' esso è, com'esso opera, vi è poco o nulla da sperare per la rinnovazione del Mezzogiorno: per necessità di cose, per ignoranza di esse, per quieto vivere, il Governo seconda il male o almeno non lo combatte,' p. 20.) By the time Nitti hits his stride in this text, no knavery is spared his pen.

> The government arrived, nay arrives, at acts that in no civilised country would be tolerated. The magistrature above all, obsequious before evil, is under the tyranny of political power. Local administrations are abandoned to the worst elements. Ministers of state have been seen (and not in one case only) to rob public documents, rescue the guilty from sentencing, falsify decrees, and impose on delicate situations persons of moral perversity and corruption. These things, a hundred times repeated, are accepted by all. Nay, many people hold them to be almost inevitable. In many respects the already bad has grown worse at an alarming rate. And if there have been inquests, they could not and cannot in such a furore of conflicting interests lead to any result.
>
> Hence Naples, which possessed in 1860 all the conditions – more than Turin, more than Milan – to transform itself into a great industrial city, for diverse reasons and because of State politics and finance, as well as customs regulations, administrative action by central government, and new lifestyles, has been pitched into a condition of growing poverty.

> Il Governo giunse, giunge ad atti che in nessun paese civile sarebbero tollerati: la magistratura sopra tutto, ossequiosa al male, è sotto la tirannia del potere politico. Le amministrazioni locali sono abbandonate agli elementi peggiori. Si son visti (e non in un caso solo) ministri di Stato rubare pubblici documenti, sottrarre colpevoli alle condanne, falsificare atti pubblici, imporre in situazioni delicate uomini di perversa morale e di vita corrotta. Queste cose cento volte ripetute sono da tutti accettate; alcuni anzi le ritengono quasi inevitabili. Sotto alcuni aspetti il male è venuto sempre più peggiorando e incalzando: e se vi sono state inchieste esse non potevano, non possono in tanto dibattersi di opposti interessi menare ad alcun risultato.
>
> Così Napoli che avea nel 1860 tutte le condizioni, più di Torino, più di Milano per trasformarsi in grande città industriale, per cause di diversa natura, per la politica finanziaria ed economica dello Stato, per il regime doganale, per l'azione amministrativa del Governo centrale, per le nuove abitudini di vita è precipitata in uno stato di crescente povertà. (pp. 64–5)

Granted this moral low point in the logic of Nitti's argument, it is always his more positive point that, however wretchedly impoverished in relation to what she once was, Naples continues to enjoy natural conditions propitious for rapid and successful industrialization, provided only that she benefit from enlightened state financing. I shall not pursue these further moves in his argumentation because something else, closer to my overall subject, arrests my attention, even though it seems almost an extraneous addition at the end of a long list of ills.

Nitti has claimed in the preceding text that even different lifestyles on the part of the Italian people (*nuove abitudini di vita*) have contributed to the decline of Naples. To what would he be referring? At one level this may be an unconscious reference back to his sense, earlier in the same quotation, that perversity and corruption in Italy's political classes have exceeded all measure. But that tendency was already there by his reckoning – perennial, so to speak – so this is hardly something *new*. I am led to deduce that Nitti is referring to a change in lifestyles since Unification, and one that as its main consequence has hardened divisions between rich and poor, North and South. Take what he had said in opening his analysis about his own region of background, the further south Basilicata: 'The inhabitants of this immense region divide into two categories: those – the masses of poor and tormented peasants – who do not grasp their condition and lead an almost bestial lifestyle; and the generally poor and ruined middle classes, who bewail everything but do nothing ...

Often every form of security, even about staying alive, is lacking.' ('Gli abitanti di questa immensa terra si dividono in due categorie: quelli che non sanno il loro male e vivono di una vita quasi bestiale, masse di contadini poveri e tormentati, e borghesi generalmente poveri e dissestati, che si dolgono di tutto e non fanno nulla ... Manca sovente ogni sicurezza, anche della vita,' p. 12.) This also may seem like nothing new, merely a radical worsening of prior conditions. What is perhaps a departure from the past is the fully lived nihilism on the part of Italy's middle classes (in this case impoverished *borghesi* of the Basilicata) – a sense that absolutely nothing can be done.

Naples's bourgeois classes too, Nitti says throughout his text, have been almost useless in turning around her misfortunes, and not merely because of private misfortunes of their own. Trained by its renowned university mainly as lawyers and doctors, or in other words in 'unproductive' professions, they are by the reckoning of Nitti (who is himself that relatively unprecedented being, an economic technocrat) unfitted for constructing and running what Naples most needs, namely, heavy industries. For this, foreigners must be brought in, and only slowly will Neapolitans learn from them. The city could learn the same from its educational institutions, including the university – but only if they were to change fundamentally their very concepts of education, so as to prioritize industrial and technocratic over legal, medical, or humanistic skills.

However, none of these initial attempts to understand what Nitti may have meant by *nuove abitudini di vita* (new lifestyles) fully satisfy me. I am led to a final set of speculations that will require the support of evidence from painting and photography, as well as some reflections on how the *belle époque* in Italy was represented long afterwards, in film.

Supposing we were to look for anything remotely resembling a Goyesque sense of horror at what some Italians experienced over the course of the nineteenth century, as new comforts and luxuries became standard for lifestyles in the wealthier classes – what would we find in painting or early photography? My personal answer to this question, based on Ottocento paintings and photographs in galleries, as well as rapidly increasing literature on the subject, is that there is little of a genuinely disturbing nature. And while it may seem strange to make this a subject of lament – as though art's main duty lay in desolating the viewer – my point is that we have by now some sense of the magnitude of distress in the daily lives of many in Italy during the period. Representation that occludes or (whether consciously or unconsciously) blunts our sense of the scale of social suffering is to some degree co-involved with other factors of cover-up in the nation at large. And this, I would claim, is the predominant impression we take from much art of the period. Painters of landscapes, cityscapes, or interiors, with the exception of those treating historical themes, rarely focus on the outrightly tragic. Latter-day rural or urban *vedutisti* are for the most part quietistic in their treatments: bent on showing degrees of harmony with nature, or of habituation to the city, however rapidly both rural and urban Italy are changing from what they have once been. Even most early photography in Italy has a greater tendency to *recommend* its many and varied locations than to draw us up short with representations of people being degraded by what is happening to them. Nor is it generally inclined to show subject matter in any other respects discomforting.

I will be more explicit about the kinds of quietism and harmoniousness I am referring to in what follows, because I want to suggest, quite straightforwardly, that what may have been at the back of Nitti's mind in casually talking of 'new habits of life' that pitched many into deeper poverty and neglect were high-bourgeois social and economic horizons that tended to exclude disturbing human experience from view. My supplementary theory is that such horizons of comfort and accommodation to change (rather than their more radical political opposites) largely characterize the work of painters and early photographers of the age.

Let us begin with a total exception to the generalization being made, indeed the strongest visual exception that I can produce from my exploration. It consists of an isolated painting, *La sala delle agitate al S. Bonifazio di Firenze* (*The Ward of the Mad Women at St Boniface in Florence*, figure 7.1), by the Florentine painter Telemaco Signorini (1835–1901), that in its intensity does indeed remind us more than a little of some of Goya's treatments of human suffering, of approximately half a century earlier and in another country. In terms of subject matter and mode of treatment, its sheer difference from what was in the main being produced around Signorini, in Tuscany or elsewhere in Italy, is resounding. There is even a departure in basic shock value from most other paintings by Signorini himself. The simple fact of its date, 1865, is interesting, being the year of the removal to Florence of capital city status.

There are represented here degrees of distress and disturbance among a group of institutionalized Florentine citizens that no amount of rapid *embourgeoisement* of the surrounding urban context in immediately succeeding years will offer the remotest hope of ameliorating. On the contrary, improvements in the city's comforts and luxuries are more

256 Italian Cultural Lineages

Figure 7.1 Telemaco Signorini, *The Ward of the Mad Women at St Boniface in Florence*. Courtesy Museo d'Arte Moderna Internazionale, Venice.

likely to have negative side effects on the situation portrayed here, as, in the event, they certainly did on so many of the more vulnerable citizens of Florence in the next few years. Herein therefore – in the utter unnegotiability of the woe it betrays – lies the work's abiding value. We do well to dwell on it, before tackling paintings and photographs more able to negotiate, or somehow attune themselves to, the changes overtaking Italy.

In Signorini's painting are some fifteen or sixteen women in drab institutional garments. Many of them sit along a bench, beyond a set of tables that aligns one side of an otherwise large and bare ward in the San Bonifazio convent. Even without knowing the painting's title, one realizes that these women are deeply distressed, either from the acute isolation showing on the faces of the many who are silent or from the shouting and gesticulation of the only one raising a protest. One woman in particular, in the foreground, standing with rounded shoulders and an absorbed, eyes-closed expression, seems by her motionlessness and the fact that, although foregrounded, she is totally in shadow, to be haunted by hopelessness or by sorrow. Another woman cowers beneath one of the tables. Two or three huddle under the cowl of their garments, their heads hanging down. Another two, their heads thrown back, are sitting as though in extreme anguish. One has her hand to her face, seeming to shield herself from some painful reality, while another sits slumped in the only doorway, weighed down by an equivalent oppression. There is not the least sign of communication between them, and with the exception of the one making protest, they are well nigh inactive. Indeed, the room seems by its bareness to afford them no *possibility* of action, let alone of interaction, were they even so inclined, which clearly they are not. Instead it bespeaks, in its monochrome whitewashed walls and its earth-toned floors, a bleakness, a despair, an absence of a single thing that might bring relief to the anguish or *anomie* that we read in every face, and in every bodily attitude.

Another artist, almost a generation younger, Angelo Morbelli (1853–1919), approaches the desolation portrayed by Signorini, again in representing *institutional* Italy, in his paintings of the Pio Albergo Trivulzio (Pious Trivulzio Hospice). This was a hospice for the elderly in Via della Signoria, central Milan, founded in 1771. Between 1883 and 1909 Morbelli produced more than twenty oil paintings and a further number of sketches and pastels of its inhabitants.[57] The first painting in the series, from 1883, gloomily entitled *Giorni ultimi* (*Last Days*),[58] shows serried ranks of the elderly sitting behind benches, all in dark brown uniforms including caps in most cases, and each incommunicado, like the women in Signorini's painting. The room has a multitude of faces, but we read each one as a study in isolation amidst the crowd. Twenty years later, in 1903, Morbelli will paint from a different angle the same room, recognizable from a stove on its wall. This time, the subject of the painting being *Natale dei rimasti* (*Those Left at Christmas*, figure 7.2), there are only five pensioners left, at dispersed points, in the room. Morbelli had already

Figure 7.2 Angelo Morbelli, *Those Left at Christmas*. Courtesy Museo d'Arte Moderna Internazionale, Venice.

treated approximately the same subject in 1892 in his painting *Holiday at the Pio Albergo Trivulzio* (figure 7.3). As in the later painting, we witness there only those inmates without relatives, or worse still – in the case of one with coat, hat, and walking stick ready on the bench before him – a pensioner whose family has failed to materialize as expected on the holiday in question.

Morbelli's series on the Trivulzio Hospice represents the pathos and loneliness of old age. Above all, it seems to suggest that individuals face impending death in mental isolation, in spite of institutions that apparently bring them together socially. Nonetheless, for all the sympathy they elicit from us by their representation of how people are abandoned in old age, Morbelli's paintings of the institutionalized elderly do not instil horror on anything like the scale of Signorini's earlier portrayal of the ward of mad women. Morbelli does represent social problems in other paintings, including a noteworthy one of a modern double suicide and another of juvenile prostitution. But such subjects are rare in the art world of late-nineteenth-century Italy. More common genres and treatments reveal established social attitudes.

In the case of portrait painting, it is of course the bourgeois classes or older aristocracy that are principally represented, for they were usually

Figure 7.3 Angelo Morbelli, *Holiday at the Pio Albergo Trivulzio*. Courtesy RMN Agence Photo, Paris.

the works' commissioners and purchasers. Domenico Morelli's 1859 portrait of his fellow artist Bernardo Celentano[59] presents the latter as an insolent-seeming man-about-town, with polka-dotted dress shirt under a cream-silk *gilet* with reveres, dark tie, and black silk top hat. Celentano, holding a dressy glove in a closed fist, stares smugly out of the picture with a half-smoked cigar projecting from his dashingly moustached mouth. Behind him is a wall advertising a performance of *Benvenuto Cellini*, almost as though Celentano were the bragging Cinquecento sculptor come back to life in the mid-nineteenth century, as 'the dandy of fall 1859' (to quote Morelli's brother Luigi's later characterization of this painting).[60] Celentano seems to be revealing his showy soul and saying to the viewer, 'Look at me – could there be anything finer?' Above all, the work suggests Celantano's utterly secure membership in the well-to-do classes. Perhaps some of the in-your-face defiance of Celantano's very dandyism constitutes a subliminal affirmation that poverty cannot and does not touch his life.

Even where the genre of portraiture explicitly takes the labouring poor as its subject matter, as in the case of Marco De Gregorio's 1873 portrait of the hoer (*Lo zappatore*), the emaciated features of the labourer's face under his simple country hat, together with his tattered clothes, seem a tribute to the stoicism by which he is seen to cope with hard work. This form of portraiture asks for *tribute* from the viewer at how reality is faced by the labouring poor, not *protest* or any sense that it should be changed. A painting by Giovanni Costa (1826–1903), *Pastore dell'agro Romano* (*Shepherd of the Roman Plain*), is an early form of anthropological documentation of the clothing styles and background landscape of a passing way of life, and in no way can be said to encourage a wish for change. There are also in gallery after gallery portraits of *banditi* of the former Kingdom of Naples and the Two Sicilies: mustachioed figures in colourful southern peasant garments, sometimes with musket over shoulder and arms akimbo in would-be threatening attitudes. Such paintings seem to relegate an urgent problem of civil dissent to the realm of costume romance.

The portrait paintings of agricultural labourers or *banditi* are cognate with what in Britain were known by the term 'fancy' paintings – initially late-eighteenth-century sentimental representations of the poor for a clientele of buyers from a different, and obviously higher, class. Into this broad category in Italy also go representations of urban chimneysweeps by Giuseppe Molteni (1800–67), the first on a commission from Count Kolowrat in 1837, and by others, among them notably the painter of urban *vedute* (view paintings) Angelo Inganni (1807–80). In such paintings of sweeps, as in the 'fancy' painting genre more generally, the urchins portrayed, although begrimed with their trade, are as plump as many a Quattrocento or Cinquecento sculpted cherub by the likes of Della Robbia or Rossellino. In fact, only their sooty faces and tatterdemalion clothes differentiate them from those earlier visual representations of the cherub.

The big eyes of the sweeps portrayed by Molteni and Inganni (see figure 7.4) prefigure the much later mutation of this sub-genre of portraiture into 'moppet' paintings of tattered children with a tear or two running down their cheeks, so popular in the West generally among nouveau riche buyers a few decades ago. So far from functioning as social protest, such paintings would seem to check any such tendency; and to channel it instead towards what Gramsci – remarking on Manzoni's (and the overall Catholic church's) attitude towards the populace – called 'condescending benevolence, not human empathy' ('un atteggiamento ... di condiscendente benevolenza, non di medesimezza umana'.)[61]

And what of cityscapes? The urban *veduta* survived as a genre from the eighteenth century into the nineteenth, and in particular picked up on novelties of architecture, transport, or lifestyle in the contexts it documented. The genre was eventually largely replaced by the photographic documentation of streets, monuments, bays, mountains, or other urban

Figure 7.4 Angelo Inganni, *Urban Chimneysweep*. Courtesy Fotostudio Rapuzzi, Brescia.

backdrops by companies such as Fratelli Alinari of Florence (who worked all over Italy), or by countless postcard views of the newly unified nation.

Whether in painted *vedute* of Italian city streets and piazzas by artists such as Giuseppe Canella and Angelo Inganni from the 1830s onwards, or in the street photography that comes later, there is a function the artists seem to have set themselves to perform: namely, to capture and to document the material fabric of streets, populated by a colourful mixture of rich and poor strollers, together with curricles or other smart carriages of the earlier age, or the trams, horse-drawn buggies, and first motorcars of the photographs. The element of social protest is entirely absent here. If the poor are included, they constitute, in Serao's terms, a kind of 'social picturesque.' And they are, in any case, balanced out by the fine buildings, the well-dressed ladies and gentlemen, and the fascinating newest forms of private and public transport. This is part and parcel of the philosophical 'quietism' that dominates the art of the period.

For example, in the well-known *Veduta di piazza del Duomo con il Coperto dei Figini* (*View of the Piazza del Duomo with the Figini Portico*, figure 7.5) of 1838, Inganni deliberately places in the centre foreground a pauper and his son, the latter munching a crust of bread. Also foregrounded and just to the left of the pair is a richly dressed youth, only a year or two older than the poor child. Groupings or isolated individuals from wealthier classes are to be seen in the right foreground as well as the far background of the painting, the bonneted ladies looking as if they have just stepped onto these streets from a different visual genre, that of the colour fashion plate. Indeed, the *veduta* and the fashion plate are contiguous visual productions, the former constantly absorbing material from the latter.

In 1879, only a year before his death, Inganni has not, after more than forty years of practising it, substantially tampered with the philosophical underpinnings of the *veduta* genre. Admittedly, in a painting of his home town of Brescia, the *Veduta di piazza della Loggia sotto la neve* (*View of the Piazza della Loggia under Snow*, figure 7.6), there are notably new contextual details, chief among them the central monument in marble to the struggles of the Risorgimento. The monument, which replaced a former one of the Lion of St Mark from the time of Venice's earlier rule over the city, specifically represents in its bas-relief panels Brescia's own heroic 'Ten Days' of uprising in January 1849 against Austrian rule. It has an inscription honouring King Victor Emmanuel for erecting it.

The way the painting is gendered is noteworthy. A well-dressed middle-aged man is inspecting the monument from one side, a similarly well-to-do but elderly man from the other. By contrast, women and children, whether of the richer or poorer classes, are going about other daily tasks, such as purchasing vegetables, carrying cooking urns over the shoulder, or just surveying the scene from a balustraded parapet. In the foreground a fashionably dressed mother with her back to the monument (probably the wife of the inspecting man close by) leads her neatly turned-out son by the hand, both of them with fur muffs to contend against the cold. Clearly, by the reckoning of this painting it is men – more specifically men of a certain social standing – who are deemed to be the absorbers and guardians of the narrative of all it had taken to construct and unify the nation. Whatever else, *their* lives as men should include this ideological focus. Women, by contrast, will tend to be engaged in a number of

Figure 7.5 Angelo Inganni, *View of the Piazza del Duomo with the Figini Portico.* Courtesy Saporetti Immagini d'Arte, Milan.

other, worldlier or simply leisure, pursuits. Their ideological attunement, whether towards shopping, labouring tasks, or the bourgeois role of child-rearing, need not include guardianship of the nation's founding narratives of unification in the same way that men's must.

Figure 7.6 Angelo Inganni, *View of the Piazza della Loggia under Snow*. Courtesy Fotostudio Rapuzzi, Brescia.

Gramsci taught us to study the entirety of a culture, in all its class manifestations, and not just concentrate on 'high cultural' phenomena. He did this by the importance he always attached to what he calls 'the *humus* of popular culture exactly as it is, with its tastes and its tendencies, etc., its moral and intellectual world, however backward and conventional' ('l'*humus* della cultura popolare cosí come è, coi suoi gesti, le sue tendenze ecc., col suo mondo morale e intellettuale, sia pure arretrato e convenzionale').[62] I am interpreting him quite widely on this point of popular culture as meaning not simply the lives and lifestyles and any revealing modes of thought of the poor; for I would contend that the important world of view painting and fashion plates, which has begun to receive due attention of late, is a case of the 'popular' acting at higher class levels.

As early as 1851, in an article entitled 'Fashions and Lifestyles from the Middle Ages to Our Own Times,' from the influential journal *Le ore casalinghe* (*Domestic Hours*), fashion had been called nothing less than 'the material expression of the needs, lifestyles and thoughts of an epoch' ('l'espressione materiale dei bisogni, dei costumi e dei pensieri di un'epoca'). And not merely that. It can 'unveil to the eye of the ob-server the political organism of the society with which it has always been intimately linked' ('essa disvela all'occhio dell'osservatore l'organismo politico della società colla quale è sempre strettamente collegata').[63] Thus, we certainly need to take note if, as seems so often the case, the best dressed men as well as women in the streets depicted by the view painters seem to have been transposed from the fashion plates of fashion journals and newspapers, for that would suggest an ideological connection of class congruity between the two visual productions in question. Such connections, when multiplied across other phenomena of cultural production, confirm as nothing else the increasing hegemony of the leisured bourgeois classes that tended to buy and consume these visual products (fashion plate journals or view paintings, as the case may be).

The popular-selling journals had titles like *Corriere delle dame* (*Ladies' Courier*), *Margherita* (after the name of the wife of Prince – later King – Umberto), *Giornale dei modelli per vestiti da donna e damigella* (*Women's and Young Women's Journal of Dress Styles*), *Illustrazione italiana* (*Italian Illustration*), *La moda di Milano e di Parigi* (*Milanese and Parisian Fashion*), *Il mondo elegante* (*The World of Elegance*), *Le ore casalinghe* (*Domestic Hours*), and many others.[64] We should remind ourselves that in certain middle and upper social strata the fashion plate (often reproduced from equivalent Parisian publications) was an important visual genre in its own right, documenting the *embourgeoisement* of Italian lifestyles; and not just documenting it, but stimulating the phenomenon to further levels. In the fashion plates, and in the surrounding or interleaving texts treating social customs, we see defined an ever-strengthening bourgeois world, one of its keenest societal markers being the very desirability of such apparel as the plates depict.

As a visual genre the fashion plate bespeaks forms of aspiration that are not remotely attuned to social problems in the newly unified nation. Nor are there articles in such journals on the lifestyles of those who, because of the trap of endemic poverty, could never conceive of dressing like the people in the plates. Nonetheless – or perhaps for this very reason of its occlusion of problems that better-off Italians would prefer not to acknowledge – this fashion magazine culture was a booming success in the mid- and late nineteenth century. While Milan tended to lead in the number and quality of output of such women's journals, most Italian cities of any standing, including the poorer southern ones, produced reviews of the latest fashions, if only in the form of newspaper 'supplements.' And always the social commentary that surrounds the plates is testimony to the changing lives of women in Italy.

In her landmark publication *Le Italiane dall'Unità a oggi: Modelli culturali e comportamenti sociali* (*Italian Women from Unification to the Present: Cultural Models and Social Behaviours*),[65] Michela De Giorgio uses articles and illustrations from these multiple fashion publications as some of the most important evidence of changing attitudes towards women, and of changes in women's own sense of their identities and lifestyles. In a more specific study of the nineteenth-century fashion journals, Silvia Franchini has shown how one city, Milan, 'became the most renowned focus of a sociality lived under the sign of elegance.' Franchini goes on to suggest how Italian fashions sought (even if without much success) to undermine 'French hegemony.'[66]

As Erica Morato's latest researches have uncovered, already in 1851, in the article of *Le ore casalinghe* to which I referred above, fashion is seen as virtually the most talismanic indicator of an age. To re-quote the crucial sentence of that article: 'It is the material expression of the needs, lifestyles and thoughts of an epoch, and it unveils to the eye of the observer the political organism of society with which it has always been intimately linked' ('è l'espressione materiale dei bisogni, dei costumi e dei pensieri di un'epoca, ed essa disvela all'occhio dell'osservatore l'organismo politico della società colla quale è sempre strettamente collegata.')[67] This judgment is one I would not wish to disavow a hundred and fifty years later, even if it crucially leaves out of account the dispossessed.

Fashion plates in journals issuing in great numbers from Milan and other Italian cities are an indication of the advent of the *haute bourgeoisie* to overwhelming dominance over Italian culture. But they are also an important artistic genre in their own right. The very fact that, as many recent studies have pointed out, contemporary journals often included instructions on how women of aspiring classes could recreate outfits approximating to or even replicating these fashions of their social superiors is an indicator of their political, as well as economic and artistic, importance. As Rita Carrarini in particular demonstrates, fashion publications grew in number and social reach. Eventually, to her reckoning, 'their objective is that of giving a *petit bourgeois* public the sensation of being able, through their dress styles, to attain parity with better-off classes. Many magazines address themselves,' she continues, quoting one such from 1911, '"to all those women who have the laudable habit of tailoring their own outfits and toilet in the home, while remaining up-to-date with directions that fashion is taking"' ('"a tutte quelle signore che hanno la lodevole abitudine di allestire i propri abiti e le proprie toilette in casa, pur mantenendosi al corrente delle novità che la moda va adottando"').[68] In terms of creative visual artistry and social penetration, fashion plate production was one of the major art forms of nineteenth-century Italy, however beholden it remained for long decades to Parisian hegemony.

Lastly, what of the retrospective account of the *belle époque* in Italy offered by film? I shall only comment on the work of one director, Luchino Visconti, whose attention to the past was important not only in a number of his best films, but in his compulsion to treat specific historical contexts in the theatre and in live opera. Visconti, who used the tailoring firm of Tirelli over and over in his productions, was known to take great care in obtaining the finest materials for costumes. As regards his punctiliousness about architectural location, scenes were either recreated from scratch, as in the case of the Venetian bridges and *calli* in an early colour film such as *Senso*, or shot on the site of actual streets and palazzi for evocations of nineteenth-century context.

The most consummate use of *belle époque* dress styles to establish and explore its characters' lifestyles occurs in Visconti's last film, *L'Innocente*. A masterly study in gender relations in the wealthiest Roman class towards the end of the nineteenth century, the film is a very loose adaptation of D'Annunzio's novel of the same title. A number of matters are therefore most evident. First, whereas D'Annunzio had spent little time describing the physical context of his characters (Rome and its environs), Visconti is punctilious about every detail of clothing, about the interiors and furnishings of rooms, and about the glories of country villas and their gardens.

In D'Annunzio the narrative consists entirely of the inner confession of the philandering Tullio Hermil, who holds a rather Nietzschean philosophy that he is above and beyond conventional morality, and who piques himself on being an 'ideologue, analyst and sophist in an epoch of decadence' ('ideologo e analista e sofista in epoca di decadenza').[69] This narrator is deeply shocked when he discovers that his wife Giuliana, in her unhappiness at the decline in intensity of his feelings for her, has succumbed to the temptation of a brief affair of her own with a well-known Roman writer, Filippo Arborio. So shocked indeed, and rendered retrospectively jealous, is Tullio when he discovers his wife is with child (which he knows could not be his own) that soon after the birth of the infant he exposes it to the cold, from which it dies.

Because the novel was written about his own period, D'Annunzio had not really troubled himself to recreate in its writing the specific cultural context. Only where Tullio Hermil is drawn into a different world, as in the case of the peasant labourers on his brother's farm, do we get close descriptions of external aspects of lifestyle, rather than the more normal mode of revelation from within. Indeed, several points in the narrative show that D'Annunzio is highly aware of Tolstoy's major fiction, and is even trying some explorations of his own on the relations between the wealthy landowning classes and their peasant tenants, a theme much treated by the older Russian novelist. Although D'Annunzio's own novel is not at its most successful in this respect, it nonetheless demonstrates a certain ambitiousness on a pan-European scale, and one that significantly is not taken up by Visconti in his film adoption.

In the novel Tullio Hermil is even encouraged by his brother Federico to take note of the 'singularly sweet smile' of one of the oldest farm labourers, who happens to have led a tough life and been cast off by his wife and children. 'Is it not extraordinary, almost incredible, this man's persistence in happiness. After all that he has suffered, he has been able to conserve the smile that you have seen! *You would do well, Tullio, not to forget that smile ...*' ('Non è straordinaria, quasi incredibile, questa pertinacia d'un uomo nella bontà? Dopo tutto quel che ha sofferto, egli ha potuto conservare il sorriso che tu gli hai veduto! *Farai bene, Tullio, a non dimenticare quel sorriso ...*')[70] D'Annunzio for his part would seem to be pitting the peasant's ability to remain happy in the face of adversity, and to exist in a state of positive wonderment at life itself (he is even given the role of godfather of the newborn child on account of this quality of his), against the cynicism and negation of life of the main character, the narrator Hermil, in his killing of the innocent child. D'Annunzio evokes scenes from Tolstoy directly in this portion of his work. Visconti for his part leaves this symbolic class contrast quite out of his film version, presumably in the belief, not entirely unfounded, that in cinematic terms the malignity of his protagonist Hermil, and to an extent his entire class, is best revealed directly, in action and expression.

Visconti does not have the main character Hermil actually narrate the story. He studies this cruel, egotistical figure, and indeed all his important characters, by use of a camera trained on their intimate expressions of reaction to what is going on in their lives. Nor can he rely on his late-twentieth-century audience to understand the story's late-nineteenth-century context. It is, therefore, lovingly created in its every material fabric, even if what Visconti mainly wishes to express is a critique of the moral decline of many of the persons living amid such luxury. This seems almost a paradox in the art film genre. On the one hand, each costume appears to be a masterpiece in its own right, meant for our appreciation as viewers. At another level, however, the drama is not so much one of how people look, as it is the original D'Annunzian one of how they behave in their class and gender roles at a particular moment in Italian culture and history. Clearly, for all Visconti's left-wing sympathies, he had retained an intense sense of an age and society of opulence approximately a generation before he was born, many remnants of which he had grown up with as a scion of one of the oldest and wealthiest Milanese noble families. In *L'Innocente* he is reaching for a critique of the degrees of moral corruption that may lie at the heart of everything that is most materially seductive about the *belle époque*. My impression, however, is that in this particular film the sheer beauties of context and of personal dress sometimes win out over the moral critique that is meant to puncture them and go to levels of more profound significance. We return to the film for its *look*, instead of for what we intuit was its intended message. In the process, that visual splendour often seems to *become* its primary message, rather than remaining merely the vessel of an essentially negative moral critique. As his life was nearing its end, Visconti seemed unable to attain the distance from all that was most questionable about the lifestyles of the wealthier classes that D'Annunzio had for the most part managed in the novel version of *L'Innocente*.

More than any other work by Visconti, *L'Innocente* seems to pay tribute to the haute bourgeoisie's dress and architectural styles. The various outfits worn by the character of the wife, Giuliana Hermil, unquestionably have nineteenth-century fashion journals as their point of inspiration, for they are recreations of the finest artistic achievements of that genre. The actress who plays this role, Laura Antonelli (figure 7.7), is

Figure 7.7 Laura Antonelli as Giuliana Hermil in Visconti's *L'Innocente*. Courtesy British Film Institute.

dressed in such a way as to seem utterly lovable, partly because she is so vulnerable to the least hint of maltreatment. Her mere looks (of which the changing tailored outfits are an integral part), because betokening an inner sweetness and vulnerability, become a criticism of Hermil for ceasing to love her passionately in return, as the devoted and innocent wife she essentially remains, even after her adultery.

Her counterpart, Hermil's on-off mistress the Countess Teresa Raffo, played by Jennifer O'Neill (figure 7.8), although similarly finely dressed in every scene in which she appears, is made to seem ruthless by contrast with the wife. The Countess's outfits and her *maquillage* imply a disturbing hardness of soul, unlike her opposite, Giuliana, whose features and costumes suggest at all times loving gentleness and an altogether finer, more generous, less egotistical temperament.

The husband Hermil's own looks and outfits are never less than immaculate. Until his wife's pregnancy by another man begins to haunt him, he is the epitome of a class of person who, not having to work for a living, displays utter complacency in a world of luxury wherein he need

Figure 7.8 Giancarlo Giannini as Tullio Hermil and Jennifer O'Neill as his mistress, the Countess Teresa Raffo, in *L'Innocente*. Courtesy British Film Institute.

never go lacking in sensual gratification. His home is a large Roman palazzo belonging to his mother, but he has two adjoining country villas to repair to also: that in which his mother actually lives and another that she has made over to the married couple for when boredom with the city sets in. Visconti did not go the further step of trying to recreate any Roman street scenes for this particular film. He had, after all, compelled us to acknowledge, if we hadn't already, the nineteenth-century fashion plate as a major art genre. In thus registering the potentiality for extraordinarily beautiful clothing and interior opulence in the *belle époque*, Visconti had paid tribute to his own class of origin, however little its artistic creations happened to express his personal politics. In saying this, we have defined a truly touching sense in which, with his last work, Visconti revealed just how little he had kicked over the traces of his wealthy upbringing. It is a work that could hardly be more different from the rural and urban losers of the film from 1943 with which he had begun his career, *Ossessione*.

Death in Venice is a far better-known film. Unlike *L'Innocente* it had explored not so much a specific Italian lifestyle, as more Europe-wide riches of the *belle époque*, and specifically as concentrated in that leisure resort of the well-to-do that by this stage Venice, for all her earlier importance, had essentially shrunk to being. In the film, the Grand Hotel of Venice's Lido is where the wealthy come to stay, a sumptuous pleasure haunt of this rich European class, the members of which circulate and interact in the finest reproduction dress styles that Visconti and his costume designer Piero Tosi could command for the production. The Lido is distinguished from Venice proper by its unalleviated finery. On day trips across the lagoon to the main city, the hotel's guests are at the mercy of distinctly more dangerous passageways, dark *campielli*, and persons of other classes who are forced to make a living off wealthy international tourists. In both real and symbolic terms the most important event is the recent outbreak of cholera: common to places that have not undergone an effective *risanamento*, even if this city's authorities are loath to publicize its presence widely for fear of damaging their livelihood.

The German protagonist Professor Aschenbach pursues through the later action of the film the Apollonian figure of the young Austrian boy, Tadzio. Aschenbach's harrowed longing for the purity and youth of the boy leads him through some of the darkest, sleaziest, and most disease-ridden haunts of Venice. Indeed, Visconti's film, for all its stress on the opulence of Aschenbach's and Tadzio's own class, takes pains to show us this seamier world with which it has come into contact. Aschenbach, as in Mann's novella, eventually resorts to a barber, who not only cuts but dyes his hair and moustache, in an encouraging attempt to help him bridge the gap between youth and age, Tadzio and himself. Towards the narrative's close Aschenbach is in an extreme state of exhaustion from the very lengths to which he has gone in his pursuit of youth. We finally witness him reaching hopelessly out to the figure of Tadzio, who wades at a distance in the sea, even as he himself eventually slumps in death, in one of the hotel's deckchairs on the beach (figure 7.9).

Almost at the end of Visconti's film, in the moments before Aschenbach's death, there is an important symbolic double meaning, which also provides a suitable image with which to finish this book on lineages in Italian cultural history. It is a double meaning that only the film world of images can capture with great intensity. Mann had not attempted it in the original novella. The image to which I refer is a disturbing one. From under Professor Aschenbach's hat there runs down his face a black liquid.

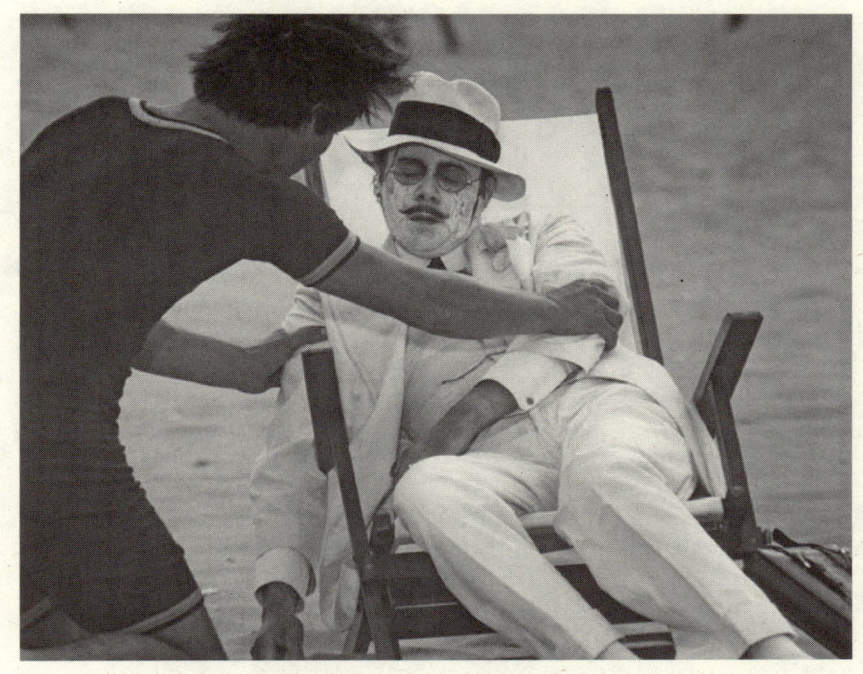

Figure 7.9 Dirk Bogarde as Professor Aschenbach, dying on the sands of the Lido, in *Death in Venice*. Courtesy British Film Institute.

Our first thought is that the dyes with which the barber has recently sought to make Aschenbach seem more youthful have instead run down his face, from an admixture of excessive perspiration caused by his tragic quest of beauty and by his worries about Tadzio amid the cholera outbreak. But a secondary notion brings us more directly to the idea of cholera itself, which also causes dark secretions. Visconti subtly implies that Aschenbach's unrequited pursuit of a world of utter perfection, as embodied in the person of Tadzio, has in the process infected him with disease and corruption – whether literally or in symbolic ways matters little – from which he cannot recover, and by which he is finally overcome. The high Apollonian ideal that we pursue throughout life reveals itself all too belatedly to include a complementary and shocking Dionysian reality, which eventually kills us.

In a not entirely dissimilar way, this long questing into lineages of Italian culture has led me to acknowledge the bleaknesses in many of her lifestyles, the moral or artistic sacrifices that accompanied her reform and rebuilding epochs, and her considerable historic failures as a 'unified' nation. These must be measured not *alongside*, but as an *integral part of* the renowned (and still to my perception far from adequately understood) achievements of her greatness.

Valediction

I reach the end of a book that has been a constant adventure of discovery to research and to write. In following my several thematized lineages I have sought to give body to old and new ways of perceiving. My own greatest challenge was to see whether there were rich *poetic* seams in this subject of a culture's varied and complex lines of historical development. I should like to think that if I have tapped any such seams, my work will in turn offer a challenge to how we tackle cultural history; not just that of Italy, but more generally.

If I have persuaded some of my readers that very diverse lineages course through a culture, I hope in the process to have proved that what we for convenience call Italian culture is in any case not one and indivisible, but many, and that these lines of development overlap, coalesce, and above all undergo transmutations, some of them withering away while others grow more strong. The viability of each is open to question, by which I do not allude solely to the economic 'base' that may or may not underpin it, but to all sorts of further conditions that may foster a given cultural tradition or, on the contrary, fail to do so, if it is one that is succumbing to time's ravages.

Simply put, cultural lineages are lines of development that are sometimes much in evidence but that sometimes equally disappear, whether accountably or unaccountably. 'Loose ends' are an integral feature of specific lineages. In talking of cultural lineages we simply cannot presuppose constant or guaranteed *linkage* over time. Survival of *all* features of a culture is not only not possible, it is not even desirable. We could all name aspects of the particular national or global culture that we could well wish would wither away. But cultures do not conform to our own desired outcomes for them. They seem to turn out the way they do because of so many and such complex influences that rarely does an individual being or movement hold much sway. Nonetheless, in the studies of this book I have singled out moments and individuals that have seemed to me of importance in the overall culture of Italy at given periods of her development.

Some mainstream currents have tended to recur in my treatment. I believe we may confidently say that these are factors that bind and unify Italians, however dispersed across the globe. Even what might appear to have vanished entirely may have been pushed out of the mainstream at some given point in history – submerged or sidetracked so to speak – only to re-emerge and form new (but never entirely new) lineages at some later point in time. Other more marginal eddies disrupt and fragment the culture, politically and socially.

However, Italy is being put through new and difficult lessons in tolerance, and enjoined to welcome the marginal into an expanded spirit of all that can count as Italian. Whether the pressures to adopt and adapt will win out over conservative movements, many of which seek to split the nation along separatist and regional lines of demarcation, is yet to be decided. Whatever the outcome, I believe that we can be sure of at least this about the nation's future: if people spoke of Italy for centuries before there was a political unit answering to that name, they will almost certainly go on doing so forever, even if there should come a day when there is again no Italian nation as such.

Notes

Introduction

1 Walter Benjamin, *The Arcades Project*, trans. Howard Eiland and Kevin McLaughlin (Cambridge, Mass., and London: Belknap Press of Harvard University Press, 1999), p. 911.
2 Ibid., p. 833.
3 Ibid., p. 834.
4 E.P. Thompson, 'The Peculiarities of the English,' in *The Poverty of Theory and Other Essays* (London: Merlin Press, 1978), p. 65.
5 Ibid., p. 64.
6 Perry Anderson, *Lineages of the Absolutist State* (London: Verso, 1974), pp. 148, 143, 151, 152.
7 The notion, put forcefully in the 1970s by Umberto Eco, that we have still not emerged from a world view and institutions that arose with the demise of feudalism (and nowhere more prominently than in Italy) is treated in detail in the introduction to my earlier book, *Italy: The Enduring Culture* (New York and London: Continuum, 2001). See esp. pp. 1–6.
8 'Big Brother: Miracle-maker or media manipulator? Martin Jacques reports from Rome on the sensational election triumph of Italy's new strong man, Silvio Berlusconi,' *The Sunday Times*, 3 April 1994, News Review section.
9 Benedetto Croce, *Philosophy, Poetry, History: An Anthology of Essays* (London and New York: Oxford University Press, 1966), p. 498.
10 Benedetto Croce, *Filosofia, poesia, storia: Pagine tratte da tutte le opere a cura dell'autore*, intro. Giuseppe Galasso (Milan: Adelphi, 1996), p. 584.
11 Croce, *Philosophy, Poetry, History*, p. 549.
12 Croce, *Filosofia, poesia, storia*, p. 644.
13 Croce, *Philosophy, Poetry, History*, pp. 571–2.
14 Croce, *Filosofia, poesia, storia*, p. 669.

15 Aijaz Ahmad, *Lineages of the Present: Political Essays* (New Delhi: Tulika, 1996), p. ix. The two chapters of this book that treat Italian realities directly are 'Fascism and National Culture: Reading Gramsci in the Days of *Hindutva*' (pp. 221–66), and 'Structure and Ideology in Italian Fascism (320–68). In the British and American edition of the book (London and New York: Verso, 2000), the quoted sentence reads slightly differently: 'no present is ever *sui generis*, no lives ever lived merely in the present tense; the lineages of historical time that went into the making of a present remain a sedimented part – often a *fatal* part – of that present' (x). Unfortunately in this latter edition the chapter entitled 'Structure and Ideology in Italian Fascism' has been left out.
16 Antonio Gramsci, *Il Risorgimento* (Turin: Einaudi, 1949), p. 55.
17 Ibid., p. 54.
18 Sir William A'Court's full title was 'Commander in Chief of the British Forces in Sicily and Plenipotentiary and Envoy Extraordinary.'
19 I explored the episode in preliminary ways in *Italy: The Enduring Culture*, pp. 295–8.
20 Sir Humphry Davy, 'Some observations and experiments on the papyri found in the ruins of Herculaneum,' in *Collected Works*, ed. John Davy (London, 1839–40), vol. 6, pp. 163–4.
21 Sir Humphry Davy, 'Report on the State of the Manuscripts of Papyrus, found at Herculaneum,' in *Quarterly Journal of Literature, Science and the Arts* 7 (1819): 157.
22 Letter from the Secretary of State, Minister for Internal Affairs, to His Excellency the Secretary of State, Minister for Foreign Affairs, Naples, 3 April 1816, in Neapolitan State Archives [hereinafter ASN].
23 Davy, 'Some observations,' p. 173.
24 Marguerite, Countess of Blessington, *Lady Blessington at Naples*, ed. Edith Clay, intro. Harold Acton (London: H. Hamilton, 1979), pp. 38–9.
25 Pietro Colletta, *Storia del Reame di Napoli*, 2 vols. (Capolago, 1834; reprinted Milan: Istituto Editoriale Italiano, n.d.), vol. 2, pp. 301–2. The reason I have not quoted from the published English translation of 1858 is that Colletta's error had in it been silently corrected to Australia. Last time that I wrote more briefly of this exchange, in my first book on Italy, I had without thinking trusted to the English translation and not checked the original. But the mistake itself – I mean General Colletta's this time – tells us something about mindset towards exotic fauna in an Old World *parco zoologico* of the 1820s and 1830s. And mindset is the very stuff of cultural history.
26 Letter from the Secretary of State, Minister for Foreign Affairs, to Sir William A'Court, Naples, 4 April 1816, in ASN.

27 *The Journal of Sir Walter Scott*, ed. W.E.K. Anderson (Oxford: Oxford University Press, 1972; reprinted Edinburgh: Canongate, 1998), p. 373.
28 Darnick is a village adjacent to Melrose, with many low-roofed labourers' and farm-workers' cottages, where Scott was referred to as 'the Duke.' The Innkeeper at Darnick in the mid to late 1820s was a Mr Harper, and perhaps our man or a near relation of his. Scott clearly imagined the whole neighbourhood descending upon Abbotsford to see the specimens from down under. *The Letters of Sir Walter Scott: 1826–1828*, vol. 10 of Centenary Edition, ed. Herbert Grierson (London: Constable, 1936), p. 255.
29 James Chandler has reminded us, by the way, that the 'equally celebrated use of *Geist der Zeit* by Arndt and *Zeitgeist* by Hegel, [come] in German writings dating from the first decade of the century.' James Chandler, from 'History' in *An Oxford Companion to the British Romantic Age*, ed. Iain McCalman (Oxford: Oxford University Press, 1999), p. 354.
30 Clifford Geertz, *Local Knowledge: Further Essays in Interpretive Anthropology* (New York: Basic Books, 1983), p. 69.
31 Theodor W. Adorno, *Quasi una Fantasia: Essays on Modern Music*, trans. Rodney Livingstone (London: Verso, 1992), p. 12.
32 From letters of May to July 1819 from William Hamilton to Joseph Planta Esq., Mr Barrow to J. Planta Esq., and from W. Hamilton to Mr Croker: Public Records Office, FO 70, no. 87, Documents 63, 76, 92, and 93.
33 Letter of 20 August 1818 from Castlereagh to A'Court, ASN, Affari Esteri, Fs. 688.
34 A cartoon by James Gilray in the National Portrait Gallery in London treats the subject of contemporary experiments with this gas.
34 Davy, 'Report on the State,' pp. 154, 156.
36 Katie Trumpener, *Bardic Nationalism: The Romantic Novel and the British Empire* (Princeton: Princeton University Press, 1997), pp. 39–66. Trumpener's chapter is entitled 'The Bog Itself: Enlightenment Prospects and National Elegies.'
37 Letter from Castlereagh to A'Court, 20 August 1818, ASN, Affari Esteri, Fs. 688.
38 Davy, 'Report on the State,' p. 157.
39 Ibid., p. 158.
40 Ibid.
41 The Superintendant of the Royal Collection of Papyrus Scrolls, Monsignor Rosini, to the Secretary of State, Minister for Internal Affairs, 7 February 1820, ASN, Affari Esteri, Fs. 688.
42 Davy, 'Some observations,' p. 176.
43 On behalf of the Secretary of State, Minister for Internal Affairs, to His

Excellency the Secretary of State, Minister for Foreign Afairs, 16 February 1820, ASN, Affari Esteri, Fs. 688.
44 Ibid.
45 Giacomo Leopardi, 'Discorso sopra lo stato presente dei costumi degl'Italiani,' in *Poesie e Prose*, vol. 2, *Prose*, ed. Rolando Damiani (Milan: Mondadori, 1988), p. 445.
46 Kenneth Burke, *A Grammar of Motives* (New York: Prentice-Hall, 1945), p. 59.
47 Sir Walter Scott, 'Introductory Remarks on Popular Poetry,' the first of two essay additions to the 1830 edition of *Minstrelsy of the Scottish Border*, ed T.F. Henderson, 4 vols. (London and Edinburgh: Oliver and Boyd, 1932), vol. 1, p. 23.

1. Modes of Viewing

1 The scholarly literature on pre-cinematic viewing devices is large. One of the best general accounts of the subject is Laurent Mannoni's *The Great Art of Light and Shadow: Archaeology of the Cinema*, trans. and ed. Richard Crangle (Exeter: University of Exeter Press, 2000). The original French edition of this work was titled *Le grand art de la lumière et de l'ombre* (Paris: Éditions Nathan, 1995). Some of the Italian writings that have most inspired the present approach are: Francesco Padovani, *Cinema: Alla ricerca degli antenati* (Feltre: Libreria Pilotto Editrice, 1995); Gian Piero Brunetta, *Il viaggio dell'icononauta: Dalla camera oscura di Leonardo alle luce dei Lumière* (Venice: Marsilio, 1997); and Carlo Alberto Zotti Minici, *Dispositivi ottici alle origini del cinema: Immaginario scientifico e spettacolo nel XVII e XVIII secolo* (Bologna: CLUEB, 1998). See also the same Zotti Minici's catalogue for an exhibition held in Bassano nel Grappa.
2 Giorgio Vasari, *Le vite de' più eccellenti pittori, scultori ed architettori*, with new annotations and comments by Gaetano Milanesi, 7 vols. (Florence: Sansoni, 1878–81), vol. 7, p. 635.
3 Juergen Schulz, 'Maps as Metaphors: Mural Map Cycles of the Italian Renaissance,' in *Art and Cartography: Six Historical Essays*, ed. David Woodward (Chicago and London: University of Chicago Press, 1987), p. 99.
4 *Cronaca Veneziana: Feste e vita quotidiana nella Venezia del Settecento*, View paintings by Gabriel Bella and engravings by Gaetano Zompini from the collections of the Querini Stampalia Foundation of Venice (Venice: Fondazione Scientifica Querini-Stampalia, 1991).
5 We have several examples of actual *mondi nuovi* in the stupendously rich collection devoted to pre-cinema in the *Museo nazionale del cinema* in Turin, finally laid out only a few years ago in the nineteenth-century landmark of

that capital city, its Mole Antonelliana. The story of how the Torino museum's founder, Maria Adriana Prolo (1908–91) picked up one *mondo nuovo* after another in flea markets, auction rooms, and antique shops across Europe makes a compelling narrative for which there is no time here to expatiate. In a different, private museum of viewing devices in Padua there is also a model of one such *mondo nuovo*, replicated from Zompini's engraving. For an account by Prolo about her collection of pre-cinematic devices and of the birth of Italy's National Museum of Cinema, see her 'Uno "spettacolo" che continua: Note sulla nascita del Museo Nazionale del Cinema,' in *Il mondo nuovo: Le meraviglie della visione dal '700 alla nascita del cinema*, ed. Carlo Alberto Zotti Minici (Catalogo di una mostra a Bassano del Grappa) (Milan: Mazzotta, 1988), pp. 51–4.

6 'Vedute ottiche e mondi nuovi: Dimensioni spettacolari di un girovagare esteso d'immagini,' in *Il mondo nuovo*, ed. Zotti Minici, pp. 34–5.
7 'Per una carta del navigar visionario,' in *Il mondo nuovo*, p. 15.
8 Carlo Goldoni, *Tutte le opere*, ed. Giuseppe Ortolani (Milan: Mondadori, 1955), vol. 13, pp. 689–702.
9 Ibid., p. 689.
10 'Per una carta del navigar visionario,' pp. 28–9.
11 Aldo Grasso, *Storia della televisione italiana* (Milan: Garzanti, 1992). Throughout much of the rest of this chapter, I use quotations from Grasso's highly useful assembly of documents. I have relied on the first edition of this fine work because of its greater usefulness for the period of first reactions by Italians to the phenomenon of television, but there exists also a valuable update, Grasso's new edition of the work (Milan: Garzanti, 2000).
12 Elena Dagrada, 'Television and Its Critics: A Parallel History,' in *Italian Cultural Studies: An Introduction*, ed. David Forgacs and Robert Lumley (Oxford and New York: Oxford University Press, 1996), pp. 233–47.
13 David Forgacs, 'Cultural Consumption, 1940s to 1990s,' in *Italian Cultural Studies*, pp. 273–90.
14 Both presented this evidence directly to the author: the former in an email, the latter in conversation.
15 'Occhio di vetro. La "prima" della televisione,' *La Stampa*, 5 January 1954. Quoted in Grasso, *Storia* (1992), p. 53.
16 See Grasso, *Storia* (1992), pp. 335–6.
17 On this point see Dagrada, 'Television and Its Critics,' p. 246.
18 For a good account of the passage from monopoly to duopoly, see Dagrada, pp. 233–47.
19 Umberto Eco, *Misreadings*, trans. William Weaver (New York: Harcourt, 1993), pp. 158–9.

20 Umberto Eco, *Diario minimo* (Milan: Mondadori, 1963), pp. 31–2.
21 For these and other directions in Eco's career, see Peter Bondanella, *Umberto Eco and the Open Text: Semiotics, Fiction, Popular Culture* (Cambridge: Cambridge University Press, 1997), pp. 19–20 and passim.
22 Leonardo Sciascia, in *Paese Sera*, 9 January 1980; quoted in Grasso, *Storia* (1992), p. 384.
23 Quoted in Grasso, *Storia* (1992), pp. 16, 410–11.
24 'Sfida ai dirigenti della televisione,' *Corriere della Sera*, 9 December 1973; quoted in Grasso, *Storia* (1992), pp. 291–2.
25 Round table discussion in Grosseto, 30 September 1962, on the theme 'Reciprocal Influences of Cinema and Television'; quoted in Grasso, *Storia* (1992), p. 157.
26 Italo Calvino, 'L'ultimo canale Tv,' *La Repubblica*, 3 January 1984; quoted in Grasso, *Storia* (1992), pp. 453–4.
27 On this point see Tullio De Mauro, *Storia linguistica dell'Italia unita*, 3rd ed. (Rome and Bari: Laterza, 1986), pp. 124–6; Forgacs, 'Cultural Consumption,' pp. 279–84.
28 De Mauro, *Storia linguistica*, pp. 458–9. For De Mauro's longer and more convincing arguments on why televisual language is so extensive, varied, and flexible, see pp. 435ff.
29 Pier Paolo Pasolini, 'Lettera aperta a Italo Calvino,' *Paese sera*, 8 July 1974, reprinted in *Scritti corsari* (Milan: Garzanti, 1975), pp. 51–5.
30 See the entries on both the former and latter of these television programs in Grasso, *Storia* (1992), pp. 295–6.
31 Quoted in Grasso, *Storia* (1992), p. 508.
32 See Grasso, *Storia* (1992), p. 530.

2. Fantasy, Science, and Hyperreality

1 Italo Calvino, *The Literature Machine: Essays*, trans. Patrick Creagh (London: Secker and Warburg, 1987; repr. London: Vintage, 1997), p. 32. From 'Due inter-viste su scienza e letteratura' (1968) in *Una pietra sopra* (1980). Repr. in Italo Calvino, *Saggi: 1945–1985*, ed. Mario Barenghi, 2nd ed. (Milan: Mondadori, 1995), vol. 1, p. 232.
2 Galileo Galilei, *Scritti letterari*, ed. Alberto Chiari (Florence: Felice le Monnier, 1970).
3 Galilei, *Scritti letterari*, p. 554. This is one instance of comparison among many between the two poets in this volume. Galileo speedily puts his general proposition about Tasso – 'that this poet is, in what he creates, beyond all measure narrow, poor, and miserable; and Aristo by contrast magnifi-

cent, rich, and admirable' ('che questo poeta sia nelle sue invenzioni oltre tutti i termini gretto, povero e miserabile; e all'opposto, l'Ariosto magnifico, ricco e mirabile,' p. 502) – and never stops criticizing the ineptitude of the one with the achievement of the other.

4 Robert Venturi, Denise Scott Brown, and Steven Izenour, *Learning from Las Vegas* (Cambridge, MA: MIT Press, 1972).

5 One of my English terms – *complexity* – is different from that of the English version of these Charles Eliot Norton lectures for Harvard, where the more literal term *multiplicity* is offered for *molteplicità*. However, what Calvino seems principally to intend by this desideratum is not merely that the world remain multiple in kind, but that that multiplicity itself be something complex, and that the complexity be admired as a cultural positive. See *Six Memos for the Next Millennium* (London: Vintage, 1996). The Italian version of the lectures, *Lezioni americane: Sei proposte per il prossimo millennio* (Milan: Garzanti, 1988), is reprinted in *Saggi*, vol. 1, pp. 627–753.

6 Calvino, *The Literature Machine*, pp. 31–2. From 'Due interviste su scienza e letteratura,' in *Saggi*, vol. 1, pp. 231–2. As students of Italian culture we might well wish to add a work that appeared in 1990, several years after Calvino's death, to the list of considerations, namely Federico Fellini's film *La voce della luna*.

7 Reprinted in Calvino, *Saggi*, vol. 1, p. 228.

8 Calvino, *Six Memos for the Next Millennium*, p. 24; *Lezioni americane*, in *Saggi*, vol. 1, pp. 651–2.

9 Giacomo Leopardi, *Operette Morali / Essays and Dialogues*, trans. Giovanni Cecchetti (Berkeley: University of California Press, 1982), pp. 118–21.

10 Saul Bellow, *The Dean's December* (New York: Harper & Row, 1982), p. 10.

11 Galileo, as quoted in Giacomo Leopardi, *Crestomazia italiana: La prosa*, ed. Giulio Bollati (Turin: Einaudi, 1968), pp. 297–8.

12 Another English translation of Galileo's work gives at this point, 'I have very often let my fancy ruminate freely upon these speculations.' Galileo Galilei, *Dialogue on the Great World Systems*, trans. T. Salisbury (Chicago: University of Chicago Press, 1955), p. 35.

13 Galilei, *Scritti letterari*, p. 578.

14 Salman Rushdie, 'Italo Calvino,' *London Review of Books*, 17–30 September 1981, pp. 16–17; reprinted in *Imaginary Homelands: Essays and Criticism 1981–1991* (London: Granta Books, 1991), p. 257. The remark, 'Like all fabulists, Calvino loves lists,' can be applied to Ariosto, to Galileo in the vein he displays here, and not least to Rushdie himself, who is deeply attuned to this fabulist tradition in many of his writings.

15 Galilei, *Scritti letterari*, p. 464.

16 *Orlando furioso di Ludovico Ariosto raccontato da Italo Calvino: Con una scelta del poema* (Turin: Einaudi, 1970), p. 171.
17 Galileo, as quoted in Leopardi, *Crestomazia*, pp. 282–3.
18 Giacomo Leopardi, *Zibaldone di pensieri*, ed. Giuseppe Pacella, 3 vols. (Milan: Garzanti, 1991), vol. 1, p. 41.
19 *Zibaldone*, vol. 1, p. 799.
20 Ibid., p. 1132.
21 Franco Gabici, 'Leopardi e Galilei,' in *Leopardi e l'astronomia: Atti del Convegno Nazionale di Studi*, ed. Luciano Romeo, Gianfranco Abate, and F. Walter Lupi (Cosenza: Progetto 2000, 2000), pp. 109–18.
22 Calvino, *Six Memos for the Next Millennium*, pp. 38–41; *Lezioni americane*, in *Saggi*, vol. 1, pp. 663–4.
23 Leopardi, quoted in Calvino, *Six Memos for the Next Millennium*, pp. 41–2; *Lezioni americane*, in *Saggi*, vol. 1, p. 665. This passage of 3 November 1821 occurs in *Zibaldone*, vol. 1, p. 1144.
24 Calvino, *Six Memos for the Next Millennium*, pp. 42–3; *Lezioni americane*, in *Saggi*, vol. 1, p. 666.
25 Rushdie, 'Italo Calvino,' p. 255.
26 Italo Calvino, *The Path to the Spiders' Nest*, trans. Archibold Colquhoun, rev. Martin McLaughlin (London: Jonathan Cape, 1998), p. 185.
27 Italo Calvino, *Il sentiero dei nidi di ragno* (1947), 4th ed. (Turin: Einaudi, 1970), p. 195.
28 Calvino, *Our Ancestors*, trans. Archibald Colquhoun (London: Pan Books, 1980), p. 287. *I nostri antenati* (Turin: Einaudi, 1960), p. 5.
29 Umberto Eco, *Travels in Hyperreality: Essays*, trans. William Weaver (San Diego: Harcourt Brace Jovanovich, 1986), p. 7.
30 Eco, *Travels in Hyperreality*, pp. 10–11, 16, 22–3.
31 Ibid., pp. 18, 38.
32 Ibid., p. 25.
33 Venturi, Scott Brown, and Izenour, *Learning from Las Vegas*, p. 53.
34 Ibid., pp. 51, 117.
35 *THE MISSION: Viva Las Venice* (BBC, 1999), directed by John Dickson.
36 I had to listen hard to the soundtrack at this moment, having first of all thought him to say 'culture fuck.' Howbeit, at the centre of the foreman's notion of what is being cluster-fucked is culture.
37 Galilei, *Dialogo sopra i due massimi sistemi del mondo, tolemaico e copernicano*, day 1, quoted in Leopardi, *Crestomazia*, pp. 304–5.
38 Calvino, *Six Memos for the Next Millennium*, p. 45; *Lezioni americane*, in *Saggi*, vol. 1, p. 667.

39 Rushdie, 'Italo Calvino,' p. 256.
40 Salman Rushdie, *Midnight's Children* (London: Jonathan Cape, 1980), pp. 245–6.
41 Noted in Douwe Draaisma, *Metaphors of Memory: A History of Ideas about the Mind*, trans. Paul Vincent (Cambridge: Cambridge University Press, 2000), p. 8. Draaisma's own reference point for the quotation is D.E. Leary (ed.), *Metaphors in the History of Psychology* (New York: Cambridge University Press, 1990), p. 43.

3. Passion in the Operatic Repertoire

1 Marta Petrusewicz, *Come il meridione divenne una questione: Rappresentazioni del sud prima e dopo il Quarantotto* (Catanzaro: Rubettino, 1998); John Dickie, *Darkest Italy: The Nation and Stereotypes of the Mezzogiorno, 1860–1900* (Basingstoke: Macmillan, 1999); Nelson Moe, *The View from Vesuvius: Italian Culture and the Southern Question* (Berkeley: University of California Press, 2002).
2 Montesquieu, *The Spirit of the Laws*, trans. A.M. Cohler, B.C. Miller, and H.S. Stone (Cambridge: Cambridge University Press, 1989), p. 233. For Nelson Moe's discussion of this issue and the specific passage, see *The View from Vesuvius*, pp. 24–7ff.
3 Montesquieu, *De l'esprit des lois* (Paris: Garnier Frères, 1973), vol. 1, p. 247.
4 *Poesie del Signor Abate Pietro Metastasio*, 10 vols. (Turin: Stamperia Reale, 1757), vol. 3, pp. 8–9.
5 Nicholas Till, *Mozart and the Enlightenment: Truth, Virtue and Beauty in Mozart's Operas* (London: Faber and Faber, 1992), p. 41.
6 Translations from Racine's preface to *Phèdre* are taken from Jean Racine, *Complete Plays*, trans. Samuel Solomon, 2 vols. (New York: Random House, 1967), vol. 2, pp. 233–5.
7 David Kimbell, *Italian Opera* (Cambridge: Cambridge University Press, 1991), pp. 186–7.
8 For commentary and documentation of Ranieri Calzabigi's part in Gluck's opera reforms, see Piero Weiss, 'Operatic Reform in Vienna: Gluck and Calzabigi,' in *Opera: A History in Documents* (New York: Oxford University Press, 2002), pp. 115–20.
9 From the dedication of *Alceste* to Grand Duke Leopold of Tuscany. Quoted in Weiss, 'Operatic Reform,' pp. 119–20.
10 Kimbell, *Italian Opera*, p. 196.
11 We know, by the way, what so transfixes our own attention about Farinelli's voice on the film bearing his name: it is a case of the modern electronic

'morphing' of two voices into *one* on the sound track. I quote a summary of relevant information by Felicia Miller: 'The filmmaker proposed ... a Baroque orchestra with two separate voices, countertenor and coloratura soprano. The recordings were then to be re-edited to form the playback for the shooting of the film ... On the computer the engineers modified the timbre of the soprano parts through audio "morphing." They selected for the "boyish" quality of the voice through global modifications, attenuating the higher frequencies to reduce breathiness and "brighten" the spectral envelope.' From '*Farinelli*'s Electronic Hermaphrodite and the Contralto Tradition,' in *The Work of Opera: Genre, Nationhood, and Sexual Difference*, ed. Richard Dellamora and Daniel Fischlin (New York: Columbia University Press, 1997), p. 79.

12 Joseph Addison, *The Spectator*, no. 5, 6 March 1711.
13 Alexander Pope, *The Dunciad*, ed. James Sutherland, 3rd ed., rev. (London: Methuen, 1963), n. to p. 346 (vol. 5 of Twickenham edition of *The Poems of Alexander Pope*, gen. ed. John Butt).
14 Hugo Meynell, *The Art of Handel's Operas* (Lewiston, Queenston: Edwin Mellen Press, 1986), p. 7.
15 Ibid.
16 Mary Hunter, *The Culture of Opera Buffa in Mozart's Vienna: A Poetics of Entertainment* (Princeton: Princeton University Press, 1999), p. 5.
17 Søren Kierkegaard, *Either/Or*, trans. D.F. Swenson and L.M. Swenson, rev. H.A. Johnson, 2 vols. (Princeton, NJ: Princeton University Press, 1959), vol. 1, p. 86.
18 Ibid., p. 121.
19 Robert Viscusi, '"Osservate, leggete con me": Leporello's Hermeneutics,' in *Lorenzo Da Ponte: Librettista di Mozart*, papers from a symposium at the Casa Italiana, Columbia University, New York, 28–30 March 1988. In *Quaderni di Libri e Riviste d'Italia* 24 (1992), p. 73.
20 Ibid., p. 78.
21 Stendhal, 'L'opéra bouffe,' in *Le rouge et le noir* (1830; reprinted Paris: Livre de Poche, 1958), pp. 362–3.
22 Stendhal, *Vie de Rossini* (1823; Paris: Gallimard, 1992), from the preface; *The Life of Rossini*, trans. Richard Coe, 2nd rev. ed. (London: John Calder; New York: Riverun Press, 1985), p. 3.
23 *Rome, Naples and Florence en 1817*: quoted in Kimbell, *Italian Opera*, p. 13.
24 Stendhal, *Life of Rossini*, p. 59.
25 Quoted in *The Faber Book of Opera*, ed. Tom Sutcliffe (London: Faber and Faber, 2000), p. 121.

4. Capital Contrasts

1. Key texts that I have used by Franco Venturi are 'The Enlightenment in Southern Italy,' in *Italy and the Enlightenment: Studies in a Cosmopolitan Century*, ed. Stuart Woolf, trans. Susan Corsi (London: Longman, 1972), pp. 198–224 [originally published as 'Il movimento rifomatore degli illuministi meridionali,' *Rivista storica italiana*, vol. 74 (1962), pp. 5–26]; *Illuministi Italiani* vol. 5 *Riformatori Napoletani*, ed. Franco Venturi (Milan and Naples: Riccardo Ricciardi Editore, 1962), which has lengthy introductory essays to the writings of each reformer it anthologizes; 'La Napoli di Antonio Genovesi,' in *Settecento riformatore: Da Muratori a Beccaria* (Turin: Einaudi, 1969), pp. 523–644; 'L'Italia anticuriale: Genova e Torino,' in *Settecento riformatore II: La chiesa e la repubblica dentro i loro limiti* (Turin: Einaudi, 1976), pp. 65–85; 'Napoli capitale nel pensiero dei riformatori illuministi,' in *Storia di Napoli* (Naples: Società Editrice Storia di Napoli, 1967–78), vol. 8, pp. 3–73.
2. 'In every era the attempt must be made anew to wrest tradition away from a conformism that is about to overpower it.' Walter Benjamin, 'Theses on the Philosophy of History' (1940), in *Illuminations*, ed. Hannah Arendt, trans. Harry Zohn (New York: Schocken Books, 1968; repr. London: Fontana, 1992), p. 247. I take Benjamin's notion of tradition to include – perhaps above all – the way history itself is practised in any given era.
3. Susan Sontag, *The Volcano Lover: A Romance* (London: Jonathan Cape, 1992), pp. 20, 115.
4. Stendhal, *Rome, Naples et Florence (1826)*, ed. Pierre Brunel (Paris: Éditions Gallimard, 1987), p. 78.
5. Stendhal, *Rome, Naples, and Florence in 1817: Sketches of the present state of society, manners, arts, literature, &c, in these celebrated cities* (London: Henry Colburn, 1818), p. 118.
6. Marta Petrusewicz, 'Before the Southern Question: "Native" Ideas on Backwardness and Remedies in the Kingdom of Two Sicilies, 1815–1849,' in *Italy's 'Southern Question': Orientalism in One Country*, ed. Jane Schneider (Oxford: Berg, 1998), p. 31.
7. Benedetto Croce, *History of the Kingdom of Naples*, trans. Frances Frenaye (Chicago: University of Chicago Press, 1965), p. 40.
8. Erich Auerbach, 'Vico and Aesthetic Historism' (1949), in *Scenes from the Drama of European Literature: Six Essays* (New York: Meridian Books, 1959), pp. 183–98, esp. 190–5. See also Benedetto Croce's much longer explications of Vico's positions in *La filosofia di Giambattista Vico* (1946), in the *Edizione nazionale delle opere di Benedetto Croce* (Naples: Bibliopolis, 1997).

One of Croce's key claims in this painstaking explication of Vico's philosophy is that he sought 'una scienza che fosse insieme filosofia dell'umanità e storia universale delle nazioni,' p. 41.

9 *The New Science of Giambattista Vico*, rev. trans. of 3rd ed. (1744), Thomas Goddard Bergin and Max Harold Fisch (Ithaca: Cornell University Press, 1968), p. 96; Giambattista Vico, *Principi di scienza nuova d'intorno alla commune natura delle nazioni* (1744), in *Opere*, ed. Fausto Nicolini (Milan and Naples: Ricciardi editore, 1953), p. 479.
10 *The New Science* (Bergin and Fisch) p. 96; Vico, *Principi di scienza nuova* (1744), p. 479.
11 Erich Auerbach, 'Contributi linguistici all'interpretazione della *Scienza Nuova* di G.B. Vico' (1937), in *San Francesco, Dante, Vico ed altri saggi di filologia romanza* (Bari: De Donato, 1970), pp. 66–77; also in *Giambattista Vico*, ed. Fulvio Tessitore and Manuela Sanna, in the series *Cento Libri per Mille Anni*, general ed. Walter Pedullà (Rome: Istituto Poligrafico e Zecca dello Stato, 2000), pp. 118–26. In terms of method, this article appears to be a prototype for chapters of *Mimesis*, which was written approximately a decade later.
12 Auerbach, 'Vico and Aesthetic Historicim' (1949), in *Scenes from the Drama of European Literature: Six Essays* (New York: Meridian Books, 1959).
13 C.G. Jung, 'Conscious, Unconscious, and Individuation' (1939), in *The Archetypes and the Collective Unconscious*, 2nd ed., trans. R.F.C. Hull (London: Routledge & Kegan Paul, 1968), p. 287.
14 *Giambattista Vico*, p. 421.
15 Ibid., pp. 1–8.
16 Auerbach, 'Vico and Aesthetic Historicism,' p. 188.
17 *Vita di Giambattista Vico scritta da sè medesimo* (1728) in *Giambattista Vico*, p. 213.
18 Wolfgang Amadeus Mozart to his sister, 5 June 1770, *The Letters of Mozart and His Family*, trans. and ed. Emily Anderson, 3rd ed. (London: Macmillan, 1985), p. 143.
19 Sontag, *The Volcano Lover*, p. 20.
20 Mozart, *Briefe und Aufzeichnungen: Gesamtausgabe* (Kassel: Bärenreiter-Verlag, 1962), vol. 1, 1755–1776, p. 369.
21 Pompeo Sarnelli, *Nuova guida de' forestieri e dell'istoria di Napoli ...* (Naples: Saverio Rossi, 1772), p. 11. Quoted in Franco Venturi, 'Napoli capitale nel pensiero dei riformatori illuministi,' in *Storia di Napoli* (Naples: Società Editrice Storia di Napoli, 1967–78), vol. 8, p. 17.
22 Wolfgang Amadeus Mozart to his sister, 19 May 1770, *Letters of Mozart and Family*, p. 137.
23 Leopold Mozart to his wife, 19 May 1770, *Letters of Mozart and Family*, p. 135.

24 Leopold Mozart to his wife, 26 May 1770, *Letters of Mozart and Family*, p. 139.
25 Iwo and Pamela Zaluski, *Mozart in Italy* (London: Peter Owen, 1999), p. 95.
26 Leopold Mozart to his wife, 19 May 1770, *Letters of Mozart and Family*, p. 135.
27 *Storia di Torino*, vol. 5, *Dalla città razionale alla crisi dello Stato d'Antico Regime (1730–1798)*, ed. Giuseppe Ricuperati (Turin: Einaudi, 2002).
28 Maria Teresa Silvestrini, 'Religione "stabile" e politica ecclesiastica,' in *Storia di Torino*, vol. 5, p. 375.
29 Duke of Noja, as quoted and summarized in Venturi, *Italy and the Enlightenment*, p. 205.
30 Donatella Balani, 'Sviluppo demografico e trasformazioni sociali nel Settecento,' in *Storia di Torino*, vol. 5, p. 631.
31 Charles de Secondat, baron de Montesquieu, *Voyages de Montesquieu*, pub. by le baron Albert de Montesquieu, 2 vols. (Bordeaux: Imprimerie G. Gounouilhou, 1894), vol. 1, p. 122.
32 Montesquieu, *Voyages*, vol. 2, p. 21, and vol. 1, p. 123. A reasonably reliable figure for Turin's population in 1737 is 63, 531, which would tend to suggest that Montesquieu had estimated somewhat on the low side nine years earlier.
33 Vittorio Alfieri, *Vita scritta da esso*, ed. Luigi Fassò (Asti: Casa d'Alfieri, 1951), p. 35.
34 Ibid.
35 Claudio Marazzini, 'Il problema della lingua,' in *Storia di Torino*, vol. 5, p. 1011.
36 G.G. Craveri, *Guida de' forestieri per la real città di Torino* (Turin: Gian Domenico Rameletti Libraio, 1753), p. 150.
37 Marazzini, 'Il problema della lingua,' pp. 1008–10.
38 Giuseppe Ricuperati and Luca Prestia, 'Lo specchio degli ordinati. La città dal tempo di Vittorio Amedeo III alla crisi definitive dell' "Ancien Régime,"' in *Storia di Torino*, vol. 5, p. 513.
39 Ricuperati, 'Lo specchio degli ordinati. La città nel tempo di Carlo Emanuele III,' in *Storia di Torino*, vol. 5, p. 15.
40 Ibid., p. 37.
41 Ibid., pp. 485–8.
42 Ibid., pp. 585–6. In *The Volcano Lover*, Sontag has written of Ferdinand that hunting was his 'ruling passion' and that for him 'the disgusting was a source of delight,' p. 36.
43 Ricuperati and Prestia, 'Lo specchio degli ordinati,' p. 495.
44 Ibid., p. 509.
45 Alfieri, *Vita*, p. 251.
46 Ibid., pp. 251–3.

47 Ibid., p. 252.
48 Ibid.
49 Ibid., p. 253.
50 Franco Valsecchi, 'Lo stato e la società piemontese da Emanuele Filiberto alla dominazione napoleonica,' in *Storia del Piemonte*, ed. Dino Gribaudi et al., 2 vols. (Turin: F. Casanova, 1961), vol. 1, pp. 291–2.
51 *Voyages*, vol. 2, p. 13.
52 Costanza Roggero, 'L'urbanistica nel secondo Settecento,' *Storia di Torino*, vol. 5, pp. 799–819; in particular the second half of this chapter, subtitled 'Il progetto unitario di Benedetto Alfieri,' pp. 802–19.
53 See *Vedute del 'Mondo Nuovo': Vues d'optique settecentesche nella collezione del Museo Nazionale del Cinema di Torino*, ed. Donata Pesenti Campagnoni (Turin: Umberto Allemandi, 2000). In the rich but unnumbered plate section of this volume, three *vedute* of Turin for showing in a *mondo nuovo* are reproduced, each shown separately in 'effetto giorno' (daylight effect) on one page, and 'effetto notte' (illuminated nighttime effect) on the facing page. Although *vedute* of other cities are designed to stress certain symmetries of design, in these three *vedute* symmetry is absolute in each case, and therefore the strongest abiding impression stimulated in the viewer.
54 Italo Calvino, *Six Memos for the Next Millennium*, trans. Patrick Creagh (1988; London: Vintage, 1996), p. 83; *Lezioni Americane: Sei proposte per il prossimo millennio*, in *Saggi: 1945–1985*, ed. Mario Barenghi, 2 vols. (Milan: Mondadori, 1995), vol. 1, p. 699.
55 Craveri, *Guida*, p. 9.
56 Venturi, *Italy and the Enlightenment*, p. 205.
57 Quoted in Francesco Cognasso, *Storia di Torino* (Milan: Aldo Martello Editore, 1960), p. 336.
58 Montesquieu, *Voyages*, vol. 1, p. 109.
59 Ibid., pp. 112–13.
60 Ibid., p. 121.
61 Ibid., p. 127.
62 Quoted in Balani, 'Sviluppo demografico,' p. 628.
63 Craveri, *Guida*, p. 95.
64 *Regole della nuova Opera pia detta il Ritiro delle Forzate, divise in regole generali, e particolari*, Archivio di Stato di Torino, 'Luoghi pii di qua dai monti,' mazzo 20, fasc. 3.
65 Ibid.
66 Ibid.
67 Ibid.

68 Ibid.
69 Ibid.
70 From 'Memoria del Senatore Ghiliossi Congiudice del Consolato circo quelle Arte, e Mestieri, che poteano essere i più convenienti per essere esercitati nelle Case di Correzione che erano per stabilirsi nella Città di Torino,' Archivio di Stato di Torino, 'Luogi pii di qua dai monti,' mazzo 17, fasc. 10.
71 Ricuperati, 'Lo specchio degli ordinati,' p. 36.
72 Valsecchi, 'Lo stato,' pp. 286, 282.
73 For the history lying behind the founding of such a chair, see Croce, *History of the Kingdom of Naples,* trans. Frenaye, pp. 150–51.
74 Giovanni Aliberti, 'Economia e Società da Carlo III ai Napoleonidi (1734–1806),' in *Storia di Napoli* (Naples: Società Editrice Storia di Napoli, 1967–78), vol. 8, p. 88.
75 Paolo Giordano, *Ferdinando Fuga a Napoli: L'Albergo dei Poveri, il Cimitero delle 366 fosse, i Granili* (Lecce: Edizioni del Grifo, 1997), p. 71.
76 Ibid., p. 80.
77 For details of this earlier building and its statutes, see Nicoletta D'Arbitrio and Luigi Ziviello, *Il Reale Albergo dei Poveri di Napoli: Un edificio per le "Arti della città" Dentro le Mura* (Naples: Edisa, 1999), pp. 19–22.
78 Giordano, *Ferdinando Fuga a Napoli,* p. 21.
79 Ibid., p. 73.
80 Quotation from Francesco Milizia is included in both Giancarlo Alisio, 'Sviluppo urbano e struttura della città,' *Storia di Napoli,* vol. 8, p. 332, and Renato de Fusco, 'L'architettura della seconda metà del settecento,' *Storia di Napoli,* vol. 8, p. 414.
81 Quoted in D'Arbitrio and Ziviello, *Il Reale Albergo dei Poveri,* p. 23.
82 Ibid.
83 'From as early as 1749 Ludovico Antonio Muratori, referring to the designated institution of the *Albergo dei poveri,* affirmed, "What has the Royal House of Savoy not done in Turin to introduce there all the skilled trades? Naples herself will also protest that she is to the highest degree beholden to the noble genius of Carlo, King of the Two Sicilies, when His Majesty, by augmentation and introduction of new skills will ensure that the poor gain their living by means of them"' ('Sin dal 1749 Ludovico Antonio Muratori, alludendo alla disegnata istituzione dell'Albergo dei poveri, affermava: "E che non ha fatto la Real Casa di Savoia di Torino per introdurvi le Arti tutte? Napoli anch'essa si protesterà sommamente tenuta al nobilissimo genio di Carlo Re delle Due Sicilie, allorché la Maestà sua coll'aumento e con l'intro-

duzione di nuove arti avrà obbligati i poveri a guadagnarsi il vitto con le medesime"'): de Fusco, 'L'architettura della seconda metà del settecento,' *Storia di Napoli,* vol. 8, p. 416.

84 Giordano, *Ferdinando Fuga a Napoli,* p. 84.
85 See D'Arbitrio and Ziviello, *Il Reale Albergo dei Poveri,* p. 39.
86 Stendhal, *Rome, Naples et Florence (1826),* p. 311.
87 There is even some evidence that the elderly of either sex were to constitute the fifth and sixth categories of the poor in the institution.
88 Venturi, 'The Enlightenment in Southern Italy,' p. 202.
89 Antonio Genovesi, 'Al gentile e cortese lettore,' from his 'Ragionamento sul Commercio in universale, e alcune annotazioni riguardanti l'economia del nostro Regno,' introduction to *Storia del Commercio della Gran Brettagna, scritta da John Cary, Mercante di Bristol, tradotta in nostra vulgar lingua da Pietro Genovesi* (1757), in Antonio Genovesi, *Scritti economici,* ed. Maria Luisa Perna, 2 vols. (Naples: Istituto Italiano per gli Studi Filosofici, 1984), vol. 1, p. 117.
90 Theories concerning the stadial development of human society were proposed by almost all of those who were active within the Scottish Enlightenment schools. Possibly the most favoured term in use now – Stadial Theory – was coined by John Millar in *The Origin of the Distinction of Ranks* (1771). In light of the comparison that I am making between Neapolitan and Scottish Enlightenment thinkers, it is fascinating that in the first of his 'Waverley' novels – *Waverley* itself, first published in 1814 – Walter Scott, himself so deeply influenced by particular figures of the Scottish Enlightenment in his Edinburgh schooling, would use Neapolitan *banditi* (as painted by Salvator Rosa in the seventeenth century) as a comparison for the lawlessness of a group of Cateran Highland depradators surrounding their chieftan, Evan Dhu: 'Waverley prepared himself to meet a stern, gigantic, ferocious figure, such as Salvator would have chosen to be the central object of a group of banditti.' *Waverley,* ed. Claire Lamont (Oxford: Oxford University Press, 1986), p. 80.
91 Venturi, 'The Enlightenment in Southern Italy,' p. 203.
92 Ibid., p. 208. See also *Riformatori Napoletani,* vol. 5 of the series *Illuministi Italiani* (Milan and Naples: Riccardo Ricciardi Editore, 1962), p. 1098.
93 Ibid., pp. 218–19.
94 Francesco Mario Pagano, *Saggi politici,* in *Riformatori Napoletani,* ed. Franco Venturi, p. 856.
95 Ibid., p. 861.
96 Ibid., p. 857.
97 Ibid.

98 Ibid., p. 858.
99 Pagano, *Saggi politici: Del civile corso delle nazioni o sia de' principi, progressi e decadenza delle società* (Naples: Gennaro Verriento, 1783)
100 Pagano, *Saggi politici*, in *Riformatori Napoletani*, p. 867. The core of the quotation in the Italian is surely constituted by the words 'niuno avea della storia formata una filosofia. Vico però ci ha mostrato più ciò che si debba fare, che non ha fatto.'
101 Ibid., pp. 897–8.
102 Ibid., p. 900.
103 Gaetano Filangieri, extract of a letter from Naples, 3 February 1781, to Domenico Pepe in Mola di Bari. Published in *Riformatori Napoletani*, pp. 768–9.
104 Extract of a letter of Domenico Pepe from Mola di Bari, to Gaetano Filangieri in Naples, 27 January 1781. Published in *Riformatori Napoletani*, n. to p. 768. I have translated the Italian term *provincia* in this passage as 'country,' since it seems to me that Pepe was very much seeking to express an Italian equivalent to the polarities that Raymond Williams, so much later in history, sought by cultural criticism to illumine in the 1970s (*The Country and the City* [London: Chatto & Windus, 1973]). For persons like Filangieri and Pepe there were Roman classical models for such a contrast between city and country. And already in the *quattrocento* Leon Battista Alberti had revisited such contrasts in his writings on the building of cities.

5. Justice and the Individual, Torture and the State

1 Alessandro Manzoni, *The Column of Infamy*, prefaced by Cesare Beccaria's *Of Crimes and Punishments*, trans. Kenelm Foster, O.P., and Jane Grigson, intro. A.P. d'Entrèves (London: Oxford University Press, 1964). English quotations in my text will be from the translations of Beccaria's and of Manzoni's texts in this volume, and page numbers will henceforth be given in parentheses after each.
2 Leonardo Sciascia, *Morte dell'Inquisitore* (Milan: Adelphi Edizioni, 2001), p. 45. Italian quotations in my text will be from this edition, and page numbers will henceforth be given in parentheses after each. Two translations are available: *Salt in the Wound* followed by *The Death of the Inquisitor*, trans. Judith Green (New York: Orion Press, 1969). English quotations will be from this edition, and page numbers will henceforth be given in parentheses after each. There is a later and very fine English version of Sciascia's text, *Death of an Inquisitor and Other Stories*, trans. Ian Thomson (Manchester: Carcanet, 1990).

3 Luciano Violante, 'I cittadini, la legge e il giudice,' in *Legge Diritto Giustizia*, ed. Luciano Violante (Turin: Einaudi, 1998), p. lxii. This is vol. 14 of the *Annali* supplements to the Einaudi *Storia d'Italia* coordinated by Ruggiero Romano and Currado Vivanti.
4 *Roma: quotidiano d'informazione*, Saturday, 13 April 2002, p. 7. The case became known as *Il giallo di Cogne – The Murder Mystery of Cogne* – after the community in the Val d'Aosta where the boy's family resided.
5 For the constitution and commentaries upon it, see *Stato della Costituzione*, ed. Guido Neppi Modena (Milan: il Saggiatore, 1995). An earlier volume of interest that also quotes the constitution in full is Giancarlo Ospitale's *Lo stato italiano e il suo ordinamento giuridico* (Padua: Casa Editrice Dott. Antonio Milani, 1967).
6 Giorgio Rebuffa, *La costituzione impossibile: Cultura politica e sistema parlamentare in Italia* (Bologna: il Mulino, 1995), p. 75.
7 Beccaria, *Dei delitti e delle pene*, ed. Franco Venturi, 3rd ed. (Turin: Einaudi, 1973). Italian quotations in my text will be from this edition, and page numbers will henceforth be given in parentheses after each. I do not concern myself with doubts that have occasionally been raised about Beccaria's authorship. Joint authorship has sometimes been attributed to Pietro Verri, another Italian Enlightenment thinker on issues of justice. (At points in *The Column of Infamy*, Manzoni takes issue with one of Verri's other texts on the judges of the *untori* in Milan, his *Observations on Torture*.)
8 For accounts of Facchinei's attack, and his coinage of the terms *socialist* and *socialism* to describe what he sees as Beccaria's dangerous prejudices, see Beccaria, *Dei delitti*, p. xii; Franco Venturi, '"Socialista" e "socialismo" nell'Italia del Settecento,' in *Rivista storica italiana* LXXV (1963), fasc. I, pp. 129ff.; and Giuseppe Ricuperati, 'The Enlightenment in Lombardy: Pietro Verri (1728–97), Cesare Beccaria (1735–94), *Il Caffè*,' in Dino Carpanetto and Giuseppe Ricuperati, *Italy in the Age of Reason: 1685–1789*, trans. Caroline Higgitt (London: Longman, 1987), p. 263. An extract of Facchinei's attack is offered in Beccaria, ed. Venturi, pp. 164–77.
9 Perry Anderson, *Lineages of the Absolutist State* (1974; London: Verso, 1979), p. 24. In subsequent pages, Anderson gives a magisterial interpretation of the importance of a revamped Roman law for the consolidation of Absolutist States throughout Europe during the Renaissance. For instance, he suggests that 'the Absolutist monarchies of the West characteristically relied on a skilled stratum of legists to staff their administrative machines ... Imbued with Roman doctrines of princely decretal authority and Roman conceptions of unitary legal norms, these lawyer-bureaucrats were the zealous enforcers of royal centrism in the first critical century of Absolutist State-construction' (p. 28).

10 Weber, *Economy and Society* (1914), as quoted in Anderson, *Lineages*, p. 24.
11 For a succinct account of this period in Milan see Dino Carpanetto, 'The Duchy of Milan under Maria Theresa and Joseph II,' in Carpanetto and Ricuperati, *Italy in the Age of Reason*, pp. 223–35.
12 Ricuperati, 'The Enlightenment in Lombardy,' p. 263.
13 Ibid.
14 Foster's English translation follows a different sequence at this point, but the two paragraphs quoted, although separated in Venturi's edition of the text, are closely connected by theme.
15 I have had to alter slightly Forster's translation of the third-last sentence, to preserve more clearly the original logic of Beccaria's argument.
16 Adriano Cavanna, *La codificazione penale in Italia: le origini lombarde* (Milan: Dott. A. Giuffrè editore, 1975) (Pubblicazioni dell'Istituto di Storia del Diritto Italiano, Università degli Studi di Milano). See the chapter entitled 'Il problema della pena della morte,' pp. 151–96; this quotation, p. 192.
17 Alessandro Manzoni, *Storia della colonna infame*, ed. Carla Riccardi (Milan: Mondadori, 1984), p. 32. Italian quotations will be from this edition, and page numbers will henceforth be given in brackets after each.
18 Leonardo Sciascia, essay on *Storia della colonna infame* in *Cruciverba* (Turin: Einaudi, 1983), pp. 101–14. This quotation is from p. 101.
19 Manzoni's work here and in much of the novel, too, is by this reckoning original in making the fate of the poor a proper subject for history. Consider in this regard his literary relationship with Scott, and both novelists' essays on the historical novel.
20 Sciascia, *Cruciverba*, pp. 110–1.
21 Ibid., pp. 104–5.
22 Ibid., p. 108.
23 Walter Benjamin, 'Theses on the Philosophy of History,' in *Illuminations*, ed. with intro. by Hannah Arendt, trans. Harry Zohn (New York: Schocken Books, 1968), p. 255.
24 Sciascia, *Cruciverba*, p. 113.
25 Trentin's term is glossed in Paolo Barile, 'Lo sviluppo dei diritti fondamentali nell'ordinamento repubblicano,' in *Legge Diritto Giustizia*, ed. Violante, p. 26.
26 Theodor Adorno, *Minima Moralia: Reflections from Damaged Life*, trans. E.F.N. Jephcott (London: NLB, 1974), pp. 27–8.
27 Quoted in Paolo Barile, 'Lo sviluppo dei diritti fondamentali nell'ordinamento repubblicano,' in *Legge Diritto Giustizia*, ed. Violante, pp. 9–10.
28 Ibid., p. 10.
29 Ibid., p. 12.
30 Quoted in Anderson, *Lineages of the Absolutist State*, p. 11.

31 Quoted in Ospitale, *Lo stato italiano*, p. 3.
32 Ibid.

6. Italy's Romantic Population

1 Quoted in C.P. Brand, *Italy and the English Romantics: The Italian Fashion in Early Nineteenth-Century England* (Cambridge: Cambridge University Press, 1957), p. 19.
2 *Storia d'Italia: Dal primo Settecento all'unità*, ed. R. Romani and C. Vivanti (Turin: Einaudi, 1973).
3 Giacomo Leopardi, 'Discorso sopra lo stato presente dei costumi degl'Italiani,' in *Poesie e Prose*, vol. 2, *Prose*, ed. Rolando Damiani (Milan: Mondadori, 1988), pp. 445–6. Page numbers from this edition will henceforth be given in the main text.
4 J.C.L. Simonde de Sismondi, *Histoire des républiques italiennes du moyen âge*, 16 vols. (vols 1–2, Zurich, 1807; 3–4, Zurich, 1808; 5–8, Paris 1809; 9–10, Paris, 1815; 12–16, Paris, 1818), vol. 16, p. 408. Quotations will in future be from this edition, with page numbers and my own translations provided in the text.
5 See Folio Classique edition of *Corinne, ou l'Italie*, ed. Simone Balayé (Paris: Éditions Gallimard, 1985) for a dateline 'Life of Mme. De Staël,' pp. 597–602, esp. 600.
6 In *Mélanges d'Art* Stendhal would call Lord Nelvil 'this cold inhabitant of the North, this sad victim of prejudices which he has neither the force to vanquish, nor the courage to pursue with abandon' ('ce froid habitant du Nord, cette triste victime des préjugés qu'il n'a ni la force de vaincre, ni le courage de suivre avec abandon'). Quoted in Michel Crouzet, *Stendhal et l'Italianité: Essai de mythologie romantique* (Paris: Librairie José Corti, 1982), p. 62, n. 106.
7 Giuseppe Parini (1729–99), author of the satirical poem *Il Giorno* (1763–1801), had of course dealt with the phenomenon of *cicisbeismo* before either of them.
8 Mme De Staël, *Corinne, or Italy*, trans. and ed. Sylvia Raphael, intro. John Isbell (Oxford and New York: Oxford University Press, 1998), p. 19. English quotations in my text will be from this translation, with page numbers given after each.
9 *Corinne*, ed. Balayé, p. 47. Quotations from the original French of this text will be from this edition, with page numbers given after each.
10 Sylvia Raphael translates 'républiques' as 'Republic,' thus giving rise to a possible misimpression that De Staël is talking about Roman times, when she has in mind the age of Dante himself. I have silently changed the word-

ing to 'republics.' Similarly, her translation of the last words reads 'more irrevocable than their eternal future.' But the French reads 'encore moins irrevocable que leur eternal avenir,' so I have silently changed her 'more' to 'less' in the English here.
11 Critics have disputed the exact date of composition. See 'Comment and notes' section on the 'Discorso' (1988), pp. 1413ff.
12 Stendhal, *Rome, Naples et Florence (1826)*, ed. Pierre Brunel (Paris: Gallimard, 1987), pp. 77–8. Translations of this and most other quoted passages from Stendhal's travel books are my own.
13 *Rome, Naples et Florence (1826)*, p. 72.
14 Journal entry dated Moscow, 30 September 1812. Stendhal, *Journal*, ed. Victor Del Litto, 5 vols. (Geneva and Paris: Slatkine, 1986), vol. 4, p. 24.
15 Letter to the Countess Beugnot of 18 October 1812, in *Correspondance générale*, ed. V. Del Litto, 4 vols. (Paris: Honoré Champion, 1997–9), vol. 2, p. 378.
16 Journal entry dated Paris, 8 March 1842. Stendhal, *Journal*, vol. 5, p. 293.
17 *Correspondence générale*, vol. 1, p. 4.
18 E.g., in *Rome, Naples et Florence (1826)*, p. 51.
19 Note du comte de Sedlnitzky, préfet de police de Vienna, adressée au chancelier d'État, prince de Metternich, Vienna, 30 November 1830, in *Correspondence générale*, vol. 3, p. 1830.
20 *The Charterhouse of Parma*, trans. C.K. Scott Moncrieff (New York: Viveright Publishing Corp., 1944), vol. 1, p. 3. *La Chartreuse de Parme* (Paris: Éditions Garnier Frères, 1973), p. 5. Henceforth quotes from these two editions will be given in parentheses.
21 Stendhal, *Pages d'Italie: L'Italie en 1818: Moeurs romaines* (Paris: Le Divan, 1932), pp. 49–50.
22 Michel Crouzet, *Le roman stendhalien: La Chartreuse de Parme* (Orléans: Paradigme, 1996), p. 11.
23 Ibid., pp. 12–13.
24 Adam, intro. to *La Chartreuse* (Garnier ed.), pp. x–xi.
25 For an account of the basis of the story as it relates to Fabrice in the history of Alessandro Farnese, and for an indication of how this eventually became updated to the Napoleonic and post-Napoleonic age in Italy, see Antoine Adam's introduction to the 1973 Garnier edition of the novel, pp. i–iv, viii–xiii.

7. Lifestyles High and Low

1 Cesare De Seta, *Napoli* (in the series *La città nella storia d'Italia*) (Bari: Editori Laterza, 1981), pp. 241, 276–7.
2 Walter Benjamin, *The Arcades Project*, trans. Howard Eiland and Kevin

McLaughlin (Cambridge, MA, and London: Belknap Press of Harvard University Press, 1999), p. 834.
3 Quoted ibid., p. 882.
4 For a good account of the importance of the Haussmann example of Paris, and of precedents set also by the likes of Vienna, Berlin, and even London for Italian urban *risanamenti* (revitalizations), see Silano Fei, *Nascita e sviluppo di Firenze città borghese* (Florence: G & G Editrice, 1971), pp. 17–21.
5 Jonathan White, *Italy: The Enduring Culture* (London and New York: Continuum, 2001), pp. 37–40.
6 Quoted in Fei, *Nascita e sviluppo*, p. 24.
7 Quoted ibid., p. 37.
8 The frenetic financial speculations on property and rebuilding during the period when Florence was briefly the capital of Italy (1865–71) are well covered in Fei, *Nascita e sviluppo*. Here I use Fei's well-presented material evidence as information inviting further interpretation. Another version of the fever to rebuild Florence in ways adequate to its new status as capital city, and of the aftermath of its sudden loss of that same status to Rome, is told by Eduardo Detti – in collaboration with Tommaso Detti – in *Firenze scomparsa* (Florence: Vallecchi, 1970), pp. 33–92. For a blow-by-blow account of what projects were inaugurated, and when, see Giovanni Fanelli, *Firenze*, in the series *La città nella storia d'Italia*, general ed. Cesare De Seta (Bari: Laterza, 1980). Fanelli's accounts, though less judgmental than either Fei's or Detti's, are illustrated with revealing photographic records of change to the essential fabric of the city.
9 Quoted in Fei, *Nascita e sviluppo*, pp. 48–49.
10 The title translates more or less as *The Florence That Has Disappeared: Historico-artistic Mementoes*. There exists a photographic reprint of it (Rome: Multi-grafica, 1979).
11 Extract from a signed letter of 12 April 1878 from nine councillors of the city of Florence, including mayor Ubaldino Peruzzi, to His Excellency the Senate President. The entire letter is given as an appendix in Fei, *Nascita e sviluppo*, pp. 190–1.
12 Detti, *Firenze scomparsa*, p. 42.
13 Antonio Gramsci, *Il Risorgimento* (Turin: Einaudi, 1949), p. 170.
14 Ibid., p. 148.
15 Fei, *Nascita e sviluppo*, p. 36.
16 Ibid., p. 27.
17 Ibid., p. 42.
18 Quoted ibid., pp. 45–6.

19 Ibid., p. 83.
20 Ibid., pp. 63, 66–7.
21 Detti, *Firenze scomparsa*, p. 42.
22 *Sui lavori per l'ingrandimento di Firenze*, a report by G. Poggi (1864–77), quoted in Detti, *Firenze scomparsa*, p. 53.
23 Fei, *Nascita e sviluppo*, p. 29.
24 Detti, *Firenze Scomparsa*, p. 53
25 Quoted in Fei, *Nascita e sviluppo*, p. 54, from 1869 plans for redevelopment of the city centre.
26 Quoted ibid., p. 163.
27 Detti, *Firenze scomparsa*, p. 57.
28 See ibid., p. 58.
29 *The Arcades Project*, p. 827.
30 Lucio Gambi and Maria Cristina Gozzoli, *Milano* (in series *La città nella storia d'Italia*) (Bari: Editori Laterza, 1982), p. 257.
31 Silvia Franchini, *Editori, lettrici e stampa di moda: Giornali di moda e di famiglia a Milano dal 'Corriere delle Dame' agli editori dell'Italia unita* (Milan: Franco Angeli, 2002), pp. 50, 55, 58.
32 Franchini, *Editori, lettrici e stampa di moda*, p. 58.
33 Honoré de Balzac, 'Traité de la vie élégante,' *La Mode*, 22 May 1830; included in *Pathologie de la vie sociale, Oeuvres complètes* (Paris: Club de l'honnête homme, 1956), vol. 23, p. 548; also available in H. de Balzac, *Traité de la vie élégante*, followed by *Théorie de la démarche* (Paris: Éditions Bossard, 1922), pp. 54–5.
34 Stuart Woolf, *The Poor in Western Europe in the Eighteenth and Nineteenth Centuries* (London and New York: Methuen, 1986), p. 69.
35 Gambi and Gozzoli, *Milano*, p. 282.
36 Quoted ibid., p. 257.
37 See ibid., figure 103.
38 Quoted ibid., p. 257.
39 From Luigi Capuana, 'La galleria Vittorio Emanuele,' from *Milano 1881* (Milan, 1881), pp. 409–17, quoted in Gambi and Gozzoli, *Milano*, p. 282.
40 *Storia d'Italia, Annali 19, La moda*, p. 841.
41 Theodor W. Adorno, *Introduction to the Sociology of Music*, trans. E.B. Ashton (New York: Seabury Press, 1976), p. 80.
42 See the treatment of attempts to restructure Naples according to a rational blueprint in De Seta, *Napoli*, chap. 9, 'Dall'Unità d'Italia alla prima guerra mondiale,' pp. 249–86. For opinions by Croce, Serao, and others about the *Risanamento* project, see esp. pp. 264–5.
43 R. De Zerbi, 'La miseria di Napoli,' in *Nuova Antologia*, 15 December 1879.

Quoted in Giovanni Aliberti, 'La "Questione di Napoli" nell'età liberale (1861–1904),' in *Storia di Napoli* (Naples: Società Editrice Storia di Napoli, 1967–78), vol. 10, p. 238. See Aliberti's further analysis of De Zerbi and other writers throughout this chapter, pp. 219–71. For more discussion of De Zerbi see Antonio Ghirelli, *Napoli italiana: La storia della città dopo il 1860* (Turin: Einaudi, 1977), p. 31. For this particular cholera attack see ibid., pp. 36–7 and Ghirelli's following chapter, 'La città del colera,' pp. 38–49. I am generally indebted to Aliberti's and Ghirelli's accounts of contemporary reflections on poverty in Naples.

44 De Zerbi, 'La miseria di Napoli,' p. 534.
45 See Ghirelli's synopsis, *Napoli italiana*, p. 33.
46 Jessie White Mario, *La miseria in Napoli* (1877), intro. and ed. Gianni Infusino with pref. by Antonio Ghirelli (Naples: Quarto Potere, 1978), p. 194.
47 Matilde Serao, *Il ventre di Napoli*, complete edition, ed. Patricia Bianchi (Cava de' Tirreni: Avagliano editore, 2nd ed., 2003), p. 37. Italian quotations in my text will be from this edition, with page numbers given in parentheses.
48 For an account of the genesis of Serao's book see the *Nota al testo* by Patricia Bianchi in *Il ventre di Napoli*, pp. 21–3.
49 Almost half a century earlier, Dickens too had commented on a tendency in those responding to Naples to concentrate only on its superficial charms and beauties, and to ignore the underlying poverty: 'Painting and poetizing for ever, if you will, the beauties of this most beautiful and lovely spot on earth, let us, as our duty, try to associate a new picturesque with some faint recognition of man's destiny and capabilities; more hopeful, I believe, among the ice and snow of the North Pole, than in the sun and bloom of Naples.' *Pictures from Italy* (1846), in the volume *American Notes, Pictures from Italy*, and *A Child's History of England* (London: Chapman and Hall, 1891), p. 326.
50 Now available in Francesco Saverio Nitti, *Edizione nazionale delle opere*, vol. 3, *Scritti sulla questione meridionale*, ed. Manlio Rossi Doria (Rome and Bari: Editori Laterza, 1978), pp. 3–185. Quotations from this work will henceforth be from this edition, with page references given in the main text.
51 Antonio Gramsci, *Selections from the Prison Notebooks*, ed. and trans. Quintin Hoare and Geoffrey Nowell-Smith (London: Lawrence and Wishart, 1971), p. 98.
52 Quoted by Doria in his preface to Nitti, *Scritti sulla questione meridionale*, p. xii.

53 We should be aware, however, that Nitti's dating of this problem is open to debate. Stuart Woolf, for instance, suggests that already by the end of the sixteenth century 'the major cities of the South had become parasites, with little or no industrial production and enormous consumption requirements extracted from the countryside.' *The Poor in Western Europe*, pp. 51–2.
54 Antonio Gramsci, 'The Southern Question,' in *The Modern Prince and Other Writings*, trans. Louis Marks (London: Lawrence and Wishart, 1957), p. 28.
55 Here also we may choose to see an anticipation of Gramsci's idea of the rich North / poor South dyad, defined by him in terms of the city–countryside relationship. For Gramsci's fuller explications, see the section in Hoare and Nowell-Smith's translation from the *Prison Notebooks* entitled 'The city–countryside relationship during the Risorgimento and in the national structure' (pp. 90–102).
56 Gramsci, 'The Southern Question,' p. 31.
57 See the entries on Morbelli in *Ottocento: Romanticism and Revolution in 19th-Century Italian Painting*, ed. Roberta J.M. Olson (New York: American Federation of Arts, 1992), pp. 236–7 and 272–3.
58 Reproduced in Barilli et al., *Il secondo '800 italiano: Le poetiche del vero* (Milan: Mazzotta, 1988), p. 294.
59 Reproduced in *I grandi maestri della pittura italiana dell'ottocento*, ed. Paolo Lecaldino, vol. 1 (Milan: Rizzoli, 1958), plate 103.
60 Quoted in the entry on the painting in *Ottocento*, ed., Olson, p. 201.
61 Antonio Gramsci, *Letteratura e vita nazionale* (Turin: Einaudi, 1950), p. 73. Gramsci's entire sentence here reads: 'L'atteggiamento del Manzoni verso i suoi popolani è l'atteggiamento della Chiesa cattolica verso il popolo: di condiscendente benevolenza, non di medesimezza umana.' I am employing Gramsci's useful distinction at the end of the sentence between two attitudes, but I would not wish to endorse the main sentence, which seems an unfair blanket judgement both as it relates to Manzoni and to the Catholic church.
62 Gramsci, *Letteratura e vita nazionale*, p. 14.
63 'Mode e costumi dal Medio Evo sino ai giorni nostri,' in *Le ore casalinghe*, vol. 1 (1851), no. 2, p. 111. Quoted in Erica Morato, 'La stampa di moda dal Settecento all'Unità,' in *Storia d'Italia: Annali*, vol. 19, *La moda*, ed. Carlo Marco Belfanti and Fabio Giusberti (Turin: Einaudi, 2003), p. 793.
64 Many further titles appear in the 'Indice delle testate' to Franchini, *Editori, lettrici e stampa di moda*, pp. 332–5. See also Rita Carrarini, 'La stampa di moda dall'Unità a oggi,' in *Storia d'Italia, Annali*, vol. 19, pp. 796–834; esp. n. 1, for identification of particular journals.

65 Rome and Bari: Laterza, 1992.
66 Franchini, *Editori, lettrici e stampa di moda*, p. 43 and passim.
67 'Mode e costumi dal Medio Evo ai giorni nostri,' quoted in Morato, p. 793.
68 Carrarini, 'La stampa di moda dall'Unità a oggi,' p. 798. The last words are taken from an advertisement for the magazine *La moda illustrata* that appeared in the 1911 *Catalogo generale della Casa editrice Sonzogno*.
69 Gabriele D'Annunzio, *L'Innocente* (1892), in *Prose di romanzi*, vol. 1, *I romanzi della rosa* (Milan: Mondadori, 1940), pp. 514–5.
70 Ibid., p. 520.

Bibliography

Addison, Joseph. *The Spectator*, no. 5, 6 March 1711.
Adorno, Theodor W. *Introduction to the Sociology of Music*. Trans. E.B. Ashton. New York: The Seabury Press, 1976.
– *Quasi una Fantasia: Essays on Modern Music*. Trans. Rodney Livingstone. London: Verso, 1992.
Ahmad, Aijaz. *Lineages of the Present: Political Essays*. New Delhi: Tulika, 1996; London and New York: Verso, 2000.
Alfieri, Vittorio. *Vita scritta da esso*. Ed. Luigi Fassò. Asti: Casa d'Alfieri, 1951.
Aliberti, Giovanni. 'Economia e Società da Carlo III ai Napoleonidi (1734–1806).' In *Storia di Napoli*, vol. 8, pp. 75–164.
– 'La "Questione di Napoli" nell'età liberale (1861–1904).' In *Storia di Napoli*, vol. 10, pp. 219–71.
Alisio, Giancarlo. 'Sviluppo urbano e struttura della città.' In *Storia di Napoli*, vol. 8, pp. 311–66.
Anderson, Perry. *Lineages of the Absolutist State*. London: Verso, 1974.
Archivio di Stato di Napoli. Lettera dal Segretario di Stato, Ministro degli Affari Esteri, Circello, al Cavaliere A'Court, Napoli, 4 April 1816.
– Lettera dal Segretario di Stato, Ministro dell'Interno, a Sua Eccellenza il Segretario di Stato, Ministro degli Affari Esteri, Napoli, 3 Aprile 1816.
– Affari Esteri. Fasc. 688. Letter of 20 August 1818 from Castlereagh to A'Court.
– Affari Esteri, Fasc. 688. Lettera dal Segretario di Stato, Ministro degli Affari Interni, a S.E. il Segretario di Stato, Ministro degli Affari Esteri, 16 February 1820.
– Affari Esteri, Fasc. 688. Lettera dal Sopraintendente della Reale Officina de' Papiri, Monsignor Rosini, al Segretario di Stato, Ministro degli Affari Interni, 7 February 1820.
Auerbach, Erich. 'Contributi linguistici all'interpretazione della *Scienza Nuova*

di G.B. Vico' (1937). In *San Francesco, Dante, Vico ed altri saggi di filologia romanza*, pp. 66–77. Bari: De Donato, 1970; reprinted in *Giambattista Vico*, ed. Tessitore and Sanna, pp. 118–26.
– 'Vico and Aesthetic Historism' (1949). In *Scenes from the Drama of European Literature: Six Essays*, pp. 183–98. New York: Meridian Books, 1959.
Balani, Donatella. 'Sviluppo demografico e trasformazioni sociali nel Settecento.' In *Storia di Torino*, vol. 5, pp. 625–88.
Balzac, Honoré de. 'Traité de la vie élégante.' *La Mode*, 22 May 1830. Included in *Pathologie de la vie sociale*, in *Oeuvres complètes*, vol. 23. Paris: Club de l'honnête homme, 1956. Also available in H. de Balzac, *Traité de la vie élégante* followed by *Théorie de la démarche*. Paris: Éditions Bossard, 1922.
Barilli, Renato, et al. *Il secondo '800 italiano: Le poetiche del vero*. Milan: Mazzotta, 1988.
Barzini, Luigi. 'Occhio di vetro. La "prima" della televisione.' *La Stampa*, 5 January 1954. Extract in Grasso, *Storia della televisione italiana*, p. 53.
Beccaria, Cesare, Marchese di. *Dei delitti e delle pene*. Ed. Franco Venturi, 3rd ed. Turin: Einaudi, 1973.
Bellow, Saul. *The Dean's December*. New York: Harper & Row, 1982.
Benjamin, Walter. *The Arcades Project*. Trans. Howard Eiland and Kevin McLaughlin. Cambridge, MA, and London: Belknap Press of Harvard University Press, 1999.
– 'Theses on the Philosophy of History' (1940). In *Illuminations*, ed. and intro. Hannah Arendt, trans. Harry Zohn, pp. 253–67. New York: Schocken Books, 1968; London: Fontana, 1992.
Bietoletti, Silvestra, and Michele Dantini. *L'Ottocento Italiano: La Storia, Gli Artisti, Le Opere*. Florence: Giunti, 2002.
Blessington, Marguerite, Countess of. *Lady Blessington at Naples*. Ed. Edith Clay, intro. Harold Acton. London: H. Hamilton, 1979.
Bondanella, Peter. *Umberto Eco and the Open Text: Semiotics, Fiction, Popular Culture*. Cambridge: Cambridge University Press, 1997.
Brand, C.P. *Italy and the English Romantics: The Italian Fashion in Early Nineteenth-Century England*. Cambridge: Cambridge University Press, 1957.
Brunetta, Gian Piero. 'Per una carta del navigar visionario.' In *Il Mondo Nuovo*, ed. Zotti Minici, pp. 13–29.
– *Il viaggio dell'icononauta: Dalla camera oscura di Leonardo alla luce dei Lumière*. Venice: Marsiglio, 1997.
Burke, Kenneth. *A Grammar of Motives*. New York: Prentice-Hall, Inc., 1945.
Calvino, Italo. 'Due interviste su scienza e letteratura' (1968). In *Una pietra sopra*. Turin: Einaudi, 1980. Reprinted in *Saggi: 1945–1985*, ed. Mario Barenghi, vol. 1, pp. 229–37. Milan: Mondadori, 1995.

– *Lezioni Americane: Sei proposte per il prossimo millennio.* Milan: Garzanti, 1988. In *Saggi: 1945–1985*, ed. Barenghi, 2nd ed., vol. 1, pp. 627–753.
– *The Literature Machine: Essays.* Trans. Patrick Creagh. London: Secker and Warburg, 1986; London; Vintage, 1997.
– *I nostri antenati.* Turin: Einaudi, 1960.
– *Orlando furioso di Ludovico Ariosto raccontato da Italo Calvino: Con una scelta del poema.* Turin: Einaudi, 1970.
– *Our Ancestors.* Trans. Archibald Colquhoun; intro. by author. London: Pan Books, 1980.
– *The Path to the Spiders' Nest.* Trans. Archibold Colquhoun, rev. Martin McLaughlin. London: Jonathan Cape, 1998.
– *Saggi: 1945–1985.* Ed. Mario Barenghi, 2nd ed., 2 vols. Milan: Mondadori, 1999.
– *Il sentiero dei nidi di ragno* (1947). 4th edition, with preface by the author. Turin: Einaudi, 1970.
– *Six Memos for the Next Millennium.* Trans. Patrick Creagh. Cambridge, MA; Harvard University Press, 1988; London: Vintage, 1996.
– 'L'ultimo canale Tv.' *La Repubblica*, 3 January 1984. Extract in Grasso, *Storia della televisione italiana*, pp. 453–4.
Capuana, Luigi. 'La galleria Vittorio Emanuele.' From miscellaneous vol. *Milano 1881* (Milan, 1881), pp. 409–17, quoted in Gambi and Gozzoli, *Milano*, p. 282.
Carocci, Guido. *Firenze scomparsa: Ricordi storico-artistici.* 1897; photographic reprint Rome: Multigrafica, 1979.
Carpanetto, Dino. 'The Duchy of Milan under Maria Theresa and Joseph II.' In Carpanetto and Ricuperati, *Italy in the Age of Reason*, pp. 223–35.
Carpanetto, Dino, and Giuseppe Ricuperati. *Italy in the Age of Reason: 1685–1789.* Trans. Caroline Higgitt. London and New York: Longman, 1987.
Carrarini, Rita. 'La stampa di moda dall'Unità a oggi.' In *Storia d'Italia: Annali*, vol. 19, *La moda*, pp. 796–834.
Catalogo generale della Casa editrice Sonzogno. 1911.
Chandler, James. 'History.' In *An Oxford Companion to the British Romantic Age.* General ed. Iain McCalman. Oxford: Oxford University Press, 1999.
Cognasso, Francesco. *Storia di Torino.* Milan: Aldo Martello, 1960.
Colletta, Pietro. *Storia del Reame di Napoli* (1834). 2 vols. Milan: Istituto Editoriale Italiano, n.d.
Consiglio Municipale di Firenze. Letter of 12 April 1878 from nine signed councillors of the city of Florence including mayor Ubaldino Peruzzi, to His Excellency the Senate President. Given as appendix in Fei, *Nascita e sviluppo*, pp. 190–1.

Craveri, G.G. *Guida de' forestieri per la real città di Torino*. Turin: Gian Domenico Rameletti Libraio, 1753.
Croce, Benedetto. *La filosofia di Giambattista Vico* (1946). In *Edizione nazionale delle opere di Benedetto Croce*. Naples: Bibliopolis, 1997.
– *Filosofia, Poesia, Storia: Pagine tratte da tutte le opere a cura dell'autore*. Intro. Giuseppe Galasso. Milan: Adelphi, 1996.
– *History of the Kingdom of Naples*. Trans. Frances Frenaye. Chicago and London: University of Chicago Press, 1965.
– *Philosophy, Poetry, History: An Anthology of Essays*. London and New York: Oxford University Press, 1966.
Cronaca Veneziana: Feste e vita quotidiana nella Venezia del Settecento. View paintings by Gabriel Bella and engravings by Gaetano Zompini from the collections of the Querini Stampalia Foundation of Venice. Venice: Fondazione Scientifica Querini-Stampalia, 1991.
Crouzet, Michel. *Le roman stendhalien: La Chartreuse de Parme*. Orléans: Paradigme, 1996.
– *Stendhal et l'Italianité: Essai de mythologie romantique*. Paris: Librairie José Corti, 1982.
Dagrada, Elena. 'Television and Its Critics: A Parallel History,' *Italian Cultural Studies*, ed. Forgacs and Lumley, pp. 233–47.
D'Annunzio, Gabriele. *L'Innocente* (1892). In *Prose di romanzi*, vol. 1, *I romanzi della rosa*, pp. 369–650. Milan: Mondadori, 1940.
D'Arbitrio, Nicoletta, and Luigi Ziviello. *Il Reale Albergo dei Poveri di Napoli: Un edificio per le 'Arti della città' dentro le mura*. Naples: Edisa, 1999.
Davy, Sir Humphry. 'Report on the State of the Manuscripts of Papyrus, found at Herculaneum,' in *Quarterly Journal of Literature, Science and the Arts*, 7 (1819).
– 'Some observations and experiments on the papyri found in the ruins of Herculaneum.' Read before the Royal Society, 15 March 1821. In *Collected Works*, ed. John Davy. London, 1839–40.
De Giorgio, Michela. *Le Italiane dall'Unità a oggi: Modelli culturali e comportamenti sociali*. Rome and Bari: Laterza, 1992.
De Mauro, Tullio. *Storia linguistica dell'Italia unita*. 3rd ed. Rome and Bari: Laterza, 1986.
De Seta, Cesare. *Napoli*. In the series *La città nella storia d'Italia*. Gen. ed. Cesare De Seta. Bari: Editori Laterza, 1981.
Detti, Eduardo. with the collaboration of Tommaso Detti. *Firenze scomparsa*. Intro. Aldo Palazzeschi. Florence: Vallecchi, 1970.
De Zerbi, R. 'La miseria di Napoli.' In *Nuova Antologia*, 15 December 1879. Quoted in Giovanni Aliberti, 'La "Questione di Napoli" nell'età liberale

(1861–1904),' in *Storia di Napoli*, 10 vols. Naples: Società Editrice Storia di Napoli, 1967–78. Vol. 10, pp. 219–71.

Dickens, Charles. *Pictures from Italy* (1846). In the volume *American Notes, Pictures from Italy,* and *A Child's History of England.* London: Chapman and Hall, 1891.

Dickie, John. *Darkest Italy: The Nation and Stereotypes of the Mezzogiorno, 1860–1900.* Basingstoke: Macmillan, 1999.

Draaisma, Douwe. *Metaphors of Memory: A History of Ideas about the Mind.* Trans. Paul Vincent. Cambridge: Cambridge University Press, 2000.

Eco, Umberto. *Diario minimo.* Milan: Mondadori, 1963.

– *Misreadings.* Trans. William Weaver. San Diego, New York, and London: Harcourt Brace & Co., 1993.

– *Travels in Hyperreality: Essays.* Trans. William Weaver. San Diego, New York, and London: Harcourt Brace Jovanovich, 1986.

Fanelli, Giovanni. *Firenze.* In the series *La città nella storia d'Italia.* Gen. ed. Cesare De Seta. Bari: Laterza, 1980.

Fei, Silano. *Nascita e sviluppo di Firenze città borghese.* Florence: G & G Editrice, 1971.

Filangieri, Gaetano. Letter from Naples, 3 February 1781, to Domenico Pepe in Mola di Bari. In *Riformatori Napoletani*, ed. Venturi, pp. 768–9.

Forgacs, David. 'Cultural Consumption, 1940s to 1990s.' In *Italian Cultural Studies*, ed. Forgacs and Lumley, pp. 273–90.

Franchini, Silvia. *Editori, lettrici e stampa di moda: Giornali di moda e di famiglia a Milano dal 'Corriere delle Dame' agli editori dell'Italia unita.* Milan: Franco Angeli, 2002.

Fusco, Renato De. 'L'architettura della seconda metà del settecento.' In *Storia di Napoli*, vol. 8, pp. 367–449.

Gabici, Franco. 'Leopardi e Galilei.' in *Leopardi e l'astronomia: Atti del Convegno Nazionale di Studi*, ed. Luciano Romeo, Gianfranco Abate, and F. Walter Lupi, pp. 109–18. Cosenza: Progetto 2000.

Galilei, Galileo. *Dialogo sopra i due massimi sistemi del mondo, tolemaico e copernicano.* Extracts in Leopardi, *Crestomazia*, in section 'Filosofia speculativa,' pp. 263–327.

– *Dialogue on the Great World Systems.* Trans. T. Salisbury, abridged text ed. Chicago: University of Chicago Press, 1955.

– *Scritti letterari.* Ed. Alberto Chiari. Florence: Felice le Monnier, 1970.

Gambi, Lucio, and Maria Cristina Gozzoli. *Milano.* In the series *La città nella storia d'Italia.* Gen. ed. Cesare De Seta. Bari: Laterza, 1982.

Geertz, Clifford. *Local Knowledge: Further Essays in Interpretive Anthropology.* New York: Basic Books, 1983.

Genovesi, Antonio. 'Al gentile e cortese lettore.' From his 'Ragionamento sul Commercio in universale, e alcune annotazioni riguardanti l'economia del

nostro Regno,' introduction to *Storia del Commercio della Gran Brettagna, scritta da John Cary, Mercante di Bristol, tradotta in nostra vulgar lingua da Pietro Genovesi* (1757). In *Scritti economici*, vol 1.
- *Scritti economici*. Ed. Maria Luisa Perna. 2 vols. Naples: Istituto Italiano per gli Studi Filosofici, 1984.

Ghiliossi, Senator. 'Memoria del Senatore Ghiliossi Congiudice del Consolato circo quelle Arte, e Mestieri, che poteano essere i più convenienti per essere esercitati nelle Case di Correzione che erano per stabilirsi nella Città di Torino.' Archivio di Stato di Torino, Luoghi pii di qua dai monti, mazzo 17, fasc. 10.

Ghirelli, Antonio. *Napoli italiana: La storia della città dopo il 1860*. Turin: Einaudi, 1977.

Giambattista Vico. Ed. Fulvio Tessitore and Manuela Sanna, in the series *Cento Libri per Mille Anni*. Gen. ed. Walter Pedullà. Rome: Istituto Poligrafico and Zecca dello Stato, 2000.

Giordano, Paolo. *Ferdinando Fuga a Napoli: L'Albergo dei Poveri, il Cimitero delle 366 fosse, i Granili*. Lecce: Edizioni del Grifo, 1997.

Gluck, Christoph Willibald. Dedication of *Alceste* to Grand Duke Leopold of Tuscany. (Actual author was Ranieri Calzabigi.) Quoted in Piero Weiss, *Opera: A History in Documents*, pp. 119–20. New York and Oxford: Oxford University Press, 2002.

Goldoni, Carlo. 'Il Mondo Nuovo' (poem). In *Tutte le opere*, ed. Giuseppe Ortolani, vol. 13, pp. 689–702. Milan: Mondadori, 1955.

Gramsci, Antonio. 'The City-Countryside Relationship during the Risorgimento and in the National Structure.' In *Prison Notebooks*, ed. and trans. Hoare and Nowell-Smith, pp. 90–102.
- *Letteratura e vita nazionale*. Turin: Einaudi, 1950.
- *Il Risorgimento*. Turin: Einaudi, 1949.
- *Selections from the Prison Notebooks*, ed. and trans. Quintin Hoare and Geoffrey Nowell-Smith. London: Lawrence and Wishart, 1971.
- 'The Southern Question.' In *The Modern Prince and Other Writings*, trans. Louis Marks, pp. 28–51. London: Lawrence and Wishart, 1957.

I grandi maestri della pittura italiana dell'ottocento. Ed. Paolo Lecaldino. Vol. 1. Milan: Rizzoli, 1958.

Grasso, Aldo. *Storia della televisione italiana*. Milan: Garzanti, 1992; new updated edition. Milan: Garzanti, 2000.

Hunter, Mary. *The Culture of Opera Buffa in Mozart's Vienna: A Poetics of Entertainment*. Princeton: Princeton University Press, 1999.

Italian Cultural Studies: An introduction. Ed. David Forgacs and Robert Lumley. Oxford and New York: Oxford University Press, 1996.

Jacques, Martin. 'Big Brother: Miracle-Maker or Media Manipulator? Martin Jacques reports from Rome on the sensational election triumph of Italy's new strong man, Silvio Berlusconi.' *The Sunday Times*, 3 April 1994, News Review section, pp. 1–2.

Jung, C.G. 'Conscious, Unconscious, and Individuation' (1939). In *The Archetypes and the Collective Unconscious*, 2nd ed., trans. R.F.C. Hull, pp. 273–89. London: Routledge & Kegan Paul, 1968.

Keats, John. *Letters of John Keats*. Selected and ed. Stanley Gardner. London: University of London Press, 1965.

Kierkegaard, Søren. *Either/Or*. Trans. David F. Swenson and Lillian Marvin Swenson, rev. Howard A. Johnson. 2 vols. Princeton: Princeton University Press, 1959.

Kimbell, David. *Italian Opera*. Cambridge: Cambridge University Press, 1991.

Leary, D.E., ed. *Metaphors in the History of Psychology*. New York: Cambridge University Press, 1990.

Legge Diritto Giustizia. Ed. Luciano Violante. Turin: Einaudi, 1998. Vol. 14 of *Annali* supplements to the Einaudi *Storia d'Italia* coordinated by Ruggiero Romano and Currado Vivanti.

Leopardi, Giacomo. *Crestomazia italiana: La prosa*. Intro. and notes Giulio Bollati. Turin: Einaudi, 1968.

– 'Discorso sopra lo stato presente dei costumi degl'Italiani.' In *Poesie e Prose*, vol. 2, *Prose*, ed. Rolando Damiani, pp. 441–80. Milan: Mondadori, 1988. (Quotations are from this edition.) See also *Discorso sopra lo stato presente dei costumi degl'Italiani*. Intro. and ed. Augusto Placanica. Venice: Marsilio, 1989.

– *Operette Morali / Essays and Dialogues*. Parallel text edition with English trans. by Giovanni Cecchetti. Berkeley, Los Angeles, and London: University of California Press, 1982.

– *Zibaldone di pensieri*. Critical editon, ed. Giuseppe Pacella. 3 vols. Milan: Garzanti, 1991.

Mannoni, Laurent. *Le grand art de la lumière et de l'ombre*. Paris: Éditions Nathan, 1995.

– *The Great Art of Light and Shadow: Archaeology of the Cinema*. Trans. and ed. Richard Crangle. Exeter: University of Exeter Press, 2000.

Manzoni, Alessandro. *The Column of Infamy*. Prefaced by Cesare Beccaria's *Of Crimes and Punishments*. Trans. Kenelm Foster, O.P., and Jane Grigson, intro. A.P. d'Entrèves. London: Oxford University Press, 1964.

– *Storia della colonna infame*. Ed. Carla Riccardi. Milan: Mondadori, 1984.

Marazzini, Claudio. 'Il problema della lingua.' In *Storia di Torino*, vol. 5, 1005–25.

Metastasio, Pietro. *Poesie del Signor Abate Pietro Metastasio*. 10 vols. Turin: Stamperia reale, 1757.
Meynell, Hugo. *The Art of Handel's Operas*. Lewiston and Queenston: Edwin Mellen Press, 1986.
Millar, John. *The Origin of the Distinction of Ranks*. 1771.
Miller, Felicia. '*Farinelli*'s Electronic Hermaphrodite and the Contralto Tradition.' In *The Work of Opera: Genre, Nationhood, and Sexual Difference*, ed. Richard Dellamora and Daniel Fischlin, pp. 73–92. New York: Columbia University Press, 1997.
The Mission: Viva Las Venice. BBC, 1999. Directed by John Dickson.
'Mode e costumi dal Medio Evo sino ai giorni nostri.' In *Le ore casalinghe* vol. 1 (1851), no. 2, p. 111. Quoted in Morato, 'La stampa di moda dal Settecento all'Unità,' p. 793.
Moe, Nelson. *The View from Vesuvius: Italian Culture and the Southern Question*. Berkeley, Los Angeles, and London: University of California Press, 2002.
Il mondo nuovo. Le meraviglie della visione dal '700 alla nascita del cinema. Ed. Carlo Alberto Zotti Minici (Catalogue of an exhibition held in Bassano del Grappa, 29 July–20 October 1988). Milan: Casa Editrice Mazzotta, 1988.
Montesquieu, Charles de Secondat, baron de. *De l'esprit des lois*. 2 vols. Paris: Garnier Frères, 1973.
– *The Spirit of the Laws*. Trans. Anne M. Cohler, Basia Carolyn Miller, and Harold Samuel Stone. Cambridge: Cambridge University Press, 1989.
– *Voyages de Montesquieu*. Pub. by le baron Albert de Montesquieu, 2 vols. Bordeaux: Imprimerie G. Gounouilhou, 1894.
Morato, Erica. 'La stampa di moda dal Settecento all'Unità.' In *Storia d'Italia, Annali*, vol. 19, *La moda*, pp. 767–834.
Mozart, Wolfgang Amadeus, et al. *Briefe und Aufzeichnungen: Gesamtausgabe*. Kassel, Basel, London, and New York: Bärenreiter-Verlag, 1962.
– *The Letters of Mozart and His Family*. Trans. and ed. Emily Anderson. 3rd ed. London: Macmillan, 1985.
Nitti, Francesco Saverio. *Napoli e la questione meridionale* (1903). In *Edizione nazionale delle opere*, vol. 3, *Scritti sulla questione meridionale*, ed. Manlio Rossi Doria, pp. 3–185. Rome and Bari: Editori Laterza, 1978.
Ospitale, Giancarlo. *Lo stato italiano e il suo ordinamento giuridico*. Padua: Casa Editrice Dott. Antonio Milani, 1967.
Ottocento: Romanticism and Revolution in 19th-Century Italian Painting. Ed. Roberta J.M. Olson. New York: American Federation of Arts, 1992.
Padovani, Francesco. *Cinema: Alla ricerca degli antenati*. Feltre: Libreria Pilotto Editrice, 1995.
Pagano, Francesco Mario. *Saggi politici: Del civile corso delle nazioni o sia de'*

principii, progressi e decadenza delle società. Naples: Gennaro Verriento, 1783; extracts in *Riformatori Napoletani*, ed. Venturi, pp. 854–900.

Pasolini, Pier Paolo. 'Lettera aperta a Italo Calvino.' *Paese sera*, 8 July 1974; repr. in *Scritti corsari*, pp. 51–5.

– *Scritti corsari*. Milan: Garzanti, 1975.

– 'Sfida ai dirigenti della televisione.' *Corriere della Sera*, 9 December 1973; extract in Grasso, *Storia della televisione italiana*, pp. 291–2.

Pepe, Domenico. Letter from Mola di Bari, 27 January 1851, to Gaetano Filangieri, Naples, in *Riformatori Napoletani*, ed. Franco Venturi, n. to p. 768.

Petrusewicz, Marta. 'Before the Southern Question: "Native" Ideas on Backwardness and Remedies in the Kingdom of Two Sicilies, 1815–1849.' In *Italy's 'Southern Question': Orientalism in One Country*, ed. Jane Schneider, pp. 27–49. Oxford and New York: Berg, 1998.

– *Come il Meridione divenne una Questione: Rappresentazioni del Sud prima e dopo il Quarantotto*. Catanzaro: Rubettino, 1998.

Pope, Alexander. *The Dunciad*. Ed. James Sutherland. 3rd ed., revised. London: Methuen, 1963. Vol. 5 of Twickenham edition of *The Poems of Alexander Pope*, general ed. John Butt.

Prolo, Maria Adriana. 'Uno "spettacolo" che continua: Note sulla nascita del Museo Nazionale del Cinema.' In *Il mondo nuovo*, ed. Minici, pp. 51–4.

Public Records Office, Kew. FO 70, no. 87, documents 63, 76, 92, and 93, Letters of May–July 1819, from William Hamilton to Joseph Planta Esq., Mr Barrow to J. Planta Esq., and W. Hamilton to Mr Croker.

Racine, Jean. *Complete Plays*. Trans. Samuel Solomon. 2 vols. New York: Random House, 1967.

Rebuffa, Giorgio. *La costituzione impossibile: Cultura politica e sistema parlamentare in Italia*. Bologna: il Mulino, 1995.

'Reciprocal Influences of Cinema and Television.' Round table discussion, Grosseto, 30 September 1962. Extract in Grasso, *Storia della televisione italiana*, pp. 156–7.

Regole della nuova Opera pia detta il Ritiro delle Forzate, divise in regole generali, e particolari. Archivio di Stato di Torino, 'Luoghi pii di qua dai monti,' mazzo 20, fasc. 3.

Ricuperati, Giuseppe. 'The Enlightenment in Lombardy: Pietro Verri (1728–97), Cesare Beccaria (1735–94), *Il Caffè*.' In Dino Carpanetto and Giuseppe Ricuperati, *Italy in the Age of Reason: 1685–1789*. Trans. Caroline Higgitt, pp. 259–72. London and New York: Longman, 1987.

– 'Lo specchio degli ordinati. La città nel tempo di Carlo Emanuele III.' In *Storia di Torino*, vol. 5, pp. 5–57.

Ricuperati, Giuseppe, and Luca Prestia. 'Lo specchio degli ordinati. La città dal tempo di Vittorio Amedeo III alla crisi definitive dell' "Ancien Régime." In *Storia di Torino*, vol. 5, pp. 477–594.

Riformatori Napoletani. Ed. Franco Venturi. Milan and Naples: Ricciardi Editore, 1962. Vol. 5 of the series *Illuministi Italiani*.

Roggero, Costanza. 'L'urbanistica nel secondo Settecento,' In *Storia di Torino*, vol. 5, pp. 799–819.

Roma: Quotidiano d'informazione. 13 April 2002.

Rushdie, Salman. 'Italo Calvino.' *London Review of Books*, 17–30 September 1981, pp. 16–17; repr. in his *Imaginary Homelands: Essays and Criticism 1981–1991*, pp. 254–61. London: Granta Books, 1991.

– *Midnight's Children*. London: Jonathan Cape, 1980.

Sacchi, Giuseppe. 'Una festa da ballo nella Galleria De Cristoforis.' In *Il Nuovo Ricoglitore* (1833), pp. 113–17; quoted in Gambi and Gozzoli, *Milano*, p. 257.

Sarnelli, Pompeo. *Nuova guida de' forestieri, e dell'istoria di Napoli ... ampliata delle molte moderne fabbriche secondo lo stato presente, ed arricchita di varie figure.* Naples: paid for by Saverio Rossi, 1772.

Schulz, Juergen. 'Maps as Metaphors: Mural Map Cycles of the Italian Renaissance.' In *Art and Cartography: Six Historical Essays*, ed. David Woodward, pp. 97–122. Chicago and London: University of Chicago Press, 1987.

Sciascia, Leonardo. From *Paese Sera*, 9 January 1980; extract in Grasso, *Storia della televisione italiana*, p. 384.

– *Death of an Inquisitor: And Other Stories.* Trans. Ian Thomson. Manchester: Carcanet, 1990.

– Essay on Manzoni's *Storia della colonna infame* in *Cruciverba*, pp. 101–14. Turin: Enaudi, 1983.

– *Morte dell'Inquisitore* (1964). Milan: Adelphi Edizioni, 2001.

– *Salt in the Wound*, followed by *The Death of the Inquisitor*. Trans. Judith Green. New York: Orion Press, 1969.

Scott, Sir Walter. 'Introductory Remarks on Popular Poetry.' Essay addition to 1830 edition of *Minstrelsy of the Scottish Border*.

– *The Journal of Sir Walter Scott.* Ed. W.E.K. Anderson. Oxford: Oxford University Press, 1972; Edinburgh: Canongate, 1998.

– *The Letters of Sir Walter Scott.* Ed. Herbert Grierson. 12 vols. London: Constable & Co. Ltd, 1932–7.

– *Waverley*, ed. Claire Lamont. Oxford and New York: Oxford University Press, 1986.

Serao, Matilde. *Il ventre di Napoli*. Complete edition, ed. Patricia Bianchi. 2nd ed. Cava de' Tirreni: Avagliano, 2003.

Silvestrini, Maria Teresa. 'Religione "stabile" e politica ecclesiastica.' In *Storia di Torino*, vol. 5, pp. 371–422.

Sismondi, J.C.L. Simonde de. *Histoire des républiques italiennes du moyen âge.* 16 vols. Vols. 1–2, Zurich, 1807; 3–4, Zurich, 1808; 5–8, Paris, 1809; 9–10, Paris, 1815; 12–16, Paris, 1818.
Sontag, Susan. *The Volcano Lover: A Romance.* London: Jonathan Cape, 1992.
Staël, Madame Anne-Louise-Germaine de, *Corinne, où l'Italie.* Ed. Simone Balayé. Paris: Éditions Gallimard, 1985.
– *Corinne, or Italy.* Trans. and ed. Sylvia Raphael, intro. John Isbell. Oxford and New York: Oxford University Press, 1998.
Stato della Costituzione. Ed. Guido Neppi Modena. Milan: il Saggiatore, 1995.
Stendhal (Marie Henri Beyle). *The Charterhouse of Parma.* Trans. C.K. Scott Moncrieff, 2 vols. New York: Viveright Publishing Corp., 1944.
– *La Chartreuse de Parme.* Text with introduction, chronology, bibliography, notes, etc. by Antoine Adam. Paris: Garnier, 1973.
– *Correspondance générale.* Ed. V. Del Litto, 4 vols. Paris: Honoré Champion, 1997–9.
– *Journal.* Ed. Victor Del Litto. 5 vols. Geneva and Paris: Slatkine, 1986.
– *The Life of Rossini.* Trans. Richard Coe. 2nd ed. London: John Calder; New York: Riverun Press, 1985.
– *Pages d'Italie: L'Italie en 1818: Moeurs Romaines.* Paris: Le Divan, 1932.
– *Rome, Naples, and Florence in 1817: Sketches of the present state of society, manners, arts, literature, &c, in these celebrated cities.* [No translator given.] London: Henry Colburn, 1818.
– *Rome, Naples et Florence (1826).* Ed. Pierre Brunel. Paris: Éditions Gallimard, 1987.
– *Le rouge et le noir* (1830). Ed. Roger Nimier. Paris: Livre de Poche, 1958.
– *Vie de Rossini* (1823). Paris: Gallimard, 1992.
Storia d'Italia. Ed. R. Romani and C. Vivanti. Vol. 3, *Dal primo Settecento all'Unità.* Turin: Einaudi, 1973.
Storia d'Italia: Annali. Vol. 19, *La moda*, ed. Carlo Marco Belfanti and Fabio Giusberti. Turin: Einaudi, 2003.
Storia di Napoli. 10 vols. Naples: Società Editrice Storia di Napoli, 1967–78.
Storia di Torino. Vol. 5, *Dalla città razionale alla crisi dello Stato d'Antico Regime (1730–1798)*, ed. Giuseppe Ricuperati. Turin: Einaudi, 2002.
Sutcliffe, Tom, ed. *The Faber Book of Opera.* London: Faber and Faber, 2000.
Thompson, E.P. 'The Peculiarities of the English' (1965). In *The Poverty of Theory and Other Essays*, pp. 35–91. London: Merlin Press, 1978.
Till, Nicholas. *Mozart and the Enlightenment: Truth, Virtue and Beauty in Mozart's Operas.* London and Boston: Faber and Faber, 1992.
Trumpener, Katie. 'The Bog Itself: Enlightenment Prospects and National Elegies.' In *Bardic Nationalism: The Romantic Novel and the British Empire*, pp. 39–66. Princeton: Princeton University Press, 1997.

Valsecchi, Franco. 'Lo stato e la società piemontese da Emanuele Filiberto alla dominazione napoleonica.' In *Storia del Piemonte*, drawn up by Dino Gribaudi et al., 2 vols. Turin: F. Casanova & Co., 1961. Vol. 1, pp. 275–309.

Vasari, Giorgio. *Le vite de' più eccellenti pittori, scultori ed architettori*. With new notes and commentary by Gaetano Milanesi. 7 vols. Florence: Sansoni, 1878–81.

Vedute del 'Mondo Nuovo': Vues d'optique settecentesche nella collezione del Museo Nazionale del Cinema di Torino. Ed. Donata Pesenti Campagnoni. Turin and London: Umberto Allemandi & Co., 2000.

Il ventre di Milano: Fisiologia della capitale morale, ed. by a society of scholars including Aldo Barilli. Milan: C. Aliprandi, 1888.

Venturi, Franco. 'The Enlightenment in Southern Italy.' In *Italy and the Enlightenment*.

– 'L'Italia anticuriale: Genova e Torino.' In *Settecento rifomatore II: La chiesa e la repubblica dentro i loro limiti*, pp. 65–85. Turin: Einaudi, 1976.

– 'L'Italia fuori d'Italia.' In *Storia d'Italia*, ed. Romani and Vivanti, vol. 3, pp. 987–1481.

– *Italy and the Enlightenment: Studies in a Cosmopolitan Century*, ed. and intro. Stuart Woolf, trans. Susan Corsi. London: Longman, 1972.

– 'Il movimento rifomatore degli illuministi meridionali.' *Rivista storica italiana* 74 (1962), pp. 5–26.

– 'La Napoli di Antonio Genovesi.' In his *Settecento rifomatore: Da Muratori a Beccaria*, pp. 523–644. Turin: Einaudi, 1969.

– 'Napoli Capitale nel pensiero dei riformatori illuministi.' In *Storia di Napoli*, vol. 8, pp. 1–73. Naples: Società Editrice Storia di Napoli, 1967–78.

– '"Socialista" e "socialismo" nell'Italia del Settecento.' In *Rivista storica italiana* 75 (1963), fasc. 1, pp. 129ff.

Venturi, Robert, Denise Scott Brown, and Steven Izenour, *Learning from Las Vegas: The Forgotten Symbolism of Architectural Form*. Rev. ed. Cambridge, MA, and London: MIT Press, 1977.

Verri, Pietro. *Osservazioni sulla tortura* (1804). Milan: Feltrinelli, 1979.

Vico, Giambattista. *Giambattista Vico*. Ed. Fulvio Tessitore and Manuela Sanna. In the series *Cento Libri per Mille Anni*. Gen. ed. Walter Pedullà. Rome: Istituto Poligrafico e Zecca dello Stato, 2000.

– *The New Science of Giambattista Vico*. Rev. trans. of 3rd ed. (1744) by Thomas Goddard Bergin and Max Harold Fisch. Ithaca: Cornell University Press, 1968.

– *Principi di scienza nuova d'intorno alla commune natura delle nazioni* (1744). In *Opere*, ed. Fausto Nicolini. Milan and Naples: Ricciardi Editore, 1953.

- *Vita di Giambattista Vico scritta da sè medesimo* (1728). In *Giambattista Vico*, ed. Tessitore and Sanna.
Violante, Luciano. 'I cittadini, la legge e il giudice.' In *Legge Diritto Giustizia*, ed. Luciano Violante, p. lxii. Turin: Einaudi, 1998. Vol. 14 of *Annali* supplements to Einaudi *Storia d'Italia*.
Viscusi, Robert. '"Osservate, leggete con me": Leporello's Hermeneutics.' In *Lorenzo Da Ponte: Librettista di Mozart.* Proceedings of a convention at Casa Italiana, Columbia University, New York, 28–30 March, 1988. *Quaderni di Libri e Riviste d'Italia* 24 (1992), pp. 73–82.
Weber, Max. *Economy and Society* (1914). Ed. by Guenther Roth and Claus Wittich from 4th German ed., trans. Ephraim Fischoff et al. New York: Bedminster Press, 1968.
Weiss, Piero. 'Operatic Reform in Vienna: Gluck and Calzabigi.' In *Opera: A History in Documents*, pp. 115–20. New York and Oxford: Oxford University Press, 2002.
White, Jonathan. *Italy: The Enduring Culture.* Continuum: New York and London, 2001.
White Mario, Jessie. *La miseria in Napoli* (1877). Intro. and ed. Gianni Infusino, pref. by Antonio Ghirelli. Naples: Quarto Potere, 1978.
Williams, Raymond. *The Country and the City.* London: Chatto & Windus, 1973.
Woolf, Stuart. *The Poor in Western Europe in the Eighteenth and Nineteenth Centuries.* London and New York: Methuen, 1986.
Zaluski, Iwo and Pamela Zaluski. *Mozart in Italy.* London and Chester Springs: 1999.
Zola, Émile. *Le ventre de Paris.* Paris: 1873.
Zompini, Gaetano. *Le arti che vanno per via nella città di Venezia.* Venice, 1753.
Zotti Minici, Carlo Alberto. *Dispositivi ottici alle origini del cinema: Immaginario scientifico e spettacolo nel XVII e XVIII secolo.* Bologna: CLUEB, 1998.
- 'Vedute ottiche e Mondi Nuovi: Dimensioni spettacolari di un girovagare esteso d'immagini.' In *Il mondo nuovo: Le meraviglie della visione dal '700 alla nascita del cinema*, ed. Zotti Minici, pp. 34–5. Milan: Mazzotta, 1988.

Index

A'Court, Sir William, plenipotentiary in Naples 10, 12–13, 18, 20, 278n18
Adam, Antoine 209–10
Addison, Joseph, and *The Spectator* 94
Adelson, Sheldon, entrepreneur of *The Venetian* 80–2
Adorno, Theodor W. 16, 55, 171–2, 237; *Minima Moralia: Reflections from Damaged Life* 171–2
Ahmad Aijaz 8, 39; *Lineages of the Present* 8
Albanian immigrants 52–3
Albergo dei Poveri ('Hotel' for the poor). *See* Naples
Alfieri, Benedetto, Vittorio's 'half-uncle,' Turin architect 117–18, 120, 125
Alfieri, Vittorio: language as class issue in Turin 117–19; 'Panegiric of Pliny to Trajan' 124; return to Turin 103, 115–18, 121–5, 130
Alinari, Fratelli, Florentine photographic firm 260–1
Amalia of Saxony, wife of Charles III of Naples 135–6
Amelio, Gianni, and *Lamerica* (film) 52–4

America 38
Amsterdam 35
ancien régime 16, 205–6
Anderson, Perry 5, 8, 149–50, 294n9; *Lineages of the Absolutist State* 8
Antonelli, Laura, actress in Visconti's *L'Innocente* 269–70
Antonioni, Michelangelo 54
Ariosto, Ludovico 50, 59, 62–3, 67–9, 85; *Orlando Furioso* 60, 67–9
Asti, birthplace of Alfieri 115
Auerbach, Erich, and interpretations of Vico 107–9
Australia 10, 17–18, 38
Avvenire, L' 220

Balbi, Venetian family 36–7
Ballarò (television program) 43
Balzac, Honoré de: *Traité de la vie élégante* 230–1
Bandello, Matteo 209
Baudrillard, Jean 60–1
BBC television. *See under* television
Beccaria, Cesare: among Enlightenment figures in Milan 206; criticized as 'Italian Rousseau' 148, 294n8; and Italian writers on justice

146; *Of Crimes and Punishments* 144, 148–56, 159–61; —, as major paradigm shift in culture 148; poverty as breeding ground of crime 152; use of terms *socialista* and *socialismo* 148, 294n8; views on capital punishment 155–7, 163; views on torture 154–5, 163
belle époque in Italy 267, 269–70, 272
Bellotto, Bernardo, view painter, nephew of Canaletto 125
Bellow, Saul: *The Dean's December* 64
Benjamin, Walter: analyses of Paris 218–19; *Arcades Project* 25; on conformism of tradition 287n2; importance of past to present 3, 169–70; 'primordial landscape[s] of consumption' 229; question re presentation of history 3, 10
Berlusconi, Silvio 43–5; 'Contract with Italians' 44
Biagi, Enzo 44
Blessington, Marguerite, Countess of: *Lady Blessington at Naples* 11–12
Boccaccio, Giovanni, and *The Decameron* 72
Bogarde, Dirk, actor in Visconti's *Death in Venice* 273
Brand, C.P.: *Italy and the English Romantics* 176
Britain (United Kingdom): compromised by celebration of Nelson 198; concerns for justice different from Italians' 147; connections with Naples in Romantic Era 10; different behavioural norms 189; different legal system 145; numerous scholars of Italy in 25
Bronte, small town in Sicily, and *Bronte: Chronicle of a massacre ...* 54

Brosses, Charles de, French visitor to Turin 126–7
Brunetta, Gian Piero 36, 38
Buona domenica (television program) 44
Burke, Kenneth, and 'representative anecdotes' 9, 25–6
Byron, Lord George Gordon 177, 202

Calabrian earthquake (1783) 138–9 141
Caldara, Antonio 89
Calvino, Italo: on Ariosto's presentation of moon 69; on Galileo as prose writer 67, 71; on Leopardi's concern with prose style 72; *Our Ancestors* (*I nostri antenati*) trilogy 73, 84, *The Baron in the Trees* 76–7, 84–5, *The Cloven Viscount* 76, *The Non-existent Knight* 74–6, 86; *The Path to the Spiders' Nest* 73; *Six Memos for the Next Millennium* 50, 61, 70–3, 77, 84, 125; —, and qualities recommended for future literature 61, 71–2, 80, 283n5; on tradition con-necting science and literature 59–63, 66; views on television 49–50
Calzabigi, Ranieri de', Gluck's librettist, writes dedication of *Alceste* 92–3
Canella, Giuseppe, urban view painter 261
Cantagiro, television program 43
Capaci, location of car-bombing of Falcone 40
capital punishment. *See* Beccaria, Milan
Capuana, Luigi 234–5
Carlo Emanuele III, King of Sardinia 120

Carocci, Guido, *Firenze Scomparsa: Ricordi storico-artistici* 221
Caroline, Queen, Marie-Antoinette's sister and Ferdinand of Naples's wife 12, 105, 110–13, 120, 141; bows to Mozart 110–12
Carrarini, Rita 267
Caserta, Royal Palace by Vanvitelli 131, 133, 136
Castlereagh, Lord, Regency foreign secretary 9, 17, 20
Catania 40
cavalieri serventi. *See* cicisbeism
Cavanna, Adriano, scholar of torture and capital punishment 157
Cavour, Count Camillo Bensodi di 170
Charles III, King of Naples 109, 133, 135–6, 141–2
Cimarosa, Domenico, composer important to Stendhal 99, 101, 200
cicisbeism, custom of *cavalieri serventi* 182, 186–7, 189–92, 205
Colletta, General Pietro 12, 15, 17–18; *History of the Kingdom of Sicily* 12–13, 17–18
commedia dell'arte 111
Constitution, Italian. *See* Italian Constitution of 1948
Cosimo de' Medici, Duke 30–1
cosmorama. *See* 'cultural cosmorama'
Costa, Giovanni, painter of *Shepherd of the Roman Plain* 260
Costanzo, Maurizio, and *Maurizio Costanzo Show* 44
Council of Trent 181
Craveri, Giovanni Gaspare, and *Guida de' forestieri* ... 116, 118–19, 126
Croce, Benedetto 6–8, 103, 106
cronaca nera (sensationalist news) 42

Crouzet, Michel 206–7
'cultural cosmorama' as metaphoric paradigm 28, 32, 39, 41, 55, 58
Cuzzoni, Francesca, soprano singer 96

Dagrada, Elena 39
D'Annunzio, Gabriele, and *L'Innocente,* source for Visconti's film 267–9
Dante Alighieri 60, 184–5, 219–20
Danti, Ignazio, painter 30
Da Ponte, Lorenzo, Mozart's librettist 16, 96, 99, 113
Da Vinci, Leonardo. *See* Leonardo Da Vinci
Davy, Sir Humphry 9, 13, 18–25, 27; invention of miners' safety lamp 19; 'literary world' 23; *Researches ... Chiefly Concerning Nitrous Oxide ...* 18; work in Naples on papyrus scrolls 18–23, 25
De Giorgio, Michela: *Italian Women from Unification to the Present* 266
De Gregorio, Marco, painter of *Lo zappatore* (hoer) 259–60
De Mauro, Tullio 51
Denina, Carlo 119
d'Entrèves, A.P. 144, 148–9, 151, 156
Depretis, Agostino, prime minister 241, 243
De Quincey, Thomas 72
Detti, Eduardo 223, 226
Dickens, Charles 161; on Naples 300n49
Dickie, John 87
Diego La Matina, Frate from Racalmuto, character in Sciascia's *Death of the Inquisitor,* protagonist of Natoli novel 163–6, 168

Diritto, Il 224
Domingo, Placido 55–6
Dossetti, Giuseppe 172–3

Eco, Umberto: on emergence of modern paradigms 277n7; employment by Bompiani 47; on hyperreality 61, 78; 'Phenomenology of Mike Bongiorno' 45–6, 48–9; television as unifying factor 51; *Travels in Hyperreality* 78
Edinburgh 105
emus given to Sir Walter Scott 14–15
England: attitudes to television 38; audience response to opera 88; Handel's visit and stay 93–4
English oratorio, musical form 94–5
English temperament, contrasted with Italian 88–9
Enlightenment 28, 103, 144, 215
Ethiopia, Italy's attempt to colonize 251–2
extracommunitari, recent immigrants 52, 175

Falcone, Giovanni, judge 40–1, 146
Farinelli, film of singer 93; and 'morphing' of castrato voice 285n11
Farnese, Alessandro, Renaissance pope (Paul III) 210, 297n25
Fascism, or Fascist epoch 8, 144, 148–9, 170–5, 185
fashion journals. *See* women's nineteenth-century fashion journals
fashion plates in journals 265–7; Visconti's recreation of look 269–71
fatti vostri, I (television program) 42–3
fatto, Il (television program) 44

Fei, Silvano: *Nascita e sviluppo di Firenze città borghese* 221, 225–6
Fellini, Federico: *La voce della luna* 283n6
Ferdinand I of Naples and Two Sicilies, formerly Ferdinand IV of Naples: diplomacy with British plenipotentiary A'Court 18, 20; enduring feudal practices 142; gift of papyrus scrolls 9–13; praise by Pagano for 'enlightened' rule 141; received in private capacity in Turin 120; residence in Palermo during 'republican' period in Naples 105; 'rough Neapolitan upbringing' (Mozart) 110–12
Ferenczi, Sándor 86
Festival Bar (television program) 43
Filangieri, Gaetano, *Scienza della legislazione* 142–3
Florence: city councillors' appeal to Senate 222–4; glass-arcaded crossroads (never built) 227; growth after Unification 219–29; Leopardi's stay 214; Mayor Ubaldino Peruzzi and councillors 223–4; Palazzo Vecchio (esp. *Sala del Guardaroba*) 30–1; Piazza Vittorio Emanuele II 219–20, 227; prefabricated houses from London firm 224; *risanamento*, urban renewal 224; speculation while capital, then downturn 221–9, 255–6, 298n8
Forgacs, David 39
fortuna in piazza, La (television program) 42
Foster, Kenelm 162
France, and different behavioural norms 189

Franchini, Silvia 230, 266
French Revolution 77
Freud, Sigmund 86
Fukuyama, Francis 5
Fuga, Ferdinando, architect of *Albergo dei Poveri* 131–3, 135

G8 Summit in Genoa (2001) 52
Gabici, Franco 71
Galilei, Galileo: appreciation by Leopardi 70–2; *Dialogue concerning the two chief world systems* 64; inspired by literary fantasy 69; part of longer tradition 60–73; passage on moon 64–7; passage on 'rapidity' of discursive thinking 70–1, 73; rewriting of Ariosto verses 67–8; 'scientist ... nourished by literary culture' (Calvino) 59; views on global intercommunicability of writing 82–5; views on Tasso vs. Ariosto 60, 282n3
Gambi, Lucio, and Maria Cristina Gozzoli: *Milano* 229–32
Garibaldi 54, 170
Garzoni, Tommaso, and *La Piazza Universale* 41
Geertz, Clifford: reciprocal interpretation of 'part' and 'whole' 15; 'thick description' 17, 113
Genovesi, Antonio 131, 137
Giannini, Giancarlo, actor in Visconti's *L'Innocente* 271
Gibbon, Edward, as 1764 visitor to Turin 126
Giordano, Paolo 132–3, 135
Gluck, Christoph Willibald: as adapter of Metastasio 89; *Alceste* and operatic reform 92–3; *Orfeo ed Euridice* 92

Goethe, Johann Wolfgang von, and 'liberation from history' 7
Goldoni, Carlo, 'Il Mondo Nuovo' (poem) 36–7
Goya, Francisco, Spanish painter 254–5
Gramsci, Antonio: '*humus* of popular culture ...' 264–5; ideas about Risorgimento 8–9; Manzoni's and Church's attitude to populace 260, 301n61; *Prison Notebooks* 8, 24, 247–8; on 'reactionary' Tuscan moderates 223–4; 'traditions' and 'mentalities' of Italian culture, 'multiple, contradictory ... individual and arbitrary' 8–9; views on 'colonization' of South contrasted with Nitti's 247–51
Graneri, G.M. 29
Grasso, Aldo 39

Hamilton, Emma 105
Hamilton, Sir William (1788–1856) 17
Hamilton, Sir William Douglas (1730–1803) 115
Handel, George Frideric: *Rodelinda* 95; Royal Academy operas in Italian, eventual loss of popularity 95–6, 100; visit to Dublin 95; visit to England, settlement in London 93–4
Hasan, Ruqaiya 39
Haussmann, Baron Georges-Eugène 219, 225–6
Hazlitt, William 15
Herculaneum 9–10, 12–13, 19, 21, 27
Herculaneum Academy 22
Herder, Johann Gottfried von 106

Hofmannsthal, Hugo von, and city as 'landscape built of pure life' 216
Hunter, Mary: *The Culture of Opera Buffa in Mozart's Vienna* 97
hyperreality 61, 78

Imbonitore. See under *mondi nuovi*
India 8, 39–40
Inganni, Angelo, painter of urban views, chimneysweeps 260; *Urban Chimneysweep* 261; *View of the Piazza del Duomo* 262–3; *View of the Piazza della Loggia* (Brescia) 262–4
Inquisition 215; in Sicily 144, 160, 163, 168
'investigative' narration or *racconto inchiesta*: concern with justice 147; Sciascia's emulation of Manzoni's use 144, 160, 168, 170
Irish cultural history 19
Italian Communist Party 173
Italian Constitution of 1948; importance of social dignity and equality 174; Italy as 'democratic Republic founded on work' 173; personal development and binding sociality 173–4; principle of nation's legal framework 175; within longer tradition re justice 144, 147, 161
Italian operatic tradition: *da capo* arias and virtuosity 93; *dramma giocoso*, form of *Don Giovanni* 96; importance of Metastasian drama 89–92; judgments of in Pope's *Dunciad* 94–5; *lieto fine* or happy ending 92; *opera buffa* 97, 110–11, 200; *opera seria* 91, 97, 100; —, reform of under Gluck 92–3; passional intensities 87; spread across Europe and worldwide 99–100; Stendhal on nuanced passions of 100–1
Italian temperament, clichés about 87–9
Italian Unification. *See* Unification

Jacques, Martin 6
Jomelli, Nicolò, composer 89, 110
Jung, Carl 108
Justinian, Emperor, and his *Corpus Iuris* 149, 153

kangaroos given to Ferdinand I 9, 12–13, 17, 26–7
Kant, Immanuel 156, 163
Kierkegaard, Søren, philosopher, and 'speculative ear' 98, 102
Kimbell, David: *Italian Opera* 91–2

Lafayette, Madame Marie-Madelaine de: *La Princesse de Clèves* 208
Las Vegas: replicas from past 78; a reshuffling of old gestalts? 61, 79; something new to be 'learned from,' thesis of Robert Venturi et al. 79–80; and *The Venetian* hotel and casino 80–2, 86
lazzaroni (Neapolitan beggars) 112, 132, 239
Leonardo Da Vinci 78, 209
Leopardi, Giacomo 177–9, 188, 193–7, 210, 212–5; *Anthology of Italian Prose* 60, 62, 64–7, 70; *Discourse on the present state of morality of the Italians* 178, 195–7, 212–15; *History of Astronomy* 60; Italian language's peculiar province the imagination 71; on Italian sensitivity vs. lack of

Index 323

love of nation 24; Italy and Hobbesian war of all against all 195; *Moral Opuscules* 60–4; —, 'Dialogue Between the Earth and the Moon' 63–4; 'poet of the moon' 63–4; —, debt to Galileo re unknowability of moon 64–6; *Popular Errors of the Ancients* 60; position in longer tradition of fantasy and speculation 59–62; Recanati (birthplace) 214; speed of travel re speed and concision of writing 72; views on torture 214–15; *Zibaldone* (*Miscellany*) 24, 60–2, 71–2

Leopold, Grand Duke of Tuscany 92

Lerner, Gad 42

lieto fine or happy ending. *See* Italian operatic tradition 92

Lisbon 35

literary republic (*repubblica letteraria*) 23

London: closer contacts with New World than Venice's 35; compared by Mozart with Naples 112; Handel's long residence in 94; popularity then decline of Handelian opera 94–6; poverty compared with Naples' 239

Lorenzo, Samuele 145

Louis XIV of France 121

magic lantern 38

Malfitano, Catherine 55, 57–8

Malta 17

Mann, Thomas. *See under* Visconti

Manzoni, Alessandro: *The Column of Infamy* 144, 158–72; —, concerns with injustice 145–6, 158, 166–8; —, overlooked in terms of his reputation 160; —, Sciascia's defence 168–70; communal 'We' vs. individualistic 'I' 162–4, 170–2, 174, 176, 178–9; —, important for *periodization* 161–3; fate of poor a proper subject for history 161, 162, 164, 295n19; *I promessi sposi* (or television adaptations) 54–5, 158; views on torture 158–62, 169; —, reference back to Beccaria 147, 159

Marazzini, Claudio 119

Marseille 13

Marx, Karl 173

Mayhew, Henry: *London Labour and the London Poor* 240

Mazzini, Giuseppe 170

Metastasio, Pietro, Italian poet and dramatist: *La clemenza di Tito* 89–91; complex passions of characters 90–1, 96; *Poesie* in ten volumes 92; shift from 'purgation to edification' (Kimbell) 92; use of *lieto fine* (happy ending) 92

Metternich, Prince Klemens Lothar Wenzel von 17, 26

Meynell, Hugo 96

Michelangelo 28, 101

Milan: Beccaria's praise of Austrian rule 150–1; capital punishment and torture 157; commercial and industrial dynamic 219; consumption levels compared with Naples's 249; Enlightenment thinkers 206; *gallerie* or arcades 228–35, 237; Habsburg rule 151; La Scala opera house 100, 213, 237; reception of French in 1796 207; setting of *I promessi sposi* 54, 158; Stendhal's

324   Index

love for 198–9, 211, 214; *Il ventre di Milano* 241
Milano-Italia (television program) 42
Milizia, Francesco: *Memorials of Architects* 134
Moe, Nelso: *The View from Vesuvius* 87–8
Molteni, Giuseppe, painter 260
mondi nuovi ('new worlds,' optic devices): artisinal production of *vedute* 35; comparison with later modes of viewing 28; day and night effects 290n53; different times and places 54; images 29, 33, 34, 37; *imbonitore* (operator) 31–3, 35; importance in pre-cinema 32; —, 'mental cinema' before cinema 125; popular name for *pantoscopi* 28; representation by Goldoni 36–8; similar devices in India in twentieth century 39; *vedute* (view projections) 35; —, representations of Turin 125
Montesquieu, Charles-Louis de Secondat, Baron de: *De l'esprit des lois,* and climate in relation to temperament 88–9, 92; response to: Naples 125, Turin 117, 126–7
Morato, Erica 266
Moravia, Alberto, and views on television 47
Morbelli, Angelo, as painter of the Pious Trivulzio Hospice, Milan 257–9; images, *Those Left at Christmas* and *Holiday ...* 258–9
Morelli, Domenico, as painter of fellow artist Celentano 259
Morris, Jonathan 235–6
Mozart, Nannerl, Wolfgang's sister 111, 113

Mozart, Wolfgang Amadeus 200; adaptation of Metastasian drama 89; with Da Ponte as librettist: *Così fan tutte* 114–15, *Die Entführung aus dem Serail* 186; *Don Giovanni* 16, 96–9, *The Marriage of Figaro* 99; importance to Stendhal 200; performance/audience dynamic 93; visit with father to Naples in 1770: new silk clothes 113–15, Queen Caroline bows to him 110–12, response to performance in San Carlo opera 110–11, scatalogical humour 111, visits to Vesuvius and other sites 112, 115
Muratori, Ludovico Antonio, Enlightenment Italian historian 135; on *Albergo dei Poveri* in Naples 291n83

National Museum of Cinema. *See under* Turin
Naples: *Albergo dei Poveri* ('Hotel' for the Poor) 131–6, 238–9; —, as 'great Reclusorium' (Milizia) 134; as 'colony of consumption' after Unification 248–9, 301n53; as 'colony of supply' before Unification 248, 250; comparative decline after Unification 219; conditions for industrialization 252–3; *gallerie* or arcades 228, 237–8; judgments re social classes by de Zerbi 238–9, 242; leisurely world along Molo 111–12; most populous city in 1861 218; Mozart's comparison with Paris, Vienna, and London 112; Museum of Archaeological Antiquities 10, 23; Nitti argues against direct train link with Rome 247–8; poorest quarters described by

Serao 241–6; population 115, 117, 218; Portici 115; portraits of *banditi* 260; poverty 134–5, 137, 143; *Risanamento* (urban renewal project) 238, 240, 246; Roman remains at Pompeii 115; San Carlo opera house 110–11, 131, 213, 237; San Gennaro Outside the Walls 132; Stendhal's love of 211, 214; —, as idealized by characters in *La Chartreuse de Parme* 213; Vesuvius 10, 19, 112, 115; Villa Floridiana 12, 17; visit of Sir Humphry Davy 19–23; Vomero (hill overlooking) 9, 12

Napoleon Bonaparte 117, 177, 179, 198, 203, 209

Natoli, Luigi, novelist of *Fra Diego la Matina* 164

Nazism 171, 185

Nelson, Lord Horatio, pejorative accounts by Stendhal and Sontag 105

New South Wales 9

New York 38

Nietzsche, Friedrich 169

Nitti, Francesco Saverio: accounts of Naples 229, 247; contrasted with Gramsci 247–51; on corrupt Italian rulers 252–3; *Naples and the Southern Question* 246–7; 'new lifestyles' of Italian people 253–5; schemes for development of Naples 248; —, against port concessions and direct train link with Rome 247

Nocita, Salvatore 54

Noja, Duke of 116, 126; *Topographical Map of the City of Naples ...* (1775) 136

Northern League 42, 251

O'Neill, Jennifer, actress in Visconti's *L'Innocente* 270–1

opera, Italian. *See* Italian operatic tradition

opera buffa, seria. See Italian operatic tradition

Opinione, L' 220

ore casalinghe, Le, fashion journal 265–6

Ormea, Marquis of 119

Paese sera 51

Paestum 115

Pagano, Francesco Mario: *Political Essays* 139–41

Pakistan 8

Palermo 40–1, 43, 105

Palmieri, Giuseppe 137–8

pantoscopi. See mondi nuovi

papyrus scrolls from Herculaneum: gift of King Ferdinand to British prince regent 9; Sir Humphry Davy's tasks of unrolling 18–23

Paris: arcades 230; Benjamin's accounts a model to emulate 218–19; called 'populous desert' in *La traviata* 237; compared by Mozart with Naples 112; contrasted with 'unplanned' Naples 126; hegemony in fashion journals 265, 267; place where Alfieri writes autobiography 123; reconfigured in Las Vegas 82; remodellings by Baron Haussmann 225; Stendhal's returns to 201–12

Parma 211, 213

Partanno, Princess, later Duchess of Floridia 12

Pasolini, Pier Paolo: against De Mauro over language issues 51; views on television 48–9, 55

Peruzzi, Ubaldino, mayor of Florence 223–4, 229
Petrarch 60, 185
Petrusewicz, Marta 87, 106
Piave, Francesco Maria, librettist of *La traviata* 237
Piazza Grande (television program) 42
Piedmont 104
Pieragostini, Augusta, proprietress of Roman silk shop 235–7
poetics of cultural history 3, 10
Poggi, Giuseppe, post-Unification architect of Florence 222, 225–7
Pompeii 19, 21, 27
Pope, Alexander, and *Dunciad* description of Italian opera 94–5
Porta a Porta (television program) 43
Pozzi, Luigi Valeriano, engraver 231
pre-cinema, history of 32; and scholarly literature on 280n1
prince regent, British 10, 13, 27
Prolo, Maria Adriana, collector of pre-cinematic devices 34, 280n5
Ptolemaic maps 30
Public Records Office in London 16
Puccini, Giacomo: *Tosca* 55–8
Puglia, coastline of 52–3
Punta Raisi, airport for Palermo 40

'quietism' of much late-nineteenth-century Italian art 262

Racalmuto, Sciascia's home town in Sicily 40, 163
racconto inchiesta. *See* 'investigative' narration
Race Laws of 1938 174
Racine, Jean: *Phèdre* 91
Rada Films 55–7
Radio Gap 52
Radio Onda Rossa 52
RAI television network. *See* television
Reina, Giuseppe 233
Renaissance *studioli* 30
Ricuperati, Giuseppe 116, 151–2; *Storia di Torino* 116
risanamento, urban renewal. *See under* individual cities
Risorgimento: account by Gramsci 8–9; —, on opposition of Tuscan 'moderates' 223–4; leaders foster common identity for Italians 170; Turin as natural focus 143
Roman law 149–50, 294n9
Rome: bolt hole from Civitavecchia for Stendhal 202, 205; capital city status after 1871 221, 228–9; contrasted with 'unplanned' Naples 126; hyperreal reproductions in Las Vegas 82; Nitti argues against direct train link with Naples 247–8; Pieragostini's silk shop on Piazza di Spagna 235–6; Teatro Parioli 44
Rosa, Salvator, painter 136
Rosini, Neapolitan Superintendant of Papyrus Scrolls 22–3
Rossini, Gioachino: *Barber of Seville* 100; *La cenerentola*, and 'inextricable knot' in plot 98; contrasted by Stendhal with Michelangelo, Beethoven, and Haydn 101; performance/audience dynamic 93; play of differences between Islamic and Italian societies, in *L'italiana in Algeri* and *Il turco in Italia* 186; seen by Stendhal as Napoleon's successor 99–100; *Tancredi* 100–1; *Thieving Magpie* 100

Royal Society 18, 27
Rushdie, Salman: detection of 'last example ... of bad sentence' in Calvino 73; fabulists' love of lists 68, 283n14; interest in 'narration as a process' in Calvino 84–5; interplay, as in Calvino, between fantastical and real 86; *Midnight's Children* 84–5

Sacchi, Giuseppe 231–5, 237
Said, Edward: *Orientalism* 251
Salzburg 111, 114
Samarcanda (television program) 42–3
San Leuccio silk works in Kingdom of Naples 113
Santoro, Michele 43–4
Saussurean linguistics 189
Schutz, Juergen 30
Sciascia, Leonardo: author's visit to surviving family members 40; *Death of the Inquisitor* 144, 146, 161, 163–70; defence of Manzoni's *Column of Infamy* 168–9; determination to build on Manzoni's example 145–7, 160; Fra Diego La Matina as *grand révolté* 164; linkage back to Manzoni and Beccaria 161; misinterpretation of Manzoni on God 165–8; views on television 47, torture 169
Sciuscia (television program) 44
Scott, Sir Walter 14–15, 27, 292n90
Second World War 39, 73–5
Seismid-Doda, 1870s finance minister 228
Senesino, Francesco Bernardi, castrato singer 95–6
Serao, Matilde, and *The Belly of Naples*: criticisms of government and prime minister 243–4; customary racial prejudices shared with Nitti 250; description of fallen women 244–6; dissimilarity with style of Nitti 248; mocks facile literature 242; plebeian sympathies 241; poor as a 'social picturesque' in others 261–2; rhetorical strategy 244
Shakespeare, William 75
Shelley, Percy Bysshe 177
Sicilian fascination with death 40
Signorini, Telemaco, Florentine painter of *Ward of Mad Women* 255–7
Silvestrini, Maria Teresa 116
Sismondi, J.C.L. Simonde de, and *History of the Italian Republics*: absolutist princes crush legality and justice 181; on changed morality evidenced in *cicisbeism* 182, 186, 189–93; different approach from Stendhal's 210, 215–16; on educational practices in Italy 181; friend of De Staël 179–80; historian of Italy's greatness and decline 177–80, 203–4; Stendhal's exaggeration of Sismondian history 206; unsparing account of Church 181
Sontag, Susan: *The Volcano Lover* 104–5
South, the Southern Question, or 'southernness' as feature of character 87–8, 91, 106, 115, 246–53
'stadial theory' of Scottish Enlightenment, cognate to Neapolitan ideas 137, 292n90

Staël, Madame Anne Louise Germaine de, and *Corinne, ou l'Italie* 216; account of Dante 184–5; account of Roman society 186–9; analytical positivism of approach to another culture 193–5; —, differences from Stendhal's approach 206, 210, 216; cicisbeism 186–8; Italian approach to decisive circumstances 193–4; lack of social bonding among Italians 186; negatives about Italy concentrated in collectivity 180; a novel-cum-travel-narration 179, 188; positives about Italy seen in individuals 180; proto-anthropological form of writing 188; psychological readings of Italy 182

Stendhal (real name Marie Henri Beyle): *La chartreuse de Parme* 178–9, 194–6, 198–217; *Chroniques italiennes* 206; *De l'amour* (*On Love*) 99; experiences on 1812 Russian campaign 198–201; the *Encyclopaedia* and Voltaire 206; French consulship in Trieste 202–3; ideas from Sismondi 206; Italian individualism 196; Italy as Sleeping Beauty at advent of Napoleon 203; judgments on Rossini 100–1; love of Cimarosa, Mozart, and Rossini 200; pejorative account of Nelson 105; relations with sister 201; *Rome, Naples and Florence* 197–9; *Le rouge et le noir* 99, 101, 202; time in Civitavecchia 202, 205, 212

Tanucci, Bernardo, Bourbon minister in Naples 134
Tasmania 9
Tasso, Torquato 60, 185; *Gerusalemme Liberata* 60
television: BBC television 81; connection with earlier viewing paradigms 31, 38–40; importance in unifying Italy 51; RAI network 44, 47, 52, 54–5; studio as a *salotto* 43; virtual piazza on various channels 41–3
Terni in Umbria, as centre of metal production 248
Thompson, E.P.: episodes in history 4–5, 8; 'molecular' research and 'macroscopic' generalization 4–5
Togliatti, Palmiro, founding member of the Italian Communist Party 173
torture. *See under* Beccaria, Manzoni, Milan, *and* Sciascia
Tosi, Piero, Visconti's frequent costume designer 272
Toulon 13
Trentin, Silvio 171
Triumph of Death (painting) 40
Trumpener, Katie 19
Turin: Accademia di Torino (and Alfieri's schooling) 116; 'amphibian city' (Alfieri) 117, 119; briefly capital city of unified Italy 222–3; commercial and industrial dynamic post-Unification 219; consumption compared with Naples's 249; 'finest city of Europe' (Stendhal) 106; Hospital for the Insane 129; Houses of Correction 129–30; Island of San Massimo 119; National Museum of Cinema 34, 280n5; *Opera delle Convertite* (Opera of the Converted) 128; population in eighteenth century 115, 117; RAI television studios 47; 'Refuge'

for Forced Women 127–9; Siege of 121; Theatre of the Prince of Carignano 118; Workhouse for Idle Vagabonds 129

Umberto I, King of Italy 237, 241
Unification 51, 103, 109, 143, 218–22, 226, 239, 246, 248, 250, 274
United Kingdom. *See* Britain
United States of America: concerns for justice different 147; legal system different 145; numerous scholars of Italy in 25
urbanization in Italy 5, 218, 298n4
urban view painters in nineteenth century 255, 260, 262–4

Valsecchi, Franco 124, 130
Vasari, Giorgio 3, 28, 30–1; description of *Sala del Guardaroba* 30–1
Venetian, The, hotel and casino. *See under* Las Vegas
Venice: cholera 272; hyperreal version of, *The Venetian* in Las Vegas 81–2; lack of an effective *risanamento* (urban renewal program) 272; *mondi nuovi* popular 32–6; representation in *Death in Venice* 272
Venturi, Franco: Beccaria's text as major paradigm shift in culture 148; key texts by 287n1; quality of writings on Bourbon Naples and Enlightenment 103–4; synopsis of Noja on unknowable quality of Naples 116; tells larger story of 'Italy outside Italy' 177
Venturi, Robert, et al., *Learning from Las Vegas* 61, 79–81
Verdi, Giuseppe 170, 237

Verona 43
Verri, Pietro 146, 151, 169, 206, 294n7
Versailles 82, 120, 133
Vespa, Bruno 43
Vico, Giambattista 103, 106–10, 139–41; exposition by Auerbach 107–8; impoverished private existence 109; influence upon later thinkers 139–41; membership of learned academies 109; objection to Cartesian philosophy 109; professor in Naples 103, 109; *La Scienza Nuova* and key points 106–9
Victor Emmanuel II, King of United Italy 220, 237, 262
Vienna 112, 114, 126
Violante, Luciano 145
Visconti, Luchino: costume designs by Piero Tosi 272; *Death in Venice*, film after novel by Mann 271–3; *L'Innocente*, film after novel by D'Annunzio 267–71; *Ossessione*, first film 271; *Senso* 267
Viscusi, Robert 98–9
Vittorio Amedeo III, King of Sardinia 119–20, 130
Voltaire 102, 206; *Essay on ancient and modern tragedy* 102

Washington, DC 38
Watteau, Jean-Antoine, painter 245
Weber, Max 150
White Mario, Jessie, *La miseria di Napoli* 239–40
Williams, Raymond, on country and city 293n104
women's nineteenth-century fashion journals 265–7

Woolf, Stuart 301n53
Wordsworth, William, lines on Italy in *Prelude* 177
World Trade Center buildings, New York 31

Zerbi, Rocco de. *See under* Naples

Zola, Émile, *Le ventre de Paris* 240–1
Zompini, Gaetano 32–3, 37; *Le Arti Che Vanno Per Via Nella Città di Venezia* 32–3
Zotti Minici, Carlo Alberto 35